D1378376

Advance Praise

"This highly informative and penetrating study of the 'fight for freedom' of Indonesian workers, and the background in which it has developed, could hardly be more timely or significant. It is an inspiring story of struggle and achievement, with important lessons for people dedicated to elementary human rights. It is also a valuable corrective to the propaganda assault that seeks to justify investor-rights agreements by portraying support for working people as an attack against them."
—Noam Chomsky

"Americans, even progressives, know precious little about the great archipelago of Indonesia, the fourth-most-populous country in the world and a major producer of goods for the U.S. market. That's why Dan La Botz's book is a must-read for those who care about global issues. Introducing us to fascinating labor activists such as Muchtar Pakpahan and Dita Sari, we see the birth of a new labor movement that is organizing the workers who make products for U.S. consumers. *Made in Indonesia* shows us how we can be conscientious supporters of this important and vibrant movement for social justice."
—Medea Benjamin, Global Exchange

"If you feel outraged by the fact that big foreign firms are still not bargaining with Indonesia's independent unions, read this book. After you read it, you'll know who to connect with. Consumer groups and human rights activists can help these courageous people win justice."
—Jeff Ballinger, Press for Change

"The resurgence of the labor movement has been one of the most breathtaking but underreported developments in Indonesia since the dictator Suharto was forced from power in 1998. Unions have asserted their presence by defending workers' rights against the background of economic crisis, widespread unemployment, and a stalled reform movement. *Made in Indonesia* tells the story through the voices of the key figures in this resurgence. It sets these developments against the background of the history of labor under the Dutch, Sukarno, and during the Suharto decades of repression. The penetration of global capital and the role of international solidarity are also analyzed. The combination of analysis and sympathetically portrayed trade unionists from across the political spectrum makes this essential reading for activists or indeed anyone who wants to understand how labor can play its role in creating a vibrant and stable democracy in the world's fourth-most-populated country."

—Carmel Budiardjo, TAPOL, the Indonesia Human Rights Campaign

Made in Indonesia

Indonesian Workers Since Suharto

Dan La Botz

South End Press
Cambridge, Massachusetts

Library of Congress Cataloging-in-Publication Data

La Botz, Dan.
Made in Indonesia : Indonesian workers since Suharto / Dan La Botz.
  p. cm.
Includes bibliographical references and index.

ISBN 0-89608-643-7 (cloth) — ISBN 0-89608-642-9 (pbk.)

1. Labor movement—Indonesia. 2. Labor unions—Indonesia. 3. Democratization—Indonesia. I. Title: Indonesian workers since Suharto. II. Title.

HD8706.5 .L32 2001
322.2'09598—dc21

               2001-020573

South End Press, 7 Brookline Street, #1, Cambridge, MA 02139-4146
www.southendpress.org

05 04 03 02 01   1 2 3 4 5

R01785475 49

Table of Contents

There were many ways, it seemed, to steal someone's country. And the objective was always the same—to win the race being run by all the colonial powers of the world to see who was the greatest thief, the greediest, the best at sucking up the riches of the earth and its people.

It made me sick.

—Pramoedya Ananta Toer,
Footsteps, Vol. III, *Buru Quartet* [i]

A change will come in our whole native world—the turning point is foreordained; it is coming. But when will it be? That is the great question. We cannot hasten the hour of revolution. For it is only we who have rebellious thoughts in this wilderness, this dark distant land, beyond which there is no land. My friends here say that we shall act wisely if we do nothing but sleep for a hundred years. When awakened, Java would be more as we would have her.

—Kartini, *Letters of a Javanese Princess* [ii]

Be careful. The mistakes of the First World can be avoided. We must not suffer the social misery and sickness that happened in Europe.

—Dr. Sutomo, 1936 [iii]

i   Pramoedya Ananta Toer, *Footsteps,* Vol. III of the *Buru Quartet* (New York: Penguin Books, 1990), 215.

ii   Raden Adjeng Kartini, *Letters of a Javanese Princess* (New York: The University Press of America and the Asia Society, 1985), 44.

iii   Quoted in Goenanwan Mohamad, *Sidelines: Thought Pieces from Tempo Magazine* (South Melbourne, Victoria: Lontar, 1994), 50.

Acknowledgments

I am indebted to many people for their help in writing this book. The interpretation of events presented here is based on dozens of interviews with Indonesian students, NGO activists, labor union organizers, and workers conducted in Indonesia in 1999 and 2000. Above all, I thank those activists and workers for sharing their experience with me. (A list of those interviewed can be found in the end of the book, before the Index.)

The AFL-CIO's American Center for International Labor Solidarity and its staff generously opened its doors to me and shared their views of the Indonesian labor movement. Tim Ryan, its director, provided me with many of the center's publications (including the invaluable monthly reports done by Roger Smith) and helped put me in touch with labor contacts.

Both Muchtar Pakpahan of the SBSI labor federation and Dita Sari of the FNPBI labor federation welcomed me into their offices, introduced me to union officials and workers, and in other ways assisted my research. Paul Keys and Lut Vasant, both of whom worked in the SBSI international department, were especially helpful in providing opportunities for me to speak with the federation's staff, officers, and members.

The research for this book was made possible in part by two grants from the Fund for Investigative Journalism, for which I am most thankful.

John Roosa originally encouraged me to travel to Indonesia, provided me with some of my contacts there, and very generously read the entire manuscript. His comments corrected many factual errors, noted omissions, directed me to important secondary sources, and frequently forced me to rethink my interpretation of events.

Loie Hayes at South End Press read the original manuscript, and made several useful suggestions for revisions. Anthony

Arnove, my editor at South End Press, was not only a most conscientious editor, but also a real partner in this editorial process. I
appreciate his advice to make stronger arguments and better explain my own views on social and political questions.

Kim Moody of *Labor Notes* read and commented on one or
another chapter of the book, as did Charlie Post. Kurt Biddle and
Malik Mia, editors of *Indonesia Alert!*, shared their knowledge of
Indonesia's social movements.

Thanks to Siusan Durst for taking the photograph used on
the author page. Thanks also to Rudy Porter and Mary Ann
Forbes of ACILS, who went to great lengths to provide the photos of Muchtar Pakpahan and Dita Sari by Anastasia Vrachnos
and the FNPBI, respectively. Kurt Biddle and Jaguar Design
helped supply the map of Indonesia printed at the opening of
Chapter 1, which was handily redesigned by Christopher
Mattison, based on the original by the United Nations Department of Public Information's Cartographic Section (Map number 4110, June 1999).

Of course, I alone am responsible for any errors of fact, for
the interpretations of Indonesian history and contemporary
events, and for the political arguments expressed here.

As always my wife, Sherry Baron, gave me her support, and
our children Traven, 13, and Reed, 10, have gotten old enough to
take an interest in their father's work, to understand the evils of
sweatshop labor, and to appreciate the importance of this book.

•

This book is dedicated to the memory of Marsinah and to all
the other women and men who suffered and died in the fight for
workers' rights in Indonesia, and to all of those who carry on
their fight today and into the future.

Introduction

In the new global economy, multinational corporations contract with firms all over the world to manufacture their electronic parts, their garments, or their footwear. The labels on our clothes tell us that they were "Made in Mexico," "Made in India," or "Made in Indonesia." We seldom stop to think about what such labels mean. One of the most notorious multinational corporations that contracts with manufacturers in Indonesia is Nike, the U.S. footwear manufacturer. In February 2001, the Global Alliance—a partnership among the Gap, Nike, the World Bank, and several U.S. universities and foundations, and an organization purportedly dedicated to "improv[ing] the lives and future prospects of workers involved in global production and service supply chains"—published a report on Nike that reveals exactly what it means when the little label says, "Made in Indonesia."

The 106-page report, titled *Workers' Voice: An Interim Report on Workers' Needs and Aspirations in Nine Nike Contract Factories in Indonesia* (hereafter "Nike Report"), represents a shocking indictment of both the U.S. corporation and its Asian partner companies.[1] Based on face-to-face interviews with 4,000 workers, most of them young adult women, in nine factories and focus group discussions with 450 workers, the study found grave violations of workers' rights. Workers reported long hours (including a six-day week), wages below the cost of living, forced overtime, verbal and physical abuse, sexual harassment, and a disregard for workers' health and safety.

The Global Alliance Nike Report disclosed that the workers' base wages were between $33.80 and $39.40 per month, or little more than $1 a day. If one included the company cost of transportation, meals, piece-rate bonuses, and overtime, then the wages rose to between $54 and $70.60. The daily pay averaged between $2.26 and $2.94, while the hourly rate was about $0.32 to

$0.42. According to the report, "These hourly wages are much higher than the overall hourly pay of the production workers in Indonesia in 1999, which was recorded at US$0.17." But the workers from the focus groups reported that "their base wage is quite low and does not adequately meet the increased cost of living and other needs."[2]

Nike workers' wages are based on a six-day, seven-hour workweek, but workers reported that in all nine factories they "receive pressure from management to sign a statement agreeing to overtime." Overtime often extends the workday from early in the morning until 10 at night, and extends the workweek through Sunday—that is, seven days a week. Not surprisingly, workers reported being exhausted. However, the Nike Report discloses that "[i]f the workers collapse, they are asked to take rest at the factory and asked to continue working when they wake up."[3]

Such horrendous conditions naturally breed discontent. One-quarter of the workers reported being dissatisfied with their direct supervisors, while one-third expressed dissatisfaction with the factory management. Some of that dissatisfaction arises from the verbal and physical abuse and the sexual harassment suffered by these workers. More than half of the workers (56.8 percent) reported having observed such abuse, and 30.2 percent reported having been the victims of it. Workers also reported sexual abuse and physical abuse. "Nearly 14 percent of the workers in the sample reported that they have observed some form of physical abuse from a line supervisor or manager, such as throwing objects, hitting, pushing, shoving," according to the Nike Report.[4]

Perhaps the most shocking aspect of the report dealt with the Nike contractors' utter disregard for the health of their workers. "In more than one focus group at one factory," the study reveals, "workers reported a line supervisor going to the dormitory to bring a sick worker back to work."[5] Two workers reportedly collapsed and died while working in the plants, and in one case the company was reported to have removed the corpse and told workers to say the individual died off the premises after leaving work. Nike and the Global Alliance report that they are investigating those allegations.

For workers, the little "Made in Indonesia" tag in our clothes means oppression, exploitation, and humiliation. For Nike, the Gap, and other manufacturers, it means enormous profits produced by unreasonably long hours of work for pathetically low wages in what are often unsafe working conditions. Faced with such shocking stories of twenty-first century wage slavery, we have to ask ourselves how this came about. How could a U.S.-based corporation like Nike engage in such apparently barbaric practices? How could a civilized country like the United States become a party to such uncivilized behavior? And, most important, what might be done to change this system of corporate oppression, exploitation, and abuse? These are some of the questions addressed in this book.

Indonesia, Globalization, and Democracy

I have written this book in hope that it will be useful to human rights activists, labor unionists, and the anti-sweatshop movement, as well as interesting to students, professors, and the general reader. I present an account of the Indonesian labor movement since the Asian economic crisis of 1997 and the popular movement that overthrew President Suharto in 1998. I describe and analyze the dynamic new labor movement that is being built in Indonesia by students, non-governmental organizations (NGOs), independent labor unions, and workers committed to democracy and social justice.

This is a book about globalization and its effects upon the people of Indonesia. I am interested in showing how the global economy affects one nation and its workers, and how those workers respond to international developments as they are expressed through their own national political and economic system. What happens in Indonesia is important not only for Indonesians, but for others around the world. Indonesia is an archipelago of 14,000 islands, the fourth most populous nation on earth, with about 210 million inhabitants, and the world's largest

Muslim country (about 85 percent of all Indonesians are Muslim). Indonesia stands astride some the world's most important sea lanes, and represents an essential source of natural resources for the economies of Korea and Japan. Such a large nation, and one so central to all of Southeast Asia and also so important to Asia proper, must inevitably affect the lives of hundreds of millions. Moreover, since the 1970s it has been a magnet for investment of billions of dollars from Japan, Korea, Taiwan, Hong Kong, Singapore, some of the nations of Europe, and the United States. Billions of dollars of direct foreign investment have constructed factories and mills and created huge industrial zones and new urban areas on the principal islands of Java and Sumatra, and on some of the other islands, as well.

There is no mystery about the reason for foreign investment in Indonesia. Capital has been attracted to Indonesia because most employers pay workers only about one dollar a day, often a 12-to-14-hour day. Labor is cheap. The cheap-labor economy was enforced for 35 years by a military dictatorship that used harassment, firings, beating, kidnapping, torture, imprisonment, and murder to keep workers in their place. Today, workers and their allies are attempting to build a new labor union movement that can raise workers' wages, improve their working conditions, and win them dignity in the workplace and in society. That movement is the focus of this book.

For Indonesian workers, globalization has meant a system of international capital control over their nation and over their lives. As the Indonesian people fight for better lives, they inevitably challenge not only their government, but the national and multinational corporations that dominate their economy and the international financial institutions, such as the International Monetary Fund (IMF), that stand behind them. They challenge capital, the concentrated wealth of billions. Capital means the power to command labor, and globalization means capital's power to command labor around the world.

The challenge of the global economy is nothing new for Indonesians. The people of Indonesia have been involved in international trade with the Arab world, India, other countries of Southeast Asia, and China for a thousand years. For most of the past 500 years, the East Indies, as they were once called, have been an important component of the world capitalist system. European imperialism turned the islands into a colony, until the Japanese took the colony in World War II. The Indonesians won their political independence in a revolutionary war against the Netherlands in 1949.

But as a politically independent nation Indonesia became drawn first into a post-war economic system that has often been described as neocolonial because it continued to be dominated economically by powerful foreign governments and corporations. The United States and Japan came to dominate Southeast Asia and, with it, Indonesia. Beginning in the early 1980s, Indonesia became drawn into the contemporary process of globalization, a new system of worldwide investment, production, and consumption. Globalization has meant that Indonesia has tended to become a low-wage industrial manufacturing export platform for offshore Chinese capital and for Japanese, European, and U.S. corporations.

Indonesian President Suharto's oppressive regime not only eliminated political democracy and civil rights, but also suppressed the press, controlled the campuses, and stifled any attempts at organization and collective action by labor. The regime became increasingly unbearable to the Indonesian people. In 1998, led by student activists, they rose up and overthrew Suharto. The mass protests forced the United States to withdraw support from the aging dictator. The Indonesian people's interests and U.S. government interests coincided for that brief historical moment, and Suharto fell from power. The question then became: would the Indonesian people be able to transform their country into a real democracy, and could they begin to move toward a more just and equitable society?

While the Suharto regime has fallen, the Indonesian people

are still a long way from achieving a genuine political democracy, full civil rights, and enforcing workers' rights. The Indonesian political system remains only quasi-democratic. The military continues to play an extensive role in politics, and the people of the archipelago suffer from repeated violations of their human rights by government officials and the military. Workers and peasants trying to exercise their labor rights have recently come under attack by private political militias and hooligans operating with the tacit support of the military. Muslim fundamentalists, some of them organized in paramilitary groups, and other religious extremists have also engaged in attacks on people of other faiths. Indonesians of various ethnicities have engaged in attacks on Chinese Indonesians, and conflicts have arisen between transmigrants and indigenous peoples. The Suharto government and the Indonesian military have frequently fomented pogroms and stirred up inter-communal violence.

Americans often have the prejudice that Indonesians are incapable of creating a democratic society because they are Asian or Muslim people. Those deep racial and religious prejudices have been reinforced by conservative intellectuals such as Samuel P. Huntington, who in a 1993 *Foreign Affairs* article, "The Clash of Civilizations?" (and in his subsequent book of the same title), suggested that Islamic civilization was incapable of creating democracy, or even of coexisting with democratic societies.[6] Especially since the end of the Cold War around 1990, there has been a tendency to create a new evil empire in the form of the Muslim societies now that the Communist regimes have collapsed. Thus, prejudice is elevated to prophecy and—indeed—becomes a self-fulfilling one.

To understand a nation like Indonesia, we have to be able to distance ourselves from the anti-Muslim propaganda that suggests that all Muslims are fanatics who easily become terrorists. Being Muslim in Indonesia is much like being Christian in the United States. While most Americans are Christians, for the vast majority of them, this is not their principal social or political definition. Most Americans do not begin thinking about economic, social, or political issues by saying, "As a Christian, I believe…" Only a small minority of Christians involve themselves in Christian social or political organizations, and a smaller number still in what we think of as Christian activist groups. Moreover, within the Christian world, there are important differences among Roman Catholics, Eastern Rite churches, and Protestants, and among the many Protestant sects. Christian fundamentalists or Evangelicals represent only one current of opinion, and political activist fundamentalists, an even smaller stream. Christianity contributes to the general social and political culture of the country, and to the ideology of many Americans, and we cannot understand contemporary U.S. history if we have no understanding of the enormous impact of Christianity. But at the same time, Christianity as culture or ideology has only limited value in explaining many of the political debates and conflicts in our own society. So similarly in Indonesia. Most Indonesians are Muslims, but not all Muslims join Muslim organizations or vote with Muslim political parties; only a small percentage belong to the Muslim fundamentalist movement, and an even smaller percentage to its more extreme political organizations.

As Robert W. Hefner has convincingly argued in *Civil Islam: Muslims and Democratization in Indonesia,* Islamic societies can be fully capable of creating a vibrant civil society. Muslim societies are diverse; Islam as a religion has many conflicting schools of thought, and Muslim intellectuals offer contradictory views of Islamic doctrine. Indonesia in particular has in various historical periods had a culturally diverse, intellectually lively, and politically pluralistic society. Hefner demonstrates that modern Indonesia has seen the emergence of a complex civil society made up of private commercial interests, non-governmental organizations, social movements, and diverse political currents. All of this, he shows, has given rise to "the emergence of a democratic, religiously ecumenical, and boldly reformist movement in Indonesian Islam in the 1980s and 1990s."[7] "Despite thirty years of authoritarian rule, Indonesia today is witness to a remarkable effort to recover and amplify a Muslim and Indonesian culture of tolerance, equality, and civility. The proponents of civil Islam are a key part of this renaissance. Civil Muslims denounce the mythology of an Islamic state."[8] Unfortunately, the democratic movement still confronts an authoritarian state.

Since the fall of Suharto, Indonesia has been confronted with many issues. Important national, ethnic, and religious struggles have arisen in East Timor, Aceh (North Sumatra), West Papua (Irian Jaya, formerly New Guinea), and the Moluccas, or Spice Islands. A new peasant and farmers' movement has also arisen, fighting for land not only on the major islands of Java, Sumatra, Sulawesi, and Kalimantan, but on many of the smaller islands, as well. The rural peasant population still makes up the great majority of Indonesia's people. About 65 percent of all Indonesians still live in the countryside, and most make their living from agriculture, particularly rice cultivation. Many of the regional and peasant conflicts have been developing at a rapid pace, even as I have been writing this book—too rapidly, in fact, to try to keep up with them all, especially from afar. I recognize the tremendous importance of these issues. Indonesia will not be able to move toward the resolution of its other social problems if it cannot solve these problems. However, I do not take up those questions in this book, which deals only with urban people; with industrial, service, and government workers; and with labor unions, workers' movements, and labor political parties.

While I do not discuss those questions here, I would argue that the labor movement will have a potentially important role in resolving them if it succeeds in becoming an important force in the country. The most important and rapidly growing democratic labor movements in Indonesia, the Indonesian Prosperity Workers' Union (SBSI) and the National Front of Indonesian Labor Struggle (FNPBI), both stand for a democratic secular state and took progressive positions on self-determination for East Timor. Their members come from many different ethnic groups and religions, but they have been able to overcome their difference, and unite in the struggle to build a new democratic labor movement. Their experience not only provides a model of social solidarity, it could also become a force to fight for the values of religious tolerance, self-determination, and autonomy within a stronger, more democratic Indonesia.

Indonesia is an incredibly complex nation and one fraught with problems that no political philosophy or party will easily resolve. The economic and social problems, and particularly the regional ethnic and religious conflicts, will not be solved with any magic wand. But a labor movement calling for an end to militarism and proclaiming the ideals of democracy and economic equality would represent a new national ethos and create an entirely new context for the resolution of those problems. Participatory democracy and workers' control of industry would release new energies, laying a human basis for economic development.

Indonesians have not only created a democratic civil society, they have also been capable historically of creating labor unions and a socialist movement of tremendous size and influence. At the opening of the twentieth century, Indonesians began to organize labor unions in industry and agriculture. By the 1920s, those unions organized powerful strike movements. While the Dutch colonial government used the military and police to suppress those movements, the unions reappeared during the independence revolution in the late 1940s, and the unions had tens of millions of members by the 1960s. The Indonesian Communist and Socialist parties played an important role in Indonesia from the 1940s until the mid-1960s, when they were violently and massively suppressed by the military with the support of some Muslim, Hindu, and Christian organizations. What this story demonstrates is not that Muslim civilization is antithetical to democracy, but rather that democratic, labor, and socialist movements existed in Muslim society in the past and can exist again in the future. In fact, as this book explains, they exist at present in a society far more complex and diverse than we generally think.

Solidarity

Why should people in Australia, Canada, England, or the United States care about what happens in Indonesia? What does it matter to us? In the new era of globalization, what happens in countries literally on the other side of the world matters very much. What happens in Indonesia has important implications for the American people, for example. Indonesia may be the site of the next big U.S. military intervention in a foreign country. It may be the place your tax money is sent to provide another economic bailout. It may be where your employer moves the plant you work in, and it may be where your job goes. As long as Indonesia has an authoritarian political system, workers will find it hard to organize labor unions or labor political parties, their wages and benefits will remain low, and Indonesia will continue to be a magnet for foreign investment seeking cheap wages. As long as workers in Indonesia remain wage slaves without basic human and labor rights, it will be impossible for them to join with labor unions and workers in other countries to fight for higher wages, to demand a more equitable division of social wealth, or to fight for an alternative organization of the world economy.

If workers in the United States hope to defend their labor unions, their contracts, and their wages and benefits, and to develop alternative political, economic, and social programs, they have every interest in supporting the Indonesian people in the struggle for their rights, too. Only once the Indonesian people have achieved democracy and labor union rights will they be able to collaborate with workers, unions, and labor parties in other countries. We have a common project. At present, the American Federation of Labor–Congress of Industrial Organizations (AFL-CIO) and its American Center for International Labor Solidarity (ACILS) offer support to Indonesian unions and workers, as do several other labor federations from countries in Asia and Europe. Whether or not that support is appropriate or effective is one of the topics discussed (in Chapter 10).

The Indonesian Working Class and Socialism

In writing this book, I have several times been torn between two approaches. On the one hand, I thought I might write a book simply about the Indonesian workers and unions mainly for human rights activists, labor unionists in other countries, and the solidarity movement. The ideal audience for the first approach would be the new student no-sweat movement made up of organizations such as United Students Against Sweatshops (USAS) that are working to end exploitative conditions in factories around the world. On the other hand, I was tempted to write a more political book aimed at the small left audience and academics involved in discussions about development, international politics, and social change. In the end, I have decided to write a book about labor for the movement, but also one that talks about the question of socialism and revolution, as well. I finally decided to do so because I felt that it was the only honest way to write the book.

The no-sweat movement and the new anti-globalization or fair trade movement, as it is sometimes called, has taken a stand against corporate domination of the economy and politics. But the fight against the corporations is in reality a struggle against the corporate system, against capitalism. The fight against corporate power can only be won when it becomes a fight to end capitalism and replace it with a more sustainable, efficient, humane, and democratic system. Historically, the name for such a system is socialism. I know that even some sympathetic readers of this book will read the word "socialism" with a feeling of irritation, a flush of embarrassment, or a sense of intellectual sophistication regarding what they see as utopian naiveté. Certainly in the United States, but also in much of the world, socialism has come to be seen as an anachronistic term, the property of sects, the shibboleth of a failed religion. Nevertheless, precisely because capitalism continues both to expand and to produce political and economic crises, socialism persists both as a term and as an alternative. I believe that those of us who are active in the various no-sweat and anti-corporate movements will be more effective when we realize and recognize that we fight not for some mystical return to nature; not for some utopia of small, local, family-owned business; nor for an inevitably unsuccessful reregulation of the corporations; but for a democratic and cooperative reorganization of the economy.

Ultimately, after we learn about the problems facing a country like Indonesia, we have to ask ourselves: what are the alternatives to corporate or, as it is sometimes called, "neoliberal" globalization? If the corporations and the governments they tend to dominate don't organize the world economy, then who will?

If Indonesian workers and workers in the United States and other countries around the world can succeed in organizing to resist the corporate globalizers, they will be well on the way to laying the foundation for a democratically organized and controlled economy. The alternative to corporate globalization is democratic socialism, and while they are just beginning to rebuild their union movement, some elements of the Indonesian labor movement have also begun to realize that.

At present, the world economy is organized around the axis of the corporations, their stockholders, and their search for profit. We would reorganize it around the axis of the human needs of the landless peasants, the urban poor, the factory workers, people working in the oil fields and mines, the school teachers and health workers. We see the reorganization of the world economy as the common task of those of us in the advanced capitalist countries together with those in the developing countries. The historic name for such a project is international socialism.

1 *Workers' Voice: An Interim Report on Workers' Needs and Aspirations in Nine Nike Contract Factories in Indonesia.* The entire report is available on both the Nike home page and the Global Alliance home page. See http://www.theglobalalliance.com/.

2 *Workers' Voice,* 30–32.

3 *Workers' Voice,* 33.

4 *Workers' Voice,* 39.

5 *Workers' Voice,* 39.

6 Samuel P. Huntington, *The Clash of Civilizations and the Remaking of the World Order* (New York: Simon & Schuster, 1996) and "The Clash of Civilizations?" in *Foreign Affairs* (Summer 1993).

7 Robert W. Hefner, *Civil Islam: Muslims and Democratization in Indonesia* (Princeton, N.J.: Princeton University Press, 2000), xvii.

8 Hefner, *Civil Islam,* 218.

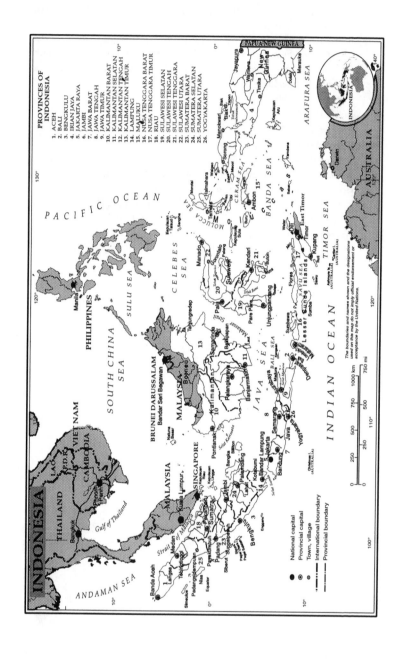

PROVINCES OF
INDONESIA

1. ACEH
2. BALI
3. BENGKULU
4. IRIAN JAYA
5. JAKARTA RAYA
6. JAMBI
7. JAWA BARAT
8. JAWA TENGAH
9. JAWA TIMUR
10. KALIMANTAN BARAT
11. KALIMANTAN SELATAN
12. KALIMANTAN TENGAH
13. KALIMANTAN TIMUR
14. LAMPUNG
15. MALUKU
16. NUSA TENGGARA BARAT
17. NUSA TENGGARA TIMUR
18. RIAU
19. SULAWESI SELATAN
20. SULAWESI TENGAH
21. SULAWESI TENGGARA
22. SULAWESI UTARA
23. SUMATERA BARAT
24. SUMATERA SELATAN
25. SUMATERA UTARA
26. YOGYAKARTA

● National capital
◉ Provincial capital
○ Town, village
▬▬ International boundary
▬ ▬ Provincial boundary

The boundaries and names shown and the designations
used on this map do not imply official endorsement or
acceptance by the United Nations.

Chapter 1

Bringing Down Suharto

Three Generations of Activists

In the midst of the greatest economic crisis in decades, in May 1998, a popular mass movement drove President Suharto from power and ended almost 35 years of military dictatorship in Indonesia. Courageous college students sparked the final conflict, risking, and sometimes losing, their lives to fight for democracy in the world's fourth largest country. After the students ignited the protests, Indonesians from many walks of life joined the demonstrations. In the capital city of Jakarta, crowds as large as 50,000 surrounded government buildings and filled public places, demanding that Suharto resign. The spreading movement gained first the assent and then the support of almost everyone but the military and Suharto's closest cronies. *Reformasi*—reform—became the word on every lip, every placard, and soon it seemed on every bumper sticker, billboard, and building. When Suharto stepped down on May 21, millions rejoiced. Democracy had triumphed, the dictator had fallen, a bright future lay ahead...

It all seemed to have happened so fast, to have taken place in an instant. But then, what were we to make of it, those of us living in other countries and on other continents, whose knowledge of Indonesia was often limited to a glimpse of a photo of exotic Bali in a travel agent's window? For many young people in Canada,

England, and the United States, Indonesia was practically a new word, a new place, and a new issue. Indonesia had never been covered on television in their lifetimes. The brief flurry of TV news coverage and newspaper headlines lasted throughout May 1998, and then Indonesia once again disappeared from the news for months at a time.

But during those few days of coverage, Indonesia appeared, ever so briefly, as a triumph of democracy. Students wearing headbands and waving banners surged around the parliament building, the dictator made the announcement of his abdication, the government promised democratic elections, and the International Monetary Fund (IMF), World Bank, and United States bestowed their approval. The TV presented those events as another success story "for our side"—Democracy victorious—and it had only taken a few days, a few bold demonstrations. A few students were killed, but it had mostly been peaceful. Youth and idealism had brought about the change, and age and wisdom confirmed the accomplishment. The U.S. government had supported the movement, hadn't it? President Bill Clinton offered his congratulations to the new president, B.J. Habibie, and sent his regards and encouragement to the Indonesian people. U.S. government officials asserted that Indonesia, by adopting democracy—and, most important, free markets—would soon achieve economic well-being. The drama subsided, and events went on in a new and hopefully democratic Indonesia.

But is that how social change really takes place? Had just a few days or weeks of popular demonstrations led to the downfall of the dictator? And did his overthrow mean that Indonesians would now live happily ever after?

Roem Topatimasang

What appeared to us as such a brief battle and one so soon victorious was viewed differently by many Indonesians. Roem Topatimasang certainly saw the fight differently, for he had spent 25 years working to empower the common people of Indonesia and to end the dictatorship of Suharto and the military. Roem was born on a small island in Sulawesi, but grew up on the island of Java in Jakarta, the capital of Indonesia, and in Jogjakarta in Central Java. He went to high school in Jogjakarta, and then to a teachers' college in Bandung in the 1970s. His fellow students elected him president of the student council, and he became a leader of the local student movement.

"[From] 1976 to 1978 students formed study clubs, and then they went to the workers," Roem remembers. "We became involved in popular education, teaching workers and peasants their rights." That was the beginning of a semi-clandestine student and worker alliance that would continue off and on throughout the Suharto dictatorship, involving three generations of students.

The students also engaged in political protests, presenting the first real challenge to Suharto's rule. "The students asked that Suharto step down," says Roem. "We were the first group of students to ask Suharto to resign. We went to the parliament and asked the legislators to impeach Suharto." The Suharto government responded harshly, he recalls:

> All of us were sent to jail at that time for two years. All of the student leaders were arrested. Forty of us were arrested in Bandung.
>
> I was tortured, not physically, but psychologically. In the first eight weeks, we were imprisoned in underground cells, right under the railroad trains, and when the train passed over our cells, it caused us to panic. Every day for three months we were taken to interrogation, and then sent back to our cells, though we never understood the reason for it.

In Suharto's Indonesia, there were no civil rights and no due process. "Some of my friends had trials, but others did not. Altogether only eight out of 40 were tried. I had no trial, but I was sent to prison for two years from 1978 to 1980. Actually, I would be arrested and held for several months, then freed, then rearrested and imprisoned again. But altogether it lasted two years."

When Roem got out of prison, he tried to go back to school, but the government had banned the student council, and because he had been the council president, the university refused to let him return.

> Well, that stopped my studies. So some friends and I founded a group in Bandung to continue our experiments in popular education with the peasants and workers of West Java. We did that work for about four years, from 1980 to 1984. It was too dangerous to try to organize, so we only did education. Even those educational meetings were underground.
>
> In south Bandung, we worked with textile workers. They had no right to self-organization, they had low salaries, and they had no grievance procedure. We tried to provide information about their rights and discuss how they could form unions by themselves.

Roem and his friends also worked with peasants on a variety of issues.

> The peasants had some of the same issues as workers, such as the right to organize. They wanted the right to choose what crops they grew. At that time, the government forced all peasants to plant only certain crops, such as rice, corn, and garden vegetables. Many peasants wanted to plant more profitable cash crops, but the government program was to achieve self-sufficiency in food. Peasants became totally dependent on the government for fertilizers and pesticides, and they couldn't make any money. Even today in Java food crops are a loss because of the cost of production inputs.

Perhaps most important was the question of the right of peasants to keep their land and work it. "Actually, most peasants are landless," says Roem. "The government or private companies have taken the land from them. In Java, for example, the government would decide to create a big sugar or tea plantation. Then the authorities would take over the land with minimal compensation, or even no compensation. This was accompanied by intimidation by the military."

The government's actions flew in the face of Indonesian law and custom. "The status of the land is still very controversial.

Historically, most of the land belonged to small units of local government, like the villages. The village owned and distributed the land to households. We have a law known as 'HGU.' That means *Halal guna usaha,* or the right to *use* land—*not* the right to *own* land. Our agrarian law states that if land is used for 25 years, it belongs to the person using it," Roem explains.

> We discussed with the peasants the history of land ownership in the village, and their perception of the government's or private companies' claims on the land. We also read the agrarian laws and interpreted them with them. But I was forced to stop this work for two good reasons. First, the military took tighter control of Bandung. Second, I had no money. So I took a job in Jakarta designing training programs for small enterprises, and did that for three or four years. I worked with the Batik cooperatives in West Java, in Ceribon and Solo.

While that was certainly useful work, Roem wanted to continue his popular education work with workers and peasants. An invitation came to him from an *ulama,* a Muslim religious leader, who headed a *pesantren,* a traditional Muslim school. Almost 90 percent of all Indonesians are Muslim, but a wide variety of political and social views exists among Muslims. This particular *ulama* wanted Roem to design a progressive educational program.

"He was not satisfied with the government's political education program, so he asked me to devise one," says Roem. "So I designed a curriculum. I began at the elementary school level, with the question: 'What is a citizen?' Civics education in Indonesia was suspended between 1965 and 1998. When I was a student in Sulawesi, before 1965, we learned about the rights of the citizen. But after the military came to power, there was only moral indoctrination in the state's ideology, which is called *Pancasila.*" Originally conceived by Sukarno, Indonesia's first president, as a statement of religious tolerance, Pancasila was used as a justification for his authoritarian rule. Roem challenged that ideology. "I wanted to return to a real civics education, so I organized and taught the course in the *pesantren.* I did that for three years."

After that, Roem spent the late 1980s and 1990s moving from one place to another, educating and organizing, supported by local communities that asked for his assistance.

> I went to West Timor for one year, and then after that to East Timor, where I was in charge of a local NGO [non-governmental organization] program organizing peasants. Then I left there and went to Irian Jaya. That was when I began to understand the indigenous people, the Papuan people with their 250 languages. I helped them to set up their own local councils, which sent representatives to local assemblies.
>
> Then I moved to the Mollucas Islands, to a very specific island called Yamdena. The government had given the forests to a big logging outfit, the Alam Nusa Segar Company, owned by Liem Sioe Liong, a friend of Suharto's. I worked with the local people to organize a campaign against this company.

The logging company's operations threatened the livelihood of the 83,000 indigenous people of Yamdena by causing soil erosion, disrupting water supplies, and threatening the coral reefs around the island, which were essential for fishing. The local protests grew until the military intervened, beating and shooting protestors. Under continued pressure from the protesters, the Forestry Ministry stopped the logging in 1993. "We won that one," says Roem.

Roem became known and respected by indigenous peoples, and received invitations to work with groups on other islands.

> I spent another four years establishing organizations on other islands. Later I went to North Sumatra. There I worked with peasants to organize unions. And just before Suharto stepped down, those peasants founded the first independent peasant union federation in North Sumatra, the SPSU, with 400,000 members.[1] The peasants in the other provinces of Sumatra imitated them, and in December of 1998 they met in Medan to found the Peasants Federation of Sumatra Indonesia, FPSI.[2] They plan to set up a national peasant union, perhaps in the next year or so. They also sent delegates to a convention of an international peasants' organization in Mexico.

In his mid-40s when I met him, Roem represented an older generation of students who had become activists in the 1970s and had gradually undermined the Suharto regime through 25 years of organizing throughout the archipelago. What turned students like Roem into lifelong activists? I think it's hard to say. Some were Muslim, some Christian. Some were genuinely religious, while others were secular humanists or leftists. In those early years of the 1970s, it seems that most were men, though some were also women, and more women became active in the 1980s and 1990s. Having talked with dozens of activists from three "generations" (of the 1970s, 1980s, and 1990s), what strikes me now is that they all held some ideal of human dignity and usually an ideal of human equality in a profound sense. The idea of equality made them democrats, and made some of them socialists, as well. Their ideals gave them courage, and their courage inspired others.

Jannes Hutahaean

Jannes Hutahaean was another Indonesian who saw the fall of Suharto differently than it appeared on the television news. For him, the struggle to overthrow the Suharto dictatorship had not been a matter of a few weeks; it had been the work of his entire adult life, almost 20 years. Jannes, a man in his late-30s with the first signs of graying hair, has a youthful energy and enthusiasm, and talks rapidly and passionately about his experiences as an environmental and labor activist. He became a student activist almost 10 years after Roem, and his story is representative of another generation of idealistic young Indonesians who laid the foundation in the 1980s for the movement that brought down Suharto in 1998.

Jannes was born in Belawan, Sumatra, on June 9, 1961, and in the late 1970s went off to study at General Sundirman University in Purwokerto, Semarang. He became vice-president of the *senat*, the student union, and, like many other students in those years, became a student activist. "Suharto was very repressive when I was going to school. My friends and I organized a demonstration to reject military involvement in the university, such as the Student Regiment."[3] Jannes also helped to organize or participated in other protests at that time against Pancasila, the state ideology, and against Golkar, Suharto's ruling political party. "We got into some trouble. The military came to my room, and the soldiers almost arrested me," he says. That was a close call, perhaps even a brush with death. Throughout the Suharto years, military arrest would almost certainly have led to beatings, and possibly to torture, imprisonment, and sometimes even murder.

As happened with many other students in Indonesia in those years, involvement in the student protests represented a first step toward participation in other social movements. "In the university, I learned about workers' and farmers' issues, but Suharto was very repressive, and it was hard to get hold of books on labor. For the government at that time, an interest in workers or farmers meant Communism, so this was very dangerous for my friends and me. The military at that time was very, very strong. But in 1983 some friends and I cautiously began to study labor."

The study of workers' and peasants' issues led Jannes and his friends to want to learn about working peoples' conditions firsthand. In Indonesia, most students come from the upper or middle classes, and most have little contact with workers or farmers. So the students had to venture into an industrial area, find a factory, and seek out workers who were willing to talk with them. "I and two other friends had our first contact with workers in 1983. They worked in a *kretek* factory, that is, a clove cigarette factory. We just talked with them about wages, conditions, and the social security system. The told us that if they worked eight hours, they only had two meals a day of rice and tempe. This was the first experience I had with workers, and it opened up my mind." At that time, workers in the cigarette factories often worked 10 or 12 hours in a single day, over 70 hours a week, and often received less than one dollar a day in wages.

After that, Jannes continued to take an interest in workers' issues. "Before I graduated, I did an academic study in Jogjakarta in

1985. It was part of a government program. I did a study of chickens, of the poultry industry, and part of that study included looking into labor conditions. I learned about the subsistence level earnings of those workers."

When Jannes finished his studies in 1986, he found a job as a journalist writing for a commercial newspaper that covered the poultry industry. "I was there about six months, and then I got hired to work as a journalist in Jakarta for the newspaper *Prioritas*. This was an opposition paper, but on the day I was to start work, the government closed it." The closing of *Prioritas* in 1987 was a famous case in Indonesia. The military detained the newspaper publisher and editor, and some reporters, and interrogated and intimidated them. With no legal justification, the government permanently shut down *Prioritas*. Management later petitioned the Indonesian Supreme Court to reopen the paper, but the case was thrown out on a technicality, and the paper was never reopened. "This was my first personal experience of the government, and it affected my views and my spirit," said Jannes. "I concluded for myself that I would fight the government."

The closing of *Prioritas* meant that Jannes found himself unemployed. With time on his hands, he explored Jakarta and went to free public events. "One day, I visited a human rights celebration. There were photos and posters on display, but there were no speakers—that would be too dangerous. I saw one poster about workers' rights, and I stood there for 15 minutes looking at it. Right then I decided that I would go to the office of the organization that made that poster. I decided I would fight for labor."

Jannes went to the office of the Urban-Rural Mission of the Protestant Batak Christian Church, known as the HKBP, and told the staff that he wanted to work with them for human rights. Led by German-educated Archbishop Dr. S.A.E. Nababan, the HKBP represented a kind of Indonesian social gospel movement or theology of liberation church. "They were one of the first organizations going to the workers in Indonesia," says Jannes. "There was great fear of going to labor, because if you did the government called you anti-government, anti-Suharto, or they called you Communist." But Jannes had decided to throw in his lot with the workers, and he joined up with the HKBP mission.

Through the church mission, Jannes went to live in Tangerang, a working class industrial suburb of Jakarta. The workers received pitifully low wages, about a dollar a day, worked in atrocious conditions, and were housed in barracks or ramshackle slums. How could these workers improve their situation? In Suharto's Indonesia, the military ran the labor unions gathered in the All-Indonesia Workers' Union (SPSI) labor federation, which existed to control workers not to fight for their rights. The same was true of public employees who had to belong to the military-run public employees' union, KORPRI (Public Employees' Corps of the Republic of Indonesia). But with the help of NGOs and of student activists, and through their own efforts, workers were beginning to organize in their communities and in their factories. "When living in Tangerang I learned that the workers had a community organization, and that they would go to the Indonesian Legal Aid, LBH, with their problems. Or they would go to the newspapers to try to publicize the issue. That was the program of the labor movement of that time. They would never go to the Indonesian Parliament, because if they went there they would be arrested."

After spending several months in Tangerang living and organizing among workers, Jannes went to live with Indonesian peasants. "I went to Siborang-Borang in North Sumatra, where I worked with a group called Community Development Initiatives Study, or KSPPM. I lived with the farmers for five years, and I became involved with them in the Inalum case," which involved a hydroelectric power plant owned by a Japanese businessman.

> The plant had closed the *sawah padi,* the wet rice fields, and the farmers had been moved from Porsea to Sioma-oma. But the people didn't like Sioma-oma because the land was not good for *padi* rice farming. I and two other activists, Indera and Asmara, organized among the farmers, and we brought the

people back to Porsea.[4] The Japanese owner and the Japanese government, as well as the Indonesian government and the military, were all very angry with the people. So the government arrested and jailed people without due process. Some people were killed.

While that was going on, Indorayon, a pulp and rayon company, came and built a factory in the area. The company had done no environmental analysis, and there was no cooperation with the people. So I organized the people to reject this. Suharto was very strong and very repressive, and the military became involved. I brought the people to the court for the hearing and to the parliament. This was one of the first environmental cases in Indonesia. So, what happened? My organization was closed. The Military District Commander closed the Urban-Rural Mission of the Protestant Batak Christian Church in 1990.

Not only did the Indonesian Army close the mission, but the military also appointed a new bishop to head the church, leading the congregations to withdraw from the church and worship in their homes.[5]

Jannes was out of a job, but was determined to keep working with workers and farmers around those same issues.

In October of that year, I went to work for the Appropriate Technology Foundation of the Indonesian Church Assembly, another non-governmental organization. I stayed in Medan and talked to church pastors and to church organizations, to students and professors at the university. I traveled to various districts of North Sumatra and talked to people in urban and rural communities. I became involved in the issue of MHP, or micro-hydropower, for drinking water systems.

The church and the government both cooperated with my organization, and we were doing some good work. But what happened? In 1991, the military attacked my office, which was owned by the church. They seized the office because it was on land that had been sold to Tommy Suharto, the president's son.

Such arbitrary land seizures by corporations or by military and government officials were common during the Suharto years. Sometimes they could be successfully resisted, but this was Suharto's own son who had taken the land and the office, and Jannes had little choice but to move on.

Once again, Jannes was out of a job, but he continued to organize, working with a network of mostly Christian activists.[6]

> I helped organize a demonstration against the military in June 1991 in Medan [North Sumatra], one of the first big demonstrations against the military in Indonesia. The military then arrested 32 professors and students and took them to jail. I escaped, thanks to the pastors and the church people who protected me. For 14 days, my friends were in prison. They were put in septic tanks, and they were given electric shocks. They were put in a room where soldiers shot at them as they ran around. Having been beaten beyond recognition, they were released in their underwear. Of course, all of this was done without due process. I came to hate the government.

The Batak Protestant Church hardened its heart against the military. In 1991, the church organized a big demonstration against the Sumatran military headquarters. Jannes, of course, was involved. "We held a very big demonstration. Some of the reverends were arrested, about 50 pastors, all without due process. I escaped to another province. I was the only one who escaped. The pastors always protected me, so I was never arrested."

Later that year, Jannes began to work with another organization, called Pondok Rakyat, or the People's House, a group that worked specifically on labor issues.

> I lived and worked with workers. I shared, discussed, and analyzed with them. We worked on analyzing labor and the community, the enterprises, the government, and the military. In Medan we organized consciousness-raising groups and an educational leadership program that lasted five years, from 1991 to 1994.
>
> In April 1994, the SBSI [Indonesian Prosperity Workers'

Union], an independent union led by Muchtar Pakpahan, the Pondok Ryat, and the Social Democratic Organization (KPS), met to organize a big demonstration.[7] On April 14 of that year, 25,000 workers demonstrated at government offices. The workers demanded higher wages and freedom of organization. The military was mobilized to suppress the demonstrations. The soldiers killed Rusli, a worker at the PT IKD plant. We had labor demonstrations in almost 200 factories for an entire month.

The April 1994 demonstrations in Medan were among the biggest labor demonstrations in Indonesia in years, and a turning point in the development of the new movement for workers' rights and democracy.[8]

"At that time Muchtar Pakpahan of SBSI, Parlin of KPS, and myself ... were arrested, together with 100 workers. Parlin and I were sentenced to 11 months, but I was released after six. U.S. President Clinton visited Indonesia for the Asia-Pacific Economic Cooperation meeting in Bogor, and I was released at that time." Once out of jail, Jannes went back to organizing, and when demonstrations around the country finally drove Suharto from power, Jannes was one of the local organizers in Medan and one of those protesting in the streets.

Dita Sari

In the 1990s, yet another student movement, one that would finally be the catalyst for the overthrow of Suharto, emerged. One young woman who joined it would become an internationally famous labor organizer and political prisoner. Dita Sari was 27 years old at the time I interviewed her. Her manner was warm and friendly, and at the same time completely open and straightforward.

I asked her about her childhood. "I was born in Medan, North Sumatra, in 1972. My father was an employee of a company, and then he was a member of parliament for Golkar (Golongan Karya, or Function Group), the government party, in 1973. He has since confessed that he was wrong," she added, smiling in a way that indicated she had won him over.

"It must have been difficult," I said, "with a father who had been in Golkar, and you a union organizer."

"No. My parents supported me in what I was doing in the union, though they were very upset when I was in prison," she explained:

> I went to high school there, in Medan, and then to the University of Indonesia in 1991, where I studied law, though I didn't finish my degree. I came from a very middle-class family. I was an ordinary student. I wanted to become a lawyer. When I got to the University of Indonesia, I started attending lots of forums, discussions, and study groups. I made friends who were political, and I joined the Free Study Forum, which was the embryo of Students in Solidarity for Democracy in Indonesia, or SMID, one of the groups that later formed the People's Democratic Party, the PRD. We talked about philosophy and theory. We read people like Karl Marx.
>
> Then, after a while, we came to the conclusion that we had to go from theory to practice. We started by organizing students to fight for human rights. Then we led the students to the parliament to demand human rights. But we realized that students cannot solve these problems alone.
>
> As students, we recognized the need to connect with workers in order to bring about democratic change. The group encouraged me to spend a month living in the workers' quarters in order to understand what their conditions were, and also to talk with them about political and economic issues in order to begin to organize them.

So, like many others of her generation, Dita went to the workers; but, unlike most, she went to stay.

> Students had already made contact with workers. But they had only done surveys and conducted research. But I went to live with them, and I said, this is not just a matter of research; this is the time to organize.
>
> This was very difficult for me, because I was pure middle class. It was hard to live in such noisy, polluted, dirty condi-

tions. At first, I just felt pity for them, because I saw them as suffering and oppressed, even if they didn't see themselves as oppressed. But my feelings of pity changed to a more emotional bond, and I saw organizing as my task.

The relationship between the student radicals and the workers was a two-way street, says Dita. "We went to the workers to educate them, but also to learn from them. It's not just workers who learn from students. Students also have to learn from the workers. We also learned from their culture and from their historical struggles." To be a successful organizer, says Dita, "you have to become part of the workers' lives and share the workers' experiences and problems. Now I identify myself so completely with my project that if I stopped I would have no idea what my life would mean or who I would be. It developed from a long process, and it is a very personal thing for me, very emotional."

Fresh from the campus and study circles reading Karl Marx, taking up the task of organizing workers was a whole new experience. "This was not just about talking or debating, it was also about organizing. So we began to organize around issues such as the workers' meal allowance or transportation allowance. We explained that they had to get together, and we organized them," she said.

> We began with those purely economic issues, such as meal and transportation allowances. But from the economic issues, we tried to show the connection between the bosses and the Ministry of Manpower, between the bosses and the state. We told them, "When you go on strike, the boss walks into the Ministry of Manpower and talks to them. But you, as a worker, have no access to the Ministry of Manpower." So we tried to explain to the workers the role of the government, of the state. It's not just between the workers and the boss; it's also between the workers and the state. We want to help make the workers a strong force before the boss and before the state.

In addition to her labor organizing, Dita was also a founding member of the PRD, the first organization since 1965 to take up the struggle for socialism in Indonesia. Since Marxism, socialism, and communism are illegal in Indonesia, the PRD defined itself as "social democratic," though no one had any doubts that the new party was far more radical than most social democratic parties and in fact aimed at a fundamental restructuring of Indonesian society. By 1994, the PRD had created three important organizations: SMID; the National Peasant Union, or STN; and the Center for Indonesian Labor Struggle, or PPBI. Dita was one of the leaders of the PPBI and active in organizing factory workers into the new union.

But organizing workers was illegal. Independent unions had been forbidden in Indonesia since 1975, and only the government-controlled SPSI could legally create a labor union. Nevertheless, Dita persisted in her efforts. In the Tandes industrial estate in southern Surabaya, Dita helped organize labor rallies involving 10,000 workers from 10 factories. At the rallies, she and other organizers called for raising wages from about one dollar to $1.25 a day. Faced with the beginning of a mass movement, the military intervened, breaking strikes and arresting Dita in early July 1996.

Dita Sari might have considered herself fortunate to have been arrested, rather than simply disappeared. Just three years earlier, in April 1993, Marsinah, a 25-year-old woman who worked at PT Catur Putra Surya, a factory in Porong, Sidoarjo, East Java, suffered a much worse fate. She had been involved in leading strikes for higher wages and better working conditions at the plant, which produced watches for export. The military, which had been sitting in on company-worker contract negotiations, came to the factory on May 2, called 12 employees into a meeting, and fired them. Marsinah loudly protested the workers' firings, but then she herself disappeared on May 5. Three days later, on May 8, her body was found about 100 kilometers from her home with indications that she had been tortured and raped before being murdered. Her throat had marks showing that she had been strangled, and some instrument had horribly damaged her vagina. The military was put in charge of investigating her murder, though human rights organizations suspected that it was the army itself that had murdered Marsinah because of her labor union activities.[9]

While not as extreme a fate, Dita's arrest led to her trial and eventual conviction. "I was arrested by the military and put on trial in a civilian court in Surabaya for four months," says Dita. "The original charge was that I had violated Article 154, that I had insulted the government, and insulted persons in the government. But after July 27, 1996, when the office of the Indonesian Democratic Party was burned, the charge was changed to violation of the Anti-Subversion Law. I was accused of trying to change the state's ideology of Pancasila." The military itself had organized the gangsters who burned the offices of the Indonesian Democratic Party (PDI), but the event was used as an excuse to outlaw opposition political parties, including the PRD. Dita herself had been in prison when the events took place, but was nevertheless held responsible for them. "In the PRD constitution, and in our labor union, the basic philosophy was not Pancasila, but 'popular social democracy.' So, because our party's philosophy was different, we were accused of trying to change the philosophy of the state. I was just an ordinary PRD member. I was not an officer or leader of the group. Yet I was now charged with subversion."

The government's case against Dita Sari and the PRD had an *Alice in Wonderland* quality about it. The PRD had made the repeal of the "five political laws" a central part of its political program. The "five laws" dealt with political parties, elections, parliament, mass organizations, and the referendum process to change the constitution. The party's proposal to amend the Indonesian constitution to remove those five laws made it guilty of subversion. After the fall of Suharto, and in the heyday of Reformasi in February 1999, the Indonesian congress (DPR) began to debate a change in those laws. But at the time Dita was arrested, the desire to change the law made one a subversive and a criminal.

"During the trial, we tried to explain the difference between social democracy and Communism," said Dita. "We tried to talk about workers' rights and conditions, such as the right to freedom of association. We argued that we shouldn't be tried because of our thoughts." But in pre-Reformasi Indonesia, she had no chance of being found innocent, and she was convicted of subversion and sentenced to six years in prison, of which she eventually served three.

Prison conditions were sometimes depressing.

> In Surabaya, prison officials accused me of organizing a riot. So they moved me to Melang. But there they started a smear campaign against me among the other prisoners and guards. They made the other prisoners afraid of me and made them not trust me. They created a space of hate and suspicion between the other prisoners and me. This put me in a corner, and I was not able to relate to anyone in a normal way. Even if I spoke about normal things, I was still haunted by the idea that other prisoners would interpret what I said in the wrong way and report it to the guards.
>
> The conditions were very bad during the seven months when I was in Melang Prison. My access to visitors was restricted. All my reading material was censored, and worst of all I was very isolated from all of the other women prisoners. This was psychologically very tiring.
>
> It was better when I was moved to Tangerang. There I was able to relate to the other prisoners. I became like an adviser to them. Since I've been released, I have sent greetings to them over the phone.

The American Center for International Labor Solidarity (ACILS), the AFL-CIO's office in Indonesia, had extended financial support to help Dita make this move from East Java to West Java so she would be closer to her family and friends and have more visitors.

While Dita remained imprisoned, her comrades in the PRD were playing a leading role in the new student movement that had begun to lead large political demonstrations calling for the overthrow of Suharto. While workers' strikes had represented the greatest threat to the regime a few years before, now it was the students who led a mass movement, first on the university campuses, and then in cities throughout the country. The student movement gradually won the support of the middle class, the independent labor unions, and then the urban poor, who also began to join the demonstrations. The pressure mounted until those days in May when Suharto finally stepped down.[10]

With Suharto's fall, the prison doors swung open for hundreds of political prisoners. But all nine PRD prisoners remained incarcerated, including Dita. The military still held crucial posts in the new government of B.J. Habibie, Suharto's handpicked successor, including the Coordinating Ministry for Political and Security Affairs, Defense Ministry, Home Affairs Ministry, and even the Attorney General. Syarwan Hamid, the Home Affairs Minister who had been largely responsible for the campaign accusing the PRD of being responsible for the riots at the PDI offices, and who had vowed to "wipe out the PRD to its very roots," strongly opposed her release, Dita explained. Apparently the military viewed the PRD as a revolutionary socialist organization, and viewed Dita Sari and her comrades as dangerous organizers and agitators. So, while other prisoners walked the streets and enjoyed their liberty, Dita remained in prison.

Many individuals and organizations helped support Dita while she was in prison, and worked for her release. Her friends and family, labor unions, women's organizations, and human rights groups spoke out on her behalf. In June 1998, Dita's parents demonstrated with the parents of other political prisoners at the offices of the Attorney General and the Coordinating Ministry for Political and Security Affairs, demanding the release of their children. The pressure from both Indonesian and international organizations gradually began to have an effect. In July 1998, Manpower Minister Fahmi Idris expressed his personal opinion to visiting labor representatives that Dita should be released from prison. U.S. Embassy First Secretary Edmund

McWillliams and Labor Attaché Greg Fergin both visited Dita in September 1998, putting more pressure on the authorities.[11]

The Habibie government attempted to make a deal with Dita in October 1998, offering to release her from prison, but on the condition that she promise to refrain from political or labor organizing or travel abroad until the end of her prison term in July 2001. But Dita rejected the offer, since she clearly intended to continue her activities once she was released. So she stayed in prison, and the visits from both foreign and domestic supporters continued. October 1998 was a busy month of activities on Dita's behalf. Phil Fishman of the AFL-CIO International Affairs Department visited Dita on October 5. On October 13, Farahdib Augustin of the Women's Department of the SBSI, another independent labor federation, led a demonstration at the Ministry of Justice demanding Dita's release. Kobar (the Workers' Committee for Reform Action), one of the PRD-initiated labor unions in the Jakarta industrial suburbs, organized protests at the Attorney General's Department on October 29 to demand her release. On January 14, 1999, Barbara Shailor, the AFL-CIO's International Affairs Director, visited Dita and promised to continue to work for her release. Three days later, Justice Minister Muladi also visited her, and indicated he supported efforts to have her released from prison. Muchtar Pakpahan, head of the SBSI, who himself had spent years in prison for union organizing, visited Dita Sari in prison on February 6, 1999. He promised to raise the issue of her release in international arenas. SBSI Secretary-General Sunarty, also a woman union organizer, visited Dita in May 1999, and promised to work for her release.

While in prison, Dita wrote letters to various prominent people around the world in an attempt to call their attention to her case and to win their support. She wrote to, among others, Nelson Mandela and Hillary Clinton. In a letter of April 17, 1999, to Mandela she wrote,

> It is only two years left, then my punishment will be over. But for my people, for my workers, it's a long way to freedom.

Freedom from fear, freedom from poverty, and freedom from
repression…. Whenever the hard times come in this prison I
try to think about the harder times that you have been
through. It does help me. My friends always tell me we should
create new Mandelas; not in South Africa, but here in Indonesia…. I am 26 years old, and most of the activists in my union
are young people. The waves of mass struggle will shape us, fill
our minds with new ideas and opinions, and, somehow,
strengthen us. It's a long way to go, Sir, and life in the struggle
does not always treat us kindly. But anyhow, I sincerely pray
for your strength and health to take care of the people, the
children of South Africa who love and admire you.

Having spent three years in prison, the Indonesian labor organizer might have been unaware of the rising conflict between
the new South African state that Mandela had created and the labor unions. While Mandela remained tremendously popular and
a national hero, many unions and workers had come to question
whether his government really stood on their side.

At the Seventh World Women's Conference of the International Confederation of Free Trade Unions on May 21, 1999, in
Rio de Janeiro, Brazil, the delegation from Malaysia proposed
and the delegation from Great Britain seconded a resolution calling on the government of Indonesia to free Dita. The
AFL-CIO's Solidarity Center helped to distribute literature about
Dita's case to the 300 delegates from 130 countries. A statement
from Dita in which she called on workers in Indonesia to take advantage of the political changes to organize labor unions was also
distributed to workshops at the conference. The conference sent
letters by fax to the new Indonesian president, Habibie, and to
General Wiranto demanding "the immediate, unconditional release of Dita Sari."

Back in Indonesia, taking Dita's words to heart, 120 worker
activists met in Lembang, West Java, from May 14 to 16 to found
the National Front of Indonesian Labor Struggle (FNPBI). The
delegates elected Dita Sari to be the front's leader, despite the fact
that she remained imprisoned. On June 20, 1999, some 100 activ-

ists from Kobar and from student groups such as Komrad and Big Family of the University of Indonesia (KB-UI) demonstrated outside the Tangerang Women's Prison, demanding her release. The Women's Committee from SPSI-Reformasi, a reformed branch of the old state-controlled unions, held another demonstration on June 28, when about 250 men and women demonstrated at the prison for two hours and then went to the Ministry of Justice to demand Dita's release. The Minister of Justice, Fahmi Idris, also visited Dita on June 28 to discuss her views of labor unionism and the new labor regulations, and agreed that she should be freed. The government finally relented and released Dita Sari from prison on July 5, 1999.

"I was released because of international pressure," says Dita. "Unions, women's organizations, and human rights organizations carried out campaigns and circulated petitions to the Habibie government demanding my release. This international solidarity, combined with campaigns by workers' and students' groups and political parties in Indonesia, was the main reason for my release."

While Dita was in prison, her mother died. A friend of hers told me that when she was released from prison, Dita went directly to her mother's grave and used her prison uniform to clean the headstone. It was her way of telling her mother that she was free, and that she had come to say good-bye. Free at last, Dita returned to her union, and began once again organizing workers.

The Struggle Continues

The fall of Suharto appeared to most as a two-minute segment on the evening news, as a flurry of demonstrations during a few days in May. But for Roem Topatimasang, Jannes Hutahaean, and Dita Sari—and for scores of other student activists, workers, and farmers—it appeared as the culmination of years of struggle. For them, the struggle meant losing jobs, moving from one city to another, and being imprisoned and tortured. For Marsinah, a factory worker from East Java, it had meant death. Because of these activists and hundreds of others like them, by the end of the

1990s, workers were involved in mass strikes, peasants had begun to step up their demands for their land, and students and citizens were demanding democracy.

For many, the Indonesian turmoil seemed to end with the fall of Suharto; the struggle seemed to be over. But for the people of Indonesia, the struggle continues, only now as a fight to make the promise of democracy and justice real.

In 1998, Roem gave up his itinerant organizing life, at least for a while, to work with a non-governmental organization called Insist, based in Jogjakarta, where I first met him. Since the fall of Suharto, Roem has concentrated on social analysis, criticism, and writing and publishing books on peasants' rights and the problems of Indonesian education.

"The main point," says Roem,

> is that we call upon the government to acknowledge the rights of the peasants in managing their own natural resources based on International Labor Organization [ILO] Convention 169 and other United Nations conventions on social and economic rights, as well as on our own national constitution, which says that all natural resources should be used for the benefit of the people.[12] I start with the thesis that the indigenous people are the most entitled to local resources. I stress that this is the basis of their rights, which have always been ignored by government since colonial times. We are trying to raise a new level of understanding in Indonesian society about these questions. For a long time, these issues couldn't be discussed. I'm trying to link issues of peasant rights and what we call customary rights, often connected to land, and cultural rights, ... to a system of local governance. This idea was destroyed by the military law and by unitary administration. Last year [1998], the indigenous communities started holding meetings, and then they held the first meeting of indigenous people in Jakarta [in 1999]. The indigenous people all together are 20 million in the outer islands and on Java. That's 10 percent of the population of Indonesia.

Most recently, Roem has become well known for his book

Schools Are Opium, a stinging critique of the Indonesian education system in which he argues that Indonesian education is a kind of dangerous drug that does more harm than good. "The public school system in Indonesia is such that people cannot be themselves," says Roem. "The people become unaware of the local social situation around them. Every Minister of Education changes the policy. Five years ago, the Minister of Education said that the curriculum should emphasize physics and engineering because the factories needed more technicians. Education is really market driven, and the idea of the university as a place for research or invention is lost."

When I talked with Jannes in Medan, North Sumatra, in June 2000, he was still organizing workers and farmers. Though Suharto had fallen, democracy had not yet been won, and economic justice remained a goal for the future. Workers still had to struggle to organize independent labor unions, fight for a living wage and decent working conditions, and organize to win democracy and civil rights.

"Now I work with the Labor Solidarity Committee of Medan and with Pondok Rakyat, which organizes fishermen, plantation workers, and factory workers," Jannes explains.[13]

> The problem in North Sumatra today is the role of the multinational corporations that have conflicts with the fishermen, laborers, and farmers of the area. For example, for five years I was involved in a boycott of the Barbie doll because of the manufacturer's hiring of child labor in North Sumatra. We have Glove company here, and we have a big Gap company plant in North Sumatra, about one hour from here by bus, and workers at both plants have low wages and poor conditions. The Gap plant is AL Ichwan, where workers are paid minimum wage or less and work 50 to 60 hours. There are 4,000 workers there.

The role of U.S. corporations is enormous, says Jannes. "Indorayon is about 8 percent U.S.-owned, PT IIO is 90 percent U.S., London Sumatra is 60 percent U.S., Goodyear Rubber is

U.S., there are 38 fish corporations here from the U.S., and 12 fishing harbors with U.S. investment." So the fight for democracy and workers' rights in Indonesia today must also be a fight against multinational corporations, particularly against U.S. corporations that exploit Indonesian workers and peasants. Jannes is now engaged in that fight, organizing workers to pressure U.S. corporations into negotiations, looking, he says, for a nonviolent method of social change.

When I interviewed her in the summer of 1999, Dita had returned to her organization and thrown herself once again into union organizing. Many things had changed during the three years she had spent in prison, particularly during the last year, and especially for union organizers. Indonesia had signed ILO Convention 87 granting the right to free association; the Ministry of Manpower had issued a statement saying it would recognize independent labor unions, and it had done so; new labor federations had been established, some of which now had more than a dozen sectoral affiliates and scores of local unions.

> In 1996, after the government outlawed the PPBI, we had to move underground; we had to become clandestine. We couldn't use the name and banner of PPBI, so we encouraged workers to build their own local struggles and local unions. We organized local unions, but then we decided it was time to unite them into a national organization, so we created the National Front for Indonesian Labor Struggle, or FNPBI. But other people had also built local unions…, so we invited them to join with us too. And so the FNPBI is now a real front, as the name implies.

Dita appreciates the new situation in Indonesia, and the increase in democratic rights, but she has also found that the changes were not all that they appeared to be. "In some ways, it is now easier to organize workers," she said:

> There is more democratic space. We can campaign and pass out leaflets. We can set up legal unions. But it is still difficult to organize at the grassroots level because the employers still use

the old methods of intimidation, firing, and blackmail to prevent workers from organizing themselves, and the government permits it. It may look like we have democracy—but we do not. The old methods are still used at the grassroots because they do not want the workers to be organized into a powerful union or to be politicized.

Both the military and the civilian bureaucracy, like the Department of Labor, try to reduce workers' involvement in union activity. This is because the military and the civilian government are in collusion with the factory owners. If the bosses think it is necessary, they can call the local police, give them a bribe, and the military will send soldiers into the factory. But the military does this not only for money ... they also see it as a way of maintaining order, the status quo.

Nevertheless, despite the threats of repression, Dita continues to organize unions and build her independent labor federation.

Dita's aspirations go beyond organizing labor unions and winning collective bargaining agreements, both of which she believes to be very important.

I have this idea of creating a "labor wing" within the political milieu so we can bargain with the regime and other political forces. Such a "labor wing" would allow the unions a way to draw other political forces closer to the working class. Workers can become a force in politics by organizing, speaking, writing, debating, just talking. Reformasi has created lots of new political spaces, and we must take advantage of them. Since Reformasi, things have changed: now workers must also become a strong force in the political arena, facing all the other forces in politics.

Roem, Jannes, and Dita represent three cohorts of student activists from the 1970s, 1980s, and 1990s who helped lay the foundation for the movement that drove Suharto from power, began to establish political democracy, and created the first independent workers' organizations.

The Reformasi movement succeeded in its aim of overthrowing Suharto precisely because it became a broad movement that successfully incorporated Muslims, Christians, and secular activists from many regions of the archipelago. The many different sorts of organizations were able to unite around a program of ending the military dictatorship, establishing political democracy, and broadening the rights of workers, farmers, and the poor. Within that context, socialists like Dita Sari and the PRD worked to promote the idea of the working class as the leading force in society to carry out a fundamental reorganization of Indonesia's economic and political system. Today, new activists, some students and NGO activists, but many of them workers, are taking up the fight for democracy and social justice, and we tell their stories in the following chapters. But first we turn to look at the role of the United States in imposing the new model of economic globalization on Indonesia.

1   Serikat Petani Sumatera Utara (SPSU).

2   Federasi Petani Sumatera Indonesia (FPSI), which should not be confused with an earlier state-controlled union with the same initials.

3   Regimen Mahasiswas, like the U.S. ROTC.

4   The two other activists, Indera Nababan and Asmara Nababan, are both brothers of Archbishop S.A.E. Nababan. Today, Indera heads the Urban Community Mission (UCM) in Jakarta, Indonesia, which supports worker organizing, while Asmara Nababan sits on Indonesia's National Human Rights Commission.

5   That was in August 1990. The KSPPM reopened two months later, but Jannes had to leave. For an account of the Indonesian military's fight with the HKBP see Gerry Van Klinken, "Battle for the pews," *Inside Indonesia* 49. Available on-line at http://insideindonesia.org/edit49/hkbp.htm. For further information, see Human Rights Watch/Asia reports: "The Limits of Openness: Human Rights in Indonesia and East Timor" (1994), "Human Rights Abuses in North Sumatra" (1993), and "Military Repression Against the Batak Church" (1993).

6   While Indonesia is about almost 90 percent Muslim, parts of Sumatra have a large Christian population.

7   Kelompok Pelita Sejahtera (KPS).

8   Rusli's body was found on March 13 in the Deli River near Medan. Police said he had fallen in the river, but his relatives and coworkers said he had been beaten and murdered. See Amnesty International, "Indonesia and East Timor, Human Rights in 1994: A Summary," 4. Available on-line at http://www.amnesty.org/ailib/1995/ASA/210395.ASA.txt.

9   Vedi R. Hadiz, *Workers and the State in New Order Indonesia* (New York: Routledge and Asia Research Centre, Murdoch University, 1997), 113.

10   For a fuller account of these events see Clare Fermont, "Indonesia: The Inferno of Revolution," *International Socialism* 80 (Autumn 1998): 3–33.

11   As they did again in February 1999.

12   ILO Convention 169 is a remarkable document dealing with indigenous peoples' rights and their relation to the environment.

13   Komite Solidaritas Buruh (KSB).

Chapter 2

Indonesia in the Grip of Global Capital

To understand developments in Indonesia, or for that matter in any other country, one must look toward the grassroots of the society but also toward the national and international economic and political elite. The truth of politics is always found in the dynamic interaction between the elite's power and the common people's acquiescence or resistance. At the same time, we have to situate both the international elite's imposition of its authority and local grassroots resistance within the context of a worldwide capitalist system that is always evolving in ways not entirely within the control of these actors. The process called globalization—capitalism's contemporary incarnation—has changed the behavior of elites and grassroots resisters, and led to new options and alternatives for both.

While it was the student activists and later other Indonesian citizens whose protests and demonstrations eventually brought down Suharto, his fall also resulted from decisions made by the U.S. government and international financial institutions. Behind those decisions was the economic crisis that swept Asia beginning in mid-1997. When the economic crisis hit, and protests began to grow in Indonesia, the United States started to reevaluate its support for Suharto. Seeing the massive student and citizen protests, and fearing that they might spread to workers, peasants, and the poor, the Clinton administration, which had backed

Suharto to the bitter end, finally decided to withdraw its support for the dictator. Perhaps nothing makes the American government's imperial role in the world as clear as events such as these.

The Clinton administration's key role in unseating Suharto should come as no surprise, for the United States had played an important part in the island nation's history ever since the end of World War II. Parts of Indonesia had been a Dutch colony since as early as 1600, and most of the archipelago had been under Dutch control since the mid-1700s. But at the beginning of World War II, the Japanese invaded and occupied the archipelago. Toward the end of the war, the Japanese—hoping to keep the Europeans from coming back to Asia—supported the Indonesians' creation of an independent nation. In August 1945, a new Indonesian nationalist government proclaimed its independence and asked the world for recognition. But, like the French in Vietnam, the Dutch refused to accept the loss of the archipelago, and sent an army to take back their colony. The Indonesians resisted and fought a revolutionary war for independence from the Netherlands that lasted form 1945 to 1949, and while the Indonesian nationalists proved incapable of defeating the Dutch, their victory over their own internal Communist rivals would eventually win them the support of the United States, and thus the war of independence.

The U.S. Role in Indonesia

The United States at first supported the Dutch, and even financed their colonial war, hoping that Indonesia's wealth flowing toward the Netherlands would help stabilize the volatile situation in Western Europe. The U.S. Government also feared that if the Netherlands lost power in Indonesia, a radical nationalist or Communist government might come to power there and threaten American economic and geopolitical interests. But when Sukarno and the nationalists succeeded in crushing the Communists in a local internal conflict in 1948, the United States switched sides and supported the Indonesian independence struggle.[1] As the dominant world power, the United States was able to determine the terms of the Dutch withdrawal from the archipelago, and ensure the international recognition of the new nationalist government in Indonesia.

Sukarno, the leader of the nationalist movement, became Indonesia's first president with the blessings of the United States, but soon fell out of favor because of his refusal to accept the Cold War division of the world. In April 1955, Sukarno's government hosted the Asia-Africa Conference, later called the Bandung Conference after the city where it took place, in an attempt to cohere a bloc of non-aligned nations, that is, countries that would back neither the Soviet Union nor the United States in the Cold War. Attending the conference were 29 leaders from Asia and Africa, including Chou En-lai of China, Jawaharlal Nehru of India, Gamal Abdel Nasser of Egypt, and Norodom Sihanouk of Cambodia. Among other decisions, the conference supported Indonesia's claim to Irian (New Guinea), which at that time had still not been resolved. Sukarno's role in convening the conference and attempting to create a non-aligned bloc made him *persona non grata* with the U.S. State Department. In an attempt to unseat Sukarno, the Central Intelligence Agency (CIA) backed rebel military forces in Indonesia from 1956 to 1958. But the CIA's various uprisings all but failed, and one of them proved to be an utter fiasco in which CIA documents were captured. As a result, the U.S. government's plans for counter-revolution had to be abandoned.[2]

Sukarno responded to these threats against his government by instituting what he called "Guided Democracy," an authoritarian regime based on martial law. But fearing that the military might attempt to remove him, Sukarno turned to the Indonesian Communist Party (PKI) as a counterbalance to the army. With Sukarno's support, the PKI grew rapidly, and its peasant organizing even faster. Under pressure from his allies in the PKI, Sukarno's government passed an agrarian reform law in 1960, and conflicts began to grow between the peasant movement and landowners, some of them Muslim temples and schools. By the early 1960s, Sukarno and the PKI were orienting more toward China, while the PKI militantly opposed the United States and other imperial powers in Indonesia. The CIA and the U.S. State Department viewed the Indonesian Communists as a very real threat, though the PKI remained subordinate to Sukarno. In that period, the Communist Party had taken power in China, and the United States found itself at war first with Communist Korea and then with Communist Vietnam. The U.S. government feared yet another Communist revolution in Indonesia, and was determined to stop it.

The earlier support for regional rebellions having failed, the U.S. government took another tack. Since the 1950s, the U.S. government had cultivated relations to Indonesian military officers, hoping some alternative to Sukarno might come from that quarter. Within a few years, the American wish came true. In the midst of an economic and social crisis, and of increasing tensions and conflicts between the Communists and the Indonesian military, an obscure general named Suharto organized a coup, overthrew the Sukarno regime, and took power in 1965. Suharto's military and its conservative Muslim allies—in some areas joined by Indonesian Nationalist Party (PNI) members, Balinese Hindus, and Javanese Catholics—proceeded to kill between 500,000 and one million Communists, labor union members, and peasant activists, while local pogroms also killed several thousand Chinese. Despite the holocaust, the U.S. government rushed to support Suharto, while *Time* magazine described the annihilation of the Indonesian Communist Party as "The West's best news for years in Asia." The United States would continue to back Suharto from the bloody 1965 coup until the Asian economic crisis of 1997.[3]

Suharto's New Order

Suharto established a military-political dictatorship that he called the New Order. The Suharto dictatorship, based on support from the military, from some Muslim clerics, and sections of the upper and middle classes, had some of the characteristics of European fascism of the 1920s and 1930s. The Suharto regime virtually eliminated political and civil rights, and gradually subordinated all important institutions, organizations, and social movements to the state. Among Suharto's first acts when he took power in 1965 was the creation of a new economic policy. He proceeded to put in place an economic system that made Indonesia into a virtual neocolony of foreign powers. First he immediately invited representations of the International Monetary Fund (IMF) and the World Bank to meet with him, and put himself on good terms with the international financial institutions, making Indonesia eligible for loans from foreign banks. Second, he hired half-a-dozen Indonesian-born economic advisors trained at the University of California at Berkeley, the so-called "Berkeley Mafia," who rewrote the nation's laws on foreign investment.

Following their suggestions, Suharto opened up oil and mineral interests to foreign investors and removed obstacles to direct foreign investment in industry and the construction of foreign-owned plants. Most important, he established an authoritarian labor regime that kept Indonesian workers down and made labor cheap. The result of these policies was in many ways a return to the kind of colonial relationship that Indonesia had to the Dutch, only now it was a subordinate relationship to Japan, the United States, and the European nations generally. In some ways, Suharto's emphasis on making Indonesia an export platform for foreign investment, and Indonesia's cheap sweatshop labor conditions, was some 20 years ahead of its time, anticipating the system of globalization and neoliberalism that would be forced upon other countries in the 1980s.

The neocolonial or neoliberal regime introduced by Suharto had important implications for the development of Indonesia's economy. Suharto and his fellow generals established business partnerships with some of Indonesia's wealthiest capitalists, most of whom were Chinese Indonesians, and soon dominated the national economy and controlled ties with foreign investors. Thus the entire Indonesian economy came to be controlled by Suharto and his cronies, a very small circle of ten or twenty of the richest men and women in Indonesia. The existence of this small political, bureaucratic bourgeoisie inhibited the growth of a real capitalist class that might have developed the nation in its own interests, such as existed in Taiwan, Hong Kong, Singapore, and Thailand. In Suharto's Indonesia, there was virtually no national capitalist class with an interest in some sort of political democracy.

Suharto's government failed to develop a national economic development plan, but instead acted as purveyor of Indonesia's riches to foreign investors from Japan, Europe, and the United States. Unlike other oil-rich nations, Indonesia never nationalized the oil industry and never created its own refineries. Instead, the government simply leased the oil to foreign companies that carried it off for refining, processing, and sale abroad. Under a unique "silent break-up" agreement, in the early 1970s the oil was divided among foreign firms, many of them American, including Union, CALTEX, Gulf, Continental, Frontier, IIAPCO-Sinclair, and Gulf Western. The Indonesian government's failure to use the oil industry as a lever for economic development reveals its profound dependence on and subordination to the multinational corporations and foreign governments. (See map below.)[4]

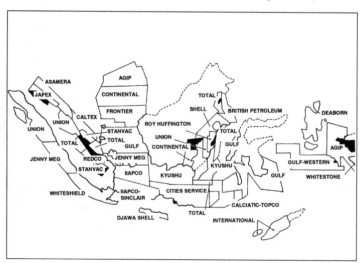

Similarly with minerals, Suharto simply turned the nation's natural resources over to foreign companies. The U.S. oil and mineral multinational, Freeport McMoRan, its Indonesian company, P.T. Freeport Indonesia, and Rio Tinto mining company were given the concession for the fabulous Grasberg gold mine in Irian Jaya (West Papua), the world's largest gold mine. Just after the coup in 1967, the Suharto government gave the company mineral rights to 1.2 million hectares of land in West Papua. The company first mined at Ertsberg (Dutch for Ore Mountain), then, when that was exhausted, moved up to Grasberg. The copper and gold mine's peak production sometimes reaches 260,000 tons per day, making it one of the most productive in the world. Freeport and Rio Tinto carry off the profits, while Indonesian workers are left with their low wages and environmental damage.[5]

Foreign capital, much of it from Japan, but also from Taiwan, Hong Kong, and Singapore, and some from Europe, arrived in the form of direct investment in factories producing for the auto, electronics, textile, garment, and footwear industries. These plants produced not only for the internal market, but also for Southeast Asia and Japan, as well as the United States. Indonesian factories eventually manufactured shoes for Nike and clothing for the Gap, Old Navy, and Banana Republic. Suharto's regime attracted foreign capital because his dictatorship and his virtually union-free environment meant low wages and big profits for foreign companies.

As this sketch indicates, Suharto and his cronies constituted a political and economic oligarchy. In the 1990s, journalists would come to call the system "crony capitalism" and students would complain about KKN, the Indonesian acronym for "corruption, collusion, and nepotism." There is certainly a good deal of truth in both of those descriptions. The Indonesian regime bears comparison with Nicaragua under Somoza or with the Philippines under Ferdinand Marcos. While the structures of the regimes were similar, the results were even more grotesque in the case of Indonesia, in which an oligarchy of a handful of generals, bankers, and industrialists controlled the fourth-largest nation in the world. Any movement for democracy had to come from elsewhere: from students, workers, and peasants who had been excluded from the political system, but whose talents and labor were needed to make it work. The forces that would change the system would be set in motion by the Asian financial crisis of 1997.

The Asian Crisis of 1997

The Asian crisis started with the collapse of the Thai currency, the baht, in early 1997, a currency and an economy destroyed by financial speculators. After that, as George Soros, the financier and one of the leading speculators, wrote, "financial markets behaved … like a wrecking ball, swinging from country to country and knocking over the weaker ones."[6] A few months later, the wrecking ball slammed into Indonesia, destroying the banking system, ruining industries, and wreaking havoc on government finances and economic planning. The financial crisis threatened to spread from Asia to Russia and Latin America, and then perhaps to the economies of Japan, Europe, and the United States.

As the Asian crisis threatened to become a worldwide depression that jeopardized the capitalist system around the world, the United States, the world's dominant economic power, and the IMF, the disciplinarian of the world economic order, intervened with demands for austerity and structural adjustment. Throughout 1997 and 1998, the United States and the IMF kept up the pressure. But the dictator alternated between resisting and capitulating, fearing that cuts would be so deep as to lead to a popular upheaval that would threaten his regime. Finally, Suharto's government signed an agreement with the IMF on October 31, 1997. Almost at once, 16 financial institutions failed, causing a classic run on Indonesia's banks and the drying up of private credit. By then, the bottom was dropping out of the economy. The Indonesian rupiah collapsed, while the inflation soared, and imports crashed. Eventually scores of banks failed (out of 238 banks before the crisis, only about 100 survived two years later). The finance sector suffered a decline of 18.6 percent in 1997. At the same time, industrial production dropped by 12.9 percent, transportation and communication by 11.6 percent, trade, hotels, and restaurants by 21.4 percent, and construction by 47 percent. Millions lost their jobs; more worked reduced hours at lower wages. It was the beginning of a great depression.[7]

Suharto's government could no longer point to an expanding economy. In fact, the gross domestic product (GDP) contracted by an astounding 13.1 percent in 1998. The Indonesian people saw promises of modernization and development wiped out overnight. Unemployment in Indonesia rose from 4 to 12 percent according to the International Labor Organization (ILO), between 1996 and 1998.[8] The World Bank reported that of 200 million Indonesians, some 40 to 50 million lived in poverty by the end of 1998.[9] For millions of urban and rural Indonesians, the crisis meant hunger; for thousands among the elderly and infants, it meant death from malnutrition or disease. In rural areas in Sumatra, some villages survived on cassava, a plant low in nutritional value alone. Unicef reported that 35 percent of Indonesian children suffered from malnutrition. Carol Bellamy, Unicef's executive director, said that around four million Indonesian children under the age of two were suffering from severe malnutrition.[10] In the late 1990s, the *Jakarta Post* and other Indonesian newspapers reported that as many as 170,000 children died every year of the crisis because their parents could not afford to feed them. In many parts of the country, despondency gave way to desperation, hunger to starvation.

The IMF nevertheless continued to demand fiscal austerity; meaning cuts in social programs and subsidies for basic necessities. But Suharto's government, instead of doing as the IMF demanded, maintained social spending and public works programs, hoping to prevent a popular rebellion. When Suharto proposed a budget at the end of 1997 still out of line with IMF policy, there was more international pressure: Chancellor Helmut Kohl of Germany, Prime Minister Hashimoto Ryutaro of Japan, and

President Bill Clinton all personally telephoned the Indonesian head of state and told him to follow the dictates of the IMF. The Clinton administration, however, also continued to oppose moves in the U.S. Congress to withdraw military support from the dictator.

Seeing no alternative, Suharto yielded on January 15, signing a new letter of intent with IMF Managing Director Michel Camdessus. Many thought that, having capitulated to the IMF, Suharto would then step down. But a few days, later he announced his candidacy for a seventh term as president, and chose his favorite, the brilliant, eccentric, but loyal Habibie, to be his vice-presidential running mate.

Suharto was no fool, and he foresaw that implementing the IMF's program of economic retrenchment would push an already impoverished and oppressed people to the point of rebellion. So he came forward with his own solution to the nation's economic problems: a currency board that would tie the domestic money supply at a fixed rate to the dollar. The idea had originated with Suharto's daughter Tutut and Steve Hanke, an American professor friend of hers. While Suharto touted it as a panacea for the country's economic crisis, others thought the scheme was intended primarily to make it easy for the Suharto clan and their cronies to transfer their funds abroad.

Camdessus immediately threatened to end IMF support for Indonesia if Suharto went ahead with the currency board plan. Clinton dispatched former vice-president Walter Mondale to pressure Suharto to drop the currency board idea and follow the IMF's program. When Suharto failed to do so immediately, the IMF announced on March 6 that it would delay a $3 billion payment expected in Jakarta by March 15 until after Suharto had picked his new cabinet. The U.S. and the IMF wanted assurance that Suharto would put the right people in the key economic posts, that is, people who would carry out the IMF policy. They also wanted to encourage the popular opposition that was beginning to speak out against Suharto.

The screws were tightening. Still Suharto held on, and began his seventh term as president of Indonesia just one week later. He defied the United States and the IMF by appointing to his cabinet several of his cronies, his daughter, and her protégés. The IMF then proposed a third agreement, demanding thoroughgoing policy reforms with much stricter timetables and monitoring procedures. Desperate for the IMF loans, Suharto's government signed the new pact on April 8. In accordance with that agreement, Suharto was forced on May 4 to announce a reduction in the fuel subsidy equivalent to a 70 percent increase in the price of gas. Popular dissatisfaction increased immediately and student demonstrations against the Suharto dictatorship, which had been confined to the campuses, now spilled into the streets. Riots broke out in Medan, North Sumatra, and continued for three days. As one foreign observer noted in his diary, "The rapid deterioration in Suharto's political control is a direct result of his decision to implement the price increases mandated by the IMF."[11]

Throughout early May, tens of thousands of students demonstrated at colleges across the nation, demanding that Suharto resign. In Bandung, West Java, 100,000 students rallied, while in Medan, North Sumatra, thousands more marched in the streets. Led by the students, from one end of the archipelago to the other, common people of Indonesia began to take to the streets and call for an end to the 35-year-old dictatorship. In the demonstrations in the larger cities, one could find representatives of the student activists of the 1970s and 1980s, small groups of workers who had participated in the strike waves of the early 1990s, and representatives of the independent labor unions such as the SBSI and the PPBI. Though they had entered into the movement at different moments, and had been involved in different struggles, gradually their protests tended to converge and their actions began to synchronize. The movement seemed to be building to a crescendo until it looked and felt like reformasi might become revolusi.

The turning point of the crisis and of the regime came when

security forces shot four students at Trisakti University on the evening of May 12, and the country erupted in protest demonstrations and then in ethnic violence. Pogroms, instigated by the military, brought violent attacks on the Chinese-Indonesian minority in Jakarta. The Chinese, a few of whom had been privileged crony capitalists under the dictator Suharto, became the targets of violence. For three days in May, hooligans ran amok, burning and looting Chinese businesses (many looters themselves died in the fires), assaulting and murdering Chinese men, and raping Chinese women and girls. Between 1,000 and 2,000 people, both Chinese Indonesians and indigenous Indonesians, died in the riots.

The disturbances created a sense of political chaos and therefore financial instability and insecurity that virtually ended all international support for Suharto. Those events also created a political opportunity for three opposition figures—Megawati Sukharnoputri, Amien Rais, and Abdurrahman Wahid (also known as Gus Dur)—all of whom appeared on television to call for an end to the burning, looting, and violence that destroyed much of Glodok, the old Chinese quarter of Jakarta. One began to see the emergence of a new political situation. All three would later be candidates in the presidential elections of 1999.

Suharto, who had been in Cairo at a summit of developing nations during the upheaval, flew back home on May 15 to find power slipping through his fingers. After the murder of the students at Trisakti, the cracks deepened between factions in the elite. On May 18, the legislators granted student protestors permission to occupy the parliament building, and General Wiranto, the most important figure in the army, declined to use troops to remove them. The very next day, Suharto appeared on national television, promising to leave office as soon as he had arranged for new elections, presumably within several months. But it was too late for such delays. The military, Muslim leaders, and even his own cabinet wanted Suharto to step down. Harmoko, the head of Golkar, told Suharto he would have to resign. General

Wiranto said he would protect Suharto, but only if he resigned at once. Still Suharto balked.

The Clinton administration, afraid of the growing opposition movement, finally determined that Suharto's continued presence was more dangerous than his removal. On May 20, U.S. Secretary of State Madeleine Albright suggested that Suharto resign and arrange for a democratic transition. That statement, indicating U.S. withdrawal of support, effectively ended Suharto's reign. The U.S. government demonstrated that in Indonesia, as in so much of the world, it had the last word. In the end, the powerful dictator was revealed to be no more than proconsul for the United States. On May 21, Suharto stepped down and handed over power to Habibie. The students left the Parliament building rejoicing. With the first stage of the political crisis past, the IMF resumed assistance to Indonesia in July. The U.S. government exulted at the fall of Suharto. After having supported his dictatorship for 35 years, it now called for democracy.

Most Americans knew little or nothing about the role of the United States in supporting Suharto's coup and tacitly approving the holocaust in 1965, in keeping Suharto in power for 37 years, or helping to bring about his overthrow in 1997. The mainstream media maintain the fiction that U.S. foreign policy is about promoting democracy. But if Clinton rejoiced at the fall of Suharto, it was not because he believed in democracy or human rights, but because he and his advisers believed that Suharto could no longer be counted on as a reliable defender of U.S. economic and geopolitical interests. Suharto proved incapable of preventing a growing popular rebellion, so he would have to go.

In the last analysis, in most cases, economic interests determine U.S. foreign policy. U.S. banks and corporations work closely with the Treasury, Defense, and State Departments and key congressional committees to set the direction of American foreign policy. Sometimes their role is completely transparent, as in the case of the oil companies' role in the Gulf War. At other times, the corporate role is more obscure because it is not about any particular corporation's interest, but rather about preserving America's hegemony over the capitalist system and the world market, as was the case in the Vietnam War. In virtually every case, though, the interests of the corporations and the U.S. commitment to the capitalist system ultimately determine diplomatic decisions. When it became clear that Suharto could not co-opt or suppress his opponents, and when it seemed as if a growing movement might draw in workers and peasants and threaten U.S. corporate interests, the U.S. government decided he must go.

Indonesia, Empire, and Globalization

At least in one sense, globalization is nothing new for Indonesia. The people of Indonesia have participated in international trading networks virtually since the founding of human civilizations on the islands. For more than one thousand years, Chinese, Indian, and Arab merchants traded in the archipelago. Then in the 1400s, Portugal appeared, followed soon by the English and the Dutch. Through military conquest, massacres, and slavery, the Dutch won out, establishing what would be a 350-year reign over Indonesia. Under the Dutch, Indonesian products such as cloves, coffee, rubber, palm oil, tin, and petroleum became a significant part of the global economy. The Dutch also developed the islands' economy by building processing plants, railroads, and harbors, and linked the archipelago to the world market centered then in London with transoceanic cables and steamships.

Nevertheless, it is true that contemporary globalization represents a new phenomenon, a new stage of world economic development, a new phase in the evolution of capitalism and imperialism that began more than a century ago. The rise of industrial capitalism in Europe in the late nineteenth century led to a new more aggressive and intrusive imperialism. The Western European powers—England, France, and Germany—together with the United States and Japan, created vast territorial empires that provided raw materials for their modern industrial economies, while simultaneously offering markets for their finished products. The industrial countries extracted the minerals, petroleum, and rubber needed for their factories and war machines from the colonies. This was the classic phase of imperialism described by J.A. Hobson, Rudolf Hilferding, Rosa Luxemburg, Nikolai Bukharin, and V.I. Lenin at the opening of the twentieth century. The rivalry between the great empires, provoked especially by the more aggressive newcomers such as Germany, Japan, and the United States, led to two world wars and, as a by-product, brought about the rise of Nazi Germany and the Stalinist Soviet Union.

That classic period of imperialism lasted from about 1870 to around 1950, collapsing after the end of World War II. By then, the old imperial system was no longer acceptable either to the colonial peoples or to the new leading capitalist power, the United States. The two world wars, sometimes described by contemporary historians as the modern thirty years' war (1914–1945), with the millions of dead and the destruction of whole regions of Europe, utterly discredited the old capitalist and imperialist system in the eyes of most of the world. A series of political and social revolutions in Mexico, Turkey, China, Persia, and Russia between 1900 and 1920, and then a host of national independence movements in colonies in Africa and Asia, challenged and sometimes defeated the imperial powers. Finally, the Asian movements for national self-determination in India, China, and Indonesia, all of which achieved national independence in the late 1940s, meant that the old order had collapsed. Those wars and revolutions brought about the eclipse of England and the rise of the United States as the new dominant world economic power, and led to a reorganization of the world political economy beginning around 1950. The rise of the Soviet Union as the dominant power in Eastern Europe and its rivalry with the United States created a bipolar world, defining the 50-year Cold War.

But the fall of the old empires was not the end of imperialism. While the powers accepted the loss of their colonies, they did not accept the end of their economic domination, and a new capitalist and imperialist system evolved. The founding of the

United Nations (UN) and the Bretton Woods agreements that created the IMF and the World Bank, together with the later establishment of the General Agreement on Trade and Tariffs (GATT) built a new framework for world capitalism. The result was the replacement of classical imperialism and colonialism by a new system of neo-imperialism and neocolonialism in which the formal political independence of the former colonies was accompanied by their actual political and economic domination by one or another of the more powerful capitalist countries. The United States displaced England as the center of the world market and took control of the largest share of the international economy and of many of the crucial economic regions, such as the oil-rich Middle East. The Soviet Union became a new sort of imperial power, as its bureaucratic command economy extracted wealth from its colonies in Eastern Europe and Central Asia.

In the neocolonial period (1950–1990), much as in the earlier classical imperialist period (1870–1950), the Europeans, Americans, and Japanese tended to see the newly independent former colonies as sources of natural resources and raw materials. In both of these periods, the imperial powers focused on the extraction of minerals, petroleum, and lumber, or agricultural products such as coffee, sugar, and rubber. Industrial investments mainly took the form of the building of an agro-industrial infrastructure for local processing, refining, and refrigeration plants, and of the construction of a transportation and communication infrastructure of railroads, harbors, and steamship lines, telegraph and telephone lines, and transoceanic cables.

After the Communists came to power in Korea and China, the United States saw Japan as a capitalist bulwark against the expansion of Communism in Asia. However, Japan's economic well being depended on natural resources that it could no longer acquire from Korea and Manchuria. The CIA suggested in 1948 that Japan should now purchase raw materials for its industry from Southeast Asia and the Philippines. The United States therefore sought to reorient Japan, turning it away from Korea and Manchuria and toward Southeast Asia, and particularly toward Indonesia, which could provide rubber, tin, and oil. By 1951, Yoshida Shigeruk, the premier and foreign minister of Japan was asserting that his country, which no longer depended on China, "intended to cooperate in developing natural resources in Southeast Asian countries."[12] While the United States encouraged Japan's leading role in Southeast Asia, and particularly in Indonesia, U.S. corporations also became involved in mining and petroleum, as did some European countries.

By 1980, however, the system began to change once again, reorienting the advanced capitalist countries from developing natural resources to the creation of foreign manufacturing export platforms. The impetus for the change really began in the late 1960s and early 1970s. By the 1960s, Germany and Japan had put the wartime destruction behind them, rebuilt their industrial infrastructure, and begun to compete with the United States. Then in the mid-1970s, the oil-producing countries created the international oil cartel OPEC and raised oil prices, causing the so-called oil shock. The reintroduction of serious international competition combined with the rising fuel prices put new strains on the Keynesian economic model, on social compacts, and on the industrial relations systems of all three of the major industrial powers. Starting around 1970, the corporations in the advanced capitalist countries began to experience a falling rate of profit that set them in search of new social and industrial models.

The worldwide depression of 1974 and 1975 and the recession from 1979 to 1981 led the elite to turn to new models both for their own economies and for the world economy. The post-war Keynesian model based on a social welfare state and industrial unions with pattern contracts and high wages which had been established by the Democrats in the United States and by the Social Democrats in Europe, was by 1980 being challenged by a new conservative ideology of hard money (monetarism) and free markets. Margaret Thatcher in England and Ronald Reagan in the United States pushed to restructure the Keynesian welfare state and to create what came to be called a neoliberal agenda. The neoliberals argued that state intervention should be reduced, allowing market forces to solve all problems. Their model called for the privatization and deregulation of the economy, drastic reductions in the social welfare budget, and a political struggle to reduce the power of labor unions.

Within a few years, the neoliberal model was also being extended to the international arena, where it took on additional characteristics. In addition to privatization, deregulation, fiscal austerity, and its anti-labor features, the neoliberals also demanded that the nationalist governments of the developing countries, the so-called Third World, and the former Communist countries reduce their tariffs and other trade barriers to permit greater foreign trade and investment.

Driven by the United States and England, the neoliberal program swept the world during the 1980s, and a new triangular geopolitical-economic system emerged. While the United States remained at the peak of the triangle as the hegemonic global power, Germany and Japan had emerged as rival powers at the two lower corners of the triad. Each of these powers now attempted to reshape its neocolonial relationships with developing countries into a new economic sphere of influence.

In Europe, Germany led in the establishment of a European common market and eventually a European Union, with a new currency, the Euro. The United States, Canada, and Mexico established the North American Free Trade Agreement (NAFTA), a free market in the Americas. Japan, while failing to create a similar political-economic structure, became the dominant economic power in Southeast Asia, exerting an important influence on the Association of South East Asian Nations (ASEAN).

All three of the leading economic powers, but particularly the United States and Japan, began to reorganize their economies on an international scale by moving industrial production abroad, especially their labor-intensive manufacturing and assembly work, which they located at first in special export zones in neighboring countries. U.S. corporations began to move garment, electronic, and automobile manufacturing plants to the Mexican maquiladora zone. By the 1990s, General Motors and its subsidiaries represented the biggest employer in Mexico. Similarly, Japan moved much of its manufacturing to special export zones in Southeast Asia. Mitsubishi electric became a major producer in Indonesia. But the tendency over the long haul was to use the neoliberal economic program as a way of turning entire nations into special export zones.

Indonesia and Globalization

When Suharto became president of Indonesia in 1965, he did so precisely at the moment that the post-war world economy began to strain under the weight of renewed competition between the United States, Japan, and Europe. While the United States was the hegemonic power in the world, it had encouraged Japan to function as the dominant economic power in Asia. Japanese capital thus led investment in Suharto's New Order Indonesia, though it was accompanied by capital from Korea, Hong Kong, Taiwan, and Singapore. Japan no longer simply developed Indonesia's natural resources, but also built industrial plants engaged in manufacture for export.

As its competition with the United States grew sharper during the late 1970s, and after the oil shocks of those years, Japan began to look to expanding its role in Southeast Asia. In 1977, Prime Minister Takeo Fukuda announced what came to be known as the "Fukuda Doctrine," the idea that Japan would take great responsibility and leadership in Southeast Asia. However, the Plaza Accord in 1985, an international agreement to revalue currencies against the dollar that resulted in a strong yen, created the strongest incentive for the Japanese to invest abroad.

The strong yen weakened the competitiveness of Japanese manufacturers in American and European markets, and pushed Japan to invest heavily in manufacturing plants in Southeast Asia. By 1993, after almost a decade of enormous economic investment in Southeast Asia, Prime Minister Kiichi Miyazawa proclaimed the "Miyazawa Doctrine," announcing Japan's leading political role in the Southeast Asian region, as well.

When Japan began establishing its new role in Southeast Asia, it found a willing partner in Indonesia. The Suharto government was anxious to break out of the economic arrangements dominated by the United States and international financial institutions, namely the Inter-Government Group on Indonesia, the IMF, and the World Bank's International Bank for Reconstruction and Development. Japanese investment would both provide a counterweight to the United States, and more opportunities for Suharto and his cronies. In the mid-1970s, General Soedjono Hoemardani, also of the Opsus Group, became the major broker of Japanese investment in Indonesia, while Suharto's wife also played a role.[13]

Japanese investment in Indonesia between 1987 and 1997 reached $25.1 billion, or 14.5 percent of aggregate foreign direct investment. While Japan invested $1 billion in 1993, by 1996 investments had grown to $8 billion. In the first ten months of 1997, before the effects of the crash, Japan's trade with Indonesia was worth $12.8 billion, more than Indonesia's trade with any other nation. Japanese companies imported from Indonesia goods and materials worth $7 billion, and exported to Indonesia nearly $6 billion (while U.S. exports to Indonesia amounted to $5.5 billion).[14]

During the 1980s and into the early 1990s, Japan seemed to be in a position to lead ASEAN in creating an integrated Asian economic bloc similar to the European Common Market and the North American Free Trade Agreement. By 1985, Japan had become the world's chief creditor nation, and American and European academics began to talk about Japan eclipsing the United States as the leading economic power on earth. Journalists and historians predicted the shift of the center of world finance from New York to Tokyo. While the United States had once looked upon Japan as a capitalist bulwark against Communism in Asia, it now saw Japan as a threat to U.S. domination of the world economy. Indonesia became a focus for competition between the United States and Japan.

In the process of industrializing, Indonesia had created a new middle class of government bureaucrats and bank and corporate employees, as well as a new urban industrial working class. The general rise in the gross national product had not been evenly distributed, but still millions of Indonesians had been lifted out of poverty and hunger. Per capita income rose from $270 in 1965 to $1,080 in 1996 (in 1996 dollars). (Per capita income is, of course, a deceptive measure, since income is so unevenly distributed, especially in a country such as Indonesia.) Most Indonesians had finished the sixth grade, almost everyone had some primary school, and virtually the entire country (90 percent) was functionally literate.

Indonesia, it seemed, had found the way to the first world—even if arrival in that modern utopia of high technology, education, and incomes still remained a distant goal. Problems and poverty remained despite the successes. In 1995, half a million children died before reaching their first birthday. In the early 1990s, millions worked for less than a dollar a day, more than a third of the population had no safe drinking water, and 15 percent of the population would die before reaching 41.

The international financial institutions certainly judged Indonesia to be a success. In mid-1997, Dennis de Tray, country director for Indonesia for the World Bank, praised Indonesia for its "sound macroeconomic fundamentals." Similarly, the World Bank's 1997 report lauded Indonesia for its fiscal policies, its prudent foreign borrowing, and its debt management. Still, at the same time, the IMF, the World Bank, and the new World Trade Organization (WTO) encouraged Indonesia to continue efforts to restructure its economy along free market and free trade lines. Led by the United States, the IMF and World Bank had undertaken to reshape all of the economies of Southeast Asia in order to open them to greater foreign investment and trade. At the center of this program was the demand for privatization, changes in rules governing foreign investment and ownership, and an opening of the financial sector. All of this was part of the process of neoliberal globalization around the world being driven by the needs of the multinational corporations and justified by a theory of free markets, free trade, and democracy. And, of course, Suharto enriched himself, his family, and his friends as they skimmed off the cream of foreign investment. If it was not the best in the best of all possible worlds, it was, at least for Indonesia's elite, very good.

International Efforts to Rescue Indonesia

The Asian economic crisis, however, threatened to destroy Suharto's regime and its ruling clique. In the summer of 1997, Suharto and his cronies, who had believed that they could successfully manipulate the ever more rapidly swirling world economic system, suddenly found themselves drifting into the maelstrom. Where the economy had seemed stable and secure only a few months before, suddenly the political and economic situation began to move, shift, and disintegrate. Indonesia's national currency, the rupiah, collapsed, the stock market crumbled, the balance of trade deteriorated, and its foreign debt became impossible. Within a few months, banks failed, industries closed, and millions of workers were laid off or forced to work reduced hours. The real estate market folded, and construction halted. Agricultural commodities could not find a market, and in many areas the peasantry fell back into poverty and despair. The Suharto government and the nation's banks and corporations suddenly found that they had no control over their own economy, and the international financial institutions, global capital, and foreign governments suddenly held the upper hand.

Indonesia's crisis affected all the other major economies in the region, particularly Japan and South Korea. Japanese banks had lent Indonesian companies about $20 billion, while South Korean banks had loaned another $12 billion. European banks had about $18 billion in loans to Indonesia, but the U.S. was less exposed with only $4.5 billion. The Southeast Asian crisis took on added dimensions of disaster because it coincided with the Japanese recession of 1997. This especially affected Indonesia, which was a major source of raw materials and parts for Japanese products, as well as a major market. The coincidence of the Southeast Asian financial crisis and the Japanese recession could easily have led to a world depression. The Indonesian crisis worsened from July to September, by which time it became clear that there would have to be a major international effort to keep the country's banks and corporations from failing and dragging the entire world economy into depression.

In June 1997, when the crisis began in Thailand, the Japanese government had proposed the creation of a $100 billion standby reserve fund for Asia, in other words a Japanese-led "Asian Monetary Fund." The Japanese called for a fund like the IMF, but moving more forcefully and quickly, and without the conditionality clauses that often require countries to cut their budget or adopt structural adjustments.

The Japanese proposal for an Asian monetary fund would have been a step in creating some sort of regional organization such as the European Economic Union or NAFTA. But the United States government and the IMF, backed by China, moved quickly to block the Japanese proposal. C. Fred Bergsten, a former U.S. Treasury official and economist, explained the U.S. Reasoning: "Japan's proposal for an Asia-only 'Asian monetary fund' … would have excluded us from the most crucial area of cooperation with the world's most dynamic economies…. The cost of any such outcome to the broad national security as well as economic interests of the United States, would play out over many years and could be huge."[15]

The attempt to rescue Indonesia revealed the latent regional competition and potential for conflict between Japan and the United States. After it had slapped down Japan, the United States mobilized to take charge of resolving the Indonesian crisis along other lines in its own interest. At the end of October, meetings took place between the government of Indonesia, several other governments, including Japan and the United States, the IMF, the World Bank, the Asian Development Bank to come up with an aid package to keep the Indonesian economy afloat. These parties originally announced a $23 billion package, which was later increased to $43 billion.[16] Altogether, rescue packages for Southeast Asia eventually totaled more than $100 billion: $17 billion for Thailand, $43 billion for Indonesia, and $57 billion for South Korea.

The United States, as the world's only superpower, and with its 18 percent voting share in the IMF, played the key role in the construction of this package and in its implementation. The Indonesia aid package, like similar programs for Mexico or Brazil, was primarily intended to reorganize financial institutions, that is, to save banks and bankers. The IMF specifically allocated $8 billion for bank reform, and the Federal Reserve Bank and the U.S. Federal Deposit Insurance Corporation worked with the Indonesian government to reorganize its banks.

But the IMF, under the leadership of the United States, also decided to take advantage of the Indonesian crisis to make a whole series of demands for structural adjustment programs and other measures. The IMF demanded that Indonesia cut its national budget and continue to open its financial system to foreign investment. The IMF's program for Indonesia can be seen as having two parts: first, keep the Indonesian capitalist economy functioning by reorganizing the banks and keeping capital in the system; and, second, take advantage of the crisis to reorganize the economy along free market and free trade lines to the advantage of foreign banks and corporations, and particularly to the advantage of U.S. corporations.

For 400 years, Indonesians had been dominated by the Dutch, and then briefly by the Japanese. Now it seemed they were to be dominated by the IMF, and the power behind it, the United States. Old-style imperialism, and even the post-war neo-colonialism, seemed to have given way to this a new form of domination by international financial institutions. "Globalization" appeared to be another avatar of the imperial and neocolonial system designed to keep millions of Southeast Asians sweating for Americans, Europeans, off-shore Chinese, and Japanese businesses. The whole system seemed calculated to keep peasants plodding through the fields and workers toiling on the assembly line for the benefit of a handful of multinational corporations. What the critics have recognized, and what they describe but often hesitate to name, is the fact that neoliberal globalization—as imposed by the IMF under the direction of the United States—represents the latest stage of imperialism. Imperialism still means, as it did in the nineteenth and early twentieth centuries, that powerful nations with great concentrations of capital politically control and economically exploit the working people of the planet. But even the imperial system is vulnerable to mass movements that become important factors in national politics.

Suharto Falls, the IMF Assumes Control, the Struggle Continues

In the end, it was the student activists who broke the impasse in the debates between Suharto and the world economic elite. They succeeded in drawing other sectors of society—the middle class, NGOs, some professionals, and even some workers—into the anti-Suharto protests. The growing size and the militant character of these demonstrations, with tens of thousands in the street, surrounding government buildings, led the United States to conclude that Suharto's regime was no longer a viable option. Though it would have preferred to keep the dictatorship in place, the Clinton administration was forced to support the opposition among the military and the civilian politicians. The change in regime meant an end to the stability-through-dictatorship of the last 35 years, but in the face of the mass movement and its growing power, the U.S. government had little choice.

Suharto's fall immediately opened up an internal struggle between all of the forces of the old regime and its opponents: B.J. Habibie, Suharto's hand-picked successor, represented the continuity of the regimes political economic project; General Wiranto stood at the head of the Indonesian army, the force which had brought Suharto to power and for 35 years had been the back-bone of the dictatorship; Megawati Sukarnoputri, the daughter of former president Sukarno, embodied the hopes but also the illusions of those who believed that her father's regime had represented a more democratic and more just model of society; Amien Rais stood for the hopes of the liberal elite who resented their exclusion from the circles of wealth, power, and influence that had surrounded Suharto; and Abdurrahman Wahid represented the millions of Muslims in the middle classes who wanted a voice in government. Those were the best known and the real contenders for the power of the presidency, but there were also other forces. Muchtar Pakpahan, the leader of the Indonesian Prosperity Labor Union (SBSI), held up the hope of a social democratic society in which labor unions and a labor political party would attenuate the evils of capitalism and imperialism. And Dita Sari, a member of the radical Peoples Democratic Party (PRD) and a leader of the radical labor union PPBI, came to symbolize the struggle for a democratic and egalitarian society that would lift up workers, peasants, and the poor.

During the coming years, Muchtar Pakpahan, Dita Sari, and many other labor union leaders and activists would attempt to give voice to the demands of workers not only for democracy, but also for social justice and dignity. The struggle would continue to be a three-cornered fight between: the masses of Indonesian people, the Indonesian capitalist class and political elite, and the U.S. government and the IMF. Within this struggle, the Indonesian elite, the United States, and the IMF are always prepared to reach a modus vivendi to prevent a victory by the Indonesian people, but the people can never find a reliable ally either in their own ruling class or in the power of international capital. If the Indonesian people have any allies, they must be found in the international labor organizations and social movements.

What makes the struggle so uneven and at present so unfair is that workers tend to struggle against the effects of globalization, while the Indonesian capitalists, the United States, and the

IMF fight over the direction of the entire process. Workers, emerging from a 35-year dictatorship and from a five-hundred year history of imperialism, have yet to create the organizations, national labor federations, workers' educational institutions and think tanks, and political parties that might challenge the system as a whole. Nor have they yet been able to create the relationships of international labor solidarity that could take on the system. Yet the fight against the effects, the fight for higher wages, the demonstrations and strikes, the creation of labor unions, and the founding of labor parties are all part of the process of developing the wherewithal to stand up to international capital, the IMF and the superpower that now dominates the world economy, the United States.

Today, Indonesia finds itself in the grip of a globalization process dominated by the United States. Capital rules: nations and peoples tremble. Global capital twitches and Indonesia convulses. Powerful forces in international capital have transformed the government and wreaked havoc with the economy. But this story is not new for Indonesia, and this is hardly the archipelago's first encounter with capital. For some four hundred years, international capital and the struggle against it has determined the course of Indonesian history. Only by understanding something of that history can we appreciate the significance of the heroic students, NGO activists, and labor union organizers who fight for freedom today.

1   The Madiun incident of 1948 was a local Communist bid for power crushed by the Indonesian Army.

2   Audrey R. and George McT. Kahin, *Subversion as Foreign Policy: The Secret Eisenhower and Dulles Debacle in Indonesia* (New York: Indonesia, 1995).

3   Noam Chomsky and Edward S. Herman, *The Washington Connection and Third World Fascism* (Boston: South End Press, 1979), 205–217, give an overview of U.S. support for Indonesia. See also 129–204 on East Timor, and Chomsky, *Year 501* (Boston: South End Press, 1993), Chapter 4.

4   Map based on Denys Lombard, *Le Carrefour Javanais: Essai d'Histoire globale* (Paris: Editions de l'Ecole des Hautes Etudes en Sciences Sociales 1990), Map 7, after *The Times* (of London), August 17, 1971.

5   Danny Kennedy, Pratap Chatterjee, and Roger Moody, *Risky Business: The Grasberg Gold Mine* (Berkeley: Project Underground, 1998).

6   George Soros, *The Crisis of Global Capitalism: Open Society Endangered* (New York: Public Affairs, 1998), 136.

7   World Bank, *Indonesia: From Crisis to Opportunity* (Jakarta: World Bank, 1999), 1.1-1.5; Pt. Data Consult Inc., *Indonesia Commercial Newsletter* (Jakarta) 259 (January 1, 1999): 3–5.

8   "ILO Governing Body to examine response to Asia crisis," and accompanying table, ILO Press Release, 16 March 1999.

9   "Indonesia from Crisis to Opportunity," World Bank, July 21, 1999, p. 1.4.

10   BBC On-Line Network, August 18, 1998.

11   Geff Forrester and R.J. May, eds., *The Fall of Soeharto* (Singapore: Select Books, 1999), 25.

12   Walter LaFeber, *The Clash: A History of U.S.–Japanese Relations* (New York: W.W. Norton & Company, 1997), 274, 295.

13   Richard Robinson, *Indonesia: The Rise of Capital* (North Sydney: Asian Studies Association of Australia, 1986), 156–58; and, Adam Schwarz, *A Nation in Waiting: Indonesia in the 1990s* (San Francisco: Westview Press, 1994), 33–34.

14   "Japanese Big Business Most Exposed to Indonesian Crisis," World Socialist Web Site, March 21, 1998, at http://www.wsws.org/news/1998/mar1998/jpn2-m21.shtml.

15   Francois Godemont, *The Downsizing of Asia,* cited in Charles Tanzer, "The Asia Crisis and the Search for a New Global Financial Architecture," *Indonesian Quarterly* 1 (2000): 61.

16   In the original package the participants were: IMF ($10 billion), World Bank ($4.5 billion), Asian Development Bank ($3.5 billion), and Indonesia's own foreign assets ($5 billion). In the second part of the package the participants were: Japan ($5 billion), Malaysia ($1 billion), Brunei ($1.2 billion), Singapore ($10 billion), and the United States ($3 billion).

Chapter 3

Global Capital and Indonesia

From Imperialism to Independence

What does it mean to look at the world in terms of globalization, the expansion of the power and control of international capital? In Indonesia today, international capital means bank loans, oil and mining concessions, and industrial investment in textile mills, clothing factories, and plants making tennis shoes. Ultimately, though, capital is a relationship between those who control the means of production and those who work at them. Capital is the power to dictate to labor and to extract wealth from it. Today, the banks and corporations of the United States control the largest blocks of capital on earth, and therefore dominate the world economy. The U.S. has so much economic—and therefore political and military—power that it sets the rules of the world economy.

But the United States is not the first country to play such a powerful role in the world economy and in Indonesia. International capital has a long and bloody history that began long before the appearance of the American colossus. Capitalism first appeared in Italy in the 1300s, and soon spread to Holland and Belgium, and later to France and England. Capital became international in the 1400s, spreading out from Europe toward Africa,

Asia, and the Americas. Merchant capital, and later industrial capital, financed and fought for control of trading posts and sea lanes, then of territory, natural resources, and labor.[1]

The story of international capital and its role in Indonesia began with the European elite's craving for cloves and silk. Beginning in the 1400s, European merchants traveled to India, China, and the Indonesian archipelago to purchase spices such as cloves and nutmeg, and textiles such as silk and damask to be sold in Europe at enormous profit. What we today call Indonesia was then a vast archipelago of 14,000 islands, which featured hundreds of different societies and languages and many different religions and faiths. Indian, Chinese, and Arab merchants had traveled and traded in those islands for centuries, buying and selling commodities, and also planting Hinduism, Buddhism, and later Islam, which became the dominant creed. But beginning in the fifteenth century, driven by international capital, the Europeans began to intrude.[2]

The Portuguese led the way, followed later by the English and the Dutch. The Portuguese controlled the Indonesian trade in spices roughly from 1400 to 1600, when they were supplanted by the Dutch. "In the early seventeenth century Holland was rapidly surpassing all other countries of the world in accumulation of capital," writes Pieter Geyl, a historian of the Netherlands.[3] That capital found an outlet in exploration and commerce abroad. Cornelis de Houtman carried out the first Dutch voyage to the archipelago, reaching Bantam in June 1596, and his success stirred others. In 1598, five more Dutch expeditions sailed to the East Indies. The overall rate of profit for all of the voyages to the East Indies that year reached 400 percent.[4] Profit drove the merchant capitalists to expand trade, and trade led to conquest and empire.

Seeing the enormous profits to be made, Dutch merchants founded the United East India Company (VOC) on March 20, 1602. The VOC—a company, a virtual government, and a commercial army on the march—would gradually extend its sway over the islands of the archipelago. The Netherlands would dominate Indonesia for almost 350 years. The conquest would prove to be a protracted and violent process based on supporting one native prince against another, dividing and conquering the indigenous peoples, and making all dependent upon the Dutch.

The Portuguese, the British, and the Dutch fought for control of the coastal trading posts of the archipelago without resolution for several years. Then Jan Pieterszoon Coen became Dutch governor of Java, and quickly took the offensive. He seized the old city of Jacatra, and built the new colonial capital he called Batavia—the future Jakarta. Coen murdered scores and enslaved hundreds of people from the islands of Lonthor and Run, and gave their lands to VOC employees. His violent subjugation of the natives established the pattern for Dutch conquest for the next 300 years.

The Dutch conquest of the Indies made no pretense of a *mission civilitrise;* it was simply based on force. Coen himself was well aware of the violence on which the whole system of conquest, land theft, and slavery was based. As he wrote home to his employers in Holland, "What honorable men will break up their home here to take employment as executioners and jailers of a herd of slaves, and to range themselves amongst those free men who by their maltreatment and massacre of the Indians have made the Dutch notorious throughout the Indies as the cruelest nation of the whole world?"[5] The Dutch gradually conquered much of Java, making nearly all of the princes and aristocrats dependent on the VOC. As Geyl summed up the experience of the VOC at the end of the century, "The Dutch East India Company was in the Indian world, the power of the sword."[6]

By 1700, the Dutch had almost unwittingly transformed their trading empire in the Indies into a vast territorial empire that included much of Java and pieces of Madura, Sumatra, Amboina, the Moluccas, or Spice Islands, and many other smaller islands. Because of the cost of its wars of conquest, the company's growing bureaucracy, and its practice of paying its stockholders dividends of 20 to 40 percent, however, the VOC fell almost 12 million guilders into debt. To deal with the looming financial crisis, the company instituted a new system of what it called "contingencies and forced deliveries," a tribute-in-kind levied on company-controlled districts. The Dutch overlords demanded tribute payments of the Indonesian princes and the nobility, the *priyayi*, who in turn squeezed crops out of their vassals. The system served to empower and enrich the Dutch, transformed the Javanese aristocracy into their dependents, and impoverished the Indonesian peasants.

At about the same time, Governor-General Zwaardekroon carried out a series of agricultural reforms aimed at strengthening the islands' economy. Most important, he introduced coffee cultivation beginning around 1700, and Dutch plantations, first in Batavia and Ceribon, and then throughout many regions in Java, turned the coffee bean into the islands' dominant crop. The shift from cloves to coffee proved momentous. Coffee cultivation quickly became the center of the economic life of the Indies, and the source of wealth and power in Holland. Coffee production, eventually involving millions upon millions of trees, changed both the economy and the ecology of the islands, and transformed the life of the peasants. The VOC set the price of coffee as low as possible, and then took the crop through forced deliveries. As a result, "the cultivator's position was worse than that of a slave."[7] The same was done on other islands with other crops. On the Banda Islands and Amboina, the Dutch licensed clove and nutmeg, and destroyed unlicensed trees. "The natives worked for a pittance, were forced to buy all their foodstuffs from the Dutch at exorbitant prices, and had to cut down their spice trees whenever the Company decided to restrict production."[8]

The Dutch role in the East Indies in the eighteenth and nineteenth centuries was little better than it had been in the two hundred years before. Jacob Haafner, a German by birth, joined his father, a surgeon in the service of the Dutch East Indies Company, and chronicled its decline and demise. In his writings, he defended the "oppressed Indians" and heaped "shame on their oppressors." In a passage from his book *Voyage from Madras to Ceylon,* he described the Dutch and other Europeans and their work among the native peoples:

> Making one's fortune! Indeed, there is not anybody who does not go East to make his fortune. That unhappy part of the world has become the prison yard of the Europeans, scoundrels, wastrels, thugs, all those who because of their crimes or for other reasons have been banished from their birthplace, bankrupts and people like that, all of them scurry to the Indies as to a common prey, all of them desiring to make their fortunes there, and how do you think they seek to realize their aim? In no other way than to rob the Company they serve, or to oppress, plunder, and kill the poor Indians. Nine out of ten who return wealthy from India have certainly gotten their loot in exactly that fashion.[9]

Other Hollanders, including those in authority, also criticized their own government and its role in exploiting the native population of the Indies in the 1820s. Governor-General Baron van de Capellen referred to his countrymen, the private investors and planters, as "parasitic plants which in their dark and crooked ways manage to get a stranglehold on the native population, choke it, and stifle its growth."[10]

The struggle in Indonesia was waged not only against native and rival European states, but Asian merchants. "Wherever there was relatively fair competition, the Asian—Arab, Persian, Indian, or Chinese—could always maintain his position. Only where the Dutchman could resort to force, as in the Spice Islands, could he gain the advantage over the Asian trader; even then he could not drive him out of the field but had to arrange a modus vivendi."[11] Cut-throat competition became more than a metaphor. With brutal force, the Dutch succeeded in ousting, or at least subordinating, the Asians and Middle Easterners, and placing themselves in a dominant position.

Within this racial caste system, the Dutch established a special role for the Chinese merchants. Coen and van Diemen, his successor, invited the Chinese to settle in the colonial capital, and promoted some to become merchant middlemen and tax farmers. While some Chinese became wealthy in the process, they also formed a particularly vulnerable ethnic minority in a system based on racial domination. Dutch and Javanese resentment against the Chinese periodically led to violence, such as the terrible massacre of Chinese in Jakarta in 1740. Anti-Chinese pogroms would be repeated many times throughout the subsequent history of Indonesia, particularly in periods of political and economic crisis. Much like the Jews in Europe, the Chinese became the scapegoats sacrificed in times of social unrest.

The VOC, preferring to pay dividends rather than pay its debts, went into crisis at the end of the eighteenth century. When the Dutch supported the American colonies' revolt against England, the British retaliated by establishing an embargo of the Dutch East Indies. The embargo exacerbated the already critical condition of the VOC, which found itself 96 million guilders in debt by 1791. Unable to negotiate new loans on the open market, the VOC was forced to turn to the government. In the end, the Dutch government decided not to renew the VOC charter, and the state took over the company's assets and its debts of 134 million guilders. On January 1, 1800, Indonesia and its people passed from the hands of the Dutch East Indies Company into the hands of the government of the Netherlands—from the frying pan into the fire.

At about the same time, however, the French Revolution and Napoleonic Wars spilled over into Holland, bringing Louis Napoleon to the throne there. With the French in power in Holland, the Netherlands once again became an enemy of the English, as the vast struggle between the two superpowers of the era was fought out. To protect India, the English attacked and seized Indonesia and installed Thomas Stamford Raffles as governor-general. Raffles proved to be a reformer who restored several native princes to their thrones, abolished torture, ended the system of forced deliveries, and made steps toward the abolition of slavery.

Raffles also instituted a series of liberal economic reforms aimed at ending government monopoly and strengthening market mechanisms and the money economy. He declared the government the owner of all land, turned the Javanese into tenants, and required them to pay land rent. At first the *desa,* or village, and later the individual landowner paid the rent. On average, the tenant had to pay two-fifths of her or his produce—usually rice—to the government. At the same time, Raffles declared the abolition of the Dutch system of forced labor on roads and bridges, though he failed in fact to end the practice for lack of an alternative. In the end, he failed to abolish slavery.

While Raffles may have been a sincere humanitarian and abolitionist, his opposition to forced labor and slavery was not altogether altruistic. As one historian noted, "Raffles also tried to introduce wages instead of forced labor, and, in general, to promote a monetary economy, and build up the consuming power of the natives so that British goods could be sold in the Indies."[12] Raffles represented the interests of British free-trade imperialism against those of Dutch mercantile imperialism. At the end of the Napoleonic wars, the British returned Indonesia to the Dutch. By that time, the Netherlands had been nearly bankrupted by the wars, and Britain, which had a good deal of investment in Holland, had an interest in seeing the Dutch survive and prosper. So the English left Indonesia, and, after a 14-year interlude, the Dutch returned. The Dutch government kept many of Raffles's reforms in place, such as his system of land rent, while ignoring his humanitarian campaign against slavery and forced labor.

The Dutch conquest of the Indies frequently met resistance. In the course of their conquest of the archipelago, the Dutch had made enemies of many people, from poor peasants to local princes. Dutch power and oppression, as well as its arrogance and exploitation, led to scores of revolts. The most famous and important was that of Prince Diponegoro, a pious Muslim who dreamed of reestablishing a Javanese kingdom. His religiously inspired rebellion led to the Java War of 1825 to 1830, which created tens of thousands of refugees in Central Java.

The Netherlands spent 20 million guilders, entirely financed by loans, on the Java War, and left the government facing a disastrous economic situation. It became clear then that Indonesia needed a new political and economic system that could make the colony pay for itself. So the Dutch government overturned the liberal principles of Raffles, and once again returned to a system of mercantilism and state monopoly that it now called the "Culture System."

The Culture System, better rendered as the Cultivation System, a system of forced crop cultivation, was the brainchild of Johannes van den Bosch, a former Indonesian planter and military man turned social reformer who rejected free-market liberalism and advocated state tutelage over the colonies. He argued that the ignorant Indonesian peasant—for her or his own good—had to be required to plant export crops such as sugar and coffee. Under the new governor-general's program, the traditional aristocrats, the *priyayi*, became government functionaries who managed the peasants. Each village was to set aside one-fifth of its rice fields for the cultivation of export crops, beginning with indigo and sugar. European and Chinese merchants contracted to pick up the crops and deliver them to the government's monopoly trading company, the Nederlandsche Handel Maatschappij (NHM), created in 1825. The system worked so well that the government soon added coffee, tea, tobacco, cotton, pepper, cinnamon, and cochineal, the insect dye. Sugar and coffee became the dominant crops. In 1833, there were 116 million coffee trees; in 1835, 242 million; and by 1840, there were 330 million. At the same time, "much of lowland Java was operated as a virtual state sugar plantation," with sugar producing between three-quarters and two-thirds of Java's exports in the mid-nineteenth century.[13]

Under the pressure of events in Europe, particularly the Bel

gian secession and civil war of 1832, the system originally introduced in Java as a progressive reform became an infernal
machine for the extraction of wealth from the people and soil of
Indonesia. In that year, each residency, as the provincial adminis-
trations were called, was required to produce the equivalent of
two guilders per head. While peasants had been told they would
have to use one-fifth of their wet-rice lands for export crops,
most soon had to dedicate two-fifths to meet production quotas.

The center of the entire Culture System was the forced labor
of the Indonesian peasant. While only about 5 percent of the
sawah, or wet-rice, land was used for the required export crops,
the impact on the people was enormous. In the 1840s when
Java's population was about 6 million, half a million families
worked in coffee cultivation. Seventy percent of all Javanese participated in compulsory cultivation, and more than half of them
worked in coffee.[14] Because both European and Indonesian officials received a percentage of the produce, they had an incentive
to increase export crop production at the expense of food production. So the tendency was for the authorities to press the peasants to dedicate more land and time to government crops, while
neglecting rice. Theoretically, peasants were required to give 60
days of labor to the government for the cultivation of export
crops each year. But in reality, some crops, such as coffee, took
much more time, a minimum of 90 days. In addition, peasants
owed forced labor for the maintenance of roads and bridges. In
many cases, they worked as many as 200 days per year for the
government. In some parts of Java, the Culture System led to
hunger and even famine, but everywhere it produced profits for
the Dutch.

The Culture System lasted until 1870, when the Dutch
passed a new Agrarian Law, though some parts of the islands and
some crops continued under the system until as late as 1917.
While it lasted, the Culture System produced enough money for
the Netherlands to pay off the national debt and finance the construction of the Dutch railway system.[15] Indonesia, and particu-

larly Java and its coffee, made Holland one of the richest nations
in Europe, indeed, one of the richest on earth. As many have observed, Holland's modern prosperity and privileged position in
the world economy resulted from the exploitation of the Javanese peasants.[16] The tiny nation of Holland sat on the back of the
great archipelago of Indonesia.

The Indonesian people, who had been defeated in countless
smaller uprisings and then decimated in the great rebellion under
Diponegoro, now found support from an unexpected quarter—the democratic and socialist labor movements of Europe.
In Holland, the Revolution of 1848 brought to power a new merchant capitalist class with a liberal ideology. The Dutch merchants and capitalists created a parliamentary government, and
began to look into matters of colonial policy. By 1864, the Dutch
parliament assumed responsibility for the budget of the Indies,
and colonial policy thus moved out of the royal chambers and
into parliament and public debate. This liberalization of the
Dutch government coincided with growing criticism of the Culture System after the first wave of famine in the Ceribon region
from 1843 to 1848, and the mass famines in Java between 1848
and 1854. By the tens of thousands, people in the Dutch East Indies were starving to death. For the first time, Dutch liberals and
radicals began to criticize Dutch imperial policy and call for both
economic and ethical reforms.

The Dutch author Eduard Douwes Dekker, also known by
his pen name, Multatuli, might be said to have launched the ethical policy with his autobiographical novel, *Max Havelaar: Or the
Coffee Auctions of the Dutch Trading Company*. This masterpiece of
modern Dutch literature exposed the government's Culture System as an economic machine that produced Holland's wealth
through the seizure of land and animals, forced labor, and virtual
slavery. Douwes Dekker's hero, Havelaar, explained to the readers that "the official reports from the functionaries to the Government, and consequently also those based upon them which
the Government sends to the Motherland, are mostly and for the

most important part *untrue*." He adds: "I have said that I can prove my charge. Where necessary, I can show that there was often famine in regions which were praised as models of prosperity, and that frequently a population that was reported to be peaceful and contented was on the point of exploding in revolt."[17] Dekker's portrayal of lying government officials, native starvation, and potential rebellion caused a sensation and helped lead to the victory of the Liberals' so-called Ethical Policy.

While often thought of primarily in humanitarian terms as a system of public health and education, the Ethical Policy had several other dimensions as well. Ethical Policy meant the introduction of liberal economic reforms, the building of a modern industrial infrastructure, the creation of a system of social welfare, the establishment of a centralized Indonesian colonial government with some consultative or representative institutions, and, finally, the extension of Dutch rule throughout all of Indonesia through a vicious and bloody imperialist war.

The economic system, as always, took precedence. The Ethical Policy was as much about opening up Java to private enterprise as it was about protecting the natives from government monopolies that oppressed them. For example, the 1870 DeWaal Sugar Law began to liberalize the sugar industry, though the process was not completed until 1917 in most of Java and not until 1920 in East Java. DeWall's law permitted private capitalists to lease government land for up to 75 years, as well as to make short-term leases with native landowners. The result was a shift from state-owned land to private investment. In 1856, the state lands produced exports worth 64.4 million guilders, while private lands exports were worth only 34.3 million. By 1885, state lands exports were producing only 16.3 million guilders, while private investors' lands were producing 168.7 million.[18] If the Culture System had represented mercantile state-capitalist oppression, the Ethical Policy stood for simple capitalist corporate exploitation, as the new privately owned corporations often continued many of the oppressive labor practices of the past.

The turn from state monopoly to private investors was eventually accompanied by a transition to wage labor. Beginning in 1882, the Dutch government abolished corvée labor and began to implement wage labor. Even then, given the long history of slavery and forced labor, wage labor often amounted to little more than wage slavery. Dutch government officials and Dutch and Chinese plantation owners and merchants held all of the power. Indonesians had virtually no political or civil rights. It would be another 20-odd years before workers began to organize labor unions to defend themselves.

The Dutch also carried out a series of terribly violent wars through which they took control of the rest of Indonesia's territory. The Netherlands' longest and most difficult war was fought against Aceh (pronounced a-cháy) in North Sumatra, and lasted more than 30 years. Beginning in 1873, it did not end until around 1904, and even then rebellions continued until as late as 1908.

The victory in Aceh completed the conquest begun in 1600, some 300 years before. The Dutch had first created a trading empire, then a territorial empire, and finally a modern industrial empire. The newly conquered areas produced not only agricultural products such as sugar, coffee, and palm oil, but also raw materials for modern industry such as tin and petroleum. Tin mining expanded to Billiton Island in the 1850s, leading to the establishment of the Billiton Tin Company. Oil had been discovered on Java, Sumatra, and Borneo, and the first concession was given to the Royal Netherlands Oil Company in 1883. The Ethical Policy, then, was the social reform policy of Dutch imperialism: it was social imperialism.

But humanitarian measures did form a significant part of the Ethical Policy. Under the influence of Christian missionaries, liberal humanitarians, and socialists, the Dutch government's Ethical Policy brought some very real benefits to some Indonesians, if principally to the old aristocracy, the *priyayi*. Most important, the Dutch government expanded education in order to train Indonesians to work in the colonial bureaucracy, a policy that would create a native intelligentsia and eventually a nationalist opposition. But, as one historian writes, it was never the intention of the Dutch to liberate the Indonesians. "Though well intentioned, it was entirely Euro-centered, and presupposed Dutch domination. The Ethical Policy was a Dutch version of the white man's burden."[19]

The Ethical Policy had three important domestic political results. First, the *priyayi* and other upper-class Indonesians who were the main beneficiaries of the new educational program learned about Western ideas of political sovereignty and democracy. They became transformed into Indonesia's future nationalists. Second, the Muslim religious leaders, the *kyai,* responded by creating their own schools, newspapers, and political parties, and thus created the Muslim social and political movement. Third, the building of an industrial infrastructure and the creation of a class of civil servants led to the creation of the first labor unions and socialist parties. By the opening of the twentieth century, one could begin to see in vague outline the three major movements of modern Indonesia: secular nationalist, Muslim, and socialist.

The Dutch conquest of Indonesia could be accomplished only by repeatedly making war against the indigenous population. For example, in the Banten region of Java alone, there were indigenous insurrections in 1820, 1822, 1825, 1827, 1831, 1833, 1836, and 1839. In 1845, the peasants in revolt wore white to indicate they were fighting a holy war. They rose up again in 1850, 1851, 1862, 1866, and 1869. The Dutch suppressed each rebellion with ruthless force, taking thousands of lives in the process.[20]

The total cost of the conquest of Indonesia will never be known. Scholars estimate the loss of life in the suppression of the Java War against Diponegoro alone at 200,000. Certainly the Dutch must also have killed tens of thousands, perhaps hundreds of thousands, in the 30-year war to subdue Aceh. As Adam Hochschild wrote about King Leopold of Belgium's atrocities in the Congo, "although the killing in the Congo was of genocidal proportions, it was not strictly speaking a genocide." Leopold's men were not trying to eliminate an ethnic group from the face of the Earth. "They were looking for labor."[21] Similarly in Indonesia, while the Dutch killed or caused the deaths of hundreds of thousands of Indonesians, they did so to control trade, take the land, and, above all, subjugate a labor force. The fact that their victims had brown skins, were Muslim, Hindu, or animist, made the murder and massacre easier, but it was not primarily the reason for the killing. The Dutch wanted a docile labor force, and only mass murder could produce the obedience they demanded.

The Dutch not only created an economic system, they also created a colonial political and social system in Indonesia based on a combination of political power, capital, and the theory and practice of racism. Indonesia was ruled as a racial hierarchy, a system sanctioned in law, established in 300 years of custom, and blessed by the church. Whites sat at the top of the system, the Chinese stood precariously on the middle levels, and the Indonesians stooped at the bottom. People of mixed race fitted into the interstices depending on their bloodlines. Race found reinforcement in religion, as the Dutch and many of the Chinese were Christians, while the Indonesians were Muslims, Hindus, Buddhists, or animists.

The Dutch and a few other white Europeans held political power over the colonies and their people. The Europeans filled all the political and administrative posts in the government, made up the officer caste in the military, and dominated all of the managerial and supervisory positions in the corporations. While the Dutch ruled through the Javanese aristocrats, the *priyayi,* they didn't trust them, and every Javanese regent had a Dutch assistant resident at his side to oversee his activities. The Dutch system of dual control reached down through lower officials in the residencies and villages. But the Europeans and Dutch remained on different levels, both literally and figuratively. Kartini, the Javanese "princess" made famous by her turn-of-the-century letters, wrote, "The most petty European [official] sits upon a chair, while native officials of any age, who are below the rank of regent, though they are often of distinguished ancestry, must sit upon the floor in their presence."[22] Even for upper-class Indonesians, life under the Europeans meant constant humiliation.

All of the Indonesian institutions were segregated, much like those in South Africa or the U.S. South. As early as 1810, Governor-General Daendels had established a system of segregated courts, with Dutch courts based on Dutch law and Indonesian courts based on *adat*, or traditional law. Later, under the Ethical Policy, there were separate schools for the Dutch, for the *priyayi*, and for the Indonesian commoners. The system of social segregation was reinforced by the custom of using different languages with different social groups: Dutch among Europeans; high Javanese with the *priyayi*; and low Javanese, other native languages, or market Malay (the future Indonesian language) with the commoners.[23] Segregated from top to bottom, everything about the system reinforced Dutch power. To be a white, Christian European, and particularly to be a Hollander, in Indonesia meant to derive power, wealth, and all the comforts and luxuries of life from the stolen land and the forced labor of millions.

From Imperialism to Independence

While Indonesians would ultimately have to fight for their own freedom, in many respects the Dutch created the Indonesian nation and Indonesian nationalism. First through trade, then by conquest, and finally with economic developments such as the telegraph, railways, and steamship lines, the Dutch forced hundreds of ethnic groups on some 14,000 islands under the rule of the Netherlands. The Royal Netherlands Indies Army (KNIL), officered by Hollanders commanding native troops, had not only conquered the islands in decades of brutal warfare that took tens of thousands of lives, but had also made Malay the lingua franca of the archipelago. The Dutch government and corporations transformed the ecology of Indonesia by forcing the Indonesians to plant cloves, coffee, sugar, and rubber. On Java, the Dutch superimposed a new colonial government on the old feudal and tributary system, but at the same time transformed the feudal lords into government bureaucrats, and their vassals into forced laborers. The Dutch destroyed the various native environmental, social, and political systems, and replaced them with a capitalist colonial regime that laid the basis for the modern Indonesian state.

Java became the central stage for the great ideological, political, and social struggles of the early twentieth century in Indonesia. There were three reasons for this. First, Java had been the site of the most economically and politically developed society in the Indonesian islands when the Dutch took control. Second, Java represented the largest and most populous island of the archipelago; with its large workforce, it was the most important economy in the islands. Finally, the Dutch had made Java the political and economic center of their colonial empire in the Indies, and had transformed the Javanese aristocrats into their colonial bureaucracy.

As many historians and anthropologists have pointed out, Javanese aristocratic society had certain cultural characteristics that made it ideally suited to its role as an instrument of Dutch rule. Historically, Javanese rulers had developed a culture of assimilation and had succeeded over several centuries in blending animism, Buddhism, Hinduism, and Islam—and later in accommodating Christianity. The *priyayi* were extremely status conscious and eager to preserve their domination over the peasantry. The Javanese nobility, as expressed in their *wayang* shadow puppet theater dramatizations of the Indian classic the *Ramayana*, sought to live lives that exhibited balance, refinement, and mastery over themselves and their subordinates. The elite dealing with the Dutch sought reconciliation and compromise—but not capitulation—while at the same time retaining its social position in the society. Within this framework, Indonesian nationalism began at the opening of the twentieth century.

The Dutch government's Ethical Policy, particularly the creation of schools and institutions of higher learning, spread European ideas of nationalism, democracy, and even socialism to a new generation of Indonesian intellectuals. A few Indonesians traveled to Europe for higher education and gained firsthand experience of European government and society, including parliamentary democracy, a free press, labor unions, and feminist movements. Why, they asked, might not Indonesians enjoy the same political rights? The newly educated Indonesians began to create newspapers in Dutch, Malay, and local languages, distributed them throughout the islands, and caused new ideas and ideals to percolate through Indonesian society.[24] While some Indonesians, particularly the children of the *priyayi*, sought to emulate the Europeans, the village holy men and the poorer peasant classes often reacted against the European, Christian civilization and asked, why should we Muslims not create a society and state based on our own cultural ideals? At the same time, the new Indonesian working classes made up of the railroad workers, miners, factory laborers, and urban service workers followed the example of the Europeans, organizing labor unions and creating first a Socialist and then a Communist Party. The Communists called upon the working class to lead the peasants toward the creation of a new socialist Indonesia, as part of world socialist revolution.

Within 50 years, there would be a national revolution. The energy for this revolution resulted from the hundreds of years of oppression of the Indonesian people of all classes by the Netherlands. The largest and most exploited groups among them were the millions of peasants who had been conquered and subdued by the Dutch—though they had periodically risen up in armed insurrections, which had been violently suppressed. The peasants had for centuries been forced to labor in the government monopoly crops, and now sought their freedom through modern social movements and political parties. But, overworked, underpaid, malnourished, mistreated, and held beneath contempt by the Dutch, those eternal victims of the system did not and could not become the leaders of the movement to overthrow the foreign oppressors.

The Javanese peasantry did organize to fight for their customary rights and, above all, for subsistence and survival in the face of increasing economic pressures. In Java, the peasants, mostly owners of small two-hectare parcels of land, faced no great landlords like the peasants in China, but did bear the weight of their own traditional Javanese aristocracy, the *priyayi*, who had been transformed into bureaucratic administrators and tax collectors by the Dutch. Indonesia had been brought into the world capitalist market, meaning the forced cultivation of staple crops for the Netherlands. The Dutch thus brought new crops that altered the environment; in some cases they introduced new technologies, and everywhere they established the domination of the imperial state. All of this threatened the traditional existence of the peasantry. At times of either capitalist economic crisis or natural disaster, the peasantry faced hunger and even starvation. In response, the peasantry organized new social movements. The most fascinating was Saminism, a millenarian movement at the opening of the twentieth century in Java that rejected Islam, opposed the state, and attacked the hierarchy of social classes. The Saminists spoke low Javanese, called each other brothers, and yearned for a classless society. A kind of folk religion in the Rembang area, Saminism became the center of a mass passive resistance movement against Dutch colonialism, the Muslim religious hierarchy, the aristocracy, and the economic elite. Interestingly, the same area later became a bulwark of the Indonesian Communist Party.

Yet the peasantry, almost entirely illiterate, with no experience of urban life or modern society, failed to produce unified leadership, wrote no program, and advanced no political party. The peasants tended to be divided geographically among the many islands; ideologically by religion, Hindu versus Muslim; and later politically between the religious and the secular. These mostly small farmers—who engaged in periodic uprisings and organized such millenarian movements as Saminism—proved incapable of providing a party, a program, or a leadership for the

Indonesian nation. It was the upper-class and middle-class intellectuals, and educated workers in the labor movement, who produced rival social and political leaderships—nationalist, Muslim, and Communist—each of which attempted to find a base of support among the peasants.

Educated Indonesians, particularly the sons of the aristocrats, experienced two apparently contradictory influences. On the one hand, Dutch education, or sometimes travel abroad, brought them into contact with European notions of national sovereignty, parliamentary democracy, and political and civil rights. Many educated Indonesians took enormous pride in learning the Dutch language as the door to a European culture that they took to be the highest expression of human civilization. Subjected to centuries of conquest, oppression, and segregation, Indonesians seized upon the great idea of the French Revolution as expressed in the Declaration of the Rights of Man: equality before the law. They looked to Europe as their model and ideal.

On the other hand, many Indonesian intellectuals simultaneously resented and hated the oppression by the Europeans. They watched with fascination the development of Asian movements against European domination such as the Boxer Rebellion in China, the Filipino independence war against Spain followed by Aguinaldo's rebellion against the United States, and the rise of the nationalist movement in India under Mahatma Gandhi. Above all, they observed with amazement and admiration the rise of Japan as it challenged and defeated Russia in the war of 1904 and became a world power. When in 1899 Japan claimed and won equal rights for Japanese with the Europeans in the Netherlands' colony of Indonesia, a wave of wonder passed through the archipelago: Asians treated as the equals of Europeans! Who could believe it? These two influences—Europe's dominant imperial civilization and Asia's rising nationalist movements—shaped the Indonesian elite's and the masses' social psychology and politics, and created what was called *pergerkan,* or "the movement." A complex interaction among nationalist, socialist, and Islamic ideas and organizations, *pergerkan* gave rise to the nationalist movement and to modern Indonesia.[25]

The first nationalist intellectuals placed their emphasis on education as the vehicle of both personal and national emancipation. Kartini's *Letters of a Javanese Princess*, posthumously published in 1911, represents one of the first Indonesian expressions of the influence of the European democratic, socialist, and feminist movements. The daughter of a regent, a provincial official, Kartini learned Dutch, received a European education, and through Dutch women friends became a feminist. Kartini expressed not only her own hopes, but the hopes of her generation when she wrote, "We wish to equal the Europeans in education and enlightenment, and the rights which we demand for ourselves, we must also give to others."[26] At the same time, she feared the government would not make educational available. "The Government believes, to my thinking, that if the people were educated, they would no longer be willing to work the land."[27] Kartini's letters represented the ideals of the first generation of Indonesian nationalists.

Dr. Waidin Sudira Usada, a retired physician, and a group of intellectuals and government officials founded the first nationalist organization, Budi Utomo (High Endeavor), in 1908. Influenced by Rabindranath Tagore and Mahatma Gandhi, they launched a national campaign to organize schools throughout Indonesia. Budi Utomo began by expressing its loyalty to the Dutch government, but by 1917 it was calling for a parliamentary government and autonomy. In 1911, Efi Douwes Dekker, the grand-nephew of Eduard Douwes Dekker (Multatuli), the author of *Max Havelaar*, organized a second nationalist organization, the Indische Partij (IP). Formed by Indo-Europeans, persons of mixed Indonesian and European parentage, it aimed to represent their interests and particularly their demand for equality with Europeans. The IP would be the first manifestation of the secular nationalist current that would later influence Sukarno and shape the ideology of the dominant secular nationalist movement.

The Muslim movement may be said to have mounted national resistance to the Dutch since at least Diponegoro and the Java war of 1825 to 1830. Throughout Indonesia, Muslim holy men, the *ulamas*, had led peasant resistance and uprisings against the Dutch. Important rebellions included the Banjermasin war of 1859, the Great Insurrection of 1888, and the Aceh wars of 1871 to 1908. All of these Muslim rebellions were put down, often with terrible violence, taking the lives of hundreds of thousands of Indonesians.[28] At the recommendation of the Dutch anthropologist Snouck Hurgronje, the government attempted to separate Islam as a religion from Islam as a political movement, promoting pilgrimages to Mecca for loyal Indonesians, while suppressing Islamic political opposition. The policy proved a political failure in the long run, since "Islam became more deeply rooted in Indonesian rural society."[29] Islamic cultural resistance would prove to be an important factor in the revolutionary movement and in future Indonesian politics.

The modern Muslim political movement began when a group of Javanese *batik* traders created Serekat Islam (the Islamic Union, or SI), a movement to resist Chinese-Indonesian domination of Indonesian commerce. SI called for the promotion of indigenous, or *pribumi*, Indonesian businesses, mutual economic support among Indonesians, improvement in the intellectual life and standard of living of Indonesians, and support for Islam. Founded to resist the Chinese, it soon began to speak out for the rights of the Islamic majority against the Dutch and their government. The leader of SI, the journalist Omar Said Tjokroaminato, pledged loyalty to the Dutch government and promised to operate within the constitution. But by 1916, when SI had some 80 local chapters and 360,000 members, its national congress called for Indonesian self-government in a federation with the Netherlands.

A second Muslim organization, Muhammadiyah, founded in 1912 by Hajji Ahmad Dahlan, organized modern religious schools that taught Arabic, Dutch, and secular subjects, and founded teacher colleges, libraries, clinics, orphanages, hospitals, and poor houses. Muhammadiyah also had an affiliated women's organization and youth and scouting groups. The more traditional Muslim religious leaders representing Muslim schools, the *pesantren*, joined together in 1926 to form Nahdlatul Ulama (NU). While formed in defense of tradition, NU also later became a modern political party.

The Muslim organizations did not confine themselves to religion and education. SI, while it began as an organization of merchants, soon turned to organizing labor unions. In 1912, SI organized the Workers' Union Council, involving workers from a variety of industries. SI member Sosrokardono organized the important union of pawn shop workers in 1916, while Surjopranoto organized the sugar refinery workers and in 1922 led them in a general strike that was quickly smashed by the government. By 1923, though, SI had gone into decline, having lost many of its most dynamic members and the political initiative to its main rival, the Indonesian Communist Party (PKI).

Europeans established the first labor unions and the socialist movement in Indonesia, though the movement soon became thoroughly Indonesian. Dutch railroad workers, with the experience of labor unions in Holland, were the first to organize industrial trade unions in Indonesia. In 1908, European workers organized the Union of Rail and Tramway Workers (VSTP), but only accepted a small number of top-level Indonesian workers into the union, and even then did not allow them to vote. Other Dutch workers also organized between 1905 and 1915—tram workers, teachers, pawn shop employees, customs officers, public workers, and treasury officials—but they were organized on the basis of racial exclusion, as well. By around 1910, however, Indonesians had begun to organize their own labor unions based on the European model. The Dutch government and employers must have scoffed at a labor movement that could not threaten their interests because it was racially divided.

In 1913, Henk Sneevliet, a Dutch Socialist, arrived in Indonesia, joined the railroad workers union, and soon became one of its leaders. Sneevliet declared that an Indonesian union, just like a European union, should organize all workers, regardless of race, to defend the workers' interests against the capitalists and the capitalist-controlled government. He not only argued that the railroad workers union should be multiracial, he also insisted that it should principally fight for the lower-paid Indonesian workers who constituted the majority of the workforce. Finally, he insisted that Indonesians be included in the union leadership. By 1914, Sneevliet had convinced the union leadership of his proposals, and the union began to recruit Indonesians at all levels, reserving three of seven positions on the executive board for Indonesians. By the 1920s, it was a powerful union of Indonesian railroad workers, with a few Europeans among the leaders.

Sneevliet, other Europeans, and Indonesians also formed the Indies Social Democratic Association (ISDV) in 1914, consistently aligning itself with the left-wing socialist opponents of World War I in Europe. In 1920, that party became the PKI.[30] During those years, the Communists worked within SI, which had also begun to organize labor unions, in an attempt to win the most important Muslim political organization over to socialism. But in 1921 SI ruled that its members could not belong to another party, forcing the Communists to leave the organization. The Communists, nevertheless, continued to be active in the SI's *serekats*, or labor unions. By 1920, the SI, PKI, and other unions among dockworkers, seamen, mineworkers, metalworkers, printers, electrical workers, and other trades and industries claimed between 60,000 and 150,000 members.

In the course of the struggle with SI, the Communists won over some influential Muslim leaders, most prominent among them Hadji Mohammad Misbach. At a Communist congress held in March 1923, Misbach explained why he had joined the Communists. The secretary of the meeting recorded:

> [B]asing himself on the Koran, [Misbach] made an argument
> for several points of agreement between the teachings of the

Koran and those of Communism. For example, the Koran declares that it is the duty of every Moslem to acknowledge the rights of human beings, and this point also appears in the principles of the Communists' program. Furthermore, it is God's command that [we] fight against oppression and exploitation. That is also one of Communism's objectives. Thus it is correct to say that he who cannot accept the principles of Communism is no true Moslem.[31]

With his scriptural arguments, Misbach won over many Islamic nationalists to the new Communist movement.

In the early 1920s, as the drive toward national independence began, the PKI was by far the most dynamic organization in the archipelago, taking bold initiatives, particularly through its leading role in the railroad workers union. Between 1918 and 1921, railroad workers, facing high rates of inflation, struck repeatedly for higher wages and won a cost-of-living clause with regular quarterly increases. But when the economy went into recession in 1922, the railroads terminated the cost-of-living payments, halved expected wage increases, and began to layoff workers. Finding the situation intolerable, the VSTP called a strike in 1923, and 10,000 railroad workers walked off the job, paralyzing the state railway and affecting private railroad lines as well. The Dutch government used the military and the police to crush the strike and destroy the union, and then sent the VSTP leader Semaun into an exile from which he did not return until 1957.

While in one sense the railroad workers' strike had simply been a labor union action for higher wages and job security, in another sense, the government was right to claim that the strike had a "revolutionary" character. The 1923 railroad workers' strike spoke out not only against economic injustice, but also against the racial discrimination that the Indonesians suffered at the hands of the Europeans. The railroad workers' union struck out against the two forces—the Dutch government and private corporations—that had dominated Indonesia for more than 300 years. The PKI leadership, which overlapped with the railroad workers union leadership, certainly saw itself building a movement to take power through such actions as the general strike. The Communists thus were, in a sense, proposing their party, the unions, and the workers as the leaders of a new and independent Indonesia.[32]

After the defeat of the railroad workers' strike, the Communists continued organizing, despite increased government repression. By 1923, the government and employers had crushed strikes by pawn shop, sugar factory, and railroad workers. In late 1923, after the suppression of the railroad workers' strike, the government began rounding up Communists throughout Indonesia. In 1925, the employers defeated a factory workers' strike in the metal industry in which the Communists had been involved.

Despite the defeats and the opposition of the Communist International then led by Joseph Stalin, the PKI leadership went ahead with plans for a revolutionary uprising. Tan Malaka, a leader of the PKI, argued against the plan, broke with the party, and provoked a split. Nonetheless, the Communists went ahead with their plans, launching the uprising at the end of 1926. The government crushed the rebellion, arrested more than 3,000 Communists, and interned 1,300 on the island of New Guinea. The defeat of the rebellion proved a disaster, and virtually eliminated the PKI as a factor in politics until the late 1940s.

The decline of SI after 1923 and the government's destruction of the PKI in 1927 cleared the way for the rise of the secular nationalist organizations that would lead Indonesia to independence. At the center of the new secular nationalist movement stood Sukarno, who would eventually issue the independence proclamation and become Indonesia's first president.

Sukarno was born in 1901, the son of a Javanese Muslim father and a Balinese Hindu mother. His father was a *priyayi*, he claimed, and his mother was a member of the *brahmana*, or priestly caste. His father, a schoolteacher, earned a very modest income, though the family was never poor, as Sukarno suggested in his autobiography. His father sent him to school in Surabaya,

for myself." When Sukarno suggested that he lived in poverty, the peasant acknowledged that was true. Sukarno wrote, "I thought to myself, this man clearly and certainly is not a member of the proletariat, he is a pauper, he is poor, he suffers much, he has not enough to live on, but he is not a member of the proletariat, for he does not sell his labor-power to another without participating in ownership of the means of production."[35]

Sukarno used the term "Marhaenism" to refer to the "little people," or the "destitute people of Indonesia." While there was a lot of truth to Sukarno's portrayal of the "little people" in the homily of Marhaen, especially on the island of Java, the story's point was intensely ideological and political. While he does not draw out the implications of this dialogue with the peasant, the story served to distinguish his politics from those of the Marxists. Clearly, Sukarno understood that nearly all of Indonesia's people were then peasants, not workers. Therefore, his dialogue suggests, Marxism, the philosophy of the working class, does not speak to most Indonesians' interests. Moreover, for Marx, the historic agent of social change in the modern era is the proletariat, an urban, literate, economically central, and powerful class that fights for its own self-emancipation, and, in doing so, fights for the emancipation of humanity. But, if there is virtually no proletariat in Indonesia, then there must be some other agent of social change. Did Sukarno believe that these rural, poor, illiterate, and isolated peasants would be the agents of the emancipation of Indonesia? Sometimes he suggested that the peasantry would liberate Indonesia. At other times, however, he suggested that a vanguard party made up of the political intelligentsia, the social group of which he himself was a member, must lead the mass of peasants to national independence and freedom.

Sukarno's parable of Marhaen also suggests that the Indonesian peasant, who owns his own land and tools and works to feed himself and his family, faces no hostile capitalist class. The Indonesian peasant is a victim of capitalism's highest stage, foreign imperialism, but supposedly not of Indonesian capitalist exploitation. As Legge writes, "The evils of capitalism were a continuing part of Sukarno's thinking certainly, but the idea that Indonesia's little people might have to fight against Indonesian capitalists was not."[36] The Marhaen homily suggests that after Indonesia had achieved its independence from the Dutch, the country would have ended oppression, exploitation, and the class struggle.

The development of Indonesian nationalism in the early twentieth century challenged Dutch domination, but the Hollanders in the colonies never accepted the Indonesians' right to political independence. In his autobiographical novel, *Country of Origin,* Edgar Du Perron depicted how the Dutch of the 1910s and 1920s felt toward the Indonesians:

> I had accepted the political outlook of *De Nieuwsbode* [a contemporary newspaper] as I had that of my father and every other Dutch citizen in the Indies: a rebellious Javanese was unquestionably the enemy. Not that people like my father thought the Javanese were wrong if they rebelled. On the contrary, it was proof of one's open-mindedness to admit that the servants of the East India Company had been thieves and that we still had no business being in Java. But having said this, they could treat any native who would not bow to their superiority with the greatest indignation.[37]

After all, the wealth of the Dutch colonists and the riches of Holland itself had been wrung from the lives of the Indonesians, and it had become impossible to imagine life without the colonies and their forced labor.

The Netherlands government saw the success of Sukarno's strategy to unite the many factions of nationalism into one powerful force, and it responded accordingly. In 1929, the Dutch government arrested Sukarno and sentenced him to a five-year prison term, though he was released two years later. The PNI was destroyed. When he got out of prison, Sukarno became a leader of a new nationalist party, Partindo, which he built into a formidable force. The Dutch arrested him again in 1933, jailed him for a time, and later exiled him to Bengkulu, Sumatra.

Sukarno was not the only victim of repression. During the 1930s, the Dutch government arrested, imprisoned, and exiled the leaders of many of the major nationalist organizations, including SI and Budi Utomo. The colonial government did its best to destroy the organizations and to halt the movement. But nationalism continued to grow. In 1936, even the staid Indonesian Volksraad, the Dutch government's official consultative assembly, adopted a petition asking for autonomy within 10 years under the framework of the Dutch Constitution.

With the rise of fascism and Nazism in Europe, and the establishment of the German-Japanese Axis, a split developed within the Indonesian nationalist movement. Some Indonesian nationalists, while still calling for independence, subordinated the struggle for independence to the struggle against fascism. Other leaders hoped to take advantage of Europe's internecine wars to win independence for Indonesia.

After the Nazis overran Holland, the Netherlands government in exile informed the Indonesian Volksraad that the question of Indonesian self-government would be postponed until after the end of the war. In 1944, Queen Wilhemina, speaking for the Netherlands government in exile, said that the relationship between metropolis and colony would have to change after the war. Exactly what that meant, she did not say. Indonesian nationalists had in any case given up on Holland.

Japan had been an imperial power expanding through Asia since the turn of the century. Japan had taken Formosa in 1895, southern Sakhalin in 1905, Korea in 1910, Germany's Pacific island possessions after World War I, and all of Manchuria in 1931. In 1940, the Japanese government announced plans to bring Southeast Asia into Japan's Greater East Asia Co-Prosperity Sphere. After the Netherlands fell to the Nazis, Japan sent diplomats to Batavia (Jakarta) to negotiate with the Volksraad, hoping to take control of Indonesia without having to deal with Holland, but by 1941 the Japanese had given up on the idea of a peaceful acquisition of the archipelago. After the attack on the U.S. base at Pearl Harbor in December 1941, Japanese troops moved through Southeast Asia and, on January 10, 1942, invaded Indonesia. Within three months, the Japanese had defeated the Dutch defensive force, and installed a military government over Indonesia on March 7. The archipelago passed from the hands of the Dutch into the grasp of the Japanese.

Many Indonesians, having lived for 350 years under Dutch imperialism, greeted the invading Japanese as liberators. Young Indonesian men ran through the streets carrying the red and white Indonesian national flag together with the Japanese banner of the rising sun. Sukarno himself believed that the war in Europe between the bourgeois democracies and the fascist countries was not a war in which Asian countries had to choose sides. For him, there was little difference between the two, since neither was genuinely democratic.

The Japanese military commander in Sumatra, Colonel Fujiyama, brought Sukarno from prison and told him that Japan intended to liberate all of Southeast Asia. He promised that Japan would grant independence to Indonesia, and asked Sukarno to work with the Japanese government. Sukarno accepted the proposal. Hatta, the second most important figure in the nationalist movement, had already accepted a similar offer. Thus Sukarno and Hatta became the heads of Indonesian national institutions under the Japanese military government in Indonesia. Sukarno chaired the "Center of People's Power," Putera, and later the "People's Loyalty Organization," known as Djawa Hokokai, and also the Central Advisory Council. In this way, the Japanese provided Sukarno with a title, with an organization, and with opportunities to travel throughout the archipelago. The Japanese created a system of village radios known as "singing trees" to tell their new subjects just what they wanted of them, but the radios also brought Sukarno's name and his speeches before hundreds of thousands of Indonesian villagers. During the course of the war, the Japanese Emperor even summoned Sukarno to Tokyo and decorated him for his services. The Japanese also gave new political importance to the Islamic organizations. They created a variety of Muslim organizations and forced all of the Muslim political parties into one party, Masyumi, thus strengthening the Islamic political presence.

Cooperation with the Japanese brought more practical benefits. Rear Admiral Maeda of the Japanese Navy established the Asrama Indonesia Merdeka, the Indonesian Freedom School, where Sukarno, Hatta, and other nationalists taught a nationalist curriculum. Later, the Japanese also created an Indonesian volunteer military force, the Peta, trained by the Japanese, but officered by young, nationalist-minded Indonesian officers, and made up of Indonesian troops. The occupation government also created a similar Muslim armed service, Hizbullah, the Army of God. The Japanese military trainers passed on to many of their Indonesian students the values of authoritarianism and militarism.

While greeted at first as liberators, the Japanese proved to be an imperial power every bit as demanding as the Dutch. The Japanese banned all independent political organizations and outlawed the flying of the Indonesian flag or the singing of the Indonesian anthem, "Indonesia Raya." They transformed the educational system, substituting the teaching of Japanese for the teaching of Dutch, and inculcated the idea of Japanese superiority in Asia. In many areas where the Dutch had required the growing of coffee, the Japanese now ordered the coffee trees to be cut down and instead had the peasants plant castor bean trees, a source of fuel oil. The Japanese also demanded forced labor from the Indonesians, including taking some 250,000 Indonesians to work outside their country, of whom only 70,000 ever returned. Some historians put the number of Indonesians who perished in forced labor for the Japanese either in Indonesia or abroad as high as between two and four million.

Sukarno, whatever his reservations, called upon the Indonesians to work for Japan's victory in the war and the crushing of the English and the Americans. Sukarno and his organization

Putera even worked with the Japanese to make production serve Japan's military needs and rounded up workers for forced labor abroad.[38] But Sukarno could argue that his actions served the Indonesian people in the long run, for on September 7, 1944, Premier Koso announced that the Japanese Diet would grant Indonesia its independence in the near future.

While Sukarno and Hatta served the Japanese, Sjarifudin and Sjahrir, leaders, respectively, of the left and right wings of the Indonesian Socialist Party (PSI), organized an underground resistance. Sjahrir was the leading intellectual of his generation, noted for his brilliant mind and his sharp tongue, while Sjarifudin was the leader of one of the most effective guerrilla forces. The PSI, with a strong base among college and high school students and Chinese Indonesians, combined romantic radicalism with European-style social democracy in a movement that really represented the left wing of Indonesian nationalism. It certainly was not a Marxist revolutionary socialist party.[39] Sukarno and the other nationalists in the government actually came to collaborate with Sjahrir and the nationalist rebels. Sukarno claimed that this division of labor had existed from the beginning, but some historians have cast doubt on this assertion. In any case, the national resistance to the Japanese occupation of Indonesia never achieved anything like the proportions of the various national resistance movements against the Nazis in Europe.

In March 1945, the Japanese established the "investigating committee for the preparation of Indonesian independence," or BPKI, with Sukarno again at the head. Perhaps the most important thing Sukarno and the BPKI did was to develop Pancasila, the five fundamental principles that would become the official ideology of Indonesia under both Sukarno and his successor, Suharto. The five principles were nationalism; internationalism, or humanitarianism; democracy, or rule by the consent of the governed; social prosperity; and belief in one God. In effect, this was Sukarno's attempt to reconcile Islam, socialism, and nationalism in a national creed.[40]

When the BPKI met to discuss a future constitution, Sukarno pressed for a unitary rather than a federal state, fearing that the Dutch or an other imperial power such as the United States would attempt to break up the Indonesian archipelago. Some nationalists, such as Mohammed Yamin, argued that a new Indonesian nation should include not only the Netherlands territories, but also British Malaya, Borneo, and even the U.S.-governed Philippines. While there was a certain ethno-cultural basis for this proposal, the idea of a Pan-Indonesia hardly seemed realistic at that time or since. In the summer of 1945, the Japanese, seeing that they were losing the war, moved quickly to create a committee to prepare for Indonesian independence in order to keep the Europeans from returning.

On August 6 and 9, 1945, the United States dropped atomic bombs on the cities of Hiroshima and Nagasaki, obliterating those cities, killing hundreds of thousands of civilians, and forcing Japan to surrender. But in Indonesia Sukarno remained ignorant of Japan's catastrophe and accepted the promise that Japan would grant Indonesia independence by August 18. The idea that Japan would grant independence, rather than that the Indonesians would declare and seize their independence, was unacceptable to those like Sjahrir in the underground resistance and anathema to a new generation of activists, the *pemuda,* or youth.

Several leaders of the *pemuda* met with Sukarno and attempted to convince him that he should proclaim independence, but he refused. Fearing that a historic opportunity might be lost, they kidnapped Sukarno and forced him to sign a declaration of independence on August 16. The document, only a couple of sentences long, simply read: "We the people of Indonesia, hereby declare Indonesia's independence. Matters concerning the transfer of power and other matters will be executed in an orderly manner in the shortest possible time."[41] On August 17, the *pemuda* seized the Japanese radio headquarters and broadcast the news of the independence proclamation.

So, Indonesia declared itself an independent nation, though

it would be another four years before it became a sovereign state in fact. British and Australian troops invaded Indonesia to drive out the Japanese, but stayed to protect the interests of the Dutch, who announced their intention to return and reclaim their colony. A state of revolutionary war then began that would last from 1945 to 1949.

Throughout Indonesia, nationalists, Muslims, Communists, and many others, including local gangsters, formed "struggle-organizations" that "gave a mass insurgency character to the revolution."[42] While the old Dutch KNIL and the Japanese Peta and Hizbullah forces came to form the core of the new army, there were also scores of independent militia groups operating throughout the archipelago. Old political parties reappeared, and new ones were organized; there were suddenly a multitude of newspapers; and everywhere people engaged in public discussion and debate, including criticism not only of the Dutch and the Japanese, but also of the new Indonesian government. The American scholar George McT. Kahin, one of the few foreigners in Indonesia at that time, remembers, "I was amazed that a state with its back against the wall under the omnipresent threat of further Dutch attack was willing to countenance such freedom. But this openness was something the leaders of the Republic were proud of."[43] Throughout the islands, Indonesians ceased to plant the crops that had been demanded by the Dutch or the Japanese and returned to the cultivation of subsistence products or cash crops for the internal market. The Indonesian revolution opened as the classic revolutionary "festival of the oppressed."

In the course of the Indonesian revolution, three political forces emerged: the PNI, headed by Sukarno; Masyumi, the Islamic Party created by the Japanese; and the PKI, which had taken on a dynamic new role in the course of the national revolution. Both Masyumi and the PKI created labor union organizations, GASBINDO and SOBSI, respectively. During the revolutionary years, nearly all Indonesian leaders and organizations—including the PNI, the PSI (which later merged with the

Communists), and even many Muslim organizations—expounded some sort of socialist ideology.

The Communist Party, operating in such a favorable environment as a national revolution espousing a socialist ideology, should have been able to grow to become a real political force. And for a while they did. But once again, as in 1927, the PKI became drawn into an adventure, attempting to turn a powerful land reform movement in Madiun into a regional seizure of power. In the Madiun Affair of 1948, Musso, the head of the PKI, attempted to challenge the power of Sukarno and Hatta, but the Indonesian army moved quickly to put down the coup. The army destroyed the PKI leadership and jailed 36,000 Communists and other rebels. The Indonesian army high command thereafter developed a profound distrust of and hatred for the Communists, sentiments that were completely mutual. (Some officers and many rank-and-file soldiers did sympathize with the Communist Party, and some proudly proclaimed their PKI sympathies even after Madiun.)

The Dutch and Indonesian forces fought for four years while Sukarno's government looked for every avenue of possible diplomatic negotiation with the Netherlands. Ultimately, however, the Indonesian revolution would be resolved through the political intervention of the United States, the new world power after World War II. For the United States, Indonesia represented a key link in its plans for Southeast Asia, for Asia as a whole, and for its new world political-economic system.

The U.S. government's view of Indonesia was determined primarily by its concerns about Europe, and particularly the fear of Socialist or Communist revolution in Western Europe. In order to stabilize the capitalist governments in Europe, the United States was prepared to allow England, France, and Holland to hang on to their colonies in Asia. Consequently, the U.S. government supported the continued British presence in Burma, Malaya, Hong Kong, and Singapore; the French return to Vietnam; and the Dutch control of Indonesia. But the United States also had concerns in Asia, where its attention focused on China. The U.S. government backed Chang Kai-shek and the reactionary Kuomintang in order to avoid a victory by the Communists led by Mao Tse-tung. The United States wanted stability in both Europe and Asia, and that seemed to mean support for the old imperial order.

In the struggle between Indonesia and the Netherlands, the United States proclaimed its impartiality. In fact, the United States systematically supported the Dutch over the Indonesians, providing Marshall Plan loans to the Netherlands government. As one historian writes, "Without these sums, the Dutch, who were also using American arms, could not have afforded their intervention."[44] When it became clear after the Madiun incident that the Indonesian nationalists and the army had no love for the Communists, the Americans shifted their support to the Indonesians, and pressured the Dutch to concede the archipelago nation's independence. At the same time, the Americans urged the new Indonesian government not to take over Dutch factories and fields and, of course, demanded that U.S. petroleum companies' properties and concessions be treated as sacrosanct. There was a tacit understanding that the new independent Indonesia would fall within the economic sphere of interest of Japan, which itself existed within the larger U.S. sphere of influence. From this point forward, Indonesia would privilege Japanese and U.S. over Dutch investment; an imperial changing of the guard had taken place. Indonesia had become a neocolony of Japan and the United States.

Yet what happened in Indonesia between 1945 and 1949 also represented a genuine national revolution. The Japanese had already destroyed the Dutch state and the Dutch army in Indonesia before the revolution began, and the Japanese themselves left, rather than be thrown out; but the Indonesian people and the Indonesian army successfully prevented the Dutch from reasserting their control over the former colony. In the course of the armed revolution, the Indonesians created their own state institutions and their own army, adopted a constitution, formed political parties, and created a new government. One of the greatest achievements of the Indonesian revolution was that it ended the Dutch and Japanese systems of forced labor. The government could no longer compel men and women to go off and labor in foreign-owned factories and fields. For the first time in its history, free wage labor prevailed in Indonesia, although the economy often could not provide work for the new free laborers, and freedom often meant hunger.

After the revolution, Indonesia ceased to be a colony of the Dutch and became an independent nation, though the role of the United States in the independence process had been an essential element. While the Indonesians had liberated themselves from the Dutch through a long military struggle, the U.S. pressure on the Netherlands had been key to the final recognition of Indonesian independence. Without U.S. approval, Indonesia might not have become an independent nation. But with it, the country would become a neocolony of the United States.

The new Indonesian state born of revolution was a very complex and contradictory institution. On the one hand, the state had been formed in struggle against foreign imperialism, above all against the Dutch. At the same time, the new Indonesian state had incorporated elements of the imperial states that had ruled the archipelago. The Dutch had given the Indonesian nationalists their European worldview and culture. The Japanese had provided the model of a rising Asian nation state. The PNI leadership, Sukarno, Hatta, and the others, had collaborated with Japanese imperialism, and the Japanese had provided them the organizational structures, titles, and resources to carry out their revolution. The Japanese had actually organized the Muslim party, Masyumi. The Indonesian army represented a patchwork quilt of the *lascars,* the popular militias, including some gangsters, and Dutch and Japanese military units. But the Dutch colonial army, the KNIL, and the Japanese colonial military forces, the Peta and Hizbullah, formed the key components of the new army. All armies tend toward authoritarianism and hierarchy, but the Dutch and Japanese both contributed particularly unfortunate models and ideals to the new Indonesian armed forces.

The contradictions of the new state were perhaps nowhere more apparent than in its ideology. All of the Indonesian political leaders espoused the ideals of *rotong-gorong,* or mutual cooperation, and expressed their belief in socialism or communism, yet at the same time, most conceived of politics as a top-down affair and felt only tepid opposition to capitalism. The state would, it promised, hand down a new cooperative arrangement to the masses below. Sukarno had created the new creed of Pancasila, an apparent reconciliation of Islam, Communism, and nationalism. In fact, the new state seemed divided among three factions: the Muslims, the Communists, and the army. The politicians sat astride the three tigers, afraid to let loose lest the big cats devour each other and the riders.

1　　Fernand Braudel, *Civilization and Capitalism, 15th–18th Century,* Vol. III, *The Perspective of the World* (Berkeley: University of California Press, 1992).

2　　The best accounts of the history of Indonesia in the period just before and then during the encounter with the West are Denys Lombard, *Le Carrefour Javanais: Essai d'histoire globale* (Paris: École des Hautes Études en Sciences Sociales, 1990), 3 vols, and Anthony Reid, *Southeast Asia in the Age of Commerce, 1450–1680* (New Haven: Yale University Press, 1988). See also J.C. van Leur, *Indonesian Trade and Society: Essays in Asian Social and Economic History* (The Hague and Bandung: W. van Hoeve Ltd., 1955). Both Lombard and Reid give a picture of the high level of development and the complexity of the Indonesian trade, civilizations, and culture before the arrival of the Europeans.

3　　Pieter Geyl, *The Netherlands in the Seventeenth Century, Part One: 1609–1648* (New York: Barnes and Noble, 1961).

4　　For accounts of these early voyages see D.G.E. Hall, *A History of South-East Asia* (New York: St. Martin's Press, 1970), 284–311, and van Leur.

5　　Geyl, *The Netherlands in the Seventeenth Century,* 182.

6　　Geyl, *The Netherlands in the Seventeenth Century,* 188.

7　　D.G.E. Hall, *A History of South-East Asia* (New York: St. Martin's Press, 1970), 331–32.

8　　Hall, *A History of South-East Asia,* 338.

9　　Jacob Haafner, *Voyage from Madras to Ceylon [Reize van Madras naar Ceilon], 1806,* cited in Rob Nieuwenhuys, *Mirror of the Indies: A History of Dutch Colonial Literature* (Singapore: Eric Oey, 1999), 21.

10　The address is cited in Nieuwenhuys, *Mirror of the Indies,* 48.

11　Geyl, *The Netherlands in the Seventeenth Century,* 315.

12　Ira M. Lapidus, *A History of Islamic Societies* (New York: Cambridge University Press, 1989), 750.

13　Richard Robinson, *Indonesia: The Rise of Capital* (Canberra and North Sydney: Asian Studies Association of Australia and Allen & Unwin, 1986), 6.

14　Robert W. Hefner, *The Political Economy of Highland Java: An Interpretation* (Berkeley: University of California Press, 1990), 41–42.

15　In addition to monopolies of such crops as sugar and coffee, the Dutch also controlled the monopolies over salt, pawnshops and opium, concessions that had earned 82.6 million guilders by 1927.

16　Multatuli (Eduard Douwes Dekker), *Max Havelaar: Or the Coffee Auctions of the Dutch Trading Company* (Amherst: University of Massachusetts Press, 1982), 212–13.

17　Douwes Dekker, *Max Havelaar,* 212–13.

18　Geyl, *The Netherlands in the Seventeenth Century,* 575, table.

19　Lapidus, *A History of Islamic Societies,* 754.

20 Lapidus, *A History of Islamic Societies,* 758. On revolts see also Sartono Kartodirdjo, *Modern Indonesia: Tradition & Transformation: A Socio-Historical Perspective,* 2nd ed. (Yogyakarta: Gadjah Mada University Press, 1991), 32; Hall, *A History of South-East Asia,* 544–45; Heffner, *The Political Economy of Mountain Java: An Interpretive History* (Berkeley: University of California Press, 1990), 40–41. This is the history of Western conquest everywhere, of course. Compare with the revolts in Chiapas, Mexico, as described in Antonio Garcia de Leon, *Resistencia y Utopía* (Mexico City: Ediciones Era, 1993), i, 89.

21 Adam Hochschild, *King Leopold's Ghost* (New York: Houghton-Mifflin Company, 1999), 225.

22 Raden Adjeng Kartini, *Letters of a Javanese Princess,* trans. Agnes Louise Symmers (New York: The Asia Society and University Press of America, 1985), 87.

23 For discussions of language, culture, and politics in the rise of Indonesian nationalism, see Benedict Anderson, *Imagined Communities: Reflections on the Origin and Spread of Nationalism,* Revised Ed. (New York: Verso, 1991) and *Language and Power: Exploring Political Cultures in Indonesia* (Ithaca: Cornell University, 1990).

24 James C. Scott, *The Moral Economy of the Peasant: Rebellion and Subsistence in Southeast Asia* (New Haven: Yale University Press, 1976), 95. For an account of Saminism, see Amrih Widodo, "Samin in the New Order: The Politics of Encounter and Isolation," in Jim Schiller and Barbara Martin-Schiller, eds., *Imagining Indonesia: Cultural Politics and Political Culture* (Athens: Ohio University Press, 1997), 261–87.

25 The best account of this period is Takashi Shiraishi, *An Age in Motion: Popular Radicalism in Java, 1912–1926* (Ithaca: Cornell University Press, 1990).

26 Lapidus, *A History of Islamic Societies,* 56.

27 Lapidus, *A History of Islamic Societies,* 57.

28 Lapidus, *A History of Islamic Societies,* 759.

29 Lapidus, *A History of Islamic Societies,* 759.

30 The best book on the origins of the PKI remains Ruth T. McVey, *The Rise of Indonesian Communism* (Ithaca: Cornell University Press, 1965).

31 Cited in Audrey R. Kahin, "The 1927 Communist Uprising in Sumatra: A Reappraisal," *Indonesia* (Cornell) 62 (October 1996): 25.

32 John Ingleson, "'Bound Hand and Foot': Railway Workers and the 1923 Strike in Java," *Indonesia* (Cornell) 31 (1981): 58–87.

33 J.D. Legge, *Sukarno: A Political Biography* (New York: Praeger Publishers, 1972), 80–83.

34 Legge, *Sukarno,* 90.

35 Sukarno, *Autobiography,* 61–62, cited in Legge, 73.

36 Legge, *Sukarno,* 133.

37   Edgar Du Perron, *Country of Origin* (Singapore: Eric Oey, 1999), 258.

38   Legge, *Sukarno,* 156, 166–67, 174.

39   Benedict Anderson, *Java in a Time of Revolution: Occupation and Resistance, 1944–1946* (Ithaca: Cornell University Press, 1972), 202–12; and George McT. Kahin, *Nationalism and Revolution in Indonesia* (Ithaca: Cornell University Press, 1952), 158.

40   Legge, *Sukarno,* 186.

41   Legge, *Sukarno,* 201.

42   Legge, *Sukarno,* 206.

43   George McT. Kahin, "Some Recollections and Reflections on the Indonesian Revolution," *Indonesia* (Cornell) 60 (October 1995): 4.

44   Gabriel Kolko, *Confronting the Third World: United States Foreign Policy, 1945–1980* (New York: Pantheon, 1988), 31.

Chapter 4

Global Capital and Indonesia

From Independence to the New Order

When Indonesia became independent, many of its people hoped that, free from the Japanese and the Dutch, the archipelago might become a prosperous nation providing a decent life for its citizens. Their country, some Indonesians believed, could avoid the evils of Europe—rapacious capitalism and its social conflicts: war, imperialism, fascism—and create a harmonious society in a better, more peaceful world. As has so often been the case following nationalist or socialist revolutions, however, the new Indonesian government faced enormous economic problems. The combination of war and revolution had devastated the Indonesian economy. Almost 200,000 Indonesian laborers had perished from Japanese forced labor, and tens of thousands of young men who labored abroad or who had fought in the Indonesian army or in the militias now had to return to civilian life. During the war, the Dutch had not invested any capital in Indonesia, and the Japanese had plundered the economy. Yet the Dutch continued to own most Indonesian plantations and industry after the war. Finally, the U.S. government insisted that, as a condition of independence, Indonesia take over some $1.13 billion of the debts of the Netherlands East Indies' debts. Ironically, some $800 million (3 billion guilders) of that amount had been in-curred as military expenses by the Netherlands in its attempt to defeat the Indonesian Republic.[1]

Nor was the economy the only issue. An Indonesian army modeled on the Dutch and Japanese armed forces had come into being, but many armed militias still existed throughout the is-lands. In the outer islands, which possessed some of the richest natural resources, there were regional rebellions, some of them led by Muslim religious groups.

Relations among the different ethnic groups also caused problems. The Javanese elite claimed pride of place in the new Indonesian institutions—in political life, civil service, and the military. The educated and privileged Javanese, mostly sons and daughters of the old aristocracy, clearly saw themselves as the heirs of the Dutch, and sometimes as the followers of the Japa-nese, a role that could only irritate and antagonize the many other Indonesian ethnic groups. In some areas, such as Sumatra and Ambon, tensions existed between Muslims and Christians. The Chinese Indonesians represented only 4 percent of the popula-tion, but wealthy Chinese owned many of the most important businesses, which made them a potential flashpoint for social dis-content.

Perhaps the biggest problem was that the revolution had not produced a political consensus about the future. The revolution-ary struggle against the Dutch had been accompanied by a de-mocratization of the society and a politicization of the peasant population, but not by a commitment to a common political pro-gram beyond national independence. Different political parties, religious leaders, and ethnic organizations presented rival pro-grams for the nation, but there was no consensus. The question arose: where was Indonesia really going?

In those first years, the leaders of nearly all the political par-ties and social movements called themselves socialists. The adop-tion of a vaguely socialist ideology was understandable. The Great Depression of the 1930s and two world wars had taken

millions of lives and had widely discredited capitalism and imperialism. In the post-war period, the colonies fought for their independence from European imperialism, and while some hoped
that with the departure of the foreigners they would make money
and enrich themselves, others believed that their societies would
become more democratic and egalitarian with the end of foreign
domination. India, China, and Indonesia all became independent
during the same historical moment, and everywhere in the former colonies the leaders talked vaguely of socialism.

Already, during the national independence revolution, the
question of socialism had been raised as a practical matter. Tan
Malaka, the former Communist who had returned to Indonesia
and founded the important Persatuan Perjuangan (Unity and
Struggle) organization, put forward a minimum program for the
nation at the group's congress in January 1946, in the midst of the
national independence revolution. Persatuan Perjuangan represented the left wing of the mass movement in the late 1940s and
remained important at least until Tan Malaka was killed in 1948.
The program called for:

- Indonesia to have 100 percent sovereignty.
- All foreign troops to leave at once.
- Establishment of a people's government (the course of gov-
  ernment to agree with the wishes of the people).
- Establishment of a people's army (the course of the army to
  agree with the wishes of the people).
- Disarming of all Japanese troops.
- Taking charge of all European internees (prisoners of the
  Japanese).
- Confiscation and management of enemy-owned planta-
  tions.
- Confiscation and control of enemy-owned industrial instal-
  lations.[2]

Not only Persatuan Perjuangan, but also the Indonesian Socialist
Party (PSI), the Communist Party (PKI), and other groups, had
popularized various versions of socialism. Tan Malaka argued

that the Republic of Indonesia should not take over the plantations and factories of the Chinese or Americans, who were not
enemies at that time, but suggested that the government would
do so at a latter date. Given that the Dutch enemy controlled
most of Indonesia's plantations and industrial plants, this program had both a revolutionary nationalist and a democratic socialist thrust. The Marxist idea of a worker-led movement for a
democratic socialist society existed among a significant number
of intellectuals and some workers, but never became a mass
movement.

A day after the independence proclamation of August 17,
1945, the new government adopted the 1945 Constitution,
though not without debate. The controversy revolved around the
role of the Muslim religion—a faith to which around 85 percent
of all Indonesians adhered—and its relation to the state. But
some Muslim parties demanded the creation of an Islamic state, a
position rejected by the nationalists, other secular and non-Mus-
lim parties, and by many Muslims, as well. Sukarno attempted to
placate the conservative Muslim groups by suggesting that the
Pancasila doctrine be amended to begin with a first principle:
"Belief in One God, with the obligation for adherents of Islam to
implement the Islamic Law (*Shariah*)."[3] This compromise, called
the Jakarta Charter, in the end proved unacceptable to the secular
groups and was removed from the draft of the constitution of
1945 just before it was adopted. Sukarno and the secular parties
thus preserved a secular state and society, but lost the trust of
some conservative Muslim groups.

Intended as a temporary document, the vaguely written 1945
Constitution gave the president enormous power, while neglecting parliament. Sukarno explicitly opposed the inclusion of a declaration of citizens' rights in the constitution, arguing that such
individual rights conflicted with the family and the collective basis of the new society.[4] Four years later, Sukarno's government
adopted a second "Federal Constitution" of 1949. But federalism
was associated with the Dutch, who, hoping to keep the Indone-

sians divided, had attempted to break-up Indonesia into a federation of separate regions just before they left. Thus nationalists rejected federalism, fearing it would mean the break up of the island nation and its piecemeal re-conquest by imperial powers.

Finally, Indonesia adopted the more substantial Constitution of 1950, which reduced the power of the president, increased the power of the parliament, and clearly subordinated the military to the civilian government. But the Constitution of 1950 was also seen as temporary, and its Article 134 provided for the calling of a Konstituante, or Constituent Assembly, to write a final permanent constitution. The Indonesian people were supposed to elect a Konstituante in 1955 to produce a new constitution by 1960. The adoption of the 1959 constitution, and then the return to the 1945 constitution, only added to the country's instability.

Indonesian politics in the mid-1950s represented a tumultuous democracy, a society grappling openly for the first time with questions of principle, politics, and power. Ordinary Indonesians attempted to make democracy work. While the nationalist party leaders, the Muslim organizations, the Communists, and the army represented the most important organized forces participating in the debates, millions of Indonesians followed the discussions. The Konstituante debates over the creation of a national constitution, and most important over the question of the role of religion in society and the state, were conducted in a reasonably rational, open, and democratic fashion. If democracy eventually failed, it was largely due to power-hungry military leaders and civilian politicians of the PSI and Masyumi (the Muslim Party) with short-term views and interests.

In the 1955 elections, believed by all observers to be the only free and fair elections in the nation's history until 1999, Sukarno's PNI won 22.3 percent of the vote, the highest of any party, while the other secular parties received about 18.4 percent of the vote (the PKI received 16.4 percent, and the PSI just 2 percent). But the two Muslim parties received a total approximately equal to the vote for the secular parties: Masyumi with 20.9 percent and

Nahdlatul Ulama with 18.4 percent, or a total of 39.3 percent. Because no party had a majority, the future of the country came to depend upon shifting parliamentary coalitions. Roughly the same sort of spread appeared in the vote in the same year for the Konstituante.

With the nation so deeply divided, seeing no possibility of reaching a consensus, faced at the same time with regional rebellions, and fearing that some faction or the military might attempt to seize power, Sukarno moved to take control. In 1957, having entered into a political alliance with General Abdul Haris Naustion, he declared martial law. Then, at the beginning of 1958, he established a new political system that he called Guided Democracy, a kind of political dictatorship with himself at the head. Under Guided Democracy, a kind of corporatist system, society was to be represented in a National Council on the basis of "functional groups." Sukarno increasingly looked to the PKI and its All-Indonesia Central Workers' Organization (SOBSI) labor union as the representative of labor, that is, of workers and peasants. So Sukarno became the arbiter of the interests of the strongest factions within society: the conservative Muslim parties, the army, and the Communists. At the same time, he put forward the idea that Indonesia should be a leader of the non-aligned or third world nations, a position that led him into conflict with the United States.

The two principal rivals within Sukarno's Guided Democracy regime, the army and the Communists, both moved to strengthen their positions. General Naustion developed a doctrine called "The Middle Way," which argued that the military should also play a role both in politics and in society. Sukarno legitimated military participation in civilian government by appointing army leaders to the cabinet, the parliament, and the administration.[5] At the same time, with Sukarno's support, the Communist Party worked to strengthen its organization among peasants in the villages. Masyumi and other conservative Muslim groups, losing political power and fearing the army and the Communists, turned to cultivate their base in their mosques and religious schools, the *pesantren*. Some of the most conservative Muslims felt a deep resentment against Sukarno and particularly against his Communist allies because they had been politically marginalized.

Sukarno created a new state ideology to attempt to reconcile these contradictions. He called it Nasakom, meaning nationalist, religious, and Communist. Like Pancasila, Nasakom was a futile attempt to reconcile through ideology and language Indonesia's deep cultural, social, and political contradictions. While these ideologies may have served for a while to reduce some sorts of conflicts, they could not resolve the underlying antagonisms between the landlords and peasants or between the military and the Communists. Sukarno used this rhetoric as part of a process of political balancing on which his whole regime was built.

Why did the Indonesian nationalists fail to create a parliamentary democracy in the 1950s? Certainly there was a strong nationalist sentiment among Indonesians—a strong national bond forged in the struggle against Dutch and Japanese imperialism—and real hope for a democratic future. Why was there no capitalist revolution, what the Europeans called a "bourgeois democratic revolution," in Indonesia? Fundamentally, there was no such development because there existed no social class at the center of the revolution to keep it together, push it forward, and give it a democratic dynamic.

When it became independent in 1949, Indonesia had virtually no native capitalist class, no national bourgeoisie. As Herbert Feith writes, "there was no *bourgeoisie* such as developed in the West and Japan, in the sense of a business class with the resources for wielding major influence over the general course of government."[6] Dutch and other European capitalists, Chinese Indonesians, and foreign Chinese businessmen dominated Indonesia's economy. The native bourgeoisie, the *pribumi*, represented small or at best medium-sized companies, often in the most marginal industries. While the Indonesian entrepreneurs did have a history of organization since the early 1900s, they did not have the economic weight and therefore the political power to shape the new Indonesia. When the Dutch and the Japanese pulled out, the political intelligentsia and the army filled the vacuum, but that did not constitute a capitalist or democratic revolution. While many of the politicians and military leaders became involved in commerce and industry, often in partnership with Chinese businessmen, they did not constitute a distinct social class with a political program.[7]

Without a strong capitalist class, a revolutionary working class might have provided an alternative social force to push forward a fight for democracy, as had been the experience in Russia between 1917 and 1925. But, first under Dutch rule and then under Japanese occupation, the proportionally small working class had been unable to create labor unions or a labor party, much less a revolutionary workers' party that might have fought for democracy en route to socialism. So, Indonesia, while it certainly remained a capitalist society, had no powerful capitalist class at the center of its national revolution, no strong bourgeois party, nor any powerful working class, and therefore it had no class basis for democratic politics.

In this situation, Sukarno's government, much like many other postcolonial states, tended toward Bonapartism, a situation where the relative weakness of all the social classes and the resulting political impasse makes it possible for a powerful individual to balance himself on the contending social classes and hold power.[8] Indonesian and Chinese capitalists, the working class, and the peasantry all proved incapable of taking power in post-independence Indonesia, so Sukarno, at the head of a group of nationalist politicians and military officers, effectively took control of the state in the Guided Democracy period. While the capitalist class did not rule, the state and society remained capitalist, and the government continued to defend the existing social system. No group—capitalists or workers, the Muslim parties or the military—had the ability to take power, and, at least for a while, each offset the other. Under Sukarno's Bonapartist regime, the society achieved a kind of fragile equilibrium.

Sukarno's government had nationalist politics, that is, a drive to bring the government, economy, and society under the control of the Indonesian elite. But it had no particular commitment to doing so democratically. The new nationalist state had needed the participation of the masses of workers and peasants in order to take control of the state and to defend itself from the Dutch. But Sukarno's government had no commitment to democratic institutions, whether capitalist or socialist. Sukarno sometimes inclined toward the Soviet Union and at other times leaned toward China, and established a kind of alliance with the PKI. But none of the Communist states or their Communist parties had any democratic ideology. Without a strong social class at its core, Indonesia's revolution had no basis for political and social coherence in the long run.

Labor Under Sukarno

The Indonesian revolution, in addition to bringing national independence, also abolished the Dutch and Japanese systems of forced labor. This important accomplishment of the Indonesian national revolution should not be minimized. The government and private employers could no longer impress workers into service on plantations, in factories, or as laborers for the military. After hundreds of years of slavery, bonded labor, debt-peonage, and forced labor, workers in Indonesia found themselves free. But freedom under capitalism proved to be a mixed blessing. Without Dutch capital, facing the tremendous destruction of war and revolution, and saddled with a large foreign debt, the economy failed to grow, and many agricultural and industrial workers found that freedom meant unemployment or low wages. No longer forced to plant export crops, some peasants reverted to rice production and improved their standard of living, but many workers suffered in the post-war economic depression.

In these critical circumstances, Indonesian workers and peasants found themselves free to organize labor unions to fight for higher wages for the first time in their history. During the revolutionary war against the Dutch, socialists in the new Indonesian government encouraged the formation of the Barisan Buruh Indonesia, or the Indonesian Workers Front (BBI), the first labor federation in independent Indonesia. After the war, political parties took the lead in organizing unions. The Socialists split from the BBI and created the Gabungan Serikat Buruh Indonesia, the Amalgamated Trade Unions of Indonesia (GABSI), a craft union federation, and the Gabungan Serikat Buruh Vertikal Indonesia (GSBVI), an industrial labor federation. But exiled Communists returning to Indonesia after the war soon took over leadership of those federations and transformed them into the Communist-led federation, SOBSI. SOBSI quickly became the most aggressive labor federation, leading the fight for the expropriation and nationalization of the Dutch companies. The PKI also created the Barisan Tani Indonesia, or Indonesian Peasant Front (BTI), which had organized around 9 million peasants and mobilized them in a massive campaign for agrarian reform by 1965.

Other political parties organized labor union federations, as well. Masyumi, the Muslim political party, created Gabungan Serikat Buruh Islam Indonesia, the Amalgamated Indonesian Islamic Labor Federation (GASBINDO). NU, the other Muslim party, established Serikat Buruh Muslimin Indonesia, the Indonesian Muslim Trade Union (SARBUMUSI), as an Islamic alternative to Marxist labor unionism. All of these labor federations, and many smaller ones, as well, competed in the workplace and in society for the loyalty of the workers. The unions also supported their parties in the elections, turning out workers to vote for Communism or Islam.

While this outpouring of labor unionism represented an enormous advance after the Dutch and Japanese suppression of unions, it was not without its problems. The state had taken the initiative to create the first labor federation, followed by the political parties; consequently, these were often top-down organizations dominated by politicians. The Communist Party labor federation, SOBSI, was the most active and dynamic of the labor unions, but SOBSI's Communist leadership took as its model the one-party states of Stalin's Russia and Mao's China. The PKI-led labor movement thus had a contradictory character: on the one hand, it expressed the democratic demands of workers and peasants; on the other hand, its leaders held a Stalinist ideology that advocated the creation of a one-party Communist state.

There were other contradictions, as well. The PKI organized and led a radical agrarian reform movement in the countryside, and often used revolutionary slogans, but the party's ambitions actually stopped well short of social and political revolution. If the Communist leadership actually hoped for revolution, it saw the path to such a revolution as running through its relationship to Sukarno. Consequently, the PKI sought to permeate and control the state, not to overthrow it, but the party's revolutionary rhetoric and radical campaigns frequently created confusion on all sides about its real intentions.

Nothing better exemplifies the contradictions of the labor movement during the Sukarno era than the issue of the expropriation of the Dutch properties. After hundreds of years of conquest, colonization, and exploitation—in which the archipelago's peasants and workers had made hundreds of millions of guilders for the Dutch and had made the Netherlands one of the richest countries in Europe—most Indonesians naturally wanted not only political independence, but also to take control of the Dutch-owned plantations and processing plants. The PKI's SOBSI labor federation led the movement to expropriate and nationalize the Dutch plants, organizing demonstrations and strikes, putting forward resolutions in the parliament, and pressuring President Sukarno. Finally, Sukarno's government decided the time was right and nationalized the Dutch industries without compensation in 1958. The PKI expected Sukarno's civilian government to take over the plant and to involve SOBSI and the other unions in the administration of the plantations and factories. Some labor union leaders expected this to be the first step toward socialism. But the army moved to take control of the plantations and factories, and Sukarno succumbed to the pressure and turned the management of the newly nationalized industries over to the military.

The military administration of the plantations, factories, and later of Pertamina, the state oil company; PT Berdikari, the state trading company; Bulog, the National Logistics Board; and Bank Dharma Ekonomi was to have a number of ramifications, all of which undermined any movement toward democracy or socialism. First, as managers of the plants and other industries, the military became involved both in ordinary business relationships and in corrupt practices with Indonesian industrialists, merchants, and bankers, many of them Chinese Indonesians. Army generals used the state industries, and later their own *yayasans,* or military foundation-owned industries, to both raise funds and supplement their salaries. Eventually the military foundations came to own every sort of industrial factory and plant, from rice mills and clothing factories to automobile assembly plants, as well as to operate joint ventures with both national and international investors. Thus began a perverse relationship between the military and the Chinese-Indonesian capitalists, with generals investing government and private money in business, and Chinese businessmen finding political support and military backing for their private ventures. These commercial generals also provided Indonesian partners for the joint ventures of multinational corporations. As Harold Crouch writes in his book *The Army and Politics in Indonesia*, "Basing their economic strength on political influence rather than entrepreneurial skill, members of the Indonesian military elite acquired the characteristics of a 'comprador' class whose interests ran parallel with those of the foreign corporations with which they were associated."[9] From 1958 forward, the Indonesian military became a major player in the economy, a role it retains to this day.[10]

Second, both as administrators of the state-owned companies and as protectors of the private companies in which they now had an economic interest, the military became locked into a structural relationship of opposition to the labor unions. The military's ideological anti-Communism now found reinforcement in its day-to-day practical opposition to the Communist-led SOBSI labor unions and BTI peasant unions that threatened the profits of military-managed businesses. Later the army even set up its own labor union, SOKSI, to compete with the Communist unions. The apparently socialist-inspired campaign to expropriate the Dutch companies thus led to an authoritarian, bureaucratic, militarized capitalism in which Indonesian army generals used their troops to protect state and private business and to oppose labor unions and workers.

The Role of the United States

The United States found the situation in Indonesia in the 1950s and 1960s completely unacceptable. The combination of radical nationalism, Communist influence, and pervasive political instability threatened U.S. investments and fueled the Cold War. Sukarno and his allies in the army and the Communist Party pursued a nationalist agenda that undermined European, Japanese, and U.S. economic interests, and deterred foreign investment. The U.S. government resented Sukarno's role in the organization of the non-aligned movement, and feared the apparent power and influence of the PKI—especially after the Communist victory in China in 1949 and the Korean War of 1950 to 1953. Direct military intervention was not out of the question. President Eisenhower and Secretary of State John Foster Dulles decided, however, that direct military involvement in Indonesia to overthrow Sukarno was not feasible, because of potential opposition both within the South East Asian Treaty Organization (SEATO) and within the United Nations (UN). Then there was the growing role of the United States in Vietnam and the fear of becoming involved in two wars in the region. The best alternative, Eisenhower and Dulles decided, was for the United States to encourage and support regional rebellions in the outer islands, where many of the most important natural resources lay. So the

U.S. president directed the CIA to foment and support rebellion in Indonesia.[11]

U.S. involvement in Indonesia was to be the largest covert operation since World War II, and would come to involve the CIA, the U.S. Navy, and a U.S.-created air force. The U.S. government also provided supplies, logistics, and intelligence for the rebel forces. Eventually, the United States would also draw in the Taiwanese Chinese Nationalist government, the Philippines, Great Britain, and Australia. Unable to dominate Sukarno and the Jakarta government, the Eisenhower administration decided to attempt to break up Indonesia, as the United States had broken up Vietnam, Korea, and Germany.

The United States focused its attention on Sulawesi and particularly on Sumatra, where U.S. corporations had oil interests. In 1956, a group of Indonesian army officers in Sumatra launched a rebellion backed by the Muslim Masyumi Party leaders, and then proclaimed an independent government in February 1958. The CIA supported the rebellion, providing hundreds of U.S. and other foreign advisors, but army officers loyal to Sukarno invaded Sumatra and suppressed the revolt. In the course of the civil war, the Indonesians shot down a plane piloted by an a U.S. CIA agent carrying documents exposing the role of the United States. Though less well known, the Indonesian affair represented an even greater fiasco than the CIA-backed Bay of Pigs invasion in Cuba. The U.S.-sponsored rebellion actually strengthened Sukarno, the army, and the Communists, while weakening democratic institutions in the country. Following the rebellion, Sukarno's government outlawed Masyumi, one of the country's principal political parties; disbanded the Constituent Assembly, which was writing a new constitution; instituted Guided Democracy in alliance with the army and the PKI; and nationalized Dutch property. The U.S. intervention that had encouraged a civil war costing thousands of Indonesian lives had been a debacle, but the Americans had not finished.[12]

Crisis and Counter-Revolution

During the late 1950s, the Indonesian economy declined precipitously. After the nationalization of Dutch property, other countries hesitated to invest, plantation exports declined, and the foreign debt rose. Then, Indonesia experienced a tremendous inflation in the 1960s that devastated many on fixed incomes, including civil servants. With the economy in a tailspin, the society became ever more polarized and divided, and Indonesian politics became extremely conflicted. In the late 1950s, the PKI peasant organization, BTI, then with approximately 7 million members, began to push for a radical agrarian reform. BTI called for the expropriation of all foreign-owned land, the break-up of large landed property, and the distribution of land to the peasants. It came into conflict not only with foreign and domestic property owners and the government, but also with Muslim landowners, including the Muslim schools, the *pesantren*. Scores died in violent conflicts between peasants and landlords, especially in West Java, and the issue took on overtones of a struggle between atheist Communists and religious Muslims. During the period between 1958 and 1965, when it led the agrarian reform movement, the BTI grew to 9 million members.[13]

Elements of the Indonesian army became alarmed at the Communist mobilization, and grew fearful because of Sukarno's apparent decision to work with the Communists to move Indonesia toward a socialist society. In Jakarta, U.S. Ambassador Marshall Green encouraged army officers to destroy the Communists, and perhaps even suggested that they overthrow Sukarno. The leadership of the army became divided into various rival factions on the basis of their attitudes toward Sukarno and the Communists. By the early 1960s, it seemed as if one side or the other might at any moment attempt a coup.

In this context, on September 30, 1965, a group of junior army officers alleged to be working with the PKI, who called themselves the September 30 Movement, kidnapped and murdered six generals and a lieutenant. The attack, supposedly intended to prevent a military coup, seemed to have the tacit support of D.N. Aidit, the head of the PKI, and perhaps also of President Sukarno. Under the leadership of General Suharto, the army reacted rapidly, quashed the coup, and accused the Communists of having attempted to seize power. That interpretation seems highly unlikely, since the Communists did not carry out a nationwide mobilization of their forces, but it subsequently became the government's official position.

Effectively holding power, Suharto and the other generals decided to take advantage of their position to destroy the PKI once and for all. The army provided arms to the NU youth organization, Ansor, and soldiers and Muslim youth moved through the countryside together, wrecking Communist party offices and newspapers, destroying labor unions and peasant organizations, and killing Communists, worker and peasant leaders, and other actual and potential opponents. In some areas, the army found allies in Muhammadiyah or the PNI.[14] Altogether, scholars estimate the number of those killed at between 300,000 and 1 million, with most estimates at around 500,000.[15] In addition, another 200,000 to 300,000 people were imprisoned, and many of them died in prison or on the infamous Buru Island. The Indonesian slaughter of 1965 represents one of the most terrible human tragedies of the twentieth century, on a scale with the Nazi atrocities of World War II. The U.S. government gave the extermination campaign its tacit approval and, well aware of the vast massacre that was taking place, gave Suharto and the Indonesian military covert support of various kinds.[16] Ambassador Green wrote to Secretary of State John Foster Dulles, that he had "made it clear that Embassy and USG [U.S. government] [were] generally sympathetic with and admiring of what [the] army [was] doing."[17] *Time* magazine said the destruction of the Communist Party was "The West's best news for years in Asia."[18]

The United States had encouraged the Indonesian military coup and the massacre to establish a new political-economic order in Indonesia, one that would safeguard U.S. investments in petroleum and create the stability to encourage U.S. and Japanese investments in other areas of the economy. How would one characterize this new regime? Suharto's New Order was a military government, but one that shared common characteristics with fascist regimes such as Hitler's Nazi Germany and Mussolini's Fascist Italy. Suharto would organize a state party, Golkar, create a political system based on that party and other officially recognized political parties, establish a state based on corporatist "functional groups," and suppress any genuine labor unions and virtually all other independent social organizations.

The New Order Regime

Suharto had not been a particularly remarkable figure before the coup. His career resembled that of many of his contemporaries in the Indonesian military. Born in Java, a veteran of the Dutch and Japanese military, he joined the Indonesian army and participated in the struggle for Jogjakarta. Later he fought against the revolts in Sulawesi and Java, and rose through the ranks to become a brigadier general. In 1965, as chief of security in Jakarta, he led the anti-Communist forces and directed the annihilation of the Communists. Now Suharto began to take power. On March 11, 1966, Sukarno was forced to hand over emergency power to Suharto. Suharto then began to round up and imprison most of the cabinet members, though Sukarno continued in the presidency. In March 1967, the People's Consultative Assembly (MPR) declared Suharto to be acting president, and only in 1968 did he become full president. For the next 32 years, Suharto would preside over the Indonesian state and the national economy.

Having taken power, Suharto established what he called the "New Order," an authoritarian, militaristic regime that served the interests of a close clique of his political allies, business partners, and friendly foreign investors. The military stood at the center of the new government. Expanding on General Nasution's "Middle Way," which had justified military participation in civilian government, the military elite created a new doctrine: *dwifungsi*, or dual function. *Dwifungsi* meant that the military should also be involved in civilian politics, not as a temporary measure, but permanently. Military leaders would take offices in parliament, serve in the civil service, and even come to run the state-sponsored labor unions. At the same time, General Ali Moertopo of Special Operations (Opsus), the intelligence service, developed the idea of the "floating mass," the idea that the state and the parties should lead the mindless masses. To do so, the state would create organizations for every group: workers, peasants, women, youth, and many others.

Soon after he took power, Suharto restructured the parliamentary system. The MPR, the body that nominates the president, was changed in 1967, giving the government the power to appoint one-third of the delegates. Similarly, the government claimed the right to appoint one-fifth of the delegates to the parliament (DPR). These alternations effectively meant the end of whatever modicum of parliamentary democracy had existed.

But it was not enough to reorganize parliament; it was also necessary to reorganize the other major institutions and the political parties. First, Suharto carried out a purge of the military to eliminate any followers of Sukarno or sympathizers with Communism. He also continued the ban on Masyumi, the Muslim party that had supported the rebellions of the 1950s. Then, working with an anti-Communist organization in the military, Suharto established Golkar, and required all government officials and employees to join it. Moertopo put the screws to government officials and peasant leaders to turn out the vote for Golkar in the first post-coup election. In 1971, Golkar won with 63 percent of the vote; NU won 18 percent; while the PNI and a new government-created Muslim party, Parmusi, each won 7 percent of the vote. Shortly afterward, in 1973, the Suharto government forced the nine existing political parties (all except Golkar) to dissolve and be reorganized into two new parties: the United Development Party (PPP), made up of the former Muslim parties, and the Indonesian Democratic Party (PDI), made up of the nationalist and Christian parties. In reality, no independent political parties existed after that period; all depended on the state.

Over the years, Suharto would exert even greater control over society and politics. After the anti-Japanese riots of 1974, the regime closed down newspapers; and, after student demonstrations in 1977 and 1978, the state suppressed student organizations. In 1984, Suharto's government decreed that all social organizations and political parties had to declare Pancasila as their only ideology. Suharto attempted to establish a state like Hitler's Germany, Stalin's Soviet Union, or Mao's China, a state that could dictate to the society. With its state party, Golkar, its army high command as a kind of Politburo, its political police, ubiquitous spies, and psychological screening tests, it had many of the earmarks of a totalitarian state. Unlike Stalin's Soviet Union and Mao's China, the state did not control the economy, so perhaps the greater similarity is to Hitler's Germany. But under Suharto, the state, like the Soviet Union, did own many firms and did attempt to establish a five-year plan, though the low levels of education and technology thwarted those efforts. In 1982, Golkar won 64 percent of the vote in national elections. By 1987, three years after NU left the PPP, Golkar won 73 percent.

Business and Foreign Investment

The purpose of government under Suharto was to promote "development," that is, domestic capitalism and foreign investment. At first, Suharto suggested that he would play by the rules of the game. The International Monetary Fund (IMF), the World Bank, Indonesian technocrats trained in the United States, and U.S. government advisers wrote the rules for the new economic order, though much that happened developed outside the formal rules. Suharto's economic team, sometimes called the Berkeley Mafia because they had all been educated at the University of California at Berkeley, wrote the 1967 Foreign Investment Law, which gave foreign corporations two important guarantees. First, the law promised there would be no nationalization of a company's assets without fair compensation. Second, it gave investors the right to convert the rupiah into foreign exchange to repatriate profits. In 1968, Indonesia signed the Convention on the Settlement of Investment Disputes, which gave foreign businesses the right to recourse outside the country if they were dissatisfied with compensation offered by the Indonesian government. With these guarantees, foreign capital soon returned. Later, however, after the oil boom of the late 1970s, Suharto became more independent and resisted U.S. and IMF control.

At the center of the new Indonesian economic order stood Suharto and his family, and their business partners such as Liem Sioe Liong and Bob Hassan. Suharto, the so-called business generals, and a small number of politically connected businessmen soon dominated the largest banks and corporations, a system that came to be called "crony capitalism." A combination of political power, shrewd business sense, and tremendous corruption made the cronies fabulously wealthy. For example, the Suharto government gave Hassan a marketing monopoly over Indonesia's forests, lumber industry, and plywood manufacture, making him a multimillionaire.[19]

As Jeffrey Winters notes in his insightful book *Power in Motion: Capital Mobility and the Indonesian State*, domestic and foreign investors, but particularly the latter, gained more influence over the Indonesian economy in the mid-1980s, after the oil boom. Under the pressure of international financial institutions and multinational corporations, the government was compelled to deregulate its economy and open its economy to foreign capital as never before.[20] The new government encouraged foreign investment, especially by the Japanese. Capital from Hong Kong, Taiwan, South Korea, Singapore, the Netherlands, and the United Kingdom also poured into Indonesia. U.S. investment was also encouraged, and U.S. capital made significant investments.[21] Under new laws, many investors held 100-percent ownership of companies in Indonesia. Other investors established joint ventures with military leaders and Chinese-Indonesian businessmen. The cronies dominated Indonesia's relations with the foreign corporations, acting as a corrupt domestic regulator of foreign investments. The combination of crony capitalism and the large involvement of Japanese capital in Indonesia led in 1974 to divisions in the ruling military elite and to a riot against the visit of a Japanese prime minister, an event known as the Malari incident. But Suharto rode out the riots, tightened his grip, and, to placate his critics, modified investment laws to outlaw 100-percent foreign ownership and instead require joint ventures. By 1975, 10 years after he seized power, Suharto had a firm hold on the state.

With the oil boom that began in the 1970s, the Suharto government borrowed abroad and built industrial infrastructure with the idea of creating a modern industrial economy. The IMF opposed Indonesia's industrial development policy, especially its plans to create its own aircraft and auto industries, but could do little about it at the time. As in Mexico, oil produced artificial buoyancy in the economy. In the mid-1980s, however, the prices collapsed, and boom turned to bust. Indonesia, like other countries around the world, found that it had to find a new source of income, and turned to manufacture for export. The earlier investments in industrial infrastructure made it possible for Indonesia to make a rapid transition from oil production to an export platform for the multinationals.

Throughout the 1960s and 1970s, Indonesia had combined a mixed economy with a relatively strong state sector and an economic model based on the substitution of imports. But in the mid-1980s, Margaret Thatcher in England and Ronald Reagan in the United States had begun to advocate new free-market policies, including privatization and deregulation. Soon the World Bank and the IMF were pushing policies that came to be called "neoliberal globalization" on developing nations. Under pressure from international financial institutions, the realities of the world market, and its own economic crisis, Indonesia, like so many other third world countries, began to deregulate its economy and open up to foreign investment.

In 1983, Indonesia liberalized its bank credit and deposit ratios. In 1986, a revision of import, export, and re-export duties and a liberalization of investment regulations took place, including the creation of a free trade zone in Jakarta. In 1987, import quotas were lifted on steel, machinery, auto parts, plastics, and textiles. The banking sector was deregulated in 1988, and other industries, agriculture, and fisheries were deregulated in 1990. Indonesia also established two free trade zones with industrial parks on Bantam Island and Tanjung Priok in the Jakarta port area. Foreign investors could own up to 100 percent of the enterprise for 10 years (they had to divest 10 percent at the end of the first 10 years, and 20 percent by the end of the second 10 years). Other free trade zones were established later in Surabaya, Semarang, Medan, Belawan, Cilacap, and Unjung Padang.

The results were remarkable, at least at first. While the petroleum sector grew at an average of 2.7 percent in the late 1980s and early 1990s, manufacturing grew at a rate of 12.2 percent during this period. By 1992, manufacturing represented the largest and most important sector of the economy, 21 percent, followed by agriculture at 19 percent, commerce at 17 percent, and gas and oil at 13 percent. By 1980, manufacture made up 13 percent of Gross Domestic Product, and about 25 percent by 1994. In 1980, manufacture made up 2 percent of exports, but represented 53 percent by 1994. At the center of this growth in manufacture was the alliance between government and military officials the Chinese-Indonesian businessmen who created huge corporate conglomerates. At the base of the system were the Indonesian workers earning little more than a dollar a day.

While Chinese Indonesians owned nearly all the big Indonesian corporations, foreign direct investment (FDI) also played a large part in the economy. Foreign corporations invested in Indonesia to take advantage of government inducements such as tax abatements, industrial infrastructure, access to natural resources, and, especially in manufacturing, low wages. FDI approvals for all countries rose from $1.5 billion in 1987 to $10.3 billion in 1992. Japan remained the nation with the largest cumulative investment in Indonesia, representing about 75 percent of all investments, followed by Hong Kong and Taiwan, with the United States fourth. U.S. investment, concentrated mainly in large-scale, capital-intensive industries such as chemicals, mining, and metallic and non-metallic manufacture, grew from less than $1 billion in 1986 to $4.7 billion in 1989 and $10.3 billion in 1992. Every conceivable kind of U.S. corporation had investments or contractors in Indonesia: AT&T and NYNEX in telecommunications; General Motors in auto; Mobil Oil in petroleum; Mattel in toys; Nike, Adidas, Fila, and Reebok in footwear; and the Gap and many major U.S. clothing manufacturers in apparel.[22] While U.S. corporations did not represent a very large part of the economy, the United States was a significant investor in Indonesia by the 1990s.[23]

Three-quarters of Indonesia's industrial development in the 1980s took place in Western Java, and over half of that in the Jakarta area. Most of the new industrial workers were young men and women from the countryside. The numbers of women entering into the urban manufacturing jobs rose dramatically throughout the 1980s and 1990s. Many of these were young women drawn from the countryside into the cities in search of higher wages and more opportunities. In 1987, for urban women between the ages of 20 and 60, more than 40 percent were economically active, while for rural women for that same age range, between 55 and 70 percent were economically active.[24] Rural women had always played an important part in peasant production, but the young female factory worker was a relatively new phenomenon. During the 1990s, these women factory workers, living in barracks and subsisting on a meager diet, often worked 12-hour days or more for as little as 14 cents an hour.

Clearly industrial development that benefited the military and businessmen did not necessarily mean economic improvement for Indonesia's population as a whole. In 1994, the United Nations Development Program's human development index ranked Indonesia 105th out of 173 countries. In the early 1990s, the UN found that infant mortality was high, at about 53 deaths per 1,000 live births; about 39 percent of Indonesia's children under five were malnourished; 58 percent of the population had no access to safe water; and 45 percent had no access to adequate sanitation. Despite the process of economic "modernization," or rather because of it, most of Indonesia's people remained poor.

The Suharto New Order and Labor

Suharto's government established an almost absolute control over labor that led Indonesia to have one of the lowest levels of union organization in the world. Out of a workforce of 80 million, less than 3 million workers were organized in labor unions, and those were government-controlled labor unions that did next to nothing to represent workers. Without labor unions, workers' wages in Indonesia were among the lowest of the industrializing countries, with workers earning on the average less than $1 per day. Occupational health and safety and environmental issues were virtually ignored.

General Ali Moertopo of the intelligence service created what became a system of state-military control over the unions. His first step was the creation in 1971 of the Indonesian Public Employees Corps (KORPRI). Government employees, both those who worked for government agencies and those in state-owned or partially state-owned companies, were required to join the state-sponsored KORPRI. Altogether KORPRI represented more than 10 million workers. KORPRI also served to mobilize votes for Golkar.

Next, Moertopo forced all of the old labor unions, whatever their political or religious basis, to join together into one state-controlled labor federation. On February 20, 1973, all existing labor unions signed a Declaration of Unity, dissolving their organizations into the All-Indonesia Labor Federation (FSBI). Controlled by the state, FSBI represented a "pure and simple" labor union concerned only about economic issues, supposedly without any political interests, and seeking cooperation with the employers. The government provided FSBI with much of its funding, while Golkar, the government party, gradually came to provide the organization's leadership.

Still unsatisfied with residual political currents remaining within FSBI, the government forced the federation to transform itself in 1985 into SPSI, the All-Indonesia Workers' Union. Controlled by Golkar, permeated by the military, and allied with the employers, SPSI could no longer be called a labor union. Workers no longer had any organizations to fight for even their most minimal needs for better conditions or higher wages. SPSI was a fascist labor front constructed to control workers, not represent them. Even more tragic, the elimination of the unions meant that when a new generation of young workers entered the factories in the 1980s, they had no labor union model to work with and had to begin organizing from scratch.

In addition to reorganizing the unions, Suharto's regime also created its own theory of labor relations known as Hubungan Perburuhan Pancasila, or Pancasila Labor Relations (HPP). This later was renamed Pancasila Industrial Relations (HIP). Both employers and workers, the theory argued, worked in service of God and humankind, striving for a just and civilized humanity, and should reach consensus through consultation between management and workers. HIP theory argued that Indonesia constituted a national "family," and that conflicts between individuals were inconceivable or unacceptable within a family. Consequently, as an Indonesian government pamphlet prepared by the Ministry of Manpower declared, "Industrial disputes shall not occur." That is, strikes were not permitted.[25] In addition, labor unions were required to limit their activities to economic questions and to eschew politics. HIP, with its organic vision of society, was a fascist theory of industrial relations.

The Ministry of Manpower, basing itself on the Pancasila ideology of cooperation, created a tripartite labor tribunal made up of government, employer, and state-controlled labor union representatives. The state created both federal and regional dispute resolution committees known as P4P and P4D. Under Law

No. 22 of 1957, disputes go before a 15-person panel made up of representative of the state, the Chamber of Commerce employer association (APINDO), and the SPSI unions. At the national level, the minister of manpower chairs the committees, while the governor chairs them at the state level. The P4P and P4D committees are simply advisory, with no power to make decisions, though the minister usually accepts their recommendations. Workers found the P4P and P4D committees to be bureaucratic, legalistic, slow, and almost always partial to management.

Under Suharto, Indonesia also established limited welfare programs, providing a social safety net of sorts for the working class. A state system of social security called JAMSOSTEK was created to provide coverage for health and pensions for workers and their families. JAMSOSTEK is based upon both worker and employer contributions; workers pay 2.3 percent of their wages, and employers pay 5.7 percent of workers' wages, for a total of 8 percent of wages overall. The government also set up PUSKESMAS, the Public Health Service for urban and rural poor, a pyramidal structure from the national down to the village level with 100,000 clinics. Finally, under Law 3 of 1996, workers are entitled to severance pay from their employers when they are terminated. Like other government programs, JAMSOSTEK was riddled with corruption; on one occasion, for example, it used welfare funds to put up politicians at fancy hotels.

Despite the ideology of labor-management harmony, the state-controlled union federation, the tripartite dispute resolution system, and the social security system, workers continued to engage in job actions, slowdowns, and strikes. During the 1980s, the government frequently turned to military and police agencies to control labor. Military and police surveillance, infiltration, and systematic harassment of labor militants were widespread. Sometimes the army kidnapped and tortured labor activists, and occasionally killed them. Not only did the military and the police spy on labor unions and workers, but military and police officials also frequently intervened to force or negotiate the end of strikes.

While the Indonesian state never proved completely successful in eliminating the various secular nationalist, Muslim, and Christian currents, it did create a very different model of unionism.

Vedi Hadiz, an authority on Indonesian labor unions, calls this an "exclusionary corporatist" system, which he defines as "the arrangement of state-society relations on the basis of state-controlled and established, monolithic and non-competitive institutions, geared to facilitate the control and demobilization of society-based organizations and movements, including those of the of the working class."[26] To put it another way, the state-controlled unions functioned much like Nazi or fascist labor fronts to control and discipline workers for capital. Under Suharto, workers had no right to organize an independent labor union, could not engage in meaningful collective bargaining with their employers, and were denied the right to strike. Those who attempted to organize strikes or independent labor unions were fired and blacklisted, beaten and tortured, and were sometimes murdered. Yet at no time did workers cease to take action to fight for higher wages and better conditions.

During the late 1980s and the early 1990s, a new era of workers' resistance began that involved both peasants and workers. The movement in the city in the early 1990s also challenged the regime. Altogether hundreds of thousands of workers struck for higher wages in the industrial suburbs of Jakarta. In East Java, a young woman organizer named Marsinah was murdered, presumably by the military, and she became the martyr of the new labor movement. New labor union organizations and organizers, such as the crusading labor attorney and union organizer Muchtar Pakpahan and the young socialist strike leader Dita Sari, nevertheless continued to appear. Suharto's government reacted by jailing both, and suppressing the latter's union as a subversive organization. Only with a full-scale political crisis could independent labor unions emerge and begin to organize openly. That crisis, which we described earlier, arrived in 1997 and 1998, and led to the fall of Suharto and the beginning of a new era.

1 George McT. Kahin, "Some Recollections and Reflections on the Indonesian Revolution," *Indonesia* (Cornell) 60 (October 1995): 15.

2 Tan Malaka, *From Jail to Jail,* trans. and ed. Helen Jarvis (Athens: Ohio University Press [Ohio University Center for International Studies Southeast Asia Series Number 83], 1991), vol. 3, 117–19. I have paraphrased Jarvis's translation.

3 Adam Schwartz, *A Nation in Waiting: Indonesia in the 1990s* (Boulder, Colorado: Westview Press, 1994), 10.

4 Goenanwan Mohamad, *Sidelines: Thought Pieces from Tempo Magazine* (South Melbourne, Victoria: Lontar, 1994), 13, 196.

5 Harold Crouch, *The Army and Politics in Indonesia* (Ithaca: Cornell University Press, 1978), 344.

6 Herbert Feith, *The Decline of Constitutional Democracy in Indonesia* (Ithaca: Cornell University Press, 1962), 104.

7 The best theoretical discussion of these issues is found in Richard Robinson, *Indonesia and the Rise of Capital* (North Sydney: Asian Studies Association of Australia, 1986); and the discussion by Jeffrey A. Winters, "Indonesia: The Rise of Capital," in *Indonesia* (Cornell) 45 (April, 1998), 109–128. For another sort of discussion, see Andrew MacIntyre, *Business and Politics in Indonesia* (North Sydney: Allen & Unwin Pty. Ltd., 1990) Chapter 2, "The Theoretical Terrain," is an excellent overview of the literature.

8 Marx first used the term to refer to Louis Napoleon Bonaparte in France, and later in discussions of Bismarck and his regime in Germany; later, Leon Trotsky applied the term at different times to Stalin, Hitler, and Lazaro Cardenas in Mexico.

9 Crouch, *The Army and Politics,* 299.

10 Dr. Indria Samego et al., *Bila ABRI Berbisnis: Buku Pertama yang Menyingkap Data dan Kasus Penyimpangan dalam Praktik Bisnis Kalagan Militer* (Bandung: Kronik Indonesia Baru, 1998), gives an overview of the military in the contemporary Indonesian economy and in particular sectors.

11 Audrey R. and George McT. Kahin, *Subversion as Foreign Policy* (New York: The New Press, 1995), give the best account of the U.S. role in the Indonesian rebellions and civil war of 1957 to 1958.

12 Vedi R. Hadiz, *Workers and the State in New Order Indonesia* (New York: Routledge and Asia Research Centre, Murdoch University, 1997).

13 Sartono Kartodirdjo, *Modern Indonesia: Tradition and Transformation: A Socio-Historical Perspective* (Yogyakarta: Gadjah Mada University Press, 1991), Chapter 2, "Peasant Mobilization and Political Development in Indonesia," 30–82.

14 John Roosa, private communication, February 2001.

15 Geoffrey Robinson, *The Dark Side of Paradise: Political Violence in Bali* (Ithaca: Cornell University Press, 1995), 273–303.

16   Robinson, *The Dark Side of Paradise,* 282–86.

17   Gabriel Kolko, *Confronting the Third World: United States Foreign Policy, 1945–1980* (New York: Pantheon Books, 1988), 181.

18   Schwartz, *A Nation in Waiting,* 22.

19   Christopher M. Barr, "Bob Hassan, the Rise of Apkindo, and the Shifting Dynamics of Control in Indonesia's Timber Sector," *Indonesia* (Cornell) (1998), 1–37.

20   Jeffrey Winters, "Capital's Power Restored, 1982 to the Present," in *Power in Motion: Capital Mobility and the Indonesian State* (Ithaca: Cornell University Press, 1996), 142–91.

21   State Minister for Research and Technology told U.S. businessmen in May 1993 that since 1967, out of a total foreign investment of $65.5 billion, U.S. corporations accounted for only $2.9 billion or around 4 percent, while Japanese corporations had invested 13.2 billion or about 20 percent. Cited in Richard R. Mann, ed., *United States Investment in Indonesia* (Toronto: Gateway Books, 1994), 13.

22   John Bresnan, *Managing Indonesia: The Modern Political Economy* (New York: Columbia University Press, 1993), Chapter 10, "Deregulating Industry," 245–269; Richard Mann, ed., *United States Investment in Indonesia* (Toronto: Gateway Books, 1994), tables, 22–29; Ilyas Saad, "Foreign Direct Investment, Structural Change, and Deregulation in Indonesia," in Nomura Research Institute and Institute of Southeast Asian Studies, *The New Wave of Foreign Direct Investment in Asia* (Singapore: Namora Research Institute and Institute of Southeast Asian Studies, 1995), 197–219.

23   Mann, *United States Investment in Indonesia.* For a general discussion, see Ilyas Saad, "Foreign Direct Investment."

24   Gavin W. Jones and Chris Manning, "Labour Force and Employment During the 1980s," in Anne Booth, ed., *The Oil Boom and After: Indonesian Economic Policy and Performance in the Soeharto Era* (New York: Oxford University Press, 1995), 368. Women of reproductive age, 20–40, were less likely to be economically active because they were giving birth, nursing, and caring for children.

25   Dr. Payaman J. Simanjuntak, *Issues on Industrial Relations in Indonesia* (Jakarta: Ministry of Manpower, 1992), 11. See also Sriharto Hardjomiguno, "Pancasila as a New Approach to Industrial Relations," in *Innovative Approaches to Industrial Relations in ASEAN* (International Labor Organization, 1985).

26   Hadiz, *Workers and the State,* 27.

Chapter 5

The Fight for Freedom

The Role of the NGOs

Non-governmental organizations (NGOs) have played an enormously important role in Indonesian society and particularly in the working-class movement for the last 10 years. Because the government-controlled All-Indonesia Workers' Union (SPSI) labor union not only failed to represent workers, but also functioned as part of the system of control used against them, and because independent labor unions were not only banned but also severely repressed, NGOs played a key role in helping workers organize. NGOs helped workers create organizations, aided them in strikes, and advised them when they engaged in informal bargaining. NGOs also helped to link the alternative labor movement to the wider effort to build a democratic movement for civil rights and political reform, what was sometimes called the new civil society.

Labor-oriented organizations represent only a small part of the panoply of NGOS that deal with every sort of economic, political, and social problem. NGOs first appeared in Indonesia in the 1970s in an attempt to create space in the New Order society for criticism and dissent, as well as for constructive social and political movements. Former student activists who sought a space for their criticism and activism in the larger society after leaving the university organized most of these NGOs. Indonesia had seen several waves or "generations" of student activism between 1970 and 2000: in 1970–1972, in 1974, in 1977–1978, 1987–1990, and again in 1996–1998. As each wave of students left the university, often following repression, expulsion, and perhaps prison, they created new organizations that took on new tasks. With each new wave, the NGO network became larger, stronger, and more sophisticated.[1]

Indonesian NGOs formed part of that elusive social phenomenon called "civil society" that appeared in countries throughout the world in the last quarter of the twentieth century. Often financed by national or international foundations and, sometimes, despite the name, by governments, NGOs seemed at times to represent some new form of elite social control or even international cultural and social imperialism. Certainly NGOs represented a retreat from radicalism in some countries, but in others, such as Indonesia, they frequently launched a new radical offensive. While Indonesia had its share of both imperial and government-financed NGOs, many Indonesian NGOs sprang up from opposition groups and served the need for social expression denied in an authoritarian society. Since the Suharto regime had eradicated all left organizations, NGOs served as incubators for radical alternatives; and since all mass-based organizations had been either co-opted or banned, they also served as small centers of resistance. Indonesian civil society and its NGOs represented the growing opposition and alternative to the 35-year dictatorship.

The older generation of NGOs tended to concentrate on development, environmental, consumers', and women's issues, and in general expressed middle-class disappointment and frustration with New Order policies. The Foundation of Indonesian Consumer Institutes (YLKI) took up the concerns of consumers, while the Indonesian Environmental Forum (WALHI) advocated environmental protection. The Institute for Economic and Social Research, Education, and Information (L3PES) studied the country's economic, political, social, and cultural issues. The

International NGO Forum on Indonesian Development (INFID) lobbied foreign aid donors in favor of projects to help the poor. Some of these older NGOs took up the causes of workers and farmers, but usually within a developmental framework. The Institute for Development Studies (LSP), for example, worked to build cooperatives among those in the informal economy, such as street vendors, while the Indonesian Rural Development Network assisted small and medium farmers.

The most important of the older generation of NGOs remains the Legal Aid Institute (LBH, pronounced el-bay-hah), or, as its coordinating center is now known, the Foundation of Indonesian Legal Aid Institutes (YLBHI). Attorney Adnan Buyung Nasution founded LBH in Jakarta in 1971, and the organization later opened its regional branches in 1978. Today LBH has branches in more than a dozen of Indonesia's major cities.

After Nasution studied law at the University of Indonesia in the 1950s, he became a public prosecutor and then a successful private attorney. His career is representative of the older generation of NGO leaders. At the time of the 1965 coup, he backed Suharto and joined a scholars' action group that worked to both support and influence the new regime. He was a member of the Indonesian Socialist Party (PSI) network that had supported Suharto and provided him with his economic elite, the so-called Berkeley Mafia. In 1971, Nasution founded LBH with the blessing of Ali Moertopo, Suharto's right-hand man. Suharto and Moertopo needed an official human rights institute to provide public defenders so it could argue that Indonesia was a state based on law, not on the whims of power-crazed generals. Ironically for the founder of a human rights organization, Nasution had never criticized the Suharto coup, nor the massacres of 1965. He adopted a human rights rhetoric intended to impress foreign funders, and found support from foundations such as Novib in the Netherlands. But things changed in 1974, when the PSI network had a falling out with Suharto. Having backed General Sumitro in the Malari affair, the PSI group found itself on the outs. Suharto's government jailed PSI student activists, and suddenly there was a real human rights issue for Nasution's associates at LBH.

Nasution eventually found himself in conflict with the authorities. In 1984, he defended Marine Lieutenant Dharsono, who had been indicted for signing a "white paper" questioning the government's account of the Tanjung Priok massacre of September 1984, and for holding a meeting with Muslim radicals a few days later. Dharsono was sentenced to 10 years in prison, later reduced to seven. Nasution, because he had defended Dharsono, lost his law license and could no longer practice. Unable to work in his own country, he left for the Netherlands. There he wrote his Ph.D. thesis on the Indonesian constitutional debate of the late 1950s, which was later published as a book. He later returned to Indonesia and was reappointed head of LBH in 1993. He retired from the LBH leadership in 1999, remaining an adviser.

While LBH provides legal representation in cases of civil and political rights, and helps many NGO, social movement, labor union, and political activists, its larger task is the promotion of progressive social change. Nasution established LBH on the basis of the concept of "structural legal aid," meaning an attempt to change the institutions that caused social, economic, and political inequalities. "Structural legal aid," Nasution said, means an approach that is "broad and political rather than narrow and legal." He explained, "The goal is not to achieve a technical victory in court (which would in all likelihood be unenforceable anyway, given the impunity with which the regime and its officials operate), but to focus domestic and international attention on abuses and to mobilize people to press for the reform of laws or procedures that discriminate against the poor and vulnerable."[2]

In the early 1990s, LBH decided to focus on labor, environmental, land, criminal, and political issues. With its national network of offices and its ties to all sorts of NGOs—whether conservative, moderate, liberal, or radical—LBH stands at the center of Indonesia's NGO organizations and represents one of the most important institutions behind the pro-democracy movement. Few social movements in Indonesia in the 1980s and 1990s developed without some sort of support or assistance from LBH and its lawyers. Because of its long history and broad base of support, the government has never suppressed LBH, though many of its employees and associated activists have been arrested and harassed.

The student activists of the 1980s and 1990s created a new generation of NGOs, more radical, more vocal, and more activist than their forerunners. The new NGOs focused on democracy and human rights, and frequently attempted to link up student and middle-class activists with workers, peasants, and the poor. The Indonesian Front for the Defense of Human Rights (Infight), the Network for Forest Conservation in Indonesia (Skephi), and the Information and Action Network for Reform (PIJAR) represented a new campaigning style of organizing, based on public forums, demonstrations, and direct challenges to the government and even the president.

To take just one example, Infight, established in 1990 to oppose the government's decision to execute several long-term prisoners, soon broadened its activities from opposition to the death penalty to a wide assortment of human rights issues, including the rights of the East Timorese and West Papuans. Indro Tjahyono, one of Infight's leading figures, explained the group's approach: "Infight undertakes political action in support of human rights. With no space within the legal system, political action is the only space we have. More importantly, at Infight we are not just concerned with the human rights of individuals, but collective rights, including the right of an ethnic group to preservation of its culture and even the right to self-determination."[3]

Infight's emphasis on political action and its campaigning approach typified the new NGOs. The new generation of NGOs represented the entire religious and political spectrum: Muslim, Christian, and secular, as well as radical, liberal, and conservative.

But, with the exception of those actually created or supported by the government, virtually all were opposed to the old regime and called for the establishment of a democratic government and society in Indonesia. The student movement and the NGOs, and later the independent labor unions, formed the backbone of the pro-democracy movement. Their fundamental goals were human rights, the rule of law, free and fair elections, and a reduction in the power of the military.[4] These fundamental principles, however, seemed unlikely ever to be conceded by the New Order regime, which responded to democratic demands with police and military repression, beatings and torture, long prison terms, and even murder.

Consequently, the new generation of NGOs was not only more activist, but also far more radical, often having given up on the notion that they could work for change within the New Order regime. Anders Uhlin, who wrote the most comprehensive account of the NGOs and new social movements in Indonesia before the fall of Suharto, writes: "Most representatives of the new generation of pro-democracy and human rights NGOs do not see any possibility of working within the rules of the authoritarian regime. They argue that authoritarian power structures and actors must be more or less directly confronted. It is not possible to reform the New Order regime."[5]

If the New Order regime could not be reformed, many of the new NGO activists decided, it must be overthrown. Some drew the conclusion that to do so would require links to the majority of Indonesia's population, who were peasants, workers, and the urban poor.

The Work of the Pro-Labor NGOs

The pro-labor NGOs provided very real services to workers and incipient labor organizations. First, they gave labor organizers and worker activists the legitimacy and protection of working for or with an NGO, a legally recognized organization. Second, they offered legal advice and legal services, teaching about labor law, for example, and helping to release workers from jail when they were arrested. Third, NGOs performed research on the economy, providing valuable information to labor activists. Finally, and perhaps most important, they helped to train labor organizers and worker activists in organizing. In fact, until real independent unions began to be formed in the late 1990s, the NGOs acted as surrogate labor organizations.

While NGOs were not the only organizations undertaking this sort of work—some student groups and political organizations also did—the NGOs were the most important source of support for workers.

The Legal Aid Institute

The Legal Aid Institute functions as one of the most important labor NGOs in Indonesia. Attorneys associated with LBH have played an important role in helping workers to defend themselves against both employers and the government, and have attempted to build independent workers' organizations. LBH has been fortunate to find several able attorneys and activists who have played a dynamic role in the defense of workers' rights.

Teten Masduki headed LBH's labor division from 1989 to 1999, when he went on to coordinate the Indonesian Corruption Watch (ICW). Teten typifies the idealistic young people who dedicated themselves to the NGOs and labor activism. Born in Limbangan Garut, West Java, in 1963, Masduki studied chemistry at the Bandung Teachers Training Institute. He worked as a vocational school teacher in Tangerang for a time, but then decided to leave. "I was disturbed about the suffering of the laborers. Although on the one hand they formed the backbone of our economic development, their standard of living did not increase accordingly. I also saw that the exploitation of laborers was not only perpetrated by capitalism, but also by the authorities through the military apparatus and civil servants," he said during an interview. "I was not satisfied teaching, and gradually became more interested in defending laborers. In 1988, LBH asked me to chair their labor rights department. So, for eight years, the organization became my law school."

Shortly after Teten joined the staff, he helped to organize a strike against the Gadjah Tunngal Company in 1989. For 10 years, he poured himself into work with workers and strikes. Teten defended scores of worker activists, and helped in organizational campaigns that involved thousands of workers. "I am fortunate that my wife was a women's rights activist, so we have a similar background. My family understands that this is my job, and I will not bend to pressure." Whether as head of the labor division or now in his work with ICW, Teten says he has worked to build a social movement for human rights. As head of ICW, Teten has had a high profile in the fight for Reformasi.[6]

Surya Tjandra succeeded Teten as head of the LBH labor division. Like his predecessor, Surya has been assisting workers as they fight through legal channels, while also helping them organize. On the second floor of the big old house on Diponegoro Street in Menteng, Jakarta that serves as LBH's office, Surya described LBH's labor work to me in the summer of 1999. "LBH, the Legal Aid Institute, has 14 branches throughout Indonesia," said Surya. "LBH provides legal aid for poor people, that is, pro bono work. The three main areas of LBH at present are labor issues, land disputes, and civil and political issues, including environmental and consumer issues. LBH has become the center of Indonesia's civil society movement."

Surya works directly on the labor issues.

LBH Jakarta has a labor office, with a staff of four and four volunteers, that serves the Jakarta area. Last year, the LBH labor division handled 550 cases involving 17,000 workers. Of those, 9,000 were involved in dismissal disputes. The rest dealt with wages, conditions, food allowances, and so on.

We work mostly with blue-collar workers. But since the crisis, we also work with white-collar workers, such as those from the banking and finance sectors. The IMF's structural adjustment problems led to mass layoffs in the banking sector. Almost 100 banks have already been liquidated. In the last wave, 17,000 workers have been laid off. Between August

1997, when the layoffs began, and July 1999, between 60,000 and 80,000 bank and finance workers were laid off in three waves. Thousands of others were also affected who were not involved in those liquidations.

Surya explained LBH's method of assisting workers: "We usually suggest to most of our clients that they *not* go through the Ministry of Manpower, except as a last resort. We also suggest that they do not go to court, because it is very expensive, and you'll lose your case anyway because the employer will pay off the judge."

While it may seem strange for an attorney to keep his clients out of court, the reasons become clear. "We have some critical problems in our system of settling labor disputes," says Surya.

> First, even if you follow the system it takes a very long time, perhaps five years or more. We have one case dealing with a man who was dismissed in 1994 that has gone on for four or five years. He went through the Ministry of Manpower dispute resolution process and won what's called the P4P decision, but the employer appealed to the court, and then to the Supreme Court. The workers themselves do not want to go through the system, knowing that the bureaucrats are corrupt.

LBH sometimes helps workers deal directly with their employer or former employer, or seeks to bring other forms of pressure to bear, says Surya.

When many workers are involved, different approaches have to be used. "In mass cases, we suggest using the system, but also simultaneously negotiating with the employer and going directly to demonstrate at the Ministry of Manpower. Workers have a better chance that way than going through the system."

"Take the Mayora candy company case for example," says Surya.

> This was a case that came to involve unions, NGOs, women's organizations, and international solidarity, through the International Union of Food Workers. Mayora had 1,500 workers, 80 percent of them women. The issues involved were higher

wages, mass layoffs, and questions of severance pay. In the spring of 1999, the workers went on strike for a week. We have a ministerial regulation that says that if a worker is gone for more than five days, the employer can dismiss him without compensation.

The workers continued their strike for three weeks. They held demonstrations at the employer's plant, at the Ministry of Manpower, at the corporate offices, and on the streets. Several times, hundreds of workers were arrested. As many as 700 were taken to police headquarters. The Ministry of Manpower ruled the workers had been legally dismissed with compensation. The workers continued their demonstrations and talked with the Minister of Manpower. He overruled the earlier decision. The company then took the case to the court. The workers still continued to demonstrate and went to the corporate headquarters—while the plant is near Tangerang, the headquarters are in West Jakarta. Once again the police arrested hundreds of workers. This time the police invited the employer to negotiate with the workers in the police station, and they reached an agreement. About 1,000 workers went back to work, and between 500 and 700 voluntarily resigned. The employers also raised their wages. The minimum legal wage is about 7,700 rupiah per day. They asked for 15 percent but didn't get it. Today they earn about 8,000 rupiah per day [less than $1.50 per day].

It took a lot of money to support that strike. They stayed for one week in the Ministry of Manpower's offices, and they had to be fed, some needed medicine, there was the issue of baths. In the Mayora case, we did not follow the system. Mayora gave us ideas for a new strategy. We can't count on the system, but we *can* count on the workers themselves.

Surya believes that NGOs continue to have a role to play assisting workers and unions. Despite nominal changes in government policy, workers still face serious problems.

Workers now have the right to organize, to form unions—but they are still not free from military intervention, not free from corruption. In reality, it is still not so easy to register a union.

The Ministry of Manpower regulation of May 1998 established a simple registry procedure for unions. But the workers still have to face employers who do not understand this law, or who do not want to understand this law. They also have to face the government-controlled federation, the SPSI. I don't think SPSI will accept a new rival union very easily.

When workers attempt to create a new union, SPSI turns the employer against the new union, and that may cause workers to be fired. SPSI also tries to turn the workers against the new union. So the government, the employer, and the old SPSI unions are all obstacles to the workers forming new unions.

But external pressures—the government, the employers, and the old unions—are not the only problems. Surya, like many of the union organizers, also commented on the workers' lack of experience, knowledge, confidence, and organization. "There is also the problem of the workers themselves," says Surya.

I don't think workers know what a union is yet. They don't know how to run a union, how to administer it. That's why we train workers. We try to teach them what a genuine trade union is, what the relationship between the employer and the workers is. We teach them about International Labor Organization (ILO) Convention 87, the freedom of association convention. We teach them about ILO Convention 98, the collective-bargaining convention, which Indonesia signed in 1954, but which has never really been put into effect.

Maybe we have the right to organize a union; we have the right *to*, but we still do not have the freedom *from*. We need freedom from the military, freedom from the bureaucracy, freedom from corruption. We need not only the right *to*, but also freedom *from*.

As long as workers need to win both their right *to* and their freedom *from*, LBH will be there to help them, says Surya.

Women's Liberation in Indonesia

During the 1980s and 1990s, a feminist movement developed

among college-educated women in Indonesia, and soon several feminist NGOs had been created. LBH created a women's rights organization called LBH APIK, and much of its general work also concerns women workers.

Sri Wiyanti joined the staff a few years ago and has been spending much of her time on women workers' issues. Born in North Sumatra in 1973, Sri is a graduate of Gadjah Mada University (UGM) in Yogyakarta, where she did a five-year degree (S1, as they call it) in law. "I was active with the law students," she explained.

> We created Mahkamah, or Law Court, the first student organi-
> zation in the law school, and I was active in that group. I
> joined an NGO, the Institute for the Study of Women and
> Children [LSPPA]. Though there were only six women in that
> organization, they were active in a wide range of issues: in-
> come-generating programs, gender training, and work with
> girl children.
>
> At first, I really didn't know about gender issues. I had been
> active in the student movement and heard them talk about
> gender, about gender and class issues. But I never thought that
> I was discriminated against. My mother and father gave me a
> good opportunity to grow and choose. But it was interesting
> to learn about discrimination and how it affected others. So
> LSPPA was my first involvement with an NGO.

After leaving law school at UGM, Sri went to work for LBH APIK. "LBH APIK is an organization for changing our law from a gender perspective. We provide legal assistance for poor women, public education, legal research, documentation, and publications. We also do networking to support others who do legal aid in other places. At present, we're working on establishing LBH APIK branches in other cities: Medan, Padang, Pontianak, Lombok, Ujung Padang, Aceh, and Malang."

There are many problems facing women in Indonesian society, says Sri. "First are cultural problems. Patriarchy still stands here, and we can see that it divides women. For example, take the case of Megawati," she says, referring to the Muslim clerics' argument at the time of the national elections that a woman could not head the Indonesian state.

Indonesia's Muslim culture also affects attitudes toward marriage, but often in ways similar to other traditional societies.

> Our concept of marriage here is that women have to marry, or they will be called *perawan tua*, an old maid. If I go the village, because of my age—I'm 26—people will say to me, "Where is your husband?"
>
> If a woman wants a divorce, people will say, "Why do you want to be a *janda*, a widow?" because there is a stigma attached to being a widow. We have a study of men and women and divorce that suggests that it is easier for men to divorce than for women. The judge is easier with men. The judge will tell the wife to follow her husband, and question why she wants a divorce, and accuse her of being a bad wife. But the judge just grants the man his divorce. It is easier for a woman to divorce today than it was five or 10 years ago, because in reality, women are now often the real head of the household.

But culture is not the only source of problems, says Sri.

> Second, there is our legal system. Take the marriage act. The marriage act says that women's role is in the domestic sphere; women should be housewives and caretakers of children. The man is to be the householder, and he provides money for the woman. Polygamy is still practiced, especially in rural areas, and a man can have up to four wives. Sometimes women don't even know the man has another wife, because he goes to another area and marries another woman.
>
> Then there are problems with the legal apparatus: the police, prosecutor, and the judge. If there are problems of rape and sexual harassment, for example, they say, "Where's the proof?" Or if a wife is beaten by her husband, the police ask, "What did she do to make him angry?"

Government policy is a third source of problems, Sri contends. "The government has contradictory positions on women. Women are supposed to be home in the kitchen, and at the same

time they are to go out and work to support development, for example, as migrant workers." The government's policies on birth
control and abortion represent yet another problematic area.
"Our critique of government policy regarding contraception is
that it focuses only on women," says Sri. "Women are given a pill
or the spiral, the IUD, as if women alone produced children, and
men had nothing to do with it." Men are not expected to take any
responsibility for birth control, she says. In addition, there is the
issue of mandatory or even forced contraception.

> Sometimes in the village they force the women to use IUDs.
> In the villages, the military sometimes intimidates women to
> make them use the IUDs, even though some women are afraid
> of the IUD because they have had friends who had cramps or
> bleeding. Similarly they're now focusing on women who are
> prostitutes and blame them for AIDS. They don't blame the
> men, because they are men.

I asked about the question of abortion. "Here women who
are pregnant before marriage will generally have an abortion,"
said Sri. Abortions, however, are illegal. "The only reason for a legal abortion here is if the doctor says the mother's life is in danger. But many women have abortions illegally, sometimes by a
doctor, or sometimes by taking traditional medicine, adminis-
tered by a *dukun beranak* [midwife]. They take traditional drugs,
what we call *jamu* [herbal medicine]."

The Indonesian state has been primarily militaristic and patriarchal in its values, but those values mesh with both the Muslim and other patriarchal religions of the society (Hinduism and
Buddhism, as well as Protestantism and Catholic Christianity),
and with the capitalist culture of corporate and managerial control. The general, the boss, the *ulama,* the priest, and the husband
all find mutual support and reinforcement in patriarchal and authoritarian values. The state, religion, home, and work have
tended to relegate women to a subordinate position in the society, though not to a position as lowly as that occupied by women
in some other Asian societies.

All of the state organizations for women are imbued not only with a patriarchal ideal, but also with a militaristic conception of hierarchy and chain of command. All power emanates from the military state and descends through the ranks to the ordinary woman at the bottom of the social pyramid. The state's Family Welfare Association (PKK) propagates the ideology of patriarchy and female subordination in domestic roles of wife and mother. The PKK has branches in both villages and urban neighborhoods throughout Indonesia, and typically the local headman's wife serves as head of the PKK chapter. The PKK emphasizes the creation of the state's ideal of the nuclear family with two children. It promotes values that tend to be "Western," middle-class, and consumerist, ignoring women's roles as workers and breadwinners. Through the PKK, the state attempts to regulate community and family values, while ignoring the needs of working-class and poor women.

Another important state organization for women, arguably the most important, is the Dharma Wanita, or Women's Association, the female auxiliary of the Public Employees' Corps of the Republic of Indonesia (KORPRI), the state-controlled union of civil servants and public employees. Dharma Wanita, an organization for the wives of civil servants, exists to encourage their support for their husbands. The organization's ideology suggests that women are and should be dependent extensions or appendages of their husbands.

In Indonesia, at least until the fall of Suharto and the New Order, all civil servants or public employees had to be members of KORPRI, and their wives were required to become members of Dharma Wanita. The state both funded and directed Dharma Wanita. Women's roles and ranks in the organization corresponded to those of their husbands, so the wives of ministers, governors, and district heads automatically assumed corresponding leadership roles in the Dharma Wanita organization. The Dharma Wanita woman's principal responsibility was "to support the official duties of her husband by creating a harmonious atmosphere, avoiding anti-Pancasila behavior, in order to create a state official who is authoritative and clean."[7] The Dharma Wanita's ideology might be summed up in the slogan *ikut suami*, follow the husband.

The state also regulates marriage, divorce, and sex among civil servants, and so KORPRI and Dharma Wanita also play an informal role in policing personal and sexual relationships. Female civil servants cannot become the second, third, or fourth wife of another civil servant, and they may not live together with a man outside of a legally sanctioned marriage. Wives of civil servants have been reluctant to file for divorce, for if they report a divorce, their husbands may be disciplined or dismissed, and then they would lose their source of alimony or child support.

The Indonesian government's women's organizations, and the patriarchal ideals that they promote, have become increasingly out of touch with the reality of women's lives in the last 25 years. During the period from 1980 to 1998, a marked change in women's educational levels and consequently in their knowledge of Indonesian society and the opportunities and alternatives available has taken place. At the same time as educational levels have risen, women have delayed marriage and childbearing, their social mobility has increased, and women's work outside the home has become more acceptable to most people in society. All of these social changes have meant a change in women's participation in the paid labor force. In 1980, only 33 percent of women participated in the paid labor force. By 1990, that figure had reached 39 percent; by 1998, that figure had reached approximately 45 percent. So the state ideology and organization have increasingly come into contradiction with social and economic reality, leading to growing individual and collective conflicts between the authorities and women.

At the center of these contradictions is women's growing participation in the workforce, particularly in industry. Women have always worked in the home and in the fields, and some women have worked in shops, as well. Since the beginning of the twentieth century, some industries have also employed women as workers, a trend that increased in the 1970s and then dramatically in the 1980s. The textile, garment, and footwear industries employ a majority of women workers. Those industries employ one-third of all workers and 45 percent of all women workers in manufacturing. Seventy-five percent of the workers in the garment and footwear industries are women, as are 53 percent of those in the textile industry.[8] Many of the women entering the workforce come from the countryside; they are farmers' daughters and often have less education than other men and women. Women workers also tend to be young and single, with little experience in the workplace. Employers take advantage of the youth, ignorance, and inexperience of the workforce, frequently violating the law, union contracts, past practices, and customs.

Women workers have ostensibly been protected by a comprehensive set of laws and regulations. As in other countries, there is an older body of female protective legislation predicated on the idea that women are different and in some ways inferior to men, cannot be equals of men in the workforce, and therefore require special protection. Some of the more recent labor legislation is based on more modern ideas of gender equality. In any case, women may use both sorts of legislation as tools to defend and advance their position in the workplace and society. The most important of these laws is Law No. 12 of 1948, which prohibits the use of women workers for a night shift, except when the conditions and nature of the job demand it. Law No.1 of 1951, Regulation No. 21 of 1954, and Act No. 1 of 1957 give women the right to two days' menstruation leave and three months maternity leave, and the right to breastfeed their babies at work. In 1984, the Indonesian government changed rules in order to eliminate gender bias in women's medical assistance and pension entitlements.[9] Like men, women are covered by the minimum wage and overtime wage laws.

Since 1965, the Indonesian government has never been aggressive about the enforcement of labor laws in general; nor has it done much for women in particular. The government does little to educate women workers about their rights in the workplace, and many other peasants coming from the countryside, poor urban women, and young female workers have little or no knowledge of their rights beyond the minimum wage. The government employs relatively few labor inspectors, and the inspectors tend to be pro-management and are reportedly lazy and corrupt. Consequently, women workers receive little comfort from special female protective legislation or from gender bias laws supposedly passed to protect them.

Women supposedly have the right to union protection, but, as with male workers, until very recently they could only join the government union, SPSI, or, in the case of public employees, KORPRI. Neither SPSI nor KORPRI really represented workers, and in fact often worked to police them. Controlled by the government, infiltrated by the police at all levels, in cooperation with the employers, committed to the state's low-wage policy, completely authoritarian, and undemocratic, the state unions were also patriarchal and sexist. Men dominated the highest and intermediate levels of the union, and discrimination against women, or simply ignorance of women's concerns, was almost universal in the old unions. Since May 1998, a whole new set of unions has begun to organize workers, some of which continue to be insensitive to women's issues and to keep women out of leadership positions. Others do better, but women have yet to achieve their rightful role in the labor movement.

Sri Wiynti believes that women workers face problems for two reasons, "because they are women, and they are also workers":

> As workers, they have the same problems as men according to their class, depending on whether or not they are white-collar workers or factory workers. Many workers are part of the lower class and work as laborers. The enterprise says women are unskilled, so they do the same kind of work every day. They have low salaries, and no protection if they are injured in

the workplace. Sometimes they have no health and safety insurance, or not enough to cover them if they are injured.

Just as in other countries, working women frequently find that they have two jobs. "Women workers work outside, but they also have a domestic duty. So they have a double duty. Even though they work outside the home, they have an obligation to do the housework. In many cases, the husband has a wife who works, but he doesn't recognize that his wife works. So she must still do the housework. We have a double burden."

Childcare, she says, is also a serious problem for women workers, especially those who are heads of households. "They have no facilities for taking care of children, so typically they leave children in the village with their grandparents and visit them every month or so."

Sri says that the crisis of 1997–98 aggravated all of these problems. "I think that because of the crisis, the situation of women is worse. The money was devalued and is worth less. Before the crisis, a woman's wages might buy two kilos of rice, fish, milk, and maybe some clothes. But after the crisis, it might buy only one kilo of rice, and no fish. There is not enough to buy milk."

Women in the workplace face a whole host of problems, she explains. "First, there is wage discrimination against women, because the government says you are not a householder, but rather a second income. So the wages are often lower, and the tax is higher for women than it is for the primary income earner, the man. A woman, married or not, must pay taxes, but a married man pays less. So the income of women is generally less than that of men."

Other problems also lead to low pay for women. "Women workers also face discrimination in the workplace. Women face difficulty in getting promoted, especially to positions usually held by men, such as being the head of an office. So women make less money than men because they can't get promoted."

Women's protected conditions represent another area of

concern. "Women's reproductive rights are not recognized," says Sri. "The right to menstruation leave and maternity leave is often not recognized by employers. Women have to prove that they are menstruating. They have to open their pants and show their underwear to their supervisors, whether they are men or women."

Women should be entitled to maternity leave, but the companies generally refuse to pay it.

> Pregnant workers just have to get out. If a woman becomes pregnant, she has to leave. That way the employers don't have to pay for her maternity leave. Under the law, women are entitled to three months' paid leave, based on their basic salary (without transportation, or food, or health allowances). Some companies make women sign a contract saying that if they get pregnant within two years, they will have to leave, so in that way they avoid maternity leave.

I asked if women who are single and become pregnant get maternity leave. "Our regulations are not clear about whether the woman has to be married or not in order to get maternity leave. We had one case of a woman who was raped by her boss, and the company made both resign. We said the woman was not guilty, and that the company had to pay her maternity leave. We won that case, but that's very rare, to get the company to pay maternity leave for a single woman."

Sexual harassment in the workplace is also common. "During recruitment to the firm, some women may have to walk around with their clothes open in front of men, or in the military the women may have to walk around in front of the officers—such cases have been reported," says Sri. "Some supervisors will touch the women whenever they feel like it. The women workers don't protest because they fear they will be fired."

Asnitriyanti Damanils, also a lawyer and the coordinator of legal services at LBH APIK, gave examples of two sexual harassment cases in Jakarta. In the first case, a Japanese company helped a woman who had been sexually harassed and punished the supervisor by transferring him to another area. But that, says

Asni, is a rare case. In the second case, the victim was asked to resign because she reported the case. The second response is far more common.

Sri says, "We have heard of cases of women who were forced to sleep with managers or supervisors, but we heard about them through friends of the women who were victims. Their friends tell us, but the women will not present the case." Even if the case gets reported, the long, drawn-out state grievance process may discourage workers. Typically, says Sri, legal cases involving sexual harassment take up to four or five years to resolve through the Ministry of Manpower's P4P and P4D grievance process.

Such sexual harassment is all too common, sexual assault is not unknown, and even rape occurs in the workplace.

> We have a case of a woman who was raped by her boss. She worked in the office, and sometimes accompanied her boss to work outside the office. One time, her boss told her to go with him to meet a client in a hotel. But there was no client at the hotel, and he raped her. There was a similar case in a Surabaya cigarette company. This case involved a girl of 16 or 17, and she was a new hire. The supervisor asked her to join him in his car. Then he asked the woman to touch his body, and to have oral sex with him.

Generally, says Sri, these cases have been very difficult to handle. Women are often reluctant to report assaults or rapes. And, she adds, "The police will not recognize the problem."

In a society in which management has often been in league with government labor authorities and with the military, women are often afraid to speak up. Experience has shown they are wise to keep their own counsel at least until they get organized and get some help. "If women protest their situation, they will be fired by the company," says Sri.

Sex Workers

Factory workers constitute the largest and most important group of urban wage laborers in Indonesia, but there are other women workers who have particular problems, such as sex workers and maids. Sex work represents a particular kind of employment that poses special problems and risks to the women workers. In Indonesia, as in many other countries, prostitution has a semi-legal status. The government tolerates prostitution in certain zones at certain times, and then forbids it in others. The semi-legal status of prostitution makes sex workers vulnerable to extortion by the military, police, government officials, and criminals.

Prostitutes usually work in specially designated areas. Kramat Tunggak, near Tanjung Priok Port in North Jakarta, was originally created as a rehabilitation center for prostitutes, offering vocational courses and psychological and social counseling. However, since the government did not provide the prostitutes with an adequate income, they returned to the practice of prostitution, turning the rehab center into a tolerated red-light district. Today, there are almost 2,000 prostitutes serving more than 2,000 men per night.

Sri Wianti explains that LBH APIK carried out a study of the so-called rehabilitation area in Jakarta, an area where prostitution is tolerated, and found that some prostitutes had to pay off as many as 20 different people, most of them some sort of government official. "Now the government is talking about closing the rehabilitation center. What will happen if it is closed? Will the sex workers go back to the street?" she asks. Health workers think that this may lead the sex workers to spread throughout Jakarta, making it more difficult to offer them health services, and increasing the risks of sexually transmitted diseases (STDs).[10]

One of the girls who works at Kramat Tunggak is Fenny, a native of Indramayu in West Java. She married at 14, and five months later her husband died, leaving her a widow. With only an elementary education, she found work at the age of 17 at Kramat Tunggak. She told a reporter, "Working here is easy, I can help my siblings. I don't want to work as a servant. Well ... working here is fun enough." She generally serves one client per day and earns 40,000 rupiah, paying her pimp 5,000 rupiah. So she clears about 35,000 rupiah, or about $4.50, about three times as much as she would make as a factory worker. Every month, she sends about 300,000 rupiah to her family. "I'll stop this once I find my mate," she says.

While Fenny may say her work is fun, sex workers face problems of extortion from government officials, violence from clients, alcohol and drug addiction, and contagion from STDs. Many prostitutes take antibiotics every day in the belief that they help to prevent STDs. Dariah, another Kramat Tunggak prostitute, says she never asks her clients to use condoms, unless they insist. "Only once in a while, when the client asks for it ... but anyway, I've protected myself," she says, referring to her daily dose of antibiotics. The fear is that the sex workers will eventually become immune to the antibiotics, according to Endang R. Sedyaningish M., health researcher at the Ministry of Health's Contagious Diseases Research Center.

Endang wrote her 1995 Harvard University Ph.D. dissertation on the problems of prostitution, which was later published in Indonesian as the book *The Women of Kramat Tunggak* (*Perempuan-Perempuan Kramat Tunggak*). She found that 459 of the 1,977 prostitutes of Kramat Tunggak did not have adequate knowledge to protect themselves from STDs. "But what most people don't realize is that the prostitutes contract these diseases from men, their customers, before transmitting them to other men seeking their services. They are only victims."[11]

Some sex workers do have organizations to work with and to represent them. Yayasan Kusuma Buma is an NGO that assists sex workers; prostitutes even have a labor union, the Bandung Wangi. Nevertheless, sex workers remain among the most vulnerable women workers in society.

Domestic Workers

Other women workers with particularly onerous conditions are domestic workers. Hendra Permana organizes migrant workers and housemaids for the Indonesia Prosperity Labor Union (SBSI). In an interview at the SBSI offices, he explained, "Most maids are between 18 and 20 years old, and they come from the countryside of Central or East Java or from the Javanese population of Lampung, Sumatra.... Maids work 12 hours a day or more, and they may earn about 180,000 rupiah [about $22] per month." Organizing maids, he says, is particularly difficult. Because they have so many employers, they usually work alone or in some cases, small groups of two or three. Young, uneducated, from rural areas, and isolated in a strange city, maids represent a particularly vulnerable group, and one without labor unions. Some NGOs have taken an interest in the problems of domestic workers, but they are extremely difficult to reach and organize.

Indonesia has an estimated 5 million domestic workers (1.5 million in the Jakarta area), the great majority of them women. Half of all domestic workers are 18 years old or younger, and one-third are under the age of 15. Most maids will work between 15 and 17 hours per day (from 5 a.m. to 8 or 10 p.m.), seven days a week, for a total of between 84 and 119 hours. There are no national laws regulating domestic workers, though Jakarta has a Municipal Regulation (No. 6 of 1993) prohibiting the hiring of maids under the age of 18 unless the employers foster parent the children and there is no evidence of its enforcement.[12]

The economic crisis that began in 1997 exacerbated all of the problems of women workers. LBH APIK conducted a survey that found that women tended to be the prime target for dismissals and layoffs. According to the survey, those most likely to be laid off from their jobs were pregnant women, women on menstrual leave, and women who were likely to lead strikes. Women as workers, as housewives, and frequently as heads of household bore the brunt of the crisis, first working for less than the minimum wage, then suffering layoffs, and finally moving into the underground economy, or even in some cases into prostitution, in an attempt to keep their families together.

One estimate is that the number of poor as a share of the population almost doubled from 11 percent in 1996 to 18 to 20 percent toward the end of 1998—approximately 40 million people. Other estimates suggest that 24 percent of the population, or 50 million people, live in poverty. When an economic crisis strikes a country like Indonesia, women often bear an disproportionate share of the burden, as men leave home to look for jobs elsewhere, but often end up abandoning their families. Women are left to take care of children and to put food on the table. While the crisis hurts all working people, women and children often suffer most. The problems facing women will require not only the activities of NGOs like LPH APIK and workers like Sri, but also stronger labor unions, political parties that fight for workers' rights, and an altogether different political system.

A Roman Catholic NGO in Indonesia

While NGOs such as the LBH and the LBH APIK are important, activists also recognized that it was necessary to build grassroots groups on the ground in local communities. The NGOs can provide resources to help local groups, but ultimately it is the grassroots activists in contact with workers and farmers who build social movements. A variety of political and religious organizations have sponsored such grassroots organizing efforts, but few have built organizations as strong and stable as the Roman Catholic Jesuits' Lembaga Daya Dharma (LDD) workers' centers.

In the center of Jakarta, opposite the imposing National Mosque, stands the equally impressive Jakarta Cathedral with its two splendid spires, the center of Roman Catholicism in Indonesia. While Catholics represent a very small part of Indonesia's population, the Archdiocese of Jakarta, headed by Archbishop Julius Cardinal Darmaatmadja SJ, plays an active role through LDD, its social action arm. As part of its social ministry, the archdiocese has also established a Bureau of Labor Service. The bureau is a pastoral ministry that also undertakes education in the areas of labor law, health and nutrition, sex and family life, vocational skills, and organizational training, including labor training. It also runs a library, theater, and credit union, and publishes a labor bulletin.

The Bureau of Labor Service assists more than 10,000 workers at 200 factories in 14 parishes of Jakarta, Tangerang, and Bekasi, the industrial suburbs known collectively as Jabotabek. The Bureau of Labor has also recently helped to found a new labor union, the Serikat Buruh Jabotabek (SBJ), which has been rapidly enrolling new members. The Catholic LDD's Bureau of Labor works to help not only the Catholic migrants who have come to work in Jabotabek, but also hundreds of thousands of Muslim workers.

The moving spirit of the LDD is a Jesuit priest, Father Padmo Harsono. Born on the last day of 1945 in Solo, Padmo, as he is called, studied at the Driyarkara Institute of Philosophy in Indonesia, and later at the Institute of Social Studies in the Hague, Netherlands, where he specialized in economics and labor. After completing his studies, he worked as a parish priest in Tullamore, Ireland, before returning to Indonesia.

Once back home, Padmo helped to found the Social Institute of Jakarta, and in 1989 was asked by the bishop to join his staff at the cathedral. "I was asked to promote the social dimension of the church," Padmo told me.

> The church isn't only a place for worship and singing. It has to have a social dimension, as well. We must also work for peace and justice. One of my jobs is to work with Lembaga Daya Dharma, an institution to help children, the homeless, the blind, and workers. We also have a special Bureau for Workers. Our approach is [to be] a social apostolate for the workers. We hold mass, we have a special catechism for the workers, and we build church "base communities." We are also becoming more open. We live in a pluralistic society. We are not just a closed Catholic community, but part of a broader human community.

The Jakarta Cathedral's LDD has put special emphasis on its program for workers. As Padmo explains,

> We train them in labor law and self-advocacy. We have classes in structural social analysis for workers. We have classes in

workers' education for consciousness-raising. We also have a gender perspective, since 75 percent of the workers are women. We use theater for consciousness-raising, and we publish a workers' bulletin.

The LDD Bureau of Labor has also supported organizing efforts of various sorts, first beginning with social events.

We think workers have to learn to organize; they have to organize picnics, festivals. They organized an Easter celebration with 4,000 Catholic workers. My approach is to prepare the workers so they can do things for themselves. But we also think it is important to develop people with a good character. What good is Reformasi if people don't have character? Many people in Indonesia are very clever, and there is a lot of corruption. We need people with character.

More recently, the LDD Bureau of Labor has supported the organization of the SBJ, an independent labor union active in the Jakarta industrial suburbs. "We have only recently begun to work with labor unions," says Padmo.

The atmosphere for the last five or 10 years was dominated by all sorts of interests—economic interests, political interests, religious interests. I didn't trust any of the existing labor movements. Unions at that time were not quite genuine unions. Then, too, the political situation was not a very good one for an open movement. Recently we helped to establish a union, Serikat Buruh Jabotabek. We are trying to facilitate for the workers to fight for themselves. I don't want to create the union for them; that is their responsibility. The most important issue is the development of good, strong unions. If they have no unions, they have no bargaining power.

Speaking to me in 1999, Padmo was both optimistic and cautious. "I think it will take a long, long time to have good unions. Sometimes I think Reformasi came too fast because we have so much to learn. But it is good that we have Reformasi .... Now we can learn by doing."

While we think of the theology of liberation as a Latin American phenomenon, it seems to have taken hold in Indonesia, too.[13] When I ask Padmo if his program is the theology of liberation put in practice in Indonesia, he answers cagily, "What we do is quite similar to liberation theology, even if we don't call it that. There are a lot of streams in Indonesia now; some call it 'development theology.' "

Padmo suggested that I talk with his staff, a few young Indonesians working on other floors in the cathedral's offices. Verena Retno, a young woman in her early 20s, works on the Bureau of Labor staff. "The Workers' Bureau was founded in 1990 in response to the economic developments in Jakarta and Indonesia. There had been a great deal of investment, and this was a response to that investment. The bishop asked us to look forward to the new millennium and to ask, what are the problems of labor in Central and East Java, in South Sumatra, in Sulawesi, and Kalimantan," she explains.

> We established what we call "Rumah Sentrum," or central houses, which service workers in Tangerang, Bekasi, Bogor, and Sunter. We have 10 such centers. They provide pastoral care. The work begins with religious activity: workers' mass, Bible study, marriage preparation. We also give vocational training: sewing, beauty care, and cooking. We provide leadership training, and we have also created a credit union.

She draws a pie and shows the various sorts of activity beginning with psychology, health care (including sex education and AIDS awareness), skills training, labor law, organizational training, general awareness, social structure analysis, religion, theater, and the bulletin. Verena explains that the LDD Workers' Bureau carries out education in a number of ways, using photographs, pictures, games, and songs. "We use pictures and photographs to show injustice." They are strongly opposed to a monologue, or what they call "pedagogy," as an approach. Instead, they call for "androgogy"—that is, for mature adult education.

When I asked about the work of the central houses, Verena introduced me to her colleague Lukas Gathy Widyanata. Lukas explained that many of the central house activities involved both Catholics and non-Catholics. He estimated that they reached between 9,000 and 13,000 workers, most of whom were Catholic. Lukas added that about 40 percent of the students in the labor law classes were Muslims. Of those attending the workers' centers, 80 percent were women. Verena explained, "We have a new perspective, which we call 'building a basic human community,' because we are all brothers and sisters as children of God."

We were soon joined by another Bureau of Labor staff person, Afra Siowarjay. "We try to get the workers to open their vision, to overcome their exclusiveness," said Afra.

> Human dignity is basic to the human community, not just to Catholics. We hope to join hand in hand to overcome our problems, especially our labor problems. We have training in awareness of our vision of brotherhood. We need to join strongly with other groups. We try to help them understand that in many respects their problem is like a cage. We have to work together to open the cage.

I asked if it would be possible to visit one of their central houses, and they invited me to accompany them to a meeting of garment workers that would take place that weekend. That Saturday, July 31, 1998, I went with Afra, Tono, and Lukas to Bekasi to visit a local workers' center. The drive took over an hour, giving me an opportunity to talk with them about a variety of issues.

Afra told me that she was born in Borneo (Kalimantan) and that she thinks she is about seventh-generation Chinese Indonesian. During May of the previous year, when anti-Chinese riots took place, she had been afraid to go to work for fear of being attacked on the streets and stayed home for a few days. Like Tono, Lukas, and Yono, another staff member whom we later met at the Rumah Sentrum, she attended a Catholic seminary.

When Padmo, Verena, and the others had told me about their various activities, I had been somewhat leery of the idea of the Roman Catholic church teaching sex education. So I asked Afra about that program. She said that their program included information on birth control. "Our archbishop of Indonesia says that contraception can be used, according to your own heart. If the wife and husband decide that it is better and don't feel guilty or don't feel that it's a sin, then it is okay," she said. "Our bishop has a pastoral book, and the appendix is about the use of contraception—but the Pope cut the appendix out because Rome rejected contraception." Abortion in Indonesia is illegal, she explained, though doctors do perform illegal abortions.

At the Workers' Center

The Rumah Sentrum, or workers' center, is located in a middle-class neighborhood of white-collar workers in Bukesi. The neighborhood is made up of houses constructed of concrete or concrete block, most of them small homes of perhaps three to six rooms with little porches and patios. Nearly every house has two or three birdcages with small songbirds, and some have larger birds such as parrots tied to perches. The street is paved with stones in some places, but is mostly a dirt road with a concrete ditch along the side. Chickens run everywhere, and a few houses have large, round wicker cages in front holding chickens. Families out for a walk wander down the street.

The workers' center itself is just a small house without furniture, but with linoleum, carpets, and mats on the floor. On the door and window of the building were stickers: one for SBSI, the independent union; another for the PNI, a liberal political party; another for Megawati, the highest vote-winner in the 1999 presidential race; and even a poster for her father Sukarno, the former president. On the porch, black bands with printed lettering had been tied to the pillars with the slogans: "Investigate the shooting of workers. Stop the layoffs. Lower prices."

While waiting for the meeting to start, I went for a walk around the block with a couple of the catechists, Tono and Yono. Like the other catechists I've met, Yono went to the seminary in Yogyakarta. I asked him why he chose to work at the Rumah Sentrum. "Because labor is the lowest class in society, and I chose the option of working with them. This is my choice as a catechist, to carry out a liberation evangelization. Perhaps this is the influence of liberation theology," he offered. We ran into their friend Tri Warti, a young woman from the local parish who invited us into her house to talk. Her family, she explained, was from Central Java. Her father had died some time ago, and her mother didn't work. She lived with her mother and 13 other people from several families in a rather large old house with three or four bedrooms. She and her mother rented out one room in the house for 80,000 rupiah per month—about a week's wages.

For the last six months, Tri had been working at the Adidas factory making shoes. Her job was to glue on the soles of the shoes. While working, she wore a paper mask, which the company replaced every third day. Sometimes, she said, the glue made her a little dizzy or nauseous. She worked eight hours a day, five days a week, for 270,000 rupiah, or $41, per month. After a short conversation, Tri walked us to the door and said goodbye with a smile and a wave.

The first person to arrive for the meeting was Rudolfus Pejkalis Dhika, the local union's advocacy chair, who walked into the room, sat down, and began talking almost at once. He was clearly interested in talking to a foreigner. Born in Flores, Rudolfus has dark skin and very curly hair. After finishing high school, Rudolfus went to Jakarta University and studied economics for two and a half years, but had to give up his studies after he was fired from the Sandang Mutiaria Era Mulia textile plant. He said that he was involved in leading a strike at the plant. In 1996, he led 2,100 workers out on strike to demand a wage increase from 136,000 to 152,000 rupiah per month. The police broke up the strike and beat and kicked him so badly that he had to spend 12 days in the hospital; then the company fired him. "That's the capitalist world," he says. "That's capitalist exploitation."

For the last 10 months, he has been advocacy director for the SBJ. "Every day I help workers who are laid off. I accompany them in fighting for their jobs or their benefits."

I asked Rudolfus about his beliefs. "I am Catholic, but I very seldom go to church. I don't go because I don't like the priests' sermons. They're too high in the sky; they never land." What he really wanted to talk about was politics. "Reformasi is not meaningful for the workers," said Rudolfus.

> Reformasi doesn't give workers a chance. The government still oppresses workers. On the one hand, labor has been given more freedom, but on the other hand, this freedom is not the result of the workers' struggle, but rather of outside pressure. The government gives freedom to form a union, but at the same time, the government controls the activities of the labor movement. The foremen report union activists to the government. There is still one hierarchical structure.

Rudolfus was clearly quite thoughtful and very angry.

> Why does Indonesia give freedom to labor? Indonesia has been economically destroyed by the crisis. It needs outside investment. The government gives freedom to labor, hoping that it will stop radical demonstrations, and then foreigners will invest in this country.
> The head of the IMF hasn't created a better situation for labor, but has made it worse. The IMF is still a capitalist organization. The condition of labor is still depressed; there is no improvement for workers. Many companies laid off workers because of the IMF's condition[s].

Rudolfus had brought along with him a young woman worker in her early 20s, Ance Hotlina. Ance worked at PT KDS Indonesia, an electronics company where she was a spot welder making components for televisions and computers. The PT KDS plant had 3,000 workers, about two-thirds of them women between 18 and 30 years old. Ance had various complaints. "To get hired, women have to sign a contract saying that if they become pregnant they will resign," Ance explained. Many of the woman were married and had children, but the company provided no child care, nor did the government. Some NGOs had opened some childcare centers, but there were none specifically for workers at her plant.

"Women have the right to two paid days off per month menstruation leave, but in reality the managers don't permit it," she said. "If a woman takes the days off, they cut her pay."

I asked about the issue of equal pay for equal work. She said that in her plant, women usually earn more than men. The reason is that the company offers a bonus of one hour overtime to women who will work a second or third shift, and does not offer any such bonus to men. But Rudolfus jumped in to say that because of gender bias, men's wages are usually higher than women's.

Ance earned 170,000 rupiah (about $21) per month in the summer of 1999, less than the 232,000 rupiah (about $29) per month legal minimum wage. She said that all of the workers knew that their employer was violating the law by paying them less than the minimum, but with the economic crisis most felt they had no alternative but to accept the lower wages. "We had strikes, but nine of my friends were threatened with being fired and then moved to other plants. If we strike again, we'll be fired for sure," she said.

At about 7 p.m., the garment workers from the PT Citra Abadi plant filed in to hold their SBJ union meeting. There were about 40 of them, all Muslims, about three-quarters of them women, some wearing the *jilbab*. Nearly all of them were in their late teens and early 20s, perhaps a few in their early 30s. We all sat in a circle on mats in the main room of the house. One of the catechists explained that I was a visiting journalist, and that I work with labor unions in the United States. He asked if they would be willing to talk with me before the meeting and answer some questions about their jobs, and the workers agreed.

I introduced myself and told them I'd be interested in learning something about their work, both the bad and the good. "Our jobs are mostly not very good for us," said one young woman. Another chimed in, "We are forced to work overtime. We work from 7 a.m. to 10 p.m. five days a week, and on Saturday we work half a day, that is, from 7 a.m. until 4 p.m. If we also work Sunday, which many of us do, we can make 400,000 rupiah a month." I calculated in my notebook that they earn about $50 for more than 90 hours of work per week, or a little more than 50 cents per hour. Another added, "We also get a free meal, but it is very low in protein and vitamins."

"The employers treat us without respect," said one young woman worker. "They just want production." Another woman added, "If we're sick, they don't care. They send us to the clinic, but they don't really treat our illnesses; they just give us vitamins."

"Old and new workers receive the same wages," said one worker, adding that she didn't think that was fair.

"If workers speak out, they are threatened with firing," one man said. "If workers obey their supervisors and do whatever they say, then they are treated well." From his tone, it was obvious that he held such pro-management workers in contempt.

One worker brought up the role of the military. "Sometimes the military police come into the factory, but we don't know why they are there. They just walk around the factory. They are bought by the company."

One woman, who seemed like a natural spokesperson, said, "Three weeks ago we had a strike to demand higher wages. We had 14 demands: higher wages, a stop to forced overtime, Saturday work to noon only, lunches with more nutrition, and we asked that the employer should stop ignoring our right to 12 days off per year. We also asked for an end to favoritism. We have had no result from the strike yet, but no one was fired because all of the workers stuck together."

The SBJ union chair, Setiyono, explained, "The military put the SBJ on their list as a subversive organization." Thus the union's organizing activities tended to have a clandestine character, even in this era of Reformasi, he said. The young, mostly female workers who sat with me in that room had the courage to attend this meeting, though they could be fired by their employer and jailed by the military. They might even be accused of subversion, a crime that carries the penalty of death in Indonesia.

Before I left, the catechists asked if the young workers could ask me some questions, and I agree. They were most curious about U.S. workers' wages. When I told them the minimum wage, the Indonesian workers gasped in disbelief. When I told them how much a unionized autoworker or steelworker makes, they were incredulous. I told them it wasn't always so. Unions in the United States were once illegal; the military and police were once—and sometimes still are—used to crush workers' unions and strikes; Americans only won the legal right to labor unions in the 1930s; unlike other countries, we have never had workers' rights written into our constitution; employers still conspire to destroy labor unions and their contracts; and our government works against the interests of unions. We are part of the same fight for workers' justice, I said, but I know that in that common fight they bore an uncommon burden and suffered an uncommon exploitation and oppression.

"Solidarity," I said in Indonesian, and they smiled and thanked me.

"We would like to be in touch with American unions," said Setiyono, handing me his card. "We could use some help."

1   Anders Uhlin, *Indonesia and the "Third Wave of Democratization":* The *Indonesian Pro-Democracy Movement in a Changing World* (New York: St. Martin's Press, 1997), 84–87. This book represents the most thorough survey of the Indonesian non-governmental organizations up to the fall of Suharto.

2   Uhlin, *Indonesia and the "Third Wave of Democratization,"* 98, citing: Nasution, "Defending Human Rights in Indonesia," *Journal of Democracy* 5: 3 (n.d): 114–23.

3   Uhlin, *Indonesia and the "Third Wave of Democratization,"* 112, citing *Inside Indonesia* 29 (n.d): 19.

4   Uhlin, *Indonesia and the "Third Wave of Democratization,"* 145. I have adapted Uhlin's somewhat longer list.

5   Uhlin, *Indonesia and the "Third Wave of Democratization,"* 138.

6   Yudha Kartohadiprodjo, "Teten Masduki, a Modest Whistle Blower," *Jakarta Post,* August 1, 1999.

7   Julia I. Suryakusuma, "The State and Sexuality in New Order Indonesia," in Laurie J. Sears, ed., *Fantasizing the Feminine in Indonesia* (Durham: Duke University Press, 1996), 99.

8   Mari Pangestu and Medlina K. Hendytio, *Survey Responses from Women Workers in Indonsia's Textile, Garment, and Footwear Industries* (Jakarta: World Bank, 1997), 1.

9   Pangestu and Hendytio, *Survey Responses from Women Workers,* 2; Yunus Shamad, *Industrial Relations in Indonesia* (Jakarta: PT. Bina sumber Daya Manusia, 1997), 240–41; Reema Nayar, *Indonesian Labor Legislation in Comparative Perspective: A Study of Six APEC Countries* (Washington: World Bank, 1996).

10   Stevie Emilia, "Brothel Complex Closure May See Rampant Spread of STDs," *Jakarta Post,* July 28, 1999.

11   Emilia, "Brothel Complex Closure May See Rampant Spread of STDs."

12   Ben White and Indrasari Tjandraningsih, *Child Workers in Indonesia* (Bandung: Akatiga, 1998), 27–30.

13   Progressive Catholic social movements found vast support after the Second Ecumenical Council, known as Vatican II (1962–1965). The council was accompanied by encyclicals arguing that human beings had a right to decent living standards, education, and political participation. In 1968, the Latin American Episcopal Conference held an extraordinary conference in Medellin, Colombia, attended by Pope Paul VI, who told the bishops, "We wish to personify the Christ of a poor and hungry people." Some interpreted that as the Christ of the workers, the savior of the working classes. The theology of liberation developed in Europe and Latin America, but also spread to Africa and Asia. While Pope John Paul II has attempted to crush liberation theology and other progressive trends in the church, they have nevertheless survived in Indonesia.

Chapter 6

The New Independent Unionism of Reformasi

Reformasi has meant not only political change in Indonesia, but also the birth of a new independent unionism. While students and other citizens struggled for political reform, workers fought for better conditions, higher wages, and—most important—the right to organize independent labor unions and bargain collectively. The fight for independent unionism has taken many forms, from clandestine meetings to public rallies, from strikes to political protests. After the fall of Suharto in May 1998, the Indonesian government signed International Labor Organization (ILO) Convention 87, recognizing the right of workers to form independent unions, and the Minister of Labor issued a decree announcing it would register independent labor organizations. Since then, dozens of labor federations or national unions have been registered by the government, and hundreds of local union organizations have been created in workplaces across Indonesia—though they still find it difficult to win union recognition or labor union contracts. The movement still represents only a small percentage of the country's tens of millions of workers (about 3 percent), but it holds the possibility of becoming a massive working-class social and political phenomenon.

The new union formations are spread across the political spectrum, from conservatives who support the employers, to moderates who seek only collective bargaining and workplace reform, and on to radicals and revolutionaries who want not only labor unions, but also real social change. Unions have been organized under nationalist, Muslim, Christian, and social democratic banners. Reformasi in the labor movement has led to the reorganization of old unions originally formed in the 1950s and banned under Suharto and to the creation of entirely new labor unions organized by student activists of the 1990s. Many unions arise not on the basis of ideology, but grow out of conditions in particular sectors, industries, firms, or plants. Though they hold a variety of philosophical positions, differ on many ideological points, and disagree strongly on political and practical postures, these unions also hold much in common.

At the center of the new union movement stands the principle of political independence from the Indonesian state. Without exception, the new unions reject control by the state; the state party, Golkar; or the military. They also demand the right to choose their own leaders, negotiate their own contracts, and set their own political course. In some cases, this is a matter of fiercely held principle; in other cases, it has arisen out of political opportunism as the collapse of the Golkar regime has virtually thrust independence upon unions. However they came to this position, though, they are now all independent unions.

In addition, all of these new labor organizations recognize that the key issue for the unions must be collective bargaining for genuine labor union contracts that can begin to raise wages and improve conditions. While this may appear to be the very definition of labor unionism, it has not necessarily been obvious to Indonesian labor union leaders or rank-and-file workers until now. During Suharto's 33 years of dictatorship, the state's official union federation—the All-Indonesia Workers' Union (SPSI), the only legally recognized labor organization—did not engage in genuine collective bargaining and contract negotiation. Moderate alternative trade unions were not allowed to organize. As a result, independent union organizing, conducted clandestinely and at great risk, often fell to radicals and revolutionaries who wanted higher wages and union contracts, but who also aimed to over-throw the Suharto regime. Now, for the first time in decades, independent labor unions oriented toward collective bargaining have emerged as the dominant form of labor organization.

Despite their areas of agreement, these independent unions retain different views on how to advance the labor movement in the social and political realm. Some would create very narrow and nominally apolitical unions that only engage in collective bargaining. Others would also attempt to influence the established parties and elite politics through interest-group pressure. Still others would attempt to create some sort of labor party on a European model. Finally, some hold to a more radical vision that foresees the creation ultimately of workers' and peasants' councils that would do away with the last vestiges of the old regime and establish a democratic and egalitarian socialist society.

All of those positions can now be debated and argued within the field of the new independent labor movement, which is a tremendous advance.

What remains most important, however, is the role to be played by the millions of unorganized workers in factories, mines, mills, plants, fields, and offices throughout Java, Sumatra, and the other major islands of Indonesia. While the new independent unionism is enormously encouraging, it will take a massive upheaval from below to transform Indonesian industrial relations. In this chapter, I will look at several new or reborn organizations of the Indonesian labor movement. The two most important new labor organizations, SBSI and the FNPBI, are not discussed here, but will be taken up at greater length in the following chapters.

SARBUMUSI: Muslim Unionism

Some of the new unions are old unions attempting to reestablish themselves after decades of repression. Serikat Buruh Muslimin Indonesia, the Indonesian Muslim trade union, best known by the acronym SARBUMUSI, represents an attempt to revive the Muslim labor movement of the pre-1965 period. One of its leaders is the veteran labor union activist and parliamentary representative Sutanto.

H. Sutanto Martoprasono—he prefers to be called simply Sutanto—is an older man. He wears glasses with heavy dark frames, and when we talked he sported a beautiful blue and gold paisley shirt made of silk. At 67, he is the representative of an older generation of Indonesian labor unionists who were put out of business by Suharto in the 1970s. Now he is back, working to rebuild SARBUMUSI.

Speaking alternately in English and Bahasa Indonesian, Sutanto told me the history of the rise and fall of Muslim unionism. Born in 1933, Sutanto was a student at Gadjah Mada University in Jogjakarta in the 1950s. There he became a member of the Indonesian Muslim Student Organization (HMI) and, as a student activist, helped to set up a union at a government-owned sugar factory in 1958. He became one of the chairs of that union, which also represented other workers in Jogjakarta.

The union with which he worked affiliated with SARBUMUSI, which had been founded in 1955. SARBUMUSI was affiliated with the Nahdlatul Ulama (NU), which was then a Muslim political party. It was also affiliated with the International Confederation of Free Trade Unions (ICFTU), an organization that represented "Western," or pro-capitalist, labor unions during the Cold War. (In that period, the pro-Communist World Federation of Trade Unions, or WFTU, represented mostly unions of the Soviet Union and Eastern bloc, as well as some unions in third world countries.)

At the December 1960 SARBUMUSI congress, Sutanto was elected one of the national chairs and moved to Jakarta. There he extended his activities from the union into politics. From 1963 to 1982, Sutanto served as a member of parliament, originally as a so-called functional member (that is, a member from a "functional organization," or social sector) but after 1971 as a representative for Java and later as a representative for East Java. As an M.P., he always served on the parliamentary labor committees.

When Sutanto first became active during the 1960s, several rival labor federations existed in Indonesia. "We fought against SOBSI in all of the factories." SOBSI, the All-Indonesia Central Workers' Organization, which was the dominant labor federation of that era, was controlled by the Indonesian Communist Party (PKI), which in turn was allied with President Sukarno. In 1965, Suharto and the military rose up, overthrew Sukarno, and, with the help of many Muslim militias, destroyed the PKI and SOBSI, and massacred hundreds of thousands of Communists.

At first Muslims like Sutanto were delighted with the elimination of the PKI and SOBSI. But Suharto's military regime was not content with having eliminated the Communists; it also wanted to eliminate all other rival political and social organizations, including the Muslim labor unions. SARBUMUSI opposed the government's attempt to control the non-Communist labor unions. "We fought against the government program to dissolve labor organizations, especially in government-owned factories and in government offices," Sutanto explained. In 1970, SARBUMUSI complained to the ILO about attempts to restrict labor unions. "But no other union supported us," he said. "We fought alone."

Sutanto and other SARBUMUSI unionists participated in talks that eventually led to the government's creation of the All-Indonesia Labor Federation (FBSI) in 1973. "We suggested that the new organization should be democratic and should recognize international labor standards established by the ILO," said Sutanto. "So we joined based on the idea that this would be a democratic union—but it was not."

After 1973, the former SARBUMUSI officials and activists maintained a network within the government-sponsored organization. But since FBSI was the only recognized union federation, SARBUMUSI could not negotiate collective bargaining agreements, and ceased to exist as a union. Looking back on those years, Sutanto says that FBSI and its government-controlled successor, SPSI, didn't help workers advance as much as they might have. "They were not good for workers. In over 20 years, only 15 percent of the workers were organized in unions," he said. And that estimate is about five times too high if one takes into account both workers and peasants.

Since Reformasi, Sutanto has been attempting to rebuild what was once one of the most powerful labor unions in Indonesia. "After the government signed ILO Convention 87 and issued its May 1998 decree stating it would register independent labor unions, those of us who had been in SARBUMUSI decided we had to build our union up again; we had to renew it. We have to rise again."

But the task facing these old union activists is daunting. "Frankly speaking," Sutanto says, "we have been absent from the labor movement for over 20 years. We lack human resources, and we find it hard to organize, so we are just beginning."

"We have organizations in East Java, in Central Java, and in South Kalimantan," he explains. He gives the example of a cigarette factory in Kediri in East Java where the union was affiliated with the Food and Tobacco Industry Union of the government-controlled SPSI. Now its members have joined SARBUMUSI. He also mentioned that one or two important labor and political figures had left SPSI and joined SARBUMUSI. "Last June," he said, "we held a conference, and more than 300 workers came from many parts of Indonesia, from East Java, Central Java, South Kalimantan, and West Sumatra."

"We are now concentrating on building up our membership again. We have a lack of funds, and we don't have money to send people to different regions. In East Java and in Central Java, we organize in the informal sector. We're also setting up cooperatives. We have set up some basic commodity shops for our members, here in Jakarta and in Central and East Java."

But the union's power is minimal. In its first year of existence since Reformasi, SARBUMUSI was registered as a union, but led no strikes and signed no collective bargaining agreements. "We're just beginning again," says Sutanto. "We recruit from students and youth," he explains, and the union now has some new, younger leaders. But while the union has an executive board of 33 members, only two of them are women. With top leaders in their 60s and 70s, only a few younger leaders, and almost no women leaders, SARBUMUSI may find that it is unattractive to the new generation of activists and workers.

I asked Sutanto what was distinctive about the Muslim philosophy of unionism, and what made a Muslim union different from nonreligious unions. His answer surprised me. "I think there is no difference. We just take care of some religious issues," he said, "for example, building a mosque for the workers and giving them an opportunity to pray."

"The name is still Indonesian Muslim Union," he said, "but the organization is not exclusive. Our members don't just come from the Muslim groups. Membership is open to all. We have no relationship to the Muslim National Awakening Party (PKB). We are independent, we are not affiliated to any party, and membership is open. We have even thought about changing the name of the union and leaving out the word Muslim."

SARBUMUSI's agenda is similar to that of the other new unions. "In my opinion," says Sutanto, "unions should fight for economic rights, for the minimum wage. The economic situation remains in crisis. But it is hard to demand higher wages when the factory might close. According to the Minister of Manpower, there are 22 million unemployed workers. So we are now in a very, very difficult situation for unions."

SARBUMUSI has joined the Union Solidarity Forum (FSU), a loose federation of independent unions inspired by and created with the assistance of the AFL-CIO's American Center for International Solidarity Center (ACILS). "The sponsorship of ACILS has been very important in getting unions together to discuss what's going on, and the national problems. ACILS's suggestion to invite many different unions to get together was a very good idea," he notes. Also participating in the FSU are the SBSI, the largest independent labor federation, led by Muchtar Pakpahan, and the radical FNPBI grouping led by Dita Sari.

Asked about Pakpahan's idea of setting up a labor party, Sutanto said, "I think it's a good idea, but there has been no time to discuss and organize around this idea."

Talking with Sutanto, one has to be impressed by the efforts of an older man from another generation who has clung to his ideals and is attempting to rebuild an organization that was obliterated by the Suharto dictatorship. Organizations like SBSI and FNPBI have connected more effectively with the new university youth movement that emerged from the struggles of the 1970s. But the chances that SARBUMUSI will prosper seem quite small. Few young people have any interest in reviving the Muslim labor union idea of the 1950s.

Marhaenism: The Sukarno Tradition

Sutanto is not the only one trying to revive the labor movement of the past. Some intellectuals and union activists have also attempted to revive President Sukarno's idea of a labor movement, what he called Marhaenism. Sukarno created Marhaenism, his populist ideology, as a way of speaking to and connecting with Indonesia's many millions of peasant toilers. To him, Marhaenism refered to the "little people," particularly the peasants of rural Indonesia, though the term was used more broadly to include workers and all laboring people. Sukarno never had much success in creating his own labor unions, but relied for support instead on the PKI labor and peasant unions. So contemporary Marhaenism is both an attempt to revive an old ideology and to create a new labor movement on a basis that failed in the past.

In the Menteng district of Jakarta, a new university was established in 1999, Bung Karno University (BKU). ("Bung," or brother, is a term of respect and endearment often attached to the name of several of the founders of Indonesia, particularly Sukarno—Bung Karno—and Hatta—Bung Hatta.) The small university campus, with only a couple of buildings and a few hundred students, represents an attempt to revive the nationalist and populist politics of the Sukarno era. At the same time, some of those involved in the BKU project are also attempting to create a distinctive Sukarnoite labor unionism.

Suhardi, the deputy rector of BKU, also doubles as the general secretary of the Marhaenist Trade Union. A man in his 40s, he could not have been involved in the labor unions in the time of Sukarno, but clearly he identifies with the ideals of that period. I met with Suhardi on registration day at the new university, sitting and talking with him as students came to sign up for classes.

"Our union was originally established in 1953," he told me, "but then abolished under Suharto. We reestablished it again in 1998. We organize workers in steel, textile, wood, food and beverages, and banks. So far, we don't have more than 5,000 members, about 40 percent of them women who work in the textile and food sector."

"We work with the International Labor Organization. I am a master trainer in the area of human rights, and I also train our people in union issues," he explains. "We have negotiated some collective bargaining agreements. We think there must be strikes to win better conditions, and we have led some strikes, for example at a lumber mill in Cikaran."

"Our ideology is the Sukarno ideology, or Marhaenism," he explains. I asked if that meant that their union was socialist or Communist, particularly since Sukarno had been close to the PKI. "Sukarno was not a Communist. How could he have been a Communist?" asked Suhardi. "He was a Muslim. He was close to labor, close to the poor."

Suhardi's attempt to recreate a Sukarnoite labor union seems even more chimerical than Sutanto's effort to reestablish the Muslim union SARBUMUSI. The Suharto dictatorship effectively eradicated all vestiges of Sukarno's social organizations, including his labor union. Few young people and almost no workers have had any connection with the values and ideas it expresses, which arose out of the independence struggles of the inter-war period. Other new organizations, such as the People's Democratic Party (PRD) and the FNPBI better represent the radical impulse in the labor movement today.

SPSI-Reformasi: State Unionism Reformed

If any of the old union organizations will survive and prosper in the new era of Reformasi, the most likely would be those coming out of the state-controlled SPSI. For over 20 years, SPSI was the only labor union organization permitted in Indonesia. Controlled by Suharto and the ruling Golkar party, permeated by military leaders at every level, and dominated by employers on the shop floor, it was fundamentally an instrument for the domination and repression of workers. Nevertheless, SPSI had a national structure that reached into the workplaces. However controlling and corrupt it was, workers had no alternative but to take their problems to SPSI. Sometimes a very few SPSI officials raised workers' issues, so occasionally it functioned to transmit workers' discontent, even if it could not be said to have represented the workers.

The 1998 upheaval and the Reformasi movement transformed official unionism. Beginning in February and March 1998, economic and political pressures on the official SPSI labor federation began to break it apart. On March 14, at a meeting of SPSI, SBSI, and several NGOs held at the home of the U.S. embassy's labor attaché, Greg Fergin, a group of SPSI officials decided to break with the government-controlled federation. Working with the State Department, ACILS decided to back the new grouping, which eventually took the name SPSI-Reformasi (SPSI-R).[1] By May 1998, several SPSI-R unions—especially in the textile/garment, tourist, chemical, plantation, and pharmaceutical industries—had begun to sever their ties with SPSI and to restructure their own organizations.[2]

Finally, at an ILO trade union workshop on August 21, 13 of the 15 sectoral unions of SPSI declared that they and their entire memberships had broken away from SPSI to form a new federation. But several of the sectoral unions waffled, and eventually not all 13 went with the SPSI-R. (At different times in the first year, nine or 11 sectoral unions supported the new reform federation.) SPSI accused the AFL-CIO's ACILS of meddling in Indonesian labor politics and of masterminding the SPSI-R split.[3] A bitter struggle developed over control of the SPSI office, with the old guard victorious in keeping control of the building and other physical assets. The SPSI-R group then moved in to share office space with the ACILS, and later moved just down the hall.

As SPSI-status quo (as the old group had come to be called by its critics) and SPSI-Reformasi battled to win the allegiance of the heads of the various sectors and fought for control of the union offices, the SPSI structure in the provinces began to break up, and the union's influence in the plants diminished. For SPSI-R, independence meant financial crisis. After the split, Golkar and the government withdrew financial subsidies to SPSI-R organizations, leading to disaffection among the union officials. Support from ACILS proved crucial to SPSI-R's survival. Mid-level officials in SPSI and SPSI-Reformasi, many of them retired Golkar or military officials, struggled to hang on to their sinecures and perquisites, thwarting reform and sowing dissension.

For several months, the survival of SPSI-R seemed doubtful. Then during October 3–6, 11 of the SPSI-R unions held a congress in Cipanas, Puncak Pass, in West Java, attended by 300 delegates, at which the officials proclaimed the founding of SPSI-Reformasi. In a dramatic break with past practice, about half the delegates were plant-level union representatives, rather than just middle- and top-level union staffers. Several international labor representatives also attended the founding congress, including Bill Jordan of the ICFTU's Brussels office, Takashi Izumi of the ICFTU-APRO office, several International Trade Secretariat representatives, and the Indonesia Director of the German Friedrich Ebert Foundation. U.S., Japanese, and German labor federations gave their blessings to the new independent SPSI-R. The congress chose Hartono of the Plantation Workers' Union as president and C. David of the Transport Workers' Union as vice-president. The SPSI-R adopted a new constitution and by-laws that did away with the bureaucracy at the branch and provincial levels.[4]

Despite the success of the founding congress, the new federation faced serious problems. SPSI-R still represented bureaucratic reform-from-above. All of SPSI-R's leaders had been the leaders of the government-controlled labor unions, and had for years functioned through an extremely hierarchical bureaucracy overseen by the state, permeated by military officials, and working closely with employers. They had moved to an independent position because the economic crisis, the political reform movement, and the rising level of working-class strikes—and finally the conversation with Fergin of the U.S. State Department—had convinced them that they must accept reform or be bypassed by history. But almost none of them had the slightest idea of what reform really meant. As an ACILS staffer noted, "Only one of the SPSI-R unions, TSK [the textile and garment union], had a clue as to what they should be doing in order to reach out to the plant-level unions and get their dues structure functioning again."[5]

The Indonesia Textile, Garment, and Leather Workers' Union (TSK), the most viable of SPSI-R unions, is led by Rustam Askam. I met with him in TSK's modern offices in Jakarta. A man in his late 50s, Pak Rustam, as he is called (Pak is a term of respect), told me that he worked in a batik company in the 1960s and became involved in the local union in 1966. At that time a multiparty and multi-union system still existed in Indonesia. His local was affiliated with the Muslim Amalgamated Trade Unions of Indonesia (GASBINDO). The law permitted more than one union in the workplace, and there were three rival unions in his shop. Over the years, he worked his way up in the union hierarchy, becoming president of the national sectoral union. At the same time, the Suharto government forced all unions to become part of SPSI, and he became one of SPSI's 15 heads of sectoral unions.

Pak Rustam explained to me how the TSK textile and garment workers' union was attempting to reorganize itself. First, he said, the union had reregistered its members.

In our union we began from the plant level and worked up through every level of our industrial union. The old SPSI opposed this because it had no officers at the federal or regional level, and they wanted that old system. Those levels are a problem because they tend to be dominated by outsiders: retired military officers, retired civil servants, and politicians from Golkar.

Today, Rustam claims, TSK has 600 plant-level unions and about 550,000 members, of whom 70 percent are women. (Other union leaders and activists dispute TSK's claim to half a million union members, arguing that TSK and other SPSI-R unions have simply counted all the workers from the old federation.) The union has recently been reorganized into four sub-sectors—textiles, garments, shoes, and toys. Because it is small, the toy sector also falls under the purview of the garment sector.

Wages in the industry were about 250,000 rupiah monthly in 1999, Rustam explained, but he claimed union wages reached 300,000 rupiah on the average (between $35 and $43 per month). In the garment industry, piece work is almost universal. "Workers are way behind in wages. Too many companies consider the minimum to be the maximum."

Rustam admits that the TSK still has many challenges. The first is the existence of so-called yellow, or company, unions within the sector and the federation. "In our federation, there are still 'yellow' unions, or half-yellow unions," he readily admits. "We are now concentrating on collective bargaining agreements, CBAs." Examining the collective bargaining agreements will allow the leadership to weed out company unions. "We will start with surveys of the existing union CBAs. Then, after that, we will look at the quality of the CBAs. We will see the weaknesses of the union and its contracts. If there is no CBA, it is hard to improve in the near future. Where there are poor CBAs, we will work to make them better."

Pattern bargaining for the entire industry does not yet exist, he said. "At present we have no industry-wide pattern agreements. But we have a letter of understanding with four employer associations," he explains.

Another challenge facing TSK, says Rustam, is how to create a new union leadership that reflects the young, mostly female workforce. "The question is how to create more young leadership coming from the workplace. Perhaps in another five years we will have people coming from the plant level at all levels of the union. Without that, there will be dangers and obstacles in the future. We lack women in the leadership, and that is also part of the problem. We are going to correct that."

While regarded as the most astute of the SPSI-R leaders, Pak Rustam remains a very cautious and conservative labor union leader, a moderate at best. He rejects the notion that Indonesian workers need to engage in mass strikes in order to win decent contracts and wages.

> I think it is not necessary to have national strikes. I think it is useless because dispute settlement is a problem, and because of the weakness of the membership. We prefer tripartite discussion. At the local level negotiations should be bipartite, but at the national level tripartite, because the government issues the regulations. We want government involvement [in collective bargaining].

Like moderate union leaders in other countries, Rustam wants to link wage gains to productivity.

> We will discuss productivity with the employers. They say productivity is low, but actually it is not. We suggest a cost-structure analysis by industry and size of the employers—large, medium, and small—looking at the relation of production to labor costs in each sector: fiber, spinning, weaving, etc. What is the percentage of labor to total costs? Labor costs are still behind. The average labor cost is less than 10 percent [of employers' costs], while in other countries it is 15 percent, so there is still room for improvement. There is still room for management to give a wage increase related to efficiency and productivity.

Rustam advocates a "flexible" wage system based on productivity rather than seniority.

> In the past, the wage structure was based on seniority. Most workers were government or agricultural workers in the early days of the 1950s and 1960s. In the 1970s, industry was growing up. Wages are still based on seniority, not on productivity as in other countries. Many young workers get low salaries because they are considered to be inexperienced newcomers. Singapore and Malaysia already have a flexible wage system.

Rustam sees the TSK and the SPSI-R as the center of a new Indonesian labor movement. He opposes the SBSI led by Muchtar Pakpahan, arguing that while Pakpahan attained international fame under Suharto, he has proven ineffective in the Reformasi period. He also criticizes Pakpahan for organizing "a political tendency," and insinuates that SBSI is a Christian labor union in an overwhelmingly Muslim country. "What we need is to create genuine unions, starting at the local level, and without any religious or political ties. We are going in that direction, organizing workers for their own benefits, not considering their politics or religion."

He takes a similar view of the FNPBI led by Dita Sari. "I think they will not be very successful because they are already affiliated to a party, the PRD. They are not really unionists. They are NGO activists. They're tough, and they're good organizers. But they don't have a union background, and what we need to do right now is educate workers about unions." He rejects the Muslim unions for similar reasons. "The Muslims have a big following because of group loyalty. But if they only want to use that mass following for political purposes, that's no good."

While Pak Rustam may represent the shrewdest of SPSI-R's leaders, his is still a union created by political pressures from above rather than grassroots action from below. Rank and file workers played little or no role in founding the new TSK. He seems to aim at the establishment of conservative business unionism, and while he talks about developing new, young union officials, incorporating women into the leadership, and involving the rank and file, still has all of those challenges before it.

While SPSI-R has been a rather conservative and cautious union, by early 2001, some sources reported that it was growing more rapidly and carrying out more demonstrations than any other union, if not necessarily leading more strikes. This was possible because SPSI-R had national and regional structures and sectoral organizations, but also because young, more active, and militant workers entered SPSI-R organizations and began to use those structures for their own purposes. In late 2000 and early 2001, SPSI-R unions and members appeared to be organizing and mobilizing more workers than any other labor union in Indonesia, despite the continuing dominance of old regime leaders, structures, and ideas. If enough new, young workers enter the SPSI-R, they will surely fight for a new kind of unionism, one more democratic and militant than before.

The FOKUBA Bank Workers' Union

If SARBUMUSI, the Marhaenist union, and SPSI-Reformasi represent the past, then FOKUBA, a finance sector union, shows us one vision of the future of labor unionism in Indonesia. Bank workers themselves organized FOKUBA from below and in confrontation with management—albeit with support from NGOs and international unions. Any labor union activist from anywhere in the world would immediately recognize FOKUBA as a genuine labor union dealing with the fundamental issues of recognition, collective bargaining, and contracts.

FOKUBA is typical of the many new labor unions that are being organized not along ideological lines but on a trade, industrial, or sectoral basis. The bank workers, emboldened by Reformasi and devastated by the economic crisis, have attempted to organize unions throughout the financial sector. Indonesia's banks and insurance companies employ tens of thousands of workers, from tellers and accountants to actuaries and adjusters. With the economic crisis of 1997 and 1998, and the collapse of much of the finance sector, bank and insurance workers have been among the hardest hit. In the new era of economic crisis and political reform, bank workers organized new independent unions to represent them. Usually well-educated, often female, the banking union activists represent a new element in the Indonesian labor movement.

Lisa Isa, a 29-year-old employee of the Sumitomo Niaga Bank, heads the FOKUBA, also known by its English name as the Indonesian Financial Sector Union (IFSU). Lisa was born in Jakarta, though her father came from Sumatra and her mother from West Java. As a teenager, she went to the American International School in the Philippines, where she learned to speak excellent English. Later she attended Stanford University in Singapore and studied communications. After leaving school, she worked for a trading house for one year and then in 1989 took a job with Sumitomo Bank, where she has worked for the last 10 years. She is married and her husband also works in a bank; they have a six-year-old daughter.

"My interest in the union arose because I work for a Japanese bank, Sumitomo," she explains:

> I am an officer in the international department. Sumitomo has a reputation as a very strict employer, exploitative to the extreme. The Japanese and Korean companies in Indonesia tend to be very exploitative of their white-collar employees.
>
> We work five days a week, but it is no 9-to-5 job. In the Japanese companies, like Sumitomo, the workday begins at 8 a.m., and employees may work 11 hours or more, sometimes as many as 15 hours, without receiving any overtime pay, which is in violation of the Indonesian Constitution.
>
> The employers psychologically manipulate and exploit the employees. The work is very stressful. Managers sometimes yell at employees. They don't treat them as professionals. They treat them as uneducated, even though they may have master's degrees.

"The salary range at Sumitomo sets a good standard," she says. And though employees at her bank do not have medical insurance, the company reimburses 90 percent of medical expenses, with certain limitations, and 100 percent in cases of hospitalization. A few foreign institutions, such as the Bank of Tokyo Mitsubishi, have pensions, but most banks and insurance companies do not. Still she says, though the pay and benefits are good, they do not compensate for the long hours and the frequent abuse that the employees experience.

"Eight years ago, I attempted to organize a union," says Lisa. "I went to SPSI [the government-controlled federation], but they would not help. SPSI has a commerce and banking sector known as NIBA, but the SPSI organizers wanted a pay-off from us before they would help with organizing."

> With Reformasi, things changed. Indonesia adopted ILO Convention 87, and there was a Ministerial Decree of May 1998, and it became easier to build a union. Though, to be frank with you, even with Reformasi, the Minister of Manpower did a very poor job of explaining about the new laws and decrees governing labor.

But Lisa found organizing bank workers still wasn't easy:

> You have to understand that in the banking sector, workers are very individualistic—sometimes they are selfish—and it is hard to convince them to join the union. They are also being exploited, even though they do not know it. In order to establish a union, you have to get 50 percent of the workers in each company to sign up. It is still psychologically difficult. You have to convince your friends of the need for a union.

Some banks had organized, even before the fall of Suharto:

> There were some banks which had established unions before Reformasi: the Bank of Tokyo Mitsubishi, Citibank, American Express Bank, Deutsche Bank, and ABN, a European bank. Those banks had unions and had been holding a common forum for four years.

In July 1998, the other bank unions, which had already been organized, held a forum to discuss collective bargaining:

A friend and I went to the forum, and after that we began to organize underground. Management would have slashed the union, just as they did eight years ago, so we had to organize secretly. We built a network. We used lunchtime and Friday evenings. Bank workers often go to a pub or a cafe on Friday nights, so we used those times to talk to our coworkers about the union. In August 1998, we registered our union.

At first Lisa found that it wasn't at all hard to organize, because "workers realized the exploitation that was going on." She got 98 percent of the workers to sign up with the union, including managers and even a vice-president!

But when we informed management, they got very angry. Before Reformasi, people had the impression that having a union in the workplace was like having bugs in your bed. They thought of the unions as extremist, radical, and impolite. So they got suspicious of our union. For two months they intimidated and threatened our members. Some members backed off. We lost about 60 percent of our original members.... We lost all the managerial level people.

But we continued to organize. We brought the issues to the Ministry of Manpower with the help of the Jakarta Legal Aid Insitute (LBH). Management told us, "We can buy and sell the Indonesian Constitution," something which—though true—is very insulting. But we forced management to obey that Constitution.

I was very militant. When the boss yelled at me, I yelled back. There was sort of a Cold War in the office. Gradually we won our members back. Management began to recognize our union. And they really did change after we established the union, though we can't trust them completely.

Union organization altered power in the office and the workplace culture.

They changed, and we changed. Nowadays everybody knows their rights. They can stand up for themselves when management is disrespectful. The environment is much better. White-collar workers don't only work for money, but they also work for respect. But then, all workers want respect.

Now I am the chairlady of the union at our company. We are working in cooperation with the American Center for International Labor Solidarity [ACILS] in developing our program. Our primary mission this year is to build a network and educate bank workers about the right to organize and bargain collectively. We will put our emphasis on education.

Lisa and her coworkers succeeded in organizing the union and winning official recognition, but they still do not have a collective bargaining agreement.

We used to just have company regulations, but such regulations were really one-sided. They just present management's side. A collective bargaining agreement represents both sides. That's the importance of having a union.

We don't just make demands on the employer. We try to achieve a win-win situation. Win-win is our principal goal. We're not against strikes, but you should negotiate first before you strike. In some sectors, strikes are the most effective means of winning your demands.

In addition to her work as chair of the union at Sumitomo, Lisa Isa has also been the head of the FOKUBA federation since September 1998. "FOKUBA is an independent federation. Today at Sumitomo we have 70 percent of the 140 employees. We have 4,000 members in the federation from 12 banks, insurance companies, and other institutions. At present, there are no workplaces where there is more than one union, but I expect that will change in the near future."

Lisa has concerns about women workers in the banking industry, in white-collar employment, and in the society in general:

Because we are a service industry, women make up 45 percent of the banking industry employees. We have equal pay for equal work, but we do not have equal chance or equal power, especially in the Japanese companies. Even if a woman is educated, she is still not treated with respect. That problem still exists. I think it is even worse in the blue-collar sector.

Not many women in Indonesia want to be active members in labor unions. Perhaps I should say the norms are Eastern. Women have to ask permission from their husbands to go to union meetings, and they are expected to take care of the children. Fortunately my husband is not like that, and fortunately he works in a bank with a union.

Lisa sees what is happening in the banking industry as part of a larger change among white-collar workers. "Those who recognized that they had the right to organize used to be just the blue-collar workers. But now it is spreading to the white-collar workers and to the middle class. Indonesia did not win the war with the Dutch fighting with bamboo and with bows and arrows. The middle class joined with the working class, and when they join their hands together, they can make a stronger force." But still the organizing work is hard, she says:

The suspicion of labor unions being Communist still exists; it is still a gray area. Even though they say we have Reformasi, the implementation is still only about 30 percent. For over 20 years we had monopoly unions and the domination of foreign investors. With the Reformasi era, we have had a lot of solidarity from Europe and from ACILS. They started to engage with us and offer cooperation. The most important thing in my mind is solidarity. Solidarity leads to unity, and that empowers you.

I asked Lisa what she thought about the labor political parties like the PRD and the National Labor Party (PBN). "I respect Muchtar Pakpahan and Dita Sari for what they have done. And I agree with the idea of labor being involved in politics; otherwise labor's voice will not be heard in parliament. But speaking on behalf of my union, right now we are not involved in politics, except as individuals. Right now we have to work on building the union. If you build a strong foundation first, you will have a stronger house."

Unfortunately, bank and insurance workers have been unable to form a single union, and several rival finance sector organizations vie for their loyalty. FOKUBA is only one among many. But given the long domination of state-controlled labor unions, it seems almost inevitable that workers will have to go through a period of experimentation, including division and reorganization, to form new industrial unions.

As Lisa experience makes clear, FOKUBA represents something quite different than the old labor unionism of the past, which was controlled from above by religious or political organizations or by the state. The bank workers created FOKUBA as an organization to defend themselves against their employers, and to fight to improve their conditions. Without any political ideology other than simple labor unionism, FOKUBA appears almost as moderate as SPSI-Reformasi. But it makes all the difference in the world that it is a union created from below by workers in conflict with management. FOKUBA's members will have to build a union structure from the bottom up, rather than having it handed down from above by the state.

While SPSI-R arguably represents the largest and most important independent union organization in Indonesia, its future remains quite cloudy, both because of its legacy of state control and because of the divisions within its own ranks. SPSI-R has depended too much on ACILS and other foreign supporters, and has failed to transform its own organization fast enough to keep up with events. The future may in fact lie not with the largest, but with the most dynamic new forces in labor, the SBSI headed by Muchtar Pakpahan and the FNPBI led by Dita Sari.

1   American Center for International Labor Solidarity (ACILS), *Monthly Report* (April 1998), 11.

2   ACILS, *Monthly Report* (May 1998), 14. At the same time, a group of SPSI-R officials—Alexander Sinaga of the Jakarta SPSI organization, Salam Sumangat, the general secretary of the timber and forestry sector, Wilhelmus Bhoka of the SPSI executive board, former Sukharno Labor Minister S.K. Trimurti, and former SPSI chairman Imam Soedarwo—formed the Partai Pekerja Indonesia or Indonesian Workers' Party (PPI). They claimed the party would work to create a democratic civil society, respect for human rights and workers' rights.

3   ACILS, *Monthly Report* (September 1998), 12.

4   ACILS, *Monthly Report* (October 1998), 12.

5   ACILS, *Monthly Report* (November 1998), 16.

SBSI leader Muchtar Pakpahan. Photo by Anastasia Vrachnos.

Chapter 7

Muchtar Pakpahan and the SBSI

With a round, dark face, his straight, black hair falling across his forehead, his *peci*—the rimless velvet cap worn by many Indonesian men—sitting somewhat askew atop his head, and wearing a blazingly bright paisley silk shirt, Muchtar Pakpahan stands in the meeting room of the Indonesian Proserity Labor Union (SBSI) Cooperative Building. The two-story, white building has a Christian church on the second floor and a meeting hall and offices on the ground floor. The cooperative distributes food, mainly rice and cooking oil, from this hall on certain days of the week. At other times, it serves as a meeting room or, as on this occasion, a classroom. The whole place is clean and neat, businesslike and professional. Two fans blow a cooling breeze through the hall, and Muchtar uses a speaker system to talk to the gathering of legal professionals who have recently been hired to work for the union, one for each of its industrial sectors.

The money to hire them, and to pay for the fans and the speakers, has come from labor unions in Europe. This is one of the reasons that the SBSI has become the most important of the independent labor unions in Indonesia. It commands resources, uses those resources to expand its staff, and uses that staff to pursue its strategic vision: the organization of a national federation with industrial sectors, the negotiation of pattern bargaining agreements and local contracts, the raising of wages, and the uplift of the Indonesian working class.

Each of the young lawyers, law students, and paralegals—15 of them altogether, five of whom are women—stands and introduces herself or himself. They come from universities all over Indonesia, including some of the best, such as the University of Indonesia and Gadjah Mada. They are clearly middle-class, neatly dressed in sports coats and business suits. Most have the bright and shiny look of recently graduated professionals. A couple of them are a little older, and one has a down-on-his-luck look about him.

Muchtar takes a piece of chalk in his hand and begins to outline the history of Indonesian labor law. Quite clearly he feels at home here, the lawyer displaying his expertise, the teacher training his students, the union leader educating and indoctrinating new staff members. He explains the history and the hierarchy of Indonesian law and diagrams it on the board, from top to bottom: the national assembly (MPRS); then the Constitution of 1945; then the legislature (MPR); then national laws; after that government regulations, and presidential and ministerial decrees, provincial and governor's decrees, and finally regional and district decrees. A ladder of law.

"Rules and regulations before 1969 were pro-labor," he says. "After 1969, they were anti-labor. You can see it in the terminology. In the old laws the term *buruh*, worker or laborer, was used. Then they began to use *pekerja*, employee. Before, they used *perjanjian*, contract, but later they used *kespakaton*, agreement, which is weaker."

A woman student raises her hand and asks a question that suggests disagreement. "What does it matter what they're called," she asks, "as long as we work to get them their rights?" Muchtar responds seriously, even sternly, almost dismissively. The change in language, says Muchtar, represented a shift in ideology, in values, in power. The worker and his contract disappeared, to be replaced by the employee and his agreement. "Before, they were workers, they were producers. Then they became employees," he says, expressing his disgust at the New Order laws.

But then, rather suddenly and unexpectedly, Muchtar began to talk not about the law, but about economic and political matters. Perhaps because he knows these are middle-class professionals, people who may not have had much exposure to critical and alternative political views, he talks about how the system has affected workers. "Suharto had the trickle-down theory," says Muchtar. "He believed that the wealth of the nation would trickle down and spread to others. If the glass was full, it would overflow. But when the glass is full, they move it to China, to Korea, to America. They keep moving the glass."

"The basic policy of the New Order was low wages," Muchtar tells the students. "Another was no freedom of association. So if you asked for high wages, then it was a violation of the regime's principles. Freedom of association didn't exist. There was only one union: SPSI [the All-Indonesia Workers' Union]. If other unions were formed, like Muchtar Pakpahan's union, they would be charged with some crime."

He moves back to the blackboard. He explains that a ministerial decree had it made unlawful to form any other union. "But that violated the law," he says gesturing at his diagram of the hierarchy of laws and regulations on the board, "because a ministerial decree cannot contradict the Constitution of 1945, Article 28."

Suddenly Muchtar switched topic and tone again and looked intently at his new staff. He gives them their marching orders: "Your first job is to understand all labor laws and regulations. Your second job is to understand all of the cases in your trade union sector. Before, we had a regional minimum wage. Our mission will be to create a sectoral regional minimum wage. Your task will be to formulate agreements with the sectoral employers' association." Muchtar sees the SBSI creating something like industrial pattern bargaining, and if he is giving the lawyers a big job, he is giving the union organizers and activists—and himself—an even bigger one. He is a man with a vision, a national plan.

Changing the agenda again, he returns to the economy, to the lives of workers. He makes a few notes, and then addresses the students. "A single worker should have a house or room no less than 10.5 meters square and a caloric intake of 2,800 calories for an Indonesian, perhaps 3,200 for a Westerner. There are also other labor benefits, transport, food, health care. Then there are social effects, organization, recreation." He pauses and walks away from the blackboard and looks at the students again. "If you use this standard, then Indonesian workers live like animals. They have no home; they don't have enough calories to live on. The goal of our organizing is to get 20 percent of total costs as pay for the workers." Today, organizers claim, labor costs make up less than 10 percent of employers' costs, while a larger percentage—some say as much as 30 percent—goes to corrupt payoffs.

Muchtar's meeting with the young lawyers has little in the way of interaction, discussion, or debate. His methods are didactic. His tone is authoritative. His manner is commanding. His language is often proprietary. If he sometimes speaks of it not as the "Indonesia Prosperity Labor Union" but as "Muchtar's union," that is, though not commendable, understandable. He created this union, he has led it through a thousand travails, and he has spent years in jail for it. How could he not think of it as "Muchtar's union"?

Muchtar Pakpahan: Labor Lawyer to Union Leader

While the morning session was winding up, lunch was served—a tasty collection of Indonesian dishes—and Muchtar offered me an opportunity to talk with him. I ask him to tell me a little about his background. "I was born on December 21, 1953, on Samosir Island in North Sumatra. My father was a farmer and worked as a plantation laborer. My mother was also a farmer and she worked with my father." At one point, rumors had circulated that Muchtar's father was a Communist, but he denies it. "I don't think he was ever even a union member."

I had one sister and three brothers, so there were five children in all, and I was raised as a Christian since childhood. After working my way through school as a *becak*, a bicycle taxi driver, I graduated from high school in Medan in 1972. My oldest brother had earned enough money to send me to medical school, so I gave up the job with the pedicab. I went to medical school at the Methodist University of Medan in 1973, and then also entered the law school in 1974. I studied both law and medicine until 1976.[1] But then my oldest brother died of a kidney problem, so I stopped medical school, but continued law school, financing myself as a pedicab driver again.

How had he become involved in labor issues? I asked. "I became an activist in 1974, in my second year of college. I was motivated by a desire for justice. I gave my attention to people who were facing injustice, peasants with land issues. We had a slogan, 'Who has the power?' Well, the employers had the power, and they violated the rights of the peasants."

So Muchtar joined the movement, like many of his generation, a dangerous proposition when the military frequently cracked down on student activists. "We had three types of activities. I helped to explain their rights to the workers, even though at that time my knowledge was minimal. We also had dialogues or seminars concerning the problems. Finally, we would go to the local parliament to protest. We called those three activities advocacy. I continued that work until I graduated in 1978 with my law degree and opened a law firm."

Muchtar pauses a moment and then adds,

It was amazing to me that I had succeeded in graduating from college. It was only through God's blessing that I graduated. So, I prayed to God, promising to repay him. I promised to dedicate my entire life to helping people and to justice. I also asked God to give me a wife to accompany me, and I told him that if he did, and gave me a son for a first child, that I would make that son a pastor who would tell the truth of the Bible. That was my promise to God.

A little more than a year later, God answered Muchtar's

prayer, he says. He married Rosintam Marparing on November 17, 1979. During the next several years, they had three children: Binsar Janathas, Yohanes Dartha, and Ruth Damaehati. True to his promise, Muchtar encouraged his eldest son to become a preacher, and Binsar is now studying theology.

Muchtar continues, "So, I opened a law firm. I had in mind that I wanted to make some money, but a majority of my clients were workers. At that time, there were virtually no labor lawyers, because there was too much risk and almost no money. But I took their cases, and since then I have worked for labor." In addition to his legal practice, Muchtar also taught classes at a university in Medan. But the local authorities disapproved of his activities as a labor lawyer and professor, and the regional military commander had him fired from the university in 1986.

Muchtar moved to Jakarta the same year and opened another law office, but once again, he says, "there were few business clients; the majority of my clients were workers." Then came a surprising break, when the attorney general hired Muchtar to advise him on labor issues in 1988. So Muchtar became a state's attorney. "But I was wasting my time there," says Muchtar. "They never took my suggestions, so I resigned in 1990."

After leaving the attorney general's office, Muchtar reflected on his experience. He had tried to help individual workers through his private law practice, but he had found he could only have a very small impact. Work through the government had proven to be useless since the system resisted reform. So he decided to become involved in one of Indonesia's NGOs. Since the late 1980s, NGOs had flourished and had become central both to the fight for democracy and for women's rights. Muchtar played a central role in the Forum for Justice and Prosperity (FAS), an organization that worked primarily with the urban poor.

In 1990, Muchtar also joined another organization, the first independent labor union since 1965. The Solidarity Free Labor Union had been founded by H.J.C. Princen. Princen himself had a remarkable history. A former Dutch soldier, he deserted the

Dutch army to fight with the Indonesian forces during the revolutionary war of independence from 1945 to 1949. Later he became an opponent of the Suharto regime, and organized the Institute for the Defense of Human Rights (LPHAM). Inspired by Solidarity, the independent labor union that had spread across Poland in 1980, he founded a union by that same name (Setiakawan) in Indonesia. But government repression and conflicts within the union among Princen, who had been the moving spirit; secretary-general Saut Aritonang, who was the principal organizer; and Indro Cahyono, a student and environmental activist who held the title of first deputy, led to the downfall of Setiakawan. Personality differences among these leaders also expressed differences over ideology and strategy, particularly over the question of the relationship between labor and politics. Princen tended to lean toward the left, and Cahyono sympathized with socialism, while Aritonang wanted to organize a labor union without a political agenda. Those differences led to the organization's collapse.[2]

The Founding of SBSI

Although Setiakawan had broken up, Muchtar felt that there was still a need for an independent labor union. So on April 25, 1992, he founded the SBSI, and launched what was to become the most important labor movement in the country in the 1990s. From the beginning, SBSI had a democratic structure. Its congresses represented the highest body, with interim leadership in the hands of the national executive board. The first 11-member board had nine worker members. Decisions were to be made democratically by the members through the principle of majority rule. In reality, however, Muchtar Pakpahan and his closest collaborators tended to provide the leadership and dominate the union's decision-making process.

Muchtar had many strengths and advantages when he began. As an attorney who had handled labor cases for more than a decade, he had great familiarity with Indonesian labor law and its serious problems. His experience as a state's attorney had given him an inside understanding of the government theory and practice with regard to labor law and labor unions. His work with FAS had given him some experience in the NGO movement, and many contacts there, as well. Finally, his involvement in the Solidarity union had shown him some of the difficulties of trying to launch an independent union movement. With his wealth of experience and his forceful personality, Muchtar would be the dominant figure in SBSI.

In launching the union, Muchtar had other social and organizational assets, as well. Because of his previous law practice in Medan, he had a base of support in North Sumatra. Since his college days, Muchtar had been an activist in the Indonesian Christian Student Association (GKMI), and he had maintained his connection to that Protestant organization. Over the next several years, he would recruit several of his leading union officials and activists from the Christian student movement.

While a Christian, Muchtar did not organize a Christian labor federation, as some of his critics have claimed. Sunarty, the union's secretary-general, was a Muslim, as were most of the union's members. Nor was it Christian philosophically. Muchtar's fundamental political positions could be called liberal or social democratic. But the unfortunate experience of the Solidarity union, which had been destroyed in part because of the debate between trade unionists and leftists, and the government's fierce and violent opposition to socialism and communism, led Muchtar—despite his social democratic convictions—to take the position that labor unions should not espouse political programs or goals. As he put it, a labor union "should not be political, although its presence may be viewed as having a political impact. But it must not aim at overthrowing the government, changing the constitution, etc. It is only an interest group." Muchtar also hoped that this self-definition of the union would not only help to keep the government at bay, but also make the union more acceptable to the unions of the International Confederation of Free Trade Unions (ICFTU) and the AFL-CIO. In fact, Muchtar's vision of unionism had more in common with the European social democratic parties and labor unions, as later became clear.

The SBSI attracted Christian and Muslim student activists, NGOs that had been helping workers organize, renegades from the government-controlled SPSI labor organization, and worker activists in various parts of Sumatra and Java. At the time of its founding, Muchtar claimed the group had representatives from 18 provinces and an initial membership of 30,000.

Muchtar believed that the SBSI would only be able to survive if it had some sort of support from Indonesian political figures and organizations, as well as foreign labor organizations and international institutions. Within Indonesia, he tried to cultivate political support from a variety of important figures, such as Megawati Sukarnoputri, the daughter of the former president, and Oka Mahendra, Sabam Sirait, and Sukowaluyo, all leading figures in the Indonesian Democratic Party. He shrewdly had Abdurrahman Wahid, better known as Gus Dur—the idiosyncratic but liberal leader of the Nahdlatul Ulama (NU), the Muslim organization with 40 million members—address the founding convention of the SBSI in 1992. Later Muchtar even cultivated ties to the military commander of Jakarta, General Hendropiryono, who at that time seemed to lean toward some liberal reforms. If Muchtar believed that his political and military contacts would protect him and his union from repression, he was wrong.[3]

Muchtar initially took a moderate position, even raising the idea of some accommodation with the SPSI or the incorporation

SBSI Membership

Year	Number
1992	30,000
1993	250,000
1994	500,000
1995-98	150,000[†]
1999	1,500,000[†] or 150,000[‡]

All SBSI figures from Vedi Hadiz, except [†] (Paul Keys, International Affairs Department SBSI) and [‡] (Roger Smith, ACILS office). See endnote 2 in this chapter.

of both SPSI and SBSI within some new government federation. At the same time, he continued to organize, believing that he could then negotiate from strength. Less than two years after its founding, Muchtar gauged that the SBSI, which he claimed had over a quarter of a million members, was in a position to test itself against the employers and the government. In 1993, he announced that SBSI would conduct a nationwide one-hour strike for higher wages on February 11, 1994, demanding a raise from 3,800 ($1.80) to 7,000 ($3.30) rupiah. The one-hour strike in February was also meant as an exercise in preparation for a national general strike in October.

The government reacted strongly against the union's strike call. Wilhelmus Bhoka, deputy secretary-general of SPSI, condemned it. The Ministry of Manpower discouraged the strike, and the military suppressed it, arresting several SPSI leaders, including Muchtar Pakpahan. Not surprisingly, given the crackdown, the February strike failed.

The SBSI still had not called off its plans for the general strike in October, and continued to organize when an unexpected explosion of working-class anger suddenly wrecked the union's plans. Workers launched a strike wave in North Sumatra in February 1994, and it grew throughout the early part of the year. NGOs had mostly been responsible for organizing the strikes, but some SBSI activists had been involved, as well. In the course of the strikes in March, the military police intervened and apparently killed Rusli, a local labor leader. That may have been the act that spurred the later events. In Medan, in April 1994, between 20,000 and 30,000 industrial workers went on a rampage through the city, destroying property and focusing their attack on Chinese businesses. Many were destroyed, and one local Chinese businessman was killed in the mayhem. The SBSI later argued that the employers' gangsters and military mismanagement of the melee had been largely responsible for the riot. Human rights NGOs eventually discovered that military officers and police agents had been involved in inciting the riots. The military and police, it appeared, had attempted to turn the workers' anger against the Chinese, lest it should turn against the government.

Muchtar Pakpahan: Political Prisoner

Following the Medan riots, the military and police arrested hundreds of activists, and dozens were given sentence of four to six months for "throwing rocks" and similar charges. The government also arrested several SBSI leaders, among them Muchtar Pakpahan, who was sentenced to three years in prison. With that arrest, Muchtar became Indonesia's best-known labor activist. Amnesty International and various European and U.S. embassies sent observers to the trial. The head of the ICFTU asked the World Bank to pressure the Indonesian government to release Muchtar. His arrest led to increasing concern about workers' rights in Indonesia, including a letter from 28 U.S. congressional representatives asking the White House to reconsider Indonesia's trade status and its eligibility for the duty-free import of U.S. goods. The U.S. embassy also expressed its concern. The International Labor Organization (ILO) strongly criticized Indonesia's human rights and trade union policies. The Netherlands Federation of Labor Unions (FNV), the French Confederation of Christian Workers (CFTC), the International Union of Food Workers (IUF), the ICFTU, the AFL-CIO, and many other unions protested. The Indonesian Supreme Court later found Muchtar not guilty. After 10 months in prison, he was freed.[4]

While Muchtar languished in prison, his union came under attack from the government. General Tanjung implied that the military had discovered that SBSI union staff and officials had connections to the Communist Party of Indonesia (PKI). General Hartono blamed the Medan riots on "Communist tactics" and suggested that Communists had caused the riots. Other Indonesian army (ABRI) generals also red-baited the SBSI.

The military's red-baiting was clearly intended to notify both SBSI and the public that the union was now anathema. But something else had happened. His arrest and incarceration had created an image of Muchtar as labor's martyr. From then on, his name and reputation became key to support from unions abroad and to the recruitment of new members in Indonesia. Muchtar defended his reputation and his principles in a book titled *The People Accuse,* a collection of documents detailing his 1994 arrest and conviction and arguing the injustice of it all.[5] The Indonesian attorney general banned the book. Muchtar nevertheless went ahead with his literary efforts, writing *Portrait of the Indonesian Nation,* in which he criticized the government's policies and expressed his support for the people's power movement that had begun to grow in the mid-1990s.

Muchtar had been free only 10 months when another riot occurred, this time in Jakarta. On July 29, military, police, and gangsters attacked the headquarters of the Indonesian Democratic Party (PDI), killing several people and injuring many more. The Indonesian government, whose military had actually responsible for organizing the attack, blamed the PRD and its affiliated student, peasant, and labor organizations (respectively the SMID the STN, and the PPBI). It outlawed the PRD and arrested about a dozen of its central leaders, including union organizer Dita Sari. But the government also blamed Muchtar and once again arrested and imprisoned him.

"I was jailed again," says Muchtar, "this time for 23 months." Much of that time in prison was spent awaiting trial or on trial. The government used his book *A Portrait of the Indonesian Nation* as evidence that he had attacked the government and sown hatred in the society. Distinguished authorities such as Professor Deliar Noer of the Political Science Department of the University of Indonesia and former PDI chair Sabam Sirait testified on Muchtar's behalf and argued that there was nothing subversive in his criticism of the government and defense of democracy. Another witness, Professor Sahetapy, attacked the Subversion Law and suggested that only a "kangaroo court" would try such matters. But with the exception of *Kompas,* most Indonesian-language newspapers ignored the trial, and the English-language daily press would not cover it.

Even while in prison, Muchtar continued to speak out and to influence labor union and political developments. In January 1998, he issued a statement from prison calling upon President Suharto to enter into a process of national repentance and dialogue in which the Indonesian government would meet and discuss issues with its critics.[6] On March 4, 1998, Muchtar, who had fallen ill, held a press conference from his hospital room in which he criticized Suharto for failing to address labor issues in a so-called accountability speech he had just delivered. Muchtar crticized the government for failing to grant workers' rights to organize and participate in protests, and for making workers the bearers of the brunt of the economic crisis. "When development went well," he said, "workers were poorly paid, and when development faltered, they were its first victims."[7]

While in prison, Muchtar received support from abroad. In March 1998, during a U.S. congressional banking committee hearing on a $18 billion contribution to IMF funding for Indonesia, independent representative Bernie Sanders of Vermont described Suharto as "a cruel dictator" whose family was worth billions. He also criticized the imprisonment of Muchtar, who sat "rotting in jail" while the dictator continued in power.[8] The Stichting Geuzenverzet, a Dutch foundation, awarded Muchtar the Geuzen Prize, an award given to persons or organizations that crusade against injustice and uphold peace and human rights, on March 13, 1999. Muchtar's wife and son accepted the award on his behalf. With help from the American Center for International Labor Solidarity (ACILS), two representatives, one from SBSI and another from the Indonesian Legal Aid Foundation (PBHI), traveled to Geneva to the United Nations Human Rights Commission to protest labor conditions and human rights violations, including Muchtar's imprisonment. Professor Spencer Zifac, a delegate of the International Commission of Jurists (ICJ), attended Muchtar's trial and called for his release in a televised press conference in Sydney on April 5, 1999.

Muchtar's own union members also pressured the government on his behalf. On March 9, 1998, for example, SBSI members staged demonstrations in front of the Sarinah department store and McDonald's on Jalan Thamrin, a major thoroughfare in downtown Jakarta. The demonstrators called for a reduction in food prices, the legal registration of SBSI, and the release of Muchtar. The government arrested four people in Jakarta, two in North Jakarta, three in Serang, West Java, and one in Lampung and charged them with offenses that carried penalties ranging from five years to death. When the police interrogated him on March 12, Muchtar took full responsibility for organizing the protest, saying he had done so to protest the MPR's reappointment of Suharto as president.[9]

Muchtar's reputation as a person willing to suffer prison for his conviction that workers had the right to independent labor unions that would fight for their rights continued to grow, though he now shared that reputation with the PRD member and Center for Indonesian Labor Struggle (PPBI) leader Dita Sari. Human rights organizations also took up Muchtar's case, and posters showing him peering out from behind bars could be found in organizations throughout Indonesia and around the world. The growth of Muchtar's reputation enhanced his union's ability to raise funds and gain other forms of support from abroad. It also caught the attention of Indonesian workers, who now began to look at the SBSI as the principal alternative to the government's SPSI federation.

By May 1998, the combination of economic crisis, student demonstrations, and the withdrawal of support by international financial institutions such as the World Bank and the International Monetary Fund, and then by the U.S. government, brought about the downfall of Suharto, who was immmediately replaced by his protégé B.J. Habibie. The SBSI joined groups such as the Coalition of Indonesian Environmental Lawyers, the Coalition of Indonesian Women for Justice and Democracy, the Indonesian Legal Aid and Human Rights Association, and many others in opposing Habibie. Nonetheless, one of Habibie's first acts was to free Sri Bintang Pamungas of the United Indonesian Democratic Party (PUDI) and Muchtar Pakpahan of the SBSI. The country's other prominent labor organizer, Dita Sari, would be kept in prison for several more months, while Muchtar and others worked for her release. With presidential amnesty, Muchtar was released from Cipinang Prison on the night of May 25, and was exculpated from any responsibility for the events of Medan in 1994 or Jakarta in 1996.[10]

Even before Muchtar's release, SBSI leaders and members had been throwing themselves into the Reformasi movement. For example, SBSI members participated in the May 18–22 occupation of the national legislature. The PRD's labor activists also began to bring workers to join the largely student demonstrations. With Muchtar back on the streets, the union became even more deeply involved in protests and in pushing reforms as far and fast as possible.

The Legalization of SBSI

The new Habibie administration indicated it would end the SPSI union monopoly and permit freedom of association and the registration of independent labor organizations. The new Minister of Manpower, Fahmi Idris, a former student activist and successful businessman, announced that Indonesia would ratify ILO Convention 87, which gives workers the right to freedom of association. Workers would be permitted to set up their own unions, with the conditions that they accept the Constitution of 1945 and the Pancasila ideology, and that they have no ties to the PKI, Idris said. On June 5, 1998, Habibie formally ratified Convention 87. Accepting these two measures, the ILO convention and the registration of independent unions, represented a revolution in industrial relations in Indonesia and meant that a new day had dawned for the SBSI and other labor organizations.

On June 1, Muchtar had already met with Idris, his friend, as he called him, who informed the SBSI leader that his organization met all the necessary requirements to be recognized and registered as a labor union by the government. Muchtar then accompanied Idris as part of the official Indonesian delegation to the ILO annual meeting in Geneva, Switzerland. Shocked that the government had invited the SBSI to attend, the SPSI leader Datoek Bagindo announced that his union would boycott the event.

Despite the government's blandishments, Muchtar became one of the most outspoken critics of the Habibie government during this period. He spoke out everywhere, criticizing the government and threatening to organize strikes by tens of thousands of workers if the legislature did not hold an extraordinary session to debate the future of the nation. While Muchtar threatened mass strikes on June 15 and again on June 22 that never materialized, his actions brought him into increasing conflict with the government and the military. When Muchtar organized a big labor demonstration against the government on June 24, the military moved to stop it by blocking chartered buses. Only a few hundred workers were able to reach the union's office. SBSI leader Tohap Simanungkalit and human rights NGOs held a press conference criticizing the government for forbidding workers to demonstrate, while students and other groups were allowed to protest.[11]

The ACILS office in Jakarta, which monitors labor in Indonesia, noted in its June 1998 report that the SBSI leadership "recognized that they were faced with the challenge to transform themselves from a militant, semi-underground activist organization into a professional trade union." SBSI organizers threw themselves into their work, finding a strong response, particularly in the crucial transportation sector.

But organizing in the new period would be tough. While Habibie and Idris had legalized the registration of new unions, government officials, the military, and employers would use every conceivable tactic to resist SBSI and the other new unions that were being recognized by the government. Ministry of Manpower officials simply refused to recognize the SBSI plant-level unions. In some cases, when SBSI filed its membership lists, the ministry turned them over to employers, who then fired or otherwise persecuted the union members. At one point, Muchtar even stopped the registration of plant-level unions and the filing of members' names to protect the workers involved.

These sorts of problems called for creative tactics. For example, in the summer of 1998, workers belonging to SBSI who lodged a complaint on behalf of a fellow worker were disciplined, in violation of labor law and regulations, at the PT Tongkyung, a Korean-owned corporation that produces for the Amanda Smith and Valerie Stevens labels in the U.S. market. Government agencies and NGOs proved unable to force the company to abide by labor law and regulations, so 20 SBSI members occupied the South Korean embassy on August 5 and refused to leave until the diplomats brought Korean company officials to explain their failure to abide by the law. The embassy helped arrange further negotiations between the Indonesian government, the company, and the union. On August 8, PT Tongkyung recognized SBSI as the union representative of its workers at that factory.

In a similar instance in fall 1998, a local official, the *bupati* of Lubu Linggau regency in South Sumatra, wrote to all local officials telling them to beware of SBSI organizing activities in the area. When SBSI challenged the official, he agreed to rescind the letters and to permit SBSI to organize within the regency. Almost everywhere SBSI organized, it encountered some difficulties, but many of them were overcome either through negotiation or demonstrations and confrontation with the authorities.

SBSI Staff and Leaders

During the 1990s, Muchtar assembled a staff of dedicated union leaders, staff members, and organizers. The senior member of the SBSI staff is Rekson Silaban, who heads of the International Department. Like Muchtar, Rekson is a Sumatran and a Christian. Rekson was born at Pematang Siantar in North Sumatra on May 8, 1966. He was educated at the University of Simalungun, where he received a degree in economics. While there he became an activist in the GKMI.

In 1992, while working as a student activist with a peasant movement to resist government land seizures, he met Muchtar Pakpahan. "Muchtar said to me that whenever I was ready to leave the university, I could join the union." Rekson went to work for the Research Department that year, and later became deputy chair and a member of the executive board. He has been the director of the International Department since 1997. Rekson remembers:

> The international community was waiting for a long time for signs of an independent union in Indonesia. For over 23 years under Suharto, there had been no independent unions. Then, in 1992, SBSI was founded. Many people thought we were crazy, because they knew how tough it would be to organize a union. At that time, there had been no democratic reforms. For example, there was no human relations commission yet.
>
> When we announced the founding of SBSI, it surprised people both here and internationally. We got letters of support from many labor unions, but no financial assistance in 1992. Not until about two years later, at the end of 1994, did we get any financial help.
>
> Because there had been many failures in the past, the international community hesitated to give us support. After two years, however, we began to get some financial support, first from NGOs in Switzerland. Then came money from labor unions and funding agencies. We have received funds from labor unions in various countries: Finland, Sweden, Canada, the United States, Belgium, France. We are especially close to trade unions in the Netherlands, perhaps because they were once here and there is an emotional link.
>
> We are affiliated with the World Confederation of Labor (WCL) based in Brussels. At one time, it was a Christian federation, but since 1968 it is nonreligious. We also work with the International Labor Organization. Muchtar Pakpahan was just elected in June of 1999 as substitute representative.

Another SBSI staff member is Patuan, who replaced Rekson as head of the Research Department. "I was a former leader of the GKMI in the Java Region," he told me. "I had been a student at the Padjadjaran State University in Bandung, and I really liked statistics. I knew Muchtar because he had also been in the same organization, as had Rekson. Muchtar impressed me because he was really a human rights activist. At that time, he was in prison and in the hospital. I went to visit him in the hospital when he was sick."

As head of the Research Department, Patuan concentrates on three areas: child labor, the "clean clothes" campaign against sweatshops in the garment industry, and Bantam, an area of Indonesia where employers have succeeded in excluding labor unions. Of course, he also does all sorts of other research for organizing and contract campaigns, as well as pitching in on other union work. The big job, says Patuan, is teaching workers just what a labor union is. "They have no idea. They know nothing about unions or collective bargaining or contracts. The job of SBSI," says Patuan, "is to accompany them in this process."

Not all SBSI staff have come out of GKMI as Muchtar, Rekson, and Patuan did. Others are workers, often workers who were laid off or fired from their jobs for union activities, and who have been hired by the union to head departments or to run organizing campaigns. Yatini Sulistyowati, chair of the food, drink, restaurant, and hotel sector of SBSI, is a young woman, apparently in her early 20s. She is a Muslim and wears a *jilbab*. She is single and explains, "I live with my parents, who support my work with the union." She speaks in a professional, sincere, and earnest manner; she gives the impression of complete dedication to her work.

Yatini previously worked for four years on the production line at the PT Monde Mahkota Biscuit company. The company runs three shifts and employs between 300 and 400 workers. When she worked there, there were two unions at the plant, the government-controlled SPSI, which she says really represented management, and SBSI, which represented the workers. In 1994, SBSI led a strike at the plant, but the military intervened and soldiers in civilian dress were sent into the plant. The strike was lost, though SBSI still represents over half the workers at the plant.

Yatini was laid off in 1996, possibly because of her work with the union, and she went to work for SBSI, becoming chair of her sector. "Organizing in these industries isn't easy," Yatini says. For example, the Wisata Hotel International is owned by the government, and the workers must belong to KORPRI, the state-controlled public employees union, so SBSI has to organize and remain underground.

Yatini and workers in her sector have been fighting hard to win contracts, but they are not always successful. Altogether, about 6,000 workers are currently organized in the sector, she says, though other SBSI members in general locals should probably also be counted in this sector. About half the workers are women. Only about 15 percent of the union members pay dues, mainly because most cannot afford them. Few have collective bargaining agreements. In many cases, management, the military, and Ministry of Labor officials have blocked their way; but in some cases they have succeeded, she says. At Novatel, a hotel in Manado, North Sulawesi, belonging to the Accord Group, SBSI waged a long fight and succeeded in winning a contract. In PT Hotan Jaya Graha, a shrimp processing plant, SBSI also won a union contract.

Yatini explains that subcontracting represents a big problem. Hotels use subcontractors to hire workers. Most hotel workers usually make the minimum wage—232,000 rupiah a month in August 1999, when I spoke to her—plus 10 percent, a little more than $1 per day. Women face problems of sexual harassment on the job, and there are also obstacles to their promotion:

> We give workers basic training, bargaining training, and leadership training. Right now, we are doing this kind of educational work at PT Budi Acid Jaya in Central Lampung, at the Kalongan Beach Hotel in North Sulawesi, and PT Kedamian and Monde Mahkota Biscuits in Jakarta.
>
> Our perspective is education. Our one-day basic training

deals with rights and organizing. We also have bargaining training where we teach between 20 and 25 people at a time, and we have recently trained 75 in bargaining.

"We want to build a union from the bottom up," says Yatini. "But we need support for our campaigns from Europe and America."

Another worker leader of SBSI is Bambang Purnomo Saeri, the vice-president of the SBSI Bank Union. "I worked for the Asia Pacific Bank [ASPAC] in financial control from 1990 until it was closed by the government in March 1999. As a result of International Monetary Fund policies, the government closed 38 banks, laying off 25,000 workers. At that time, I became unemployed and went to work for SBSI," he explained.

Purnomo, as he calls himself because there are two other people named Bambang in the SBSI office, joined the union in 1996. "In March of 1998, we had 4,000 members. Then, after the government closed the banks, we had only 1,000 members. Now we are up to 1,200 members. At present, we have no collective bargaining agreements."

Bank workers, at least those who have jobs, represent a rather privileged part of the Indonesian working class. "Workers work eight hours a day, five days a week, though in the Japanese banks they may work longer. Many bank workers have good salaries. Fresh recruits earn about 750,000 rupiah monthly, while managers make between 10 and 40 million rupiah.

"If the owner is Chinese, there is almost sure to be discrimination against the non-Chinese workers. We can't always prove it—but we can feel it," he says. Surprisingly, he says that there is "no discrimination against women workers" in the banks, though women banks workers tell me otherwise.

His main job, says Purnomo, is union organizing, and the strategy is simple:

Usually we organize in the bank's head office, and then reach out to the branches. This is easier than having to go to each branch, which would take a lot more time and money. We train the head office people to reach out to the branches. We have training for managers, training for trainers. This is our strategy for organizing. It's like multilevel marketing. Recruit one by one, and in just four days you have 16 new members.

"I just recruited 45 new members from an insurance company, PT Asuransi Axa Indonesia, in Jakarta," says Purnomo. "I gave them basic training. We introduce the union. We tell them what SBSI is. We explain the sectors, the structure of SBSI, and the aim of our organization. At our second-level training course, we deal with collective bargaining agreements." Purnomo is confident that as the economy improves somewhat, the SBSI bank workers' union will make headway.

Staff members like Rekson, Patuan, Yatini, and Purnomo, a combination of former student activists and worker leaders, all dedicated to organizing, have made it possible for the SBSI to grow rapidly in the Reformasi period.

The National Labor Party

In July 1998, Muchtar gave an interview to *Ummat* magazine in which he criticizied the Indonesian Association of Muslim Intellectuals (ICMI), headed by Habibie. The article immediately led to a smear campaign against Muchtar, attacking him as anti-Muslim. *Ummat* later issued an apology. After reviewing the recording, the magazine admitted it had misrepresented his remarks, but by then it was too late. Muchtar, his wife, and their children received death threats; Muslim youths demonstrated at SBSI offices in provincial cities; and pro-ICMI newspapers such as *Republika* published articles strongly criticizing him. Pamphlets circulated that claimed his father had been a Communist. The Minister of Justice, Muladi, warned Muchtar that he could be re-arrested if he tried to overthrow the government.[12]

Muchtar responded to the attack by launching an offensive of his own. On August 28, Muchtar, other SBSI leaders, and some 200 supporters launched the Partai Buruh Nasional (PBN), or National Labor Party, at a ceremony in Jakarta. While Muchtar was clearly the moving spirit, Tohap Simanungkalit was chosen as chair. Muchtar took a seat on the national advisory board, but later declined to be a candidate for the legislature. The PBN called for the democratization of Indonesian politics, economic reforms to improve the lives of Indonesian citizens, rights for workers and unions, and an end to the military's dual function as security force and as part of the government. While several other so-called labor parties would be formed in anticipation of the 1999 national elections, only the PBN really deserved that name.

Muchtar clearly had a social democratic conception of labor politics: workers would organize in the economic arena through SBSI and in the political arena through PBN. Though he did not discuss it at the time, he hoped the PBN would affiliate with the Socialist International, an alliance of labor and socialist parties that includes the British Labor Party, the French Socialist Party, the German Social Democratic Party, and the Israeli Labor Party.[13] He suggested at the time that the PBN might ally with the National Awakening Party (PKB), headed by Gus Dur, and the Indonesian Democratic Party of Struggle (PDI-P), led by Megawati Sukarnoputri. By proposing such alliances, Muchtar intended to place the PBN in the mainstream of opposition to the Suharto and Habibie governments, but also on the left.

Having launched the party, Muchtar left for the United States and the Netherlands to acknowledge international support while he was in prison, but also to attempt to make contacts and raise funds for future organizing efforts. In the United States, Muchtar met with AFL-CIO leaders and thanked them for their help during his incarceration. In the Netherlands, he met with Dutch union and Labor Party officials, and garnered commitments for further financial support for the union.

While Muchtar toured the United States and Europe, the government and military continued their pressure on the SBSI. In August, SBSI treasurer Rusmina was robbed at gunpoint of 80 million rupiah (more than $6,000) while leaving a bank. Such armed robberies are rare in Indonesia, where the military has kept a strict control on firearms, leading to suspicion that the military itself organized the robbery. At the same time, military personnel approached Tohap, the SBSI and PBN leader, and told him that he and his organizations must stop calling for an end to *dwifungsi*. But the PBN did not back off. A PBN spokesperson told the *Jakarta Post* on November 16, 1998, "The MPR decrees must be rejected and Habibie resign immediately. [General] Wiranto and National Police Chief Lieutenant General Roesmanhadi should be brought before military tribunals."

Upon his return in September, Muchtar found that he faced a rebellion in his own ranks. The ACILS office's report noted, "SBSI also suffered some internal tension during the month [of September]. This tension was largely caused by demands for greater autonomy from the sectors and what was perceived by some as a tendency for Muchtar Pakpahan to treat SBSI like his own personal organization."[14] In fact, from time to time, there were various protests from staff members, union sectors, and union activists, some of which developed into mutinies and even attempted coups against Muchtar. At the staff lawyers' meeting that I attended in August 1999, Muchtar alluded to one of these. Talking to the new legal staff, Muchtar told them,

> The most important thing is your commitment to do this work. That's the most difficult part. Commitment and consistency are the most important. Our work depends on your consistency and commitment. For example, we once had 10 people in our law office. Now we just have four. Some of them tried to make a coup d'etat against me to throw me out. Eliasa Budianto, for example, he raised the religious issue. He said that Muslims could not be organized by non-Muslims. He made a campaign for a coup d'etat. Then he joined the Center for Information and Development Studies [(CIDES), an organization linked to Habibie.]

But while various opposition movements have arisen within the SBSI, Muchtar has been able to defeat them and hold the organization together.

While fighting the rebellion in his own ranks, Muchtar also continued his ambitious program of expanding SBSI's influence. In September, he launched Bapera, the union's distribution cooperative. SBSI officials were joined by abassadors from Sweden and Finland at the inauguration ceremony. Bapera established 42 distribution points throughout Indonesia to provide discounted rice to 200 families at each point. In addition, the cooperative created 67 new jobs. Muchtar's organization now operated on three levels, with the Bapera cooperative reaching working-class communities, the SBSI union organizing in factories, and the PBN serving as labor's political arm. Within a month, the PBN informally nominated Megawati as its presidential candidate. (She was also the candidate of her own party, the PDI-P.)

While Ministry of Manpower officials, military commanders, and employers continued to place obstacles in the path of union recognition, SBSI's local organizers plowed ahead. By September 1999, SBSI had 60 active branches throughout Indonesia, and each one of them had at least three plant-level unions that had applied for union recognition, though many had been ignored or rejected. By November 1998, SBSI had seen its membership double in many areas. For example, in Jambi, Sumatra, the membership jumped from 5,000 to 11,000, of whom 1,000 were dues-paying members. In Lampung, the SBSI had 1,457 members in 13 plant-level unions. In Palembang, it had 700 members in plant-level unions. In East Java, there were 21 plant-level unions in various cities. In East Surabaya alone, there were 420 members. SBSI also established new branches in Sulawesi and East Kalimantan. The Bapera cooperative also expanded. By November, it reported 219 distribution points in East and North Jakarta, each providing discounted rice to 1,000 people, in addition to creating 429 jobs. While continuing their organizing, SBSI activists also found time to participate in the demonstrations in November against the Special Session of the MPR.[15]

In December 1999, Muchtar left the country again. First he went to Australia to attend a meeting of the Australian Council of

Trade Unions (ACTU) in Lorne, Victoria. In his address to the ACTU, he excoriated the Australian government for its role in supporting Suharto, referring to it as the dictator's public relations organization, and bitterly condemned it for its defense of Indonesia's human rights record at the UN Human Rights Commission's annual meeting. From Australia, Muchtar flew to Paris to receive the Prize of Defender of the Rights of Man of the French Republic on the occasion of the 50th anniversary of the signing of the Universal Declaration of Human Rights on December 10, 1948. In his acceptance speech, Muchtar called for Suharto's arrest and trial, and also attacked the military and *dwifungsi.*

On January 7, 1999, Muchtar opened the SBSI's four-day National Working Meeting, or *Rakernas,* which was attended by 107 union officials—national executive board members, 10 department heads, 14 sector leaders, 24 regional coordinators, several union advisers, Bapera cooperative representatives, and leaders of the PBN. Also in attendance were representatives of the WCL, the Brotherhood of Asian Trade Unionists (BATU), the AFL-CIO's ACILS office, the French General Confederation of Labor (CGT), Senegalese unionists, and diplomatic representatives from the United States, Australia, New Zealand, France, and Brazil.

"The main purpose of the *Rakernas* was to help realize the goal of turning SBSI from a militant, semi-underground movement into a professional trade union with a target of achieving a fully dues-paying membership of 1 million within three years. The union would then become fully self-sufficient," ACILS noted.[16] While the campaign for 1 million members was a challenging one, it was not unrealistic. The ACILS office reported in February 1999 that "the best estimate of the SBSI strength is approximately 120 unions registered, 180 in the process to become legally registered units. The SBSI stands between 204,000 and 300,000 members."[17] In some areas, SBSI grew by leaps and bounds. In Malang, East Java, the SBSI chapter increased from a small underground organization of just 12 members to 700 members and nine registered plant-level unions by May 1999. At the same time the Lampung chapter had grown to 7,400 members in 16 plant-level unions.[18]

While Suharto had fallen and the military had begun to withdraw from interference in labor union activities, the situation remained difficult, and the SBSI faced constant opposition from employers, the old state-controlled SPSI labor federation, the police and military, and hired gangsters and paramilitary organizations. In the spring of 2000, the SBSI published an account of dozens of cases of employer, rival union, and government interference in organizing campaigns. While most simply involved firing, several were real atrocities involving violent attacks on union leaders and workers.

Take the case of the workers at the Riau Pulp and Paper Company (PT RAAP). When the company announced it was going to reduce its employees' wages and medical benefits, the workers protested at the workplace. Management called the police and the military, who soon arrived on the scene. Officers of the Riau Police Mobile Brigade (Brimob) and Army Brigade 132 ordered their troops to disperse the workers by shooting tear gas, firing blanks and bullets, and chasing and kicking workers. The attack continued for three and a half hours, and resulted in serious injuries to several workers. Five—Parapat, Aprijat, Gultom, Simamora, and Marbun—were stuck by bullets in the head or leg. Thirteen other workers disappeared, though they were later found in custody in the Riau police station, where they had been kicked and beaten. Later the company had the SBSI branch chairman from Kampar, Kaspar Sibuea, arrested on spurious charges. At the time of publication of the SBSI book several months later, he remained in jail. The story of the Raiu Pulp and Paper workers is just one of many such incidents against SBSI activists.[19] Despite this sort of repression, SBSI continued to organize and to gain strength throughout the country.

As the national election approached, Muchtar and the PBN continued their attack on the role of the military. In January 1999,

Muchtar blasted the military, declaring that he opposed ABRI's continued presence as unelected representatives in the DPR legislature, and contending that if the PBN won a significant number of seats in the coming legislature, it would demand their expulsion. In February, Muchtar announced the PBN's nomination of Megawati as its presidential candidate. He described her as "attuned to the needs and problems of the oppressed masses" and as an honest and patriotic fighter. He reiterated his call for an alliance with the PKB of Gus Dur and Megawati's PDI-P. The *Indonesian Observer*, formerly a pro-government newspaper, described the potential coalition as one with "formidable strength."[20] Ironically, not long after Muchtar endorsed Megawati, she appeared to reconcile with leaders of the military.

While the SBSI union grew in strength in the Reformasi period, its affiliated labor party, the PBN, failed to take root. Many SBSI officers and staff members declined to support, participate in, or vote for the new party, and ordinary workers proved equally uninterested. Most working-class people and the poor who might have been attracted to the PBN gave their votes to Gus Dur's PKB, Megawati's PDI-P, or to one of 40 other political parties. As Yatini Sulistyowati told me, "Workers just weren't interested in the PBN." When the elections came, the PBN received 0.011 percent of the vote, or less than 100,000 votes.[21]

The SBSI held its third congress and celebrated its eighth anniversary from April 25–30, in Cileungsi-Bogor. It was the first time that the SBSI had been able to hold an open and democratic convention without government harassment and intimidation. Some 859 people participated in the congress, 22 of them international guests, mostly from European and Asian labor federations. Now a legal organization operating in a democratic society, SBSI had grown enormously from the 55 branches it had during the Suharto years to 163 registered branches. While many expected the congress to be difficult because of a number of scandals and conflicts in the preceding year, in fact it was an open and democratic event with a healthy airing of differences.

A U.S. observer from the ACILS office reported, "While the discussions were animated at times, the delegates never appeared reluctant to express their honest concerns with their leadership. The open exchange, while sometimes off target, was a cathartic exercise for the delegates who for the first time had a free and open venue to share their frustrations." Eventually all the reports passed as read or amended with only one region refusing to give its endorsement to the proceedings. As the ACILS observer concluded, "In all, the SBSI congress appeared to run democratically and without harassment or intimidation according to schedule and according to the rules, displaying a newfound maturity and professionalism on the part of its leadership."[22]

The SBSI congress passed a dozen resolutions on labor, economic, social, and political issues. As might be expected of a progressive labor federation, the resolutions included a call for May 1 to be recognized as international labor day in Indonesia and a demand for pay hikes for civil servants. But SBSI also advanced a social and political agenda, calling for cuts in the military budget, criticizing the World Bank and International Monetary Fund, and calling for the cancellation of the debts of developing countries. The federation condemned the Suharto regime for its corruption, collusion, and nepotism, and called for cultural autonomy in the troubled province of Aceh.[23] The SBSI's third congress demonstrated that it had not only become the nation's largest and most important independent union, but also a major force for democracy and social justice in Indonesia.

While the SBSI was proving to be a viable and vigorous organization, Muchtar was not content, for he still held the hope of organizing a Social Democratic Party in Indonesia. Despite the dismal failure of the PBN in the 1999 national elections, he intended to give political organization another try. In the spring of 2000, at the same time as he was organizing the SBSI congress, he convened the first national congress of his new project, the Indonesian Social Democratic Forum (Sosdem Forum). Participants in the Sosdem Forum congress, which took place from April 23 to 24 in Jakarta, included six existing Indonesian labor parties, the three independent labor federations (SPSI-Reformasi, SBSI, and the FNPBI), and two NGOs, the People's Foundation and the Kantata Foundation.[24]

Muchtar expressed his reasons for forming the party in a letter to social democratic and labor parties in other countries:

> To present, the SBSI, other independent trade unions, and left-of-center parties are labeled in the press as quasi-Communist and are constantly on the defensive over such allegations. Moreover, sectarianism is unmistakably on the rise, reflected in the growth of Islamic parties and sectarian violence—from Christians and Muslims alike—in Aceh, [the] Mollucas, and Indonesia at large. Unions can of course blunt sectarianism by uniting Christians, Muslims, transmigrants and locals in the same trade union—[and] point out their shared interests as workers—but they are limited in scope; they can only combat sectarianism where they are already active. A wider movement is also needed. These are the reasons for forming the Social Democratic Study Forum.

Muchtar indicated that his goal was the formation of a new party somewhat like the Workers' Party (PT) of Brazil.[25]

Regional Organizing: SBSI and Local NGOs

Among its other achievements, SBSI has succeeded in finding allies among local activists and NGOs. In Medan, North Sumatra, for example, the Institute for Social Transformation (Lembaga Transformasi, or ELTRANS) has played an important role in advising and organizing workers, and works closely with the SBSI. Daulat Sihombing and Timbul Simanungkalit, two men in their 30s, work with 10 other ELTRANS staff members in the Pematang Siantar industrial suburb about 160 kilometers from Medan. ELTRANS undertakes worker education, organizing, and systematic cadre training, and works to create labor unions. In general, it helps move workers from the old state-controlled SPSI unions to the independent SBSI by supporting workers as they fight for their rights and for better contracts and conditions.

Timbul, an attorney who works as an organizer and negotiator for ELTRANS, told me a little about how the group works. "We teach workers their rights by discussion and by campaigns. We also have a magazine for workers called *Galak,* a word that means 'angry' in English. In addition we write brochures on workers' rights, and we produce posters." The magazine, brochures, and posters spread the word about campaigns, such as the current campaign to fight for the minimum wage in all Pematang Siantar factories.

Daulat told me that ELTRANS works largely through campaigns on "normative" and "non-normative" issues. "Normative means demanding the minimum government standards," he explained. "Many workers are still paid less than the minimum wage, for example. We also demand maternity leave, menstrual leave, and 12 days off each year." But beyond these demands, said Daulat, are the "non-normative" issues, such as proper treatment, justice on the job, and a wage higher than the current minimum wage of $1 a day.

How does ELTRANS help workers with these issues? Dault explained that it uses both formal and informal education to raise workers' consciousness about these issues. The formal education involves classes for workers that are offered in the community. But more important may be the informal education that takes place when ELTRANS organizers visit workers' houses. "Often as many as 12 workers live in a house, and we go and visit and talk with them. We may stay overnight in their houses in order to carry on these informal discussions."

Pematang Siantar, where Daulat and Timbul work, has about 20 large industrial plants producing cigarettes, matches, plastic, food and beverages, cassava, and rubber, among other products. ELTRANS has been involved with workers at many of these plants, and Daulat speculates that the organization is now known to half the workers in the area. For example, it has been very involved in organizing workers at the Sumatra Tobacco Trading Company owned by Chinese-Indonesian capital. The tobacco factory employs 8,000 workers, 70 percent of whom are women, and wages averaged between 254,000 and 264,000 rupiah in May 2000. With the help of ELTRANS, workers have now begun to transfer their membership from the old state-controlled SPSI labor federation to the independent SBSI. Both unions are now present in the plant. On the day that I interviewed him, Daulat explained that he just gone into the factory and put up the new SBSI bulletin board. "That's the first time in 35 years some other union besides SPSI has its bulletin board in the plant," he said proudly.

"Before the fall of Suharto everything had to be done by confrontation, but now there are often negotiations, lobbying, mediation, and collaboration. But if that doesn't work, then we still strike," Daulat explained. He gave me the example of a cassava, or tapioca, factory that makes powder for medicine, chemicals, and paint and paper production. The company, PT Bumi Sari Prima (BSP) of RGM Group (Roger Garuda Mas), also has financial involvement by Indorayon Pulp and Paper, which is owned by Sukanto Tanoto, one of Indonesia's wealthiest men. "The company's 300 workers often work in water. They have no safety equipment, no boots or masks," says Daulat. The factory has also damaged the environment. In the spring of 2000, the factory killed tons of fish and had to pay a fine of millions of rupiah. ELTRANS, which works closely with SBSI, helped the workers negotiate with the company, using the environmental issues as leverage. Before negotiations, the company was paying 9,000 rupiah daily for a 10-hour day, but afterward it raised wages to 9,955 rupiah daily for seven hours' work. Happy with the improvement in their hours and wages, the workers then moved from SPSI into SBSI. In this way, with the help of the NGO, workers are moving into independent unions.

Timbul gave another similar example of a rubber-processing factory called PT ADEI (Aceh-Deli Export Import), a plant with 300 workers that also had environmental problems. "Five delegates came to the ELTRANS office to ask for help," said Timbul.

They asked for a wage based on their minimum needs. They were being paid 245,000 rupiah, with no subsidy for housing or food. "I had negotiations with the owner of the factory, and since I know he has a lot of money, I threatened him with bringing an environmental suit, because his company has done a lot of environmental damage. We threatened that we would create an international campaign against his company. We also threatened demonstrations and strikes." Management gave in to these pressures. The factory raised wages to 295,000 rupiah plus 100,000 yearly for housing, 5,000 daily for food, 1,000 daily for transport, and menstrual leave. In addition, workers would be paid the "13th month," that is, one month's pay for the Ramadan holiday. "This strategy only works with the rich factories," said Timbul. After winning that settlement, he suggested that the workers join SBSI, which they agreed to do. Often in these factories, the white-collar or management employees stay in SPSI, while the industrial workers move into SBSI.

SBSI Facing the Future

Rekson told me in 1999 that he believed the union's key task was

> to develop trade-union consciousness through education and training. For almost 30 years, we've been absent from the scene. So the workers' minds have been filled by government's ideas: that unions are no good, that strikes are not necessary, that one must have Pancasila or harmony in union-employer relationships. Look at the results. We have 74 million people in the labor force, and yet only 3 million are organized. Most workers have no protection; they have no collective bargaining agreements. Many of our members cannot read, or have only a primary school education. It's a big job to make them aware of their rights.

"Our next step is internal consolidation, to make my union the biggest and the strongest," says Muchtar. But organizing isn't the union's only goal. "In addition, we want to see the reform of all labor laws—trade union laws, the labor courts, labor rights laws." Clearly, Muchtar also has political ambitions. In mid-1999, the rumor spread that if Megawati became president, she might make Muchtar the Minister of Manpower. Muchtar himself spread the word, delighted in the flattering prospect of being asked to join the first reform cabinet in Indonesia. A union adviser later told me that, in fact, he had thought better of the idea and turned down the offer.

Without a doubt, the SBSI represents the most important independent labor union project in Indonesia, at least in organizational and numerical terms. During the 1990s, Muchtar became the symbol of the struggle for independent unionism in Indonesia around the world. He had the political perspicacity to turn the liability of imprisonment into a political asset, making his name and reputation as a man of principle jailed for his beliefs and activities on behalf of Indonesia's underdogs. Throughout the last decade, whether in jail or out, and especially since the crisis of 1997, Muchtar spoke out against the Suharto regime and the military, and demanded labor rights. At the same time, he found foreign funding from the international labor movement, organized a dedicated staff, and attracted union organizers and activists.

In the late 1990s and especially after the fall of Suharto in 1998, the SBSI was able to rise out of the underground, and began to organize scores of new plant-level unions and register them with the government, as tens of thousands of new members were recruited. Whether the union has 100,000 or 1 million members, it is far and away the largest independent union in the country. Muchtar also expanded the union's activities to include the Bapera cooperative and the founding of the PBN, and later the Sosdem Forum. If the PBN proved an electoral failure, it was nevertheless a bold move that showed Muchtar's commitment to both labor organization and political and economic reform. No other independent labor organization in Indonesia has accomplished as much as Muchtar and the SBSI.

But the union is not without its problems and its difficulties. Muchtar dominates the SBSI almost to the exclusion of its other leaders, such as Sunarty, the national chair. Muchtar's personalistic leadership style and his proprietary attitude toward the union have not only led to problems such as the internal rebellions and splits of 1999, but also and more importantly represent an obstacle to the building of a democratic union. As long as a single, powerful personality so completely dominates the union, the development of a genuinely democratic decision-making process will be hampered. The SBSI has a democratic structure, with its congresses and national board meeting, and majority-rule votes on important matters, but Muchtar monopolizes information and contacts, and controls the staff and leadership in a way that works against a fully democratic union.

The leadership by Muchtar and a largely male staff means that the union conveys a macho image. While women occupy between one-third and one-half of all national leadership posts, and while there are women on the national staff, one tends to see Muchtar and Rekson conferring with other men at union gatherings. SBSI does have women organizers, and does actively recruit women members, some of whom, like Yatini, become organizers. But the union's atmosphere is one of male dominance, if not domination. When I asked a woman NGO activist what she thought of the SBSI, she sighed in exasperation and said, "Gender-blind and gender-biased."

All of that having been said, the SBSI staff, leaders, organizers, and activists have spent 10 years organizing a union in the underground. They are mostly young, enthusiastic, and dedicated people who can fight for their views and make the union more democratic if they so choose. While Muchtar dominates the union through the force of his personality and his centrality to the organization, the SBSI can hardly be called a union with a hardened bureaucracy. But the issue of the union's officialdom also raises another question about the future of the union. The SBSI of the 1990s represented a social movement for labor justice in the process of transforming itself into a standard labor union. Life under a military dictatorship, with high penalties for labor activism—from prison to murder—tended to select out those sincerely dedicated to the cause of labor. In the 1990s, the SBSI acted as a voice for oppressed and exploited workers and attracted workers throughout Indonesia dedicated to the cause of defending workers on the job and in society. Today all of that is changing as the SBSI attempts to win legal registration and negotiate collective bargaining agreements. Legal recognition and union contracts are important both for the union as an organization and for workers, who stand to benefit by written agreements that can codify gradual improvements in their wages, benefits, and conditions. But if legal status and contracts become the be-all and end-all of a union, they threaten to dampen its fighting spirit and to turn it into another institution of Indonesian capitalism.

Muchtar's model of labor unionism has been inspired by European social democracy, or more generally by the kind of labor unions that exist today in capitalist societies such as the European countries or the United States. The historical record of such liberal countries indicates that, under capitalism, labor unions tend toward bureaucratization. First, they exist under one or another system of labor laws meant to institutionalize a union as a hierarchical organization and part of the capitalist system. Second, they make union officials into mediating agents between workers and bosses, and attempt to strike a balance between them. The usual result—we might say the almost universal result—has been the creation of bureaucratic labor unions. Such bureaucratic unions tend quickly to give up their vocation for social justice. They tend to squelch internal democracy, while at the same time becoming the enforcers of the contract. From there, it is not a long step to becoming the employers' enforcer.

How, then, can a union avoid becoming a bureaucratic obstacle to the goal of workers' justice? Only by remaining a social movement in the struggle not only for labor unions and contracts, but also to build a movement for democratic socialism, a society without capital or bureaucracy. In his own way, Muchtar has addressed this issue with the idea of the National Labor Party, modeled after the European labor parties. But European labor parties have never—not even in their youth in the late nineteenth century, and less with every passing decade—established a socialist society. From about the year 1918, European social democracy has adopted the goal of managing capitalism, ostensibly to make it more humane. After World War II, the labor and socialist parties took on the task of constructing the modern welfare state as the expression of that humane capitalism. But the social democratic welfare state never included all of the poor, exploited, and oppressed, and long ago gave up the goal of banishing capitalism, exploitation, and oppression. By the 1980s and 1990s, the European social democracies changed their objectives altogether, and began to become parties dedicated to a neoliberal agenda, giving up on the state regulation and welfare programs that had defined them in their heyday. Muchtar's endorsement of Megawati and the PDI-P, even as she and her party moved to reach a modus vivendi with the military and indicated their willingness to be responsible leaders of a capitalist Indonesia, may indicate the similar trajectory of his politics.

All of this, of course, begs the question of whether Indonesia's military–state capitalist regime can structurally permit such reforms, and of whether its small, powerful, avaricious, and brutal elite will allow them. The Reformasi movement has not yet broken the power of the military-industrial complex and its relationship to the multinational corporations, and that nexus is the tie that holds the entire system together. Will a standard labor union, tending toward bureaucratization, and a moderate European labor party, a party that has yet to be established, have the will and the power to challenge and smash that system? It hardly seems likely that they will. Labor unions and social democratic parties have modest tendencies toward reform. They do not have the revolutionary strategy, agenda, will, and vision necessary to transform such a society and restructure the state. So we turn in the next two chapters to another union-party alliance—between the People's Democratic Party with the National Front of Indonesian Labor Struggle—to see what alternative it offers.

1   Unlike the system in the United States, where students generally take liberal arts courses for four years before spending two years or more in professional specialization, Indonesian students enroll directly in professional programs such as law or medicine.

2   Vedi R. Hadiz, *Workers and the State in New Order Indonesia* (New York: Asia Research Center, Murdoch University, 1997), 145–47.

3   Hadiz, *Workers and the State*, 147–50.

4   Hadiz, *Workers and the State*, 151, 171. See also the appendix to Muchtar Pakpahan, *Rakyat Menggugat* (Jakarta: Pustaka Forum Adil Sejahtera, 1996), "Penutup," 230–63.

5   Pakpahan, *Rakyat Menggugat*.

6   American Center for International Labor Solidarity (ACILS), *Monthly Report* (January 1998), 13.

7   ACILS, *Monthly Report* (March 1998), 11.

8   ACILS, *Monthly Report* (March 1998), 7.

9   ACILS, *Monthly Report* (March 1998), 10.

10   At first both Sri Bintang and Muchtar refused to accept the amnesty, demanding total exoneration instead. Eventually they both accepted the amnesty with the understanding that all other political prisoners would be released in stages and that the government would make a written apology for the acts of the Suharto regime. In fact, however, some political prisoners, such as the PRD leaders, remained in jail, and some are still in prison as of early 2001.

11   ACILS, *Monthly Report* (June 1998), 11.

12   ACILS, *Monthly Report* (July 1998), 12.

13   Author's interview with Rekson Silaban, SBSI International Affairs Director, Jakarta, August 1999.

14   ACILS, *Monthly Report* (September 1998), 14.

15   ACILS, *Monthly Report* (November 1998), 19.

16   ACILS, *Monthly Report* (January 1999), 14.

17   ACILS, *Monthly Report* (February 1999), 19.

18   ACILS, *Monthly Report* (May 1999), 17.

19   SBSI, *Violations of Freedom of Association in 1999* (Jakarta: SBSI, 2000), 49–51. (I use the English language title. The book is bilingual and carries the same title in English and in Bahasa Indonesian.)

20   ACILS, *Monthly Report* (February 1999), 20.

21   Interview with Roger Smith, July 1999, Jakarta.

22   ACILS, "SBSI Congress Report," Jakarta, May 2000. This report is not part of the ACILS monthly reports, but an unsigned and undated manuscript given to me by ACILS staff.

23   "Resolusi" in "Serikat Buruh Kuat, Rakyat Sejahtera: Laporan Pertanggungjawaban," Panitia Kongres Nasional III, Cileungsi Bogor Jawa Barat, April 21–May 1, 2000.

24   The six participating parties are the Indonesian Democratic Alliance
     Party (PADI), Workers Solidarity Party (WSP), People's Party (Murba),
     PRD, Indonesian Workers' Party (PPI), and, of course, the PBN.
25   Letter sent by Muchtar Pakpahan to international invitees to the Social
     Democratic Forum Congress, March 14, 2000.

FNPBI leader Dita Sari addressing a rally. Photo courtesy of FNPBI.

Chapter 8

Dita Sari and the FNPBI

Making Unions a Political Force

When I visited Indonesia in the summer of 1999, the National Front for Indonesian Labor Struggle (FNPBI) still shared offices with one of its affiliates, the Kobar union, located in the town of Depok, a suburb of Jakarta. The fastest and cheapest way to get there was by the light-rail train, so I bought a ticket and boarded the train at Cikini Station. I had an appointment to interview Dita Sari, the union's famous leader, who had only recently been released after spending three years in prison. The Suharto regime jailed her supposedly for insulting the government and for subversion, but in reality for organizing a labor union and leading strikes. Even a year after the fall of the dictator, Dita had languished in prison because of her association with the People's Democratic Party (PRD), a leftist political party made up mostly of students. But now she had been freed, and once again was leading what some thought to be the most dynamic organization in the new independent union movement.

The train to Depok is on a very busy commuter line. Each train coach had four or five oscillating fans on the ceiling, some of them working, which blew a little hot air over the sweltering passengers who sat, or more often stood, sweating beneath them. But the best spot was not under the little fans, but in front of the coach's big double doors, which remained open throughout the trip. There men squatted or stood, smoking clove cigarettes and staring at the passing landscape, cooled by the breeze.

Depok must once have been a small town far from Jakarta, but now it is a suburb on the city's edge. Through the open doors, one could see the neighborhoods, mostly small white houses with tile roofs, but also some rather pathetic little tumble-down buildings. In the open spaces between the houses tropical plants grew. Banana trees casually waved their broad leaves, while the more sedate papaya trees stood at attention.

The car was filled with men, women, and children. Most of the men wore long pants and short-sleeved shirts, though a few wore T-shirts. Only one old man wore a sarong, looking like a relic of the past. The women dressed in a wide variety of fashions. Some women wore a *jilbab,* and a few also wore a longer, even more modest version, a kind of shawl that comes down to the waist. Other women dressed in skirts and blouses, but many wore short-sleeved blouses and blue jeans, and could be taken for young women on the streets of Mexico City or New York.

Boys, some as young as 10 years old, walked through the cars selling candy, cold bottled drinks, newspapers, and toys. Such child labor is widespread in Indonesia, and it has replaced school for many children of the crisis. The vendors shouted out their merchandise: "Cold Pop," "Candy," "Read All About It," or more or less that in Bahasa Indonesian. One man sold a toy, a mechanical centipede that scuttled along the floor of the train. A blind woman passed through the car, singing into an electric amplifier turned up full blast to magnify her weak voice into a shrill scream, accompanied by some terrible imitation of piano bar melodies on a synthesizer. As she moved on through the crowd, another vendor found himself halted. A small boy, maybe nine or 10 years old, with a heavy bucket filled with ice and bottles of water and soft drinks, pressed between several large adults, was unable to move through the car and peddle his wares. He stood and waited patiently for someone to get off the train and open up a space so he could continue his day's work.

The Depok stop is at Guna Dharma University, and I had to walk through the campus to get to my destination. Students walked along together chatting or were sprawled on the steps of one of the buildings, studying or relaxing. While this is a Catholic university, most of the students are Muslim, as I could see from the many women who wore *jilbabs*. Most of the students dressed very casually in blue jeans and sports shirts, though some of the young men wore slacks, and a few women dressed in more expensive, stylish clothes. But unlike Mexico or New York, where young people like these would be playfully pushing and pulling each other, or occasionally embracing and kissing, I saw no physical contact among the Muslim students.

Coming out the other side of Guna Dharma University, I crossed a busy thoroughfare, running between buses and motorcycles, and then entered into one of the narrow lanes of the neighborhood, a little alleyway perhaps 12-feet wide. After walking for a few blocks, I realized that I was lost and stopped at the Wartel, the telephone kiosk, and called the office to ask someone to come help me. A young man who called himself Sangsu came and found me and led me to the nearby union headquarters.

The FNPBI offices then occupied a little house with a small yard on one side where a few scrawny chickens hunted for something to eat. Several stickers had been pasted on the union office door. One read: Koalisi Perempuan Indonesia, the Coalition of Indonesian Women.

Once inside, I saw how small the house was, with only a living room, a kitchen, one bedroom, and a bathroom. The living room served as the principal office of both Kobar and the FNPBI. Two young men were at work on the computer. They shared the only chair, which constituted the office's furniture. One fellow was typing some document into the computer, while the other watched and occasionally pointed at the screen, making some suggestions. A couple of other people were also in the office, one napping on a mattress in the bedroom, and another eating rice and vegetables with chopsticks out of a plastic bowl while watching MTV Asia. We were all introduced to each other and shook hands, and then everyone went back to their activities.

These young people lived and worked in this office almost day and night, coordinating one of the most dynamic forces in the Indonesian labor movement. It seemed hard to believe that this was the headquarters of a labor organization that coordinated half a dozen regional unions, organized dozens of plant-level unions, and sometimes led thousands of workers in strikes and confrontations with the military.

The office had various pictures, posters, and calendars on the walls. One poster over the computer desk read, "Free Xanana Gusmão," referring to the then-imprisoned leader of the East Timor liberation movement. Another poster from the Surabaya Press Club read, "Freedom to get information is every citizen's right." High up on another wall hung a portrait of a young woman, whom I supposed must be Dita Sari, or perhaps Marsinah, the young woman labor organizer who had been murdered by the military a few years ago. But when I asked, no one knew who the woman in the picture was, and they suggested it was an art student's work left behind by the previous owners.

I noticed that on another wall was a calendar with a portrait of Lenin, the Russian revolutionary leader, and on the edge of the page displaying the month of July was the slogan in French: "Le vote ne change rien; la lutte continue" (The vote changes nothing, the struggle continues), which seemed an apt slogan for that moment, shortly after the national elections which had given a plurality of about 35 percent to Megawati Sukarnoputri. After winning that election, Megawati had suddenly been transformed from the leader of the opposition to the dictatorship into a conservative defender of the status quo and, not long after, she became the vice-president in the new Wahid government.

A book lying on the computer desk caught my attention, and I walked over to see what it was: *Lenin on the Trade Unions*. The book was in English, and the title page indicated it had been published by the Moscow Foreign Language Publishing House. I had once read that very edition of the book, in which Lenin argues the need for socialists to organize their own highly disciplined factions within the union, to take control of the unions, and to combat tendencies toward economism or liquidationism, that is, the tendencies of socialist labor union officials to give up the struggle for socialism. Looking down from the calendar on the wall and speaking out of the book on the desk, Lenin was there advising the young Indonesian revolutionaries. I wondered what they made of his advice.

While waiting for Dita Sari, I asked to talk with Augustinus Santoso, one of the FNPBI staff members. He was eating his lunch and watching MTV Asia's "100 Percent Indonesia" show, which blasted rock music in the background. I had the impression he would have preferred watching the young singers and dancers on the screen to talking to a foreign journalist, but he kindly offered to be interviewed, though he continued to glance at the screen out of the corner of his eye throughout the conversation. Agus, as he prefers to be called, a small, lean man with thinning hair, works as the FNPBI secretary of education and propaganda. Then 32 years old, making him five or 10 years older than most of the rest of the staff, he attended the University of Indonesia and studied law, but until now had been a labor activist rather than a lawyer. He explained that he planned to take the bar exam the next time it was offered, because the movement needed legal expertise.

I was curious to know how he became a labor organizer. "As a student, I joined a study club, and we discussed social conditions," he said.

> We talked about the need for action to do something about those conditions. Three years ago, I really got involved in labor issues when I joined up with a friend who was organizing workers. From the University of Indonesia we began to organize workers in many different industries in the Jakarta area.
>
> We met with the workers and discussed with the workers the real conditions of their lives. The workers told us about

their situation, and we explained to them why their conditions weren't improving, and why they would have to do something for themselves. We explained why they couldn't change the conditions by themselves as individuals, but must join with other workers and together deal with the employer. We explained about the workers' position, and the employer's position. We explained that the workers' position was very weak, and they must show their power through a strike. At that time, there were a number of strikes taking place. The strikes were usually over demands for increased wages. Sometimes they won those strikes, but if the unity broke down, then they lost.

Agus was one of hundreds of students throughout Indonesia who had gone to the workers to help them organize with the goal of overthrowing the Suharto government. I asked him about his experience in the strike movements.

"As a student activist, I was personally involved in two strikes," he said.

One took place at the Fajaindo company in 1998. Fajaindo is a zipper company that employs 800 workers, most of them women. The strike lasted three days, and the workers won some of their demands. Another strike was at the HDX Company, which makes tape cassettes. That was a plant with 1,000 workers, again mostly women. The workers struck, won some demands, and lost others. Unfortunately, in both cases, after the strike ended, the employers fired the leaders. At Fajaindo, for example, they fired 10 worker leaders.

While the workers were fired, the students were threatened by the military and finally had to move their union office to another location, Agus explained.

For a few months now, Agus had been working for the FNPBI. "We have our strongest base in North Jakarta, an industrial area mainly made up of garment factories, but that is not a very strategic area since it is too far away from the rest of the city. I am the FNPBI secretary of education and propaganda, and we plan to do mass education among workers, by distributing our bulletin and educating the workers."

Many of the FNPBI staff are former student activists, though some are workers. Sometimes fired workers come to work for the FNPBI, but after a few weeks or months they either find new jobs or return to their villages in the countryside, I was told. Consequently, most of the FNPBI's permanent national staff came from the PRD or from one of the organizations that it originally formed: SMID, founded in 1991; the National Peasant Union (STN), founded in 1993; or the Center for Indonesian Labor Struggle (PPBI), founded in 1994. Those organizations later came together as the People's Democratic Union, and then became the PRD in 1996. Almost all of the young men and women who work with the FNPBI began their political activities as student activists, and then turned to peasant or labor organizing.

The PRD's earlier labor organization, the PPBI had been banned, together with its parent party, after the government-organized riot at the PDI offices in July 1996. Several of the PRD and PPBI leaders had been arrested and jailed. The PRD labor activists had gone underground, and couldn't emerge until many months later. While organizing clandestinely, they had led several strikes and organized some independent unions. They had also met other student and worker activists who had been organizing new unions, and in 1998 brought those groups together as FNPBI. The FNPBI then represents a genuine united front, that is, an alliance between unions with different and independent origins.

In 1999, the FNPBI was made up of several regional affiliates in Sumatra, the Jabotabek area, Jakarta, and its industrial suburbs, Bandung, Semarang, Surakarta, Surabaya, and Bitung.[1] Each of these unions was engaged in organizing local labor unions in plants in its own area.

The affiliated groups represented mostly manufacturing and transport workers, particularly garment workers. Because of the concentration on the garment industry, most of the union's members were women workers, though many men are also involved. The union's key issues have been low wages, job security in the face of widespread layoffs, and firings for union activity. The FNPBI does not organize rural workers, though its sister organization, the STN, does.

Unlike the PPBI, which had formed part of the PRD, the FNPBI has no political affiliation. While activists from the PRD helped to found the FNPBI and several PRD members lead it, the union is organizationally independent. The FNPBI has its own offices and its own staff and publications, and makes decisions through its own leadership bodies. Many other student and worker activists who are not PRD members are members and activists of FNPBI, which, like most labor unions, is open to all workers who wish to join. But, however genuine the organizational independence—and I believe it is quite real—these PRD union organizers think of themselves as revolutionaries and see the FNPBI as part of their revolutionary project. The leaders are PRD members first and FNPBI members second. At the same time, it should be said, they see no contradiction between the two; they are simply two closely related projects for advancing the working class to power.

One PRD leader who works within the FNPBI told me,

> We recruited some workers to the PRD, but only a very small number. We want workers to accept the PRD program, not because they are PRD members, but because they see the PRD program as their own program. We must organize workers and increase their awareness of their conditions, and we want them to understand that those conditions would change if workers joined in the seizure of power. This is the strategy. But tactically, we must organize day to day to solve the workers' problems. Organizing unions and getting collective bargaining agreements is important—but it is not the main goal. Trade union organization is a tactic, but we must link the trade union to economic and political issues. We understand the tendency of trade union organization to lead to "trade unionism." But sometimes we must have moderate demands to meet the lower consciousness of backward workers. After the

workers accept us, then we can educate those workers politically.

The FNPBI functioned in 1999 as a labor union, a social movement, and an incipient political project, a revolutionary political project. Kobar, the flagship of the FNPBI, had been one of the most dynamic new workers' organizations in Indonesia. The AFL-CIO's American Center for International Labor Solidarity (ACILS) in Jakarta, which monitors labor developments throughout the country, reported in July 1998 that Kobar "was arguably the most active union in Jabotabek (Jakarta, Bogor, Tangerang, Bekasi) in terms of mobilization of workers." For example, Kobar brought 1,200 workers from various factories it organizes to demonstrate at the Ministry of Manpower on July 8, 1998. Kobar's supporters demanded a doubling of the minimum wage, an end to military interference in labor disputes, a halt to layoffs, a repeal of the Manpower and Demonstration laws, and an end to collusion between the Ministry of Manpower and the employers. The next day, Kobar carried out a coordinated strike around the same demands at 14 factories in North Jakarta, Tangerang, and Bogor that involved 10,000 workers.[2] The next month, Kobar held training sessions for its members and produced an eight-page newspaper with a circulation of 10,000 that it distributed throughout the Jabotabek industrial area.

In September 1998, Kobar's newspaper was encouraging workers to take advantage of Reformasi and new changes in labor laws to register their independent unions. Employers frequently resisted Kobar's efforts. For example, when Kobar-affiliated workers at PT Polystar attempted to register their independent union with the local Ministry of Manpower office, the ministry informed the company about the existence of the new union. The employer and the government-controlled All-Indonesia Workers' Union (SPSI) then worked together to try to squelch the union through intimidation. The company fired one worker and reported others to the police and military authorities. SPSI officials told the new union's officers that independent unions were banned and that they had better resign. In August 1998, at another factory, PT Osaga Mas Utama, the company posted a notice that "within the grounds of the factory, every employee is prohibited from organizing or engaging in non–work-related activities, except for SPSI." Nevertheless, Kobar continued its organizing efforts in many factories in the Jakarta area. By October 1998, Kobar had succeeded in registering one of its unions at the PT Golden Swallow plant. In November, it registered two others, at PT Fajar Indo and PT Kapasindo. By December, Kobar had registered several other plants in North Jakarta, including PT Binoli, with 400 workers, representing almost the entire workforce; PT Kapasindo I and II; and PT NUP, with 500 members, representing the entire workforce. At the same time, it registered PT Ganda Guna Indonesia in Kalideres and PT Polystar in Bogor. In some plants, Kobar competed with both the SPSI and with the SPSI-Reformasi textile union, the Indonesia Textile, Garment, and Leather Workers' Union, but held its own. Rank-and-file workers responded to Kobar's militant unionism.

But Kobar was not only a labor union; it was also part of a political movement. ACILS reported in November 1998, "Kobar played the most active role of all unions in opposing the Special Session of the MPR" by participating in mass protest from November 10 to 13 and that "Kobar totally rejected the results of the MPR Special Session and called for the establishment of a provisional government to lead Indonesia to democratic elections next year." In the course of the protest, eight Kobar workers were injured, and one was beaten unconscious.[3] Kobar also engaged in other activities demanding a change in labor laws and other government policies. Kobar and the legalized and briefly reactivated PPBI organized a demonstration of hundreds of workers at the Proclamation Monument in Jakarta in September 1998 to declare the establishment of the Indonesian Workers Solidarity Action (ASBI). The new coalition demanded an end to military interference in labor disputes, the repeal of *dwifungsi,* a halt to layoffs, and lower prices.[4]

Kobar took the lead in organizing the FNPBI, drawing together other PRD-inspired labor unions and some independent unions looking for national connections. The FNPBI has tried to reclaim the traditions of the Indonesian and the international labor movement, such as May Day. Since the 1880s, May 1, which commemorates the labor union activists known as the Haymarket Martyrs of Chicago, has been celebrated as international labor day in virtually all countries in the world, except, ironically, the United States, where Labor Day is celebrated in September. In many countries, workers march on May 1 with their union banners and red flags in a show of solidarity and working-class power. Because the Socialist International and later the Communist International generally organized the event, celebration of May Day was prohibited in Indonesia after the overthrow of Sukarno in 1965.

So, determined to take another step to legitimize the labor movement and its radical traditions, some 300 students, NGO activists, and workers rallied on the May 1 weekend at the campus of the University of Indonesia in Central Jakarta in 1999. Students arrived first and forced open the gates of the university so that the workers could join them. A couple of hundred workers from several companies in West and North Jakarta arrived shortly afterwards, wearing red headbands with the words "MAY DAY." Also present were activists from the Jakarta Legal Aid Institute (LBH) and other NGOs that work with labor.

The organizers of the event declared a free speech forum and opened the microphone. A woman factory worker said: "Today is our day. We should unite in our struggle to advance our demands to employers and the government officials who back the employers." She and others put forward the group's demands: a 100 percent pay increase, an end to the firing of workers for union activities, an end to layoffs, a reduction in the prices of basic commodities, and the right to organize labor unions without interference. Students and workers cheered the speakers.

The PRD and the FNPBI had played a key role in organizing

the event, working through the student organizations in which they are influential, such as the Big Family of the University of Indonesia. They had also drawn in labor groups such as the Greater Jakarta Workers' Union and the Workers' Committee for Reform, and they had involved Surya Tjandra, an attorney with LBH. Though the military police questioned the students, none were arrested. The event represented another small victory for the FNPBI.[5]

In 2000, the FNPBI organized a May Day demonstration in Jakarta in which 1,500 workers took part, and it looked as if the celebration of May 1 as international labor day was gradually becoming part of Jakarta's labor union culture.

The activities of the PRD labor activists, first in the PPBI, later in Kobar, and most recently in the FNPBI, have kept them at the forefront of militant labor union activism—and always under the surveillance of the police and military. Dita Sari was not the only PRD labor activist who had been in prison. To be a union activist in Indonesia, and especially a PRD activist, almost certainly led to some sort of run-in with the military. But the student leaders of the FNPBI continued their activities. Driven by their deep political commitment, the worker activists engaged in actions on the job, demonstrated, and struck out of the need to defend themselves from employers and the desire for a decent life. Between the two groups, a bond of mutual respect had developed; they had created a labor union together.

The FNPBI puts opposition to the military's role in labor issues at the center of its agenda, says the youthful Sangsu. The FNPBI calls for an end to *dwifungsi* and for the complete elimination of the military from labor matters. Despite some reforms, says Sangsu, the military frequently intervenes in strikes, it sometimes detains worker leaders and activists, and it frequently interrogates them and thus intimidates them. Historically, the military has been a very repressive force and has arrested, tortured, and sometimes killed worker activists. Sangsu explains that while the Indonesian government signed the convention granting workers the right to strike, "In reality, no right to organize independent labor unions exists. And there is no right to strike." The only union federation that is really tolerated is the SPSI, the government-sponsored labor federation, and that, says Sangsu, is a "yellow union." "Workers," he argues, "cannot build their own independent organizations."

While the FNPBI publicly calls for a united front with other union federations and joins them in temporary alliances and more public coalitions, its leaders are quite critical of rival unions and contemptuous of their leaders. One top FNPBI leader says, "If we joined SBSI, all the vital decisions would be made by Muchtar and the reformists. They claim thousands or millions of workers in their organizations. But they have to prove it. They have to prove that the masses are really there. If they are, we will go there, too. We have 70 or 80 million workers in Indonesia, and how many are really organized? Two million? Or perhaps 5 million? But the rest are not; they are untouched."

Regarding Muchtar Pakpahan and the SBSI, another FNPBI activist says, "The SBSI is an independent union, and so to that extent it is a good development for workers. But the SBSI doesn't really organize the mass of workers." In fact, the SBSI has organized many more workers than the PPBI, Kobar, or the FNPBI, but the activist either doesn't know or doesn't care. He adds, "The SBSI has been built on Muchtar Pakpahan's name and on his fame. The SBSI structure is very elitist. Muchtar Pakpahan and a small number of people in the leadership of the union make all of the decisions. Their character is politically elitist. They just use strikes to increase his popularity." It is difficult to tell whether the young radicals' contempt for Muchtar Pakpahan is a question of generational differences, differences in style and sophistication, or real political differences.

I finished talking with Agus and the others and stepped outside to watch the chickens peck and the construction workers mix mortar. About that time, Dita Sari came along, walking alone down the narrow street, carrying a couple of bundles. She had just come from a meeting with ACILS, which would be giving FNPBI some financial support, and she had been discussing the matter with ACILS chief, Tim Ryan. While she had been in prison, ACILS had helped to fund some FNPBI projects.

"Well," she said, smiling and extending her hand to me, "you're the first *bulai* journalist to come to our office by train. Most of them come in cabs." *Bulai* means albino in Indonesian, but is used to refer to white people, that is, to Caucasians, sometimes in a derogatory way—but in this case it was clearly meant warmly and in fun.

We entered the office and, since there was no furniture, sat on the floor and talked. Agus had finished eating his lunch, and Dita reached over and turned off MTV Asia so we could have a more pleasant conversation. But the roosters she couldn't turn off, and they fought, crowed, and complained throughout the entire interview, sometimes so loudly I could hardly hear her.

Dita told me about growing up the daughter of a Golkar congressional representative, her involvement in the student movement, and her labor organizing activities. She described the workers' miserable conditions, and the strikes for higher wages that she had helped to lead. She talked about her trial and imprisonment, and about all of the support she received from women, workers, and students around the world. She recounted the history of the PPBI and its transformation into the FNPBI, and the new challenges it faced in the post-Suharto era.[6]

Dita looks to the transportation industry as being strategically key. "We will continue targeting transportation and manufacturing, especially textiles and garment," she says.

> Transportation is important strategically because when the workers go on strike and it stops, production in many sectors will be disrupted. The service sector is also important, but we cannot take on that area at this time. We have to think strategically about the sectors where we already have influence. We have a base in manufacturing and transportation. We are still small and must use our energy and resources in the best way.

Asked how her strategy differs from Muchtar Pakpahan's SBSI or from SPSI-Reformasi, Dita answers, "We see the workers' struggle as political and economic. The two cannot be separated. The SBSI does not have a perspective to mobilize the mass of the working class. It is not their tactical priority. Its priorities are more in terms of negotiations and legal advocacy—they are experts at that. But they must combine those skills with mobilizing the workers themselves."

Dita says that the FNPBI is not reluctant to join in coalitions with other unions.

> We recently held a joint meeting of several independent unions, and we formed the Union Solidarity Forum [FSU]. Through FSU we hope to be able to find commonalities between the struggles of the workers represented in our unions, and to come up with common solutions. This will be the first step in developing a close relationship between all of the unions. From now on, the most important thing is to give the best of ourselves to the union movement, instead of trying to badmouth other unions. If another union can do what we cannot do, we must learn from them. I think we can make a confederation of unions with common goals.

But Dita's aspirations go beyond organizing labor unions and winning collective-bargaining agreements, both of which she believes to be very important.

> I have this idea of creating a "labor wing" within the political milieu so we can bargain with the regime and other political forces. Workers can become a force in politics by organizing, speaking, writing, debating, just talking. Reformasi has created lots of new political spaces, and we must take advantage of them. Since Reformasi, things have changed. Now workers must also become a strong force in the political arena, before all the other forces in politics. Such a labor wing would allow the unions a way to draw other political forces closer to the working class.

But she believes that it will only be possible to create such a political force if there is greater unity in the labor movement.

> There have been a lot of polemics between unions. It is not the time to give black names and reputations to unions. We need to create a workers' wing in the political field, a political force that really belongs to workers. This is my principle, that workers' struggles are also political struggles. It cannot be done by the FNPBI, or by SBSI, or by SPSI-Reformasi. It will take all of us. Instead of fighting like political parties, we must work together. People see the political parties fighting, and they say, what's the use? So the unions have to work together to build a political wing. Then, perhaps in 10 or 15 years, building on that, we can establish a labor party. This would be a place for workers to take charge now and maybe later to take power.

In terms of national political parties, Dita remained critical of the whole election process. "Even though we know the [1999 presidential] elections were fraudulent, a lot of people thought the elections were fair because the presence of international observers made them think so. People have illusions, and there is nothing we can do to change it until a new government is in place and we can show the people what kind of government it will be in reality."

Dita told me that in 1999 most Indonesians put their hope in Megawati and the PDI-P.

> Most people supported and still support Megawati and the PDI-P, and they are not willing to do otherwise. It is a matter of time until we can prove to people, so they can see with their own eyes, hear with their own ears, feel with their own bodies, and recognize for themselves that the government will not bring about the changes that they need.
>
> The elections represented a new departure for Indonesia. The people's support for PDI-P is a giant wave, the sea. After PDI-P comes into power, it will be easier to show the people the reality of the situation. We say Megawati won the election because of the votes of the workers, so now she must listen to the workers. We are the workers. We are millions. We build

everything in this society. So we should have a voice in society as a whole.

When I returned to visit Dita and the FNPBI a year later in the summer of 2000, their situation had changed remarkably. The union was housed in new offices in the Tebet district of Jakarta, in a two-story house. The casual student style had been replaced by a more professional organization. In the year and a half after the fall of Suharto, the FNPBI had grown rapidly. At its first congress in the spring of 1999, it had had nine regional affiliates, but it had 15 regional organizations a year later. The FNPBI began with just six affiliated unions in 1999, but had over 20 by the year 2000. Several independent unions organized by workers or local activists had joined Dita, took great pride in her union's accomplishments, and saw its national congress as a milestone.

The FNPBI held its second congress in Salatiga, Central Java, from July 24 to 26, 2000. It was attended by 250 participants from 11 of the federation's 14 regional affiliated organizations. Delegates from far-flung regions such as West Kalimantan and South East Sulawesi were unable to attend because of prohibitive transportation costs. Dita had been unable to attend the founding convention in May 1999—where she was elected chairperson—because she had been in prison at the time. Now she presided over a much larger and more effective federation, one recognized by many of the world's most important labor organizations. The congress opened with greetings from the International Confederation of Free Trade Unions, from the Trade Union Congress of Great Britain, the United Auto Workers of the United States, LO-Norway, the Australian Manufacturing Workers' Union, and the KMU federation of the Philippines.

The second FNPBI congress showed a marked growth in maturity. While Dita and Ilham Syah were reelected to their posts of chair and general secretary, a new leadership team was chosen that incorporated more workers, while a majority of the executive board were women. In most regions, workers now played the leading role in the organization, though students still dominated in Bandung and Surabaya. In little more than a year the FNPBI had transformed itself from a loose front or alliance of independent unions into a labor federation with four levels, all of which would seek registration as legal trade unions.

The union adopted dues of 1,000 rupiah per month, with most of that going to the plant-level union, and only 50 rupiah going to the national federation. The union sets its goals as developing its four levels—plant, industrial zone, province, and national—and organizing in new areas such as Riau, known for its oil fields and refineries. Since most Indonesians continue to work in agriculture, the FNPBI decided to expand its organizing efforts among plantation workers. Finally, the FNPBI adopted a program calling for a 32-hour workweek, a 100-percent increase in the minimum wage, support for continued government subsidies of food and fuel, and a commitment to fight for better labor legislation. The FNPBI also called upon the Indonesian government to give assistance to East Timor to compensate for its destruction by the Indonesian military.[7]

The unions and workers that joined the FNPBI were not radicals like the PRD-affiliated founders of the union. "Mostly they are workers who have heard our name and agree with our opinions," explained Dita. "Or they are workers we have helped who are grateful, thankful, and comfortable with our organization."

How, I asked, was the FNPBI winning these workers over?

> First, we carry out intensive propaganda campaigns where we not only introduce our organization, but also explain our program. And since I was freed from prison, my personal popularity has helped our organization. Second is our direct approach to the masses. Where there are strikes, we try to participate. We offer solidarity, and we introduce our organization. We say, if you need help, just call on us. We distribute our leaflets and pamphlets and explain our views.

When asked to name the biggest challenge her federation faced, Dita explained it was organization:

The biggest challenge is how to coordinate this rapidly grow-ing union effectively. We need to increase the organizational capacity of the union and of the individual leaders and staff members. We need more officials from the regions to help us coordinate. We need a new organization based not on geogra-phy but on industrial sectors.

I think that building a union is not as easy as building a party, because the consciousness is different. In a party, such as the PRD, everyone has the same idea of socialism and de-mocracy.... A union represents workers who are concerned about wages and conditions, but otherwise they do not have the same ideas. So it is a lot harder to organize.

Despite the FNPBI's growing professionalism and its legal activities, the Indonesian government has still refused to recog-nize and register the federation and most of its affiliated unions. High civilian and military leaders within the Indonesian govern-ment still view the FNPBI, with its informal ties to the PRD, as a Communist and subversive organization, and have done every-thing possible to put obstacles in its path. FNPBI activists also face new forms of repression, now that the military has with-drawn from active involvement in most labor conflicts.

"The military has been largely withdrawn from industrial re-lations, but we still face repression," says Dita. The overthrow of Suharto, the loss of East Timor, and the investigations of war crimes and other military misbehavior by the new civilian govern-ment have humiliated the Indonesian military (formerly known as ABRI, and now as the TNI) and driven it back into its bar-racks. But today there are new problems. "Now we face a new phenomenon," says Dita. "The employers are now hiring and paying civilians to protect the company. They hire the unem-ployed to fight the workers. Or they bring in the PDI-P Satgas or the NU's Banser to attack the workers." Since troops are no lon-ger as available as they once were to discipline the working class, employers have increasingly turned to other alternatives. Some companies hire security guards who may be used as armed union busters and strikebreakers. Other companies hire street gangs made up of unemployed neighborhood youth. But the most dangerous development has been the growing role of religious and party paramilitary organizations. The PDI-P has a paramilitary organization known as Satgas that dresses in red and black military uniform. Golkar's youth group, Pemuda Pancasila, also wears military uniforms as it struts through the streets. But the group that has received the most attention and the most criticism is Banser, the paramilitary organization of Nahdlatul Ulama (NU), and the National Awakening Party (PKB) of President Abdurrahman Wahid.

Banser has its origins in NU, Indonesia's largest Muslim organization, with a membership estimated around 30 million. In 1965, with the support of the Indonesian military, the NU youth group Ansor participated in the violent attacks on Communists, labor unionists, and peasant activists, which killed at least 500,000 people. Three years later, in 1968, the NU and Ansor created Banser, short for Barisan Serba Guna, which means all-purpose troops. Banser claims to have 520,000 members, about 170,000 of them in East Java. Most Banser members are agricultural workers; motorcycle, taxi, or truck drivers; public employees; or small businessmen. Many are unemployed workers and peasants. The Banser members wear military uniforms resembling those of Kopassus, Indonesia's special army forces; Kostrad, the army strategic reserves command; the Indonesian Marines; and other military officers. They purchase their own uniforms, and arm themselves with clubs and other weapons.[8]

Throughout the period from 1968 to 1999, Banser was more of a social club than a dangerous paramilitary organization. However, after NU leader Wahid (Gus Dur) created the PKB, Banser became more involved in politics, evolving into something like the party's police. Since Gus Dur's election, the paramilitary troops have become even more active. When Indosiar, the private television station, aired a comedy show that made fun of Gus Dur, protestors, including Banser members in uniform, showed up to protest at the station. In May 2000, when the *Jawa*

Pos newspaper reported on alleged corruption involving NU executives, Banser paramilitary troops "visited" the newspaper. The *Jawa Pos* had reported that NU General Chairman Hasyim Muzadi and Gus Dur's brother, Hasyim Wahid, had been implicated in embezzling about $4 million from Bulog, the State Logistics Agency. The Banser members then occupied the *Jawa Pos* building, forcing the paper to cancel its May 7 edition. After that action, Gus Dur declined to criticize his party's paramilitaries, stating instead that the *Jawa Pos* story had been intended to topple his government.[9]

Labor unions and worker activists have been concerned because Banser and Satgas have been used as strikebreaking forces. Several union officials and workers reported to me that these two paramilitary groups had been used to attack workers' picket lines, attack union offices, and intimidate workers. Ironically, the parent organizations of Satgas and Banser, that is, respectively, the PDI-P and the PKB, are the two most important democratic parties in Indonesia. Yet their paramilitary youth groups engage in activities we associate with right-wing or even fascist parties. Local chapters of these groups rent themselves out as guards for religious and political affairs, and sometimes to employers, and then use the proceeds to buy uniforms and other supplies for their clubs.

When they take on these police functions, the paramilitary organizations usually work closely with the police or military. Whatever the motivation, the rise of these paramilitary organizations represents a dangerous development. We have seen such paramilitary organization in Latin America lead to "death squads" and the torture and murder of labor activists and leftists. The accounts in Indonesia are frighteningly familiar.

The proliferation of all of these forms of organized gangsters, from security guards to party paramilitaries, threatens not only labor unions and workers' rights, but also endangers democracy in Indonesia. Nevertheless, Dita and the FNPBI remain undeterred in their efforts.

Dita and most of the other leaders of the FNPBI represent a student social movement that has attempted to turn itself into a working-class movement, and more recently into a coalition of labor unions and a national labor union coalition. What is equally exciting about their labor movement is its character as a radical social movement with both economic and political aims. The FNPBI has taken several big steps in the process of becoming a genuine labor federation. While originally organized by students, it first recruited labor activists to join in organizing quickie protest strikes, and then convinced them to organize real labor unions. In the last two years the FNPBI has recruited a number of independent unions that had been organized by local activists and workers in various parts of the country. The FNPBI brought those unions together to create a new federation, with local worker leaders, most of them women, on its executive board. More militant and more radical than other unions, the FNPBI faces even greater opposition from the government and employers than the Muchtar Pakpahan's SBSI or unions such as Pak Rustam's TSK-SPSI-R. Nevertheless, the FNPBI has succeeded in registering some independent unions and is negotiating some collective bargaining agreements on the basis of its strength in the plants and in the communities.

The FNPBI's leaders also want to make the union a political force in society. Those who came out of the PRD want to link the labor unions to their project of building a socialist party with the aim of carrying out a revolutionary transformation of Indonesia to make it both a democracy and a socialist society. To understand just what they mean by that, we have to turn to an examination of the PRD itself.

1   The affiliates were the Dewan Buruh Sumatera Utara in Sumatra; the Komite Buruh untuk Aksi Reformasi (Kobar) in the Jabotabek area, Jakarta's and its industrial suburbs; the Solidaritas Buruh Indonesia in Bandung; the Persatuan Buruh Semarang in Semarang; the Pusat Perjuangan Buruh Surakarta in Surakarta; the Pusat Perjuangan Buruh Surabaya in Surabaya; and the Pusat Perjuangan Buruh Bitung in Bitung.

2   American Center for International Labor Solidarity (ACILS), *Monthly Report* (July 1998), 12.

3   ACILS, *Monthly Report* (November 1998), 12.

4   ACILS, *Monthly Report* (September 1998), 16.

5   "300-Strong Rally to Laud Labor Day," *Jakarta Post*, May 3, 1999.

6   Dita Sari's story is told in the last part of Chapter 1 of this book.

7   See ACILS, *Monthly Report* (July 2000), 18–19, which contains a report on the FNPBI second congress.

8   Ainur R. Sophiaan, "Banser Told to Dump Legacy of Militarism, Mob Politics," *Jakarta Post*, June 8, 2000, 5.

9   ACILS, *Monthy Report* (May 2000), 3.

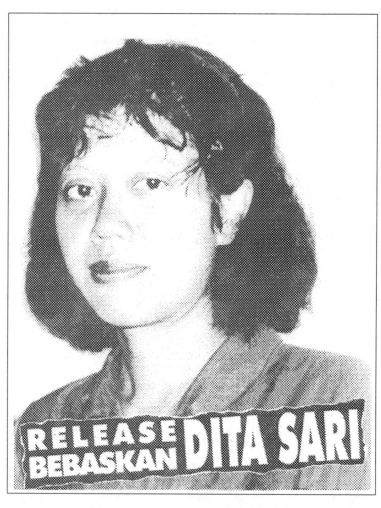

"Jailed for Daring to Struggle." Poster demanding the release of Dita Sari. "Dita Indah Sari — Indonesia's only woman political prisoner today — was sentenced to five years jail on 22 April, 1997. Her 'crime' was daring to fight alongside Indonesian workers struggling for a better life." Poster by Pelayanan Buruh Jakarta.

Chapter 9

The People's Democratic Party

A Socialist Alternative

The People's Democratic Party (PRD) celebrated its third anniversary on the evening of July 22, 1999, in the historic Building of the Generation of 1945. A complex of several buildings, one structure stands surrounded by bronze busts of the nationalist leaders who won independence from the Dutch in August 1949. But on this night in July, another generation—the generation of 1997 one might call them—assembled to commemorate the founding of their party and the overthrow of Suharto, and pledged to end the military regime that still dominated the politics of their country.

The meeting hall upstairs in the main building had chairs for about 150 people, but dozens of others had crowded in, jamming the aisles and standing in the back of the room. Still others filled another room across the hall, and then the landing and the staircase. Perhaps altogether there were 400 people at the event, almost all young men and women in their late teens or early 20s. Probably two-thirds of those in attendance were men dressed casually in blue jeans and T-shirts, some carrying backpacks. Some of the women wore a *jilbab,* but most did not. There were also a few older men and women, and one Catholic nun walked, smiling and waving, through the group. Although a young man, an activist in the PRD, told me that the attendees were not just students, but that some were workers and others had come from organizations of the urban poor, they seemed to be overwhelmingly students.

The PRD is clearly a youth group, a student party. Some of those present wore PRD T-shirts, shirts with PRD patches, or PRD buttons. A few had T-shirts with portraits of Che Guevara, the Argentinian who had thrown in his lot with the Cuban Revolution and had become an icon of revolution and internationalism after his murder in Bolivia. A few people brought video cameras to film the events, and a number of photographers had come, though the mainstream press seemed to ignore the celebration.

At the front of the room hung the PRD flag, a socialist version of the Muslim star and crescent. The flag is a large red banner with a yellow star, the gray gears of a machine in the shape of a crescent, and the number 16, the PRD's place on the ballot in the recent elections. The dozens of people smoking kretek clove cigarettes made the overcrowded room, the 90-degree temperature, and the tropical humidity even more unbearable. The room was almost asphyxiating to me, but the young people present hardly seemed to notice. They had come to celebrate their party, their people, and themselves. They had come to celebrate the coming revolution.

Several young people surrounded an old European man in a wheelchair who had been given a place of honor toward the front of the room. H.J. Princen was a former Dutch soldier who deserted the Dutch Army and joined the Indonesian revolution in the 1940s to help fight for Indonesia's independence from his country. Later, unable to return to the Netherlands, he became an Indonesian citizen. After the fall of Sukarno in 1965, Princen became an outspoken opponent of the Suharto dictatorship. In 1990, he helped to organize the Solidarity trade union, the first attempt at establishing an independent labor union. Since the founding of the PRD in 1997, he had been a strong supporter of the new party. The PRD has also attracted the support of other prominent opponents of the regime, among them Pramoedya Ananta Toer, the famous novelist who spent 14 years in prison, including a long stint on Buru Island.

The meeting began. One after another, various PRD leaders, all young men and women, rose and spoke, denouncing the former Suharto regime, attacking the still powerful ruling party, Golkar, and demanding an end to *dwifungsi*. Periodically everyone rose and chanted "End *dwifungsi* now!" with raised fists. Speakers also emphasized the need to involve not only students, but also peasants, workers, and the urban poor in a struggle for genuine democracy. This was a student group aiming at developing a broad popular movement and organizing a working-class party.

On the occasion of its third birthday, the PRD received fraternal greetings from the Democratic Socialist Party (DSP) of Australia and from Solidarity, a socialist group from the United States. Delegates from the dissident nationalist movements of East Timor, Aceh, and West Papua (Irian Jaya) also brought their salutations. At the time of a referendum on independence for East Timor, the PRD supported self-determination. The party has also called for an end to military repression in Aceh and West Papua.

Plates of yellow rice, a traditional Javanese ceremonial food, were given to several people as a symbol of recognition and appreciation. Jefri Aries Linggu, a PRD activist who had been beaten by the military and suffered permanent brain damage, was one of those recognized. Another PRD member accepted a bag of rice on behalf of four party members who had been disappeared and murdered by Kopassus, a special Indonesian military unit dedicated to covert operations and repressing radicals. The military had admitted that General Prabowo and Kopassus had "mistakenly" carried out an order from an unnamed higher officer to kill the PRD members.

The group stood to sing its anthem, "Revolution Until Death," with arms raised and fists clenched. The meeting upstairs ended with the singing of another PRD hymn, "Blood of Struggle." Still, the ceremonies continued. Several young men and women distributed candles, and then one candle lit the other until one thought the whole hall would soon be ablaze. The group marched out of the building and into the courtyard for more speeches, short political plays, and revolutionary poetry.

Light from the candles of the socialist revolutionaries of 1997 shone on the bronze busts of the nationalist revolutionary leaders of 1945. Young men and women held up the light of the present to the faces of the dead men of the past. A poet spoke, the young people cheered, and the meeting finally ended in another chant and one last song, and then they all drifted out onto the boulevard and back into the multi-millions of Jakarta.

If there is going to be another wave of radical upheaval in Indonesia to complete the process of reform begun in 1997, the PRD intends to play a role in it. If there is going to be a socialist revolution in Indonesia—the idea sounds like an anachronism at the beginning of the twenty-first century, after so many counter-revolutions and reactionary developments—then the PRD is the one group that aspires to lead it.

A Different Kind of Party

The PRD represents a response to the Indonesian economic and political crisis that is qualitatively different from that of the NGOs, labor unions, and labor parties considered so far. While all of those organizations are attempting to organize peasants, workers, and women, as well as other oppressed groups, and working to protect the oppressed and to ameliorate the lot of the majority of the Indonesian people—and while some of those organizations call for an end to *dwifungsi*—no other organization in Indonesia has so consistently and actively opposed the role of the military in state and society. No other organization calls for such a complete transformation of Indonesian politics and society.

Nearly all of the parties formed in the wake of the fall of the New Order were exclusively electoral organizations, aiming at electing their candidates to office. The National Labor Party

(PBN) of Muchtar Pakpahan, in addition to running candidates for office, hoped to spur the organization of workers into its sister labor federation, the Indonesian Prosperity Labor Union (SBSI). In addition to taking its electoral activities quite seriously and striving to be at the center of the unions it had inspired—which were later gathered together as the National Front of Indonesian Labor Organizations (FNPBI)—the PRD aspires to be the party of all the working people of Indonesia.

The PRD takes the position that it fights today for a social democratic program, for democracy and social improvements for the masses, and that it will fight for more radical change in the future. In a society that has proscribed Communism and socialism, to take up the fight for social democracy represents a daring and radical act. The very existence of the PRD as a legal political party expands the political spectrum and shifts it to the left. The PRD, with its social democratic definition, is far more grassroots, democratic, egalitarian, and activist than any other political organization in Indonesia.

The PRD presents a radical vision of working people and citizens democratically organizing both the economy and politics. Though they do not themselves use the word, some would call such a vision revolutionary socialism.

At the same time that it has inspired thousands of students and other young people with a radical vision in the aftermath of the fall of Suharto, the economic crisis, and the first year of a quasi-democratic parliamentary democracy, the PRD pursued a cautious strategy. While mobilizing students against Golkar, *dwifungsi,* and the military, the PRD moved to shore up the existing semi-democratic system, and even entered into an alliance with President Abdurraman Wahid (Gus Dur) and his National Awakening Party (PKB). The PRD's support for Gus Dur and the parliamentary system was based both on its theoretical view that Indonesia's "feudal" military regime had to be replaced by democracy before there could be a struggle for socialism, and on its perception that in practice Indonesia's fragile democracy

was threatened by a return of the military or a right-wing fundamentalist Muslim movement.

The Origins of the PRD

Unlike Asian, European, or Latin American socialist and Communist parties that trace their lineage back to the late nineteenth
and early twentieth centuries, the PRD has grown up as a new socialist party out of the experiences of the last 20 or 30 years. As
discussed earlier, the Indonesian Communist Party (PKI), which
had been founded in 1920 and had been a significant force in Indonesia between the 1920s and the 1960s, was crushed by the reactionary terror of 1965 in which Sukarno was overthrown and at
least half a million people lost their lives. Suharto and the New
Order regime not only outlawed Communist organizations, but
also outlawed Communist and socialist ideology. Communist
books were burned, and new ones were banned. Between 1965
and the fall of Suharto in 1997, at least two generations of people
were raised in Indonesia with virtually no exposure to leftist
ideas. The Suharto regime largely succeeded in eliminating socialist organization and ideology from Indonesia.

Because the PKI was destroyed, an Indonesian left had to be
created on a new political basis. After 1965, neither Soviet Stalinism nor Chinese Maoism had any direct influence in Indonesia;
nor did the followers of the dissident Indonesian Communist
Tan Malaka, or any other Indonesian leftists for that matter.
Communism was dead. When some 25 years later Indonesian
student radicals began to find their way to socialism in the late
1970s and early 1980s, they did so on a new and independent basis. The students' search for socialism would lead to the rediscov-
ery of revolutionary Marxism and the founding of the PRD.

The Student Movement in Search of a Theory

Beginning in the early 1970s, successive waves of student protests questioned the legitimacy of the Suharto regime and demanded greater democracy and even an end to the dictatorship.
Student upheavals in late 1973 and early 1974 were violently sup-

pressed by the government, but broke out again just four years later. The government also crushed the 1978 student movement, though many veterans of those years later became active as reformers in Indonesian NGOs. A few of the students who had participated in the movements of 1978 became radicalized and exposed to socialist or Communist ideas of one sort or another. In the early 1980s, they formed student study clubs and began to investigate various socialist theories. Out of the student study clubs came the PRD.

Hendrik Kuok, the PRD's representative to the 1999 Elections Commission, the multiparty commission that oversaw the 1997 elections, explained how this happened:

> A few former activists returned to Indonesia from the United States, and they brought with them a "new theory." Actually, dependency theory was an old theory in other countries, but it was new to us in Indonesia. This theory was introduced by Arief Budiman, who had studied at Harvard University, and by Adi Sasono and others like them. Since then, Budiman has become pro–International Monetary Fund and World Bank, and Adi Sasono has become a minister in the government.

Whatever became of them afterward, those academics introduced a theoretical framework for trying to understand Indonesia's place in the world of capitalism and the reasons for its repressive dictatorship, a tool that gave the students a way to begin to grapple with their nation's problems. First developed in the late 1950s and 1960s by theorists such as Paul A. Baran, Andre Gunder Frank, Pierre Jalee, A. Emmanuel, and Samir Amin, and originally applied to the former French colonies and to Latin America, dependency theory argued that monopoly capital in the metropolitan states increasingly dominated and controlled third world countries through mechanisms of neocolonialism. The metropolitan monopoly capitalists did not export capital to develop industry in the third world, said the dependency theorists; they only encouraged the development of extractive industries such as mining, oil drilling, logging, or the production of certain agricultural products. Metropolitan monopoly capital tended to "underdevelop" or to distort the development of its neocolonies. Only a socialist revolution could end the imperialist domination and the structural deformation, distortion, and underdevelopment of the third world. Many of these theorists put their hope in a third-world socialist revolution such as those that had taken place in China, Vietnam, or Cuba.[1]

The attractions of this theory to the Indonesian students are apparent. Here was a theory that seemed to explain how the Netherlands, Japan, the United States, and other capitalist countries could dominate Indonesia. Moreover, the theory tended to give a central role to third-world peoples and looked to the Asian revolutions in China and Vietnam as the vanguard of progressive forces. But it soon became apparent to Indonesian students that this theory did not apply to their country, at least not anymore. While it was true that Indonesia historically had been a producer of raw materials for the developed world, Indonesia had been the locus of an enormous amount of foreign direct investment by capital from Singapore, Hong Kong, Taiwan, Japan, Europe, and the United States at least since the early 1980s. Multinational corporations had moved into the country to build enormous factories, producing textiles, garments and shoes, electronics, and auto parts. Just as the Indonesian students encountered dependency theory, it no longer seemed to explain their world.

In some places, the study clubs first encountered the theories of the Frankfurt School, the Hegelian Marxists who emphasized the role of capitalist culture in controlling class conflict. Amir, one of the principal leaders and theoreticians of the PRD, remembered that some of his professors had first introduced one of the study groups to the Frankfurt School. The Frankfurt School had first arisen at the Institute for Social Research in Frankfurt, Germany, in the 1930s. As Hitler and the Nazis rose to power in Germany—and Stalin consolidated his bureaucratic counter-revolution in the Soviet Union—the Frankfurt School intellectuals were horrified by capitalism's apparent transforma-

tion into systems of totalitarian control, but also increasingly dis-
illusioned with the revolutionary potential of the working class.
In general, these writers—Theodor Adorno, Max Horkheimer,
Franz Neumann, and Herbert Marcuse—turned away from the
Marxist emphasis on economics and politics to focus on the role
of culture, ideology, and psychology in controlling society's dissi-
dents and muting class consciousness. By the 1960s, Marcuse, for
example, no longer looked to the working class to lead a revolution, but turned instead to the lumpen-proletariat, ghetto gangs,
or students.[2] But if the Frankfurt School seemed to explain a society like the United States, where millions of workers lived a
middle-class lifestyle, it was less useful for understanding Indonesia, where workers worked or lived in conditions much like those
Marx and Engels had described in nineteenth-century England.
While the Indonesian students learned much from their studies
of dependency theorists and the Frankfurt School, all of this
study tended to lead them back to what they came to call "the
classics," Marx, Engels, Lenin, Stalin, and Mao. Surprisingly,
Trotsky was not then on their list, perhaps because of the historical weakness of the Trotskyist movement throughout the world,
and in Asia in particular. Only later did the student activists dis-
cover Trotsky through their contacts with Australian, U.S., and
European socialists.

But how could they read those classics, which were banned
in Indonesia. Owning a book by Marx, Lenin, or Mao could lead
to the charge of Communist subversion, punishable by death.
One had to get the books, but what was to be done?

Amir, PRD Founder and Leader

Amir, one of the PRD's leading intellectuals, was the driving
force behind organizing the study of "the classics." A
young-looking man with a clean-shaven face and a crew cut who
dresses in blue jeans and a T-shirt, Amir has spent the last 25
years as a radical and then a revolutionary.

"I was born in 1955 in Ceribon," says Amir, at 44 by far the
oldest of the PRD leaders. He adds,

but my family moved to Bandung shortly after I was born. I
have some Chinese blood. My grandmother ran away from
home to marry my Indonesian grandfather. People say we
have noble blood in our family, but I have always been poor.
My family was Muslim, but not religious.

My father, my mother's third husband, came from South
Sumatra. He later went to West Java where he was a guerrilla
fighter in the national revolution. He became an army intelligence instructor, but retired from the military early because of
the corruption. My mother later divorced him and then
worked in a student dormitory. As a child, I was poor and had
to do odd jobs such as sell newspapers. My family was so poor
that I was sent out to live with other family members. Every
year I had a different family, sometimes in different cities. I
sometimes lived with families that were not even related to us.

Because of my family situation, I went to high school for a
while in Bandung, then in Jakarta, and then back to Bandung,
where I graduated. While I was in high school, someone in the
student movement gave me a pamphlet that talked about our
previous President Suharto's wealth.

With his mother's help, Amir was able to attend college.

I took the exams to enter the University of Indonesia, and I
had to choose one of five state university campuses. I chose to
study political science at Gadjah Mada University. But my
mother said, "I won't pay for you to go into politics, because
politics is dirty. I won't give you money for that." So, I entered
the Christian University of Indonesia instead. I chose to study
management, because at that time I thought that poverty was
due to mismanagement.

Amir went off to college at a critical moment, the peak of
university protests. "In 1974, I became involved in the student
movement, and I was chosen as a courier to take a code to people
in the provinces. The codes were centralized in Java, and we had
to take them to the provinces so people could communicate. But
the military came to my place and searched me, and after that I
left school."

After leaving school in 1974, Amir worked a series of odd jobs and even engaged in criminal activities. "I worked as carpenter's assistant, a petty drug dealer selling morphine and heroin, and later as a truck driver." But, driven by a thirst for knowledge and a desire for justice, Amir returned to the university in 1978. "Just as I got back to school, there was another student movement. We failed again; we were defeated again."

Still, Amir continued his studies. "In 1983, I dropped economics at the Christian University of Indonesia and moved to the University of Indonesia, where I studied history. A professor of Chinese literature gave me Mao Tse-tung's books to read, and I studied Mao." The encounter with Mao's writings was the beginning of Amir's long study of Marxism.

Mao, a leader of the Chinese Revolution of 1949, had developed a theory and practice of political and social revolution that, while it had its origins in Marxism, eventually diverged and finally departed radically from it. After the failure of a workers' revolution in China in 1927, Mao retreated to the countryside and organized a Communist-led national liberation army. Mao's army led the Chinese peasants to fight against the great landlords and warlords and to defeat the Kuomintang, the reactionary nationalist government. After the revolution of 1949, Mao and the Communist Party established a Stalinist-style one-party state in China.

But could Mao's revolutionary approach work in Indonesia? Unlike China, Indonesia had no landlords or warlords. With the exception of the Dutch and later state plantations, some of the land owned by Islamic schools, and some corporate plantations on Sumatra, there were few big landlords in Indonesia. Most peasants were parcelary farmers with small holdings of between about one-half and three hectares. On Java, even the wealthiest farmers had only about four or five times as much land as the poorest farmers. The kind of peasant revolution against the great landlords that Mao led in China did not seem to have much of a future in Indonesia. Moreover, while Mao did carry out a successful political and social revolution that swept away the old regime and laid the basis for modernization, at no point in modern China's history did Maoism lead to anything even remotely resembling either democracy or socialism. Today it seems quite clear that Mao's modernizing revolution laid the basis for a transition to authoritarian capitalism. But for the Indonesian students at that time, study of the classics began with Mao, and he led back to Stalin, who led to Lenin, and Lenin led to Marx. The trajectory of their study led from socialism's totalitarian present to its democratic origins.

What Is to Be Done?

"With my friends, I set up study clubs," Amir explains:

> Study clubs were the only alternative for us because the government had dismantled the student unions. There were two kinds of study clubs, and there was a division between us. Some clubs were academic study clubs, and others were in the tradition of what we call the Indonesian study club. The Indonesian study clubs published newspapers and bulletins; the academic study clubs did not. The Indonesian study clubs talked about politics and workers' strikes, and criticized the government, but the academic study clubs never did. Our club was in the Indonesian study club tradition.
>
> So that was the first split, between the academic study clubs and the Indonesian study clubs. But then we split again. We decided that we had to be democratic, and we had to decide what we would read. Some just wanted to read contemporary books: Andre Gunder Frank, Henrique Cardoso, the Brazilian dependency theorist, or the Frankfurt School. But some of us wanted to read what we called classic books: Mao Tse-tung, Marx and Engels, Lenin, and books by Indonesian Communists. So we split again.
>
> We had a hard time getting the classic books, since they had been banned in Indonesia. How did we get them? Well, we would go the secondhand book stores and comb through them until we found one.

But it was hard to keep the study groups going. Periodically the government would repress the student study clubs; the leaders would be detained and perhaps jailed or even tortured. The students' books, the rare and cherished classics, would be confiscated and taken away as evidence, or simply because they were banned. "But," Amir says, chuckling, "the corrupt district attorneys would take them back to the secondhand book stores to sell. So within a few weeks, we would go to the bookstores, comb through the shelves, and buy them back. This happened more than once."

But there were also other ways to get proscribed books, he explains. "Sometimes we went and talked to the Jesuits, and asked them when they went abroad if they would buy us books. They would say, 'Well, we'll buy you books, but not the classics.' They were afraid that they would get in trouble, too." But perhaps sometimes the Jesuits, against their better judgment and at the risk of their freedom, brought back one or two of the classics.

The study of the classics led the Indonesian students back to the great Russian revolutionary Vladimir Lenin and particularly to Lenin's most famous and most controversial work, *What Is to Be Done? Burning Questions of Our Movement.* Lenin had argued that a socialist party should be made up of professional revolutionaries operating under the direction of a centralized organization. While those of us living in other countries may read Lenin as an interesting historical document, Indonesian students reading Lenin's *What Is to Be Done?* felt as if they were reading about their own country and their own movement. After all, they lived under what was virtually a monarchy. They had been student radicals like Lenin and his comrades. They had made contacts with factory workers and had helped them to begin to organize labor unions. They had seen some people begin to work with labor unions and become completely engrossed in that work, to the exclusion of building a revolutionary movement. So, the students asked, like Lenin before them: "What is to be done?"

"We split after reading Lenin's *What Is to Be Done?*" Amir explained.

Some of us decided we were Leninists, and some of our friends weren't Leninists. But being a Leninist had practical implications. The days of their student study circles were over, because for Leninists the key issue was the creation of a party of professional revolutionaries. It was time to organize a party. So, between 1983 and 1985, we set up what we called a Marxist-Leninist pre-party formation. Then we dispersed to different cities ... no, dispersed is not the right word; we deployed our members to different cities to organize. My friends asked me to go to Jogjakarta.

I went to Jogjakarta and organized at the Universitas Islam Indonesia, because at that time it was more radical than Gada Madja University. Because I was going there, I had to read religious books in order to smash ahistorical religious dogmatism. I read the Koran. I studied the Pakistani Islamic modernist Fazlur Rachman, a Muslim writer who became a "Chicago boy." I read Ashghar Ali Egineer. After that, I read the Islamic Communist Hadji Misbach, who says, "You're not a Muslim if you're not Communist."

Then our pre-party formation entered into a debate on the question of whether or not it was time to enter into action. But at that time, in 1985, I had to go to the United States to help my sister. Her husband had died of cancer, and I needed to be with her. While there, I went to Tulsa University as an international student. I studied English, and I enrolled in classes, but I never attended them. I just went to the library and read. When I returned to Indonesia, our group decided to send me to the Philippines to study the movement there.

Into the Revolution in the Philippines

In the early 1980s, the Philippines had the fastest growing revolutionary movement in the world, led by the Communist Party of the Philippines (CPP) and the thousands of soldiers in its New People's Army (NPA). The Philippines was relatively close by, virtually part of the same chain of islands; most Filipinos were of the same ethnic stock as many Indonesians; and some spoke similar languages. Like the Indonesians who had been ruled by the Dutch, the Filipinos also shared a history of imperialism, having been ruled by Spain and the United States. Both Indonesia and the Philippines had become independent at the end of World War II, and later both had fallen under the rule of powerful dictators, Suharto in Indonesia and Ferdinand Marcos in the Philippines. But while Suharto had succeeded in putting down the student movement in the early 1970s in Indonesia, students in the Philippines established links with peasants and workers and had built a powerful revolutionary movement to challenge the Marcos dictatorship.

The revolutionary movement in the Philippines was Maoist, with its origins going back more than two decades. During the early 1960s, the Soviet Union and China began to come into conflict, and those conflicts spilled over into the Communist Parties of many countries. The Chinese argued that the Soviet Union's bureaucracy had carried out a quiet capitalist counter-revolution in Russia, while in China, they claimed, Mao's revolutionary Red Guard kept any such thing from taking place. While in fact neither the Soviet Union nor China had much to do with socialism and had far more in common with capitalism, the image that China cultivated of an anti-bureaucratic socialist revolution held an attraction for young people around the world. In many countries, the Communist Parties split, and young people went off to found new parties, often called Maoist or Marxist-Leninist.

In the Philippines, an intellectual named Jose Maria Sison left the old pro-Soviet Communist Party, the Partido Komunista ng Pilipinas (PKP), to found a new Maoist party, the CPP. The CPP was founded in the province of Pangasinan on the island of Luzon on December 26, 1968, calling itself a party of Marxist-Leninist-Mao-Tse-tung Thought. During the 1970s, as Mao embraced Richard Nixon and China became an ally of the United States, the CPP dropped its Chinese connection, if not all of its Maoist ideology. Shortly thereafter, in March 1969, the CPP established the NPA as its fighting arm, under the leadership of Bernabe Buscayno, better known as Kumander Dante. The NPA began with just 35 soldiers, but it had 25,000 full-time fighters by the early 1980s. At about the same time, the CPP established the so-called National Democratic Front (NDF), though it was not really a united front of independent organizations. Later the party organized a peasants' union, a teachers' union, an artists' union, and a labor union federation, as well as a student and youth organization, a women's organization, and organizations for Christians. By 1985, the CPP was estimated to have not only 25,000 fighters, but as many as 1.5 million sympathizers and influence over 20 percent of the population of the Philippines. No other revolutionary organization espousing a socialist or Communist program has experienced such remarkable growth in recent memory.

Amir had gone to the Philippines in the mid-1980s while the CCP was quite influential. He joined both the party and the NPA. "My Indonesian organization asked that I join the party and that I get military training and fight in at least one battle. So I received military training, and in fact I fought in two battles." While he does not say much about it, participating in the CPP and the NPA must have had an enormous impact on his political views at the time. His participation in the CPP had given him a taste of what it meant to be part of a mass revolutionary party in a nation in crisis, something most of his comrades had only dreamed about. In any case, the CPP's conception of building a revolutionary party had become an important influence within the Indonesian radical student movement.

But the CPP lost its influence suddenly and sharply in 1986. The "people's power" movement led by Corazon C. Aquino was growing, the United States was withdrawing its support for the dictator, and many Filipinos felt that the time for change had come. In late 1985, Marcos called for national elections to be held in February 1986, taking the CPP by surprise. While other groups in the opposition greeted the elections as an opportunity, the CPP believed they would be a farce controlled by Marcos, the military, election boards, and the mass media. Consequently, the CPP leadership decided to organize a boycott of the elections.

While most dissident groups moved toward the electoral option, the CPP moved away. Thus the CPP's boycott quickly cut them off from the rest of the political opposition movement, and more important, from the majority of the people of the Philippines.

After Aquino won the election, she released CCP leader Sison from prison and her government entered into a ceasefire with the NPA that lasted from November 1986 to January 1987. During that time, the CPP began to participate in elections, but by then it was too late. Many local notables began to move toward the government, and the CPP's popular support was drying up. The party had become separated from the mainstream of the opposition and was quickly losing its influence. After the ceasefire broke down, Aquino and her chief of staff, Fidel Ramos, launched an intense and systematic attack on the NPA, a far more successful offensive than any conducted under Marcos. With U.S. support, the offensive, combined with the strategy of "low-intensity conflict"—economic, political, and psychological pressures, combined with the use of unofficial paramilitary organizations—began to turn the tide against the CPP. By the early 1990s, the CPP's power and influence had been seriously reduced; it was no longer a significant factor in national politics.[3] But by then Amir had returned to Indonesia.

While Amir was gone, the student groups continued to develop. "From the middle of the 1980s, we began to turn to action," Ma'ruf, another PRD leader, told me. "We established student action committees. We took up student issues such as student fees, students' rights, and academic freedom. We also began to take up social issues." Many students became activists and gradually became involved in the new movement of the NGOs.

"I returned to Indonesia, and our group split again, this time over the issue of the NGOs," said Amir.

> That year, 1987, was the moment when the NGOs mushroomed. In 1987, there were some 1,400 NGOs, excluding those we called "red plate" NGOs, which had been created by the government. Most of our comrades were involved in the

NGOs, bringing charity to the villages, working on human rights, or helping with women's organizations. We concluded that it was difficult to radicalize the NGOs. We believed that we had to create the political conditions that would make the NGOs more radical.

The NGOs were good for reaching the masses, because they had so many links throughout society. But, we told our friends, "You are not the head of the NGO. The NGOs are not democratic organizations. If you organize the masses, you will be fired." As we saw it, the NGOs absorbed idealistic people and took them out of the movement. So we split again, and this time there were only two of us left: I and one of my friends. So it was very frustrating.

The NGO debate virtually destroyed that particular generation's party-building efforts. The student activists went their separate ways, most of them into the NGOs. As Amir says, "We were two people beginning again from nothing. My friend went to Jakarta, and I went to Jogjakarta, and we started all over again, slowly, step by step, setting up study clubs again."

The Turn to Agitation

Within a year or two, Amir and his only remaining comrade had rebuilt their study clubs. They revisited the debate over Leninism. Then, during the next five years, between about 1987 and 1993, they not only built up the study clubs, but also began to establish a network of activists. Activism represented a new stage for the Indonesian student movement. "We concluded that it was time to move to practice, to direct action—but we knew the brutal character of the military. So we decided to engage in direct action over local issues on campus," says Amir.

> The biggest victory of the New Order had been to crush the militancy and radicalism of the people. Compare the situation today with that of the period of the Indonesian Revolution when people would fight the military without guns. One man with a rifle would be followed by an unarmed man, and when the man with [the] gun fell, his friend would cry out, "Are you

dead yet? Or are you still alive?" And, if he was dead, the other would take his gun and continue the fight. That courage which existed during the Indonesian Revolution was lost under the New Order. We had to recreate that courage, but we had to begin with local issues.

So the study groups that Amir had organized and led began to deal with local issues.

We took up tuition fees or decadent professors. We went after professors who drank and went out with women, and appeared in class for only one hour and then left the class in the hands of the teaching assistant. We went after professors who developed university projects with private corporations, and then took the money for themselves. We actually investigated those professors, just like the police. We waited at the professor's house early in the morning to see where he went, just like the military intelligence. Then we would leaflet in the restrooms with two or three other comrades to protect us.

Student activism grew gradually at various university campuses. By 1991, the movement was strong enough to call a convention and establish a national organization, Students in Solidarity for Democracy in Indonesia (SMID). SMID chapters were organized on various campuses. The organization produced leaflets and pamphlets, and published a magazine, *Ablaze: Critical and Creative Reflections*. The magazine's reflections on Indonesian society and politics, attacking the Suharto dictatorship and the military, were red hot stuff.

The next step, Amir explains, was to take the movement off the campuses and into the society. Women students first took that step.

Women students had also became involved, and with them we created Gerakan Kesadaran Perempuan, or the Movement of Conscious Women. They proposed direct action off campus to defend in court a woman who had burned her husband. They said that she had not done it because she was brutal or sadistic, but actually it was her husband who had beaten her.

But, they said, he was not brutal or sadistic either. He became sadistic only after he lost his job. So they blamed the economic conditions, and they blamed the government for creating those economic conditions.

It surprised us when the judge after hearing those arguments, said, "You are like the Communists." We had never come upon such a clever government official before. There was no jury trial, and the woman was found guilty and punished by the judge. The military broke up the Movement of Conscious Women, but there were no injuries.

The student movement had ventured off campus and survived.

Their confidence boosted by their successful venture into the broader world, the students began to take up other projects. Amir remembers, "We began to defend people who lost their land in the Borobudur Temple area." Borobudur is a Buddhist temple built by the Sailendra dynasty on the plain of Kedu in Central Java between 750 and 850 A.D. After the fall of that civilization, the temple was abandoned, buried, and consigned to oblivion for hundreds of years. Sir Thomas Stamford Raffles, the British governor of Java during the brief British interlude, uncovered the temple in 1815. Since then, there have been a variety of restorations. Borobudur represents one of the greatest religious monuments on earth, in a class with the pyramids of Egypt, and certainly deserved attention. After Suharto came to power, the government, with assistance from the United Nations, turned the temple into a tourist attraction. In the judgement of some archaeologists, the government has also done significant damage by altering its original setting, including demolishing some nearby ancient buildings to put up tourist facilities.

One of the victims of this cultural project was the local peasantry that had farmed in the vicinity of the ruin. "The government confiscated their land and paid them very little in compensation, all in order to develop the temple area for tourism. So we organized protests." The government responded by attempting to implicate the student protestors in a murder. "Someone put the body of a dead man—a [body] covered with tattoos, probably the body of a street person—in front of the house of an activist, to intimidate us."

Ecological and peasant concerns combined in student protests over other issues. "We also defended peasants in Kedung Omba. The government, with financing from the World Bank, built a big dam there, and kicked the people out, again with very low compensation. We organized about 100 students for a 'long march' to the village. This became a big international issue—and then the NGOs came. We had opened up the political space, but they got more funding. That's why we call them political parasites," says Amir.

In their work at Borobudur and Kedung Omba, student activists had begun to make links with the peasantry and had even begun to lead peasant protests. Hendrik Kuok explains the next step:

> We had organized SMID for the students in 1991. Our second organization was the National Peasant Union (STN), founded in 1993. Students had been organizing with peasants to defend their land in Central Java, East Java, and Sumatra. In the course of this organizing, we met Imam Bui Sanyoto, a peasant leader from Ambarawa, Central Java. He had been in the Indonesian Communist Party and had been exiled in 1965 to Buru Island. When he got out of prison, he became an activist again and a peasant leader, and we worked with him to organize the STN. He became the head of the organization.

"Because we went to the peasants, it might seem like we're Maoists," says Amir, "but it was only a tactical thing. We know we have to go to the workers—but we are also aware of how the government guards the industrialization project. So we had to go to the students and peasants *first* in order to change the political atmosphere. *Then* we could go to the workers."

While the student movement had begun to go off campus and into society, the students still hesitated to create permanent organizations, Amir explained. "We knew that creating permanent organizations was dangerous—so between 1987 and 1993 we created temporary organizations, what we call Komite Komite Aksi, or action committees. They were formed around one action, and then, after that action, they disbanded."

From work with peasants, the students began to turn to the working class.

> In 1993, we carried out a deeper analysis of labor issues. There were 4 million industrial workers in Jabotabek, which includes Jakarta and the suburbs of Bogor, Tangerang, and Bekasi. We saw that in 1993 there were 1,240 strikes nationally, about 80 percent of them in Java and about 60 percent in Jabotabek, the industrial suburbs of Jakarta. There was a time when one strike involved thousands of workers, and the capitalists lost billions of rupiah per day. In 1993, there were 87 million workers, including agricultural workers, in the entire country. So, seeing this level of worker resistance, we deployed most of the prepared comrades to industrial areas.

The students were radicals and many of them were revolutionaries. Many had spent years studying the great debates of revolutionary literature from Misbach and Lenin to Mao and Sison. Still the students were completely unprepared for their encounter with the workers. "We were quite frustrated by the level of consciousness of the workers," Amir remembers. "We seldom found books in the homes of workers. It was hard to find even an old magazine."

> That's why in the beginning we chose to work with workers who had lived longer in Jakarta. Jakarta, with its pornographic and violent films from Hong Kong or the United States, with its prostitutes, tends to liberalize workers. The positive aspect of all of this is that it breaks down all of the taboos of the village. Here workers become more mobile, more open, and braver. In Jakarta, workers are merged with other ethnics from other areas. After a while, they don't pray anymore.

The radical students decided that they had to teach the workers about socialism. If the workers were to become part of this revolutionary process, they also had to be politically educated and trained. The students had to explain to them the nature of imperialism and capitalism, the history of the world socialist movement, the struggle for independence and for social justice in Indonesia, and the history of the Indonesian labor movement.

> So we created intensive classes for the workers. We brought the students to the cities, to the workers' rooms. Sometimes the neighbors were suspicious, because the students didn't look like the workers who lived in the neighborhood. Social classes here, you know, are really materialized. Workers have different clothes and different faces. The worker's face is a village face. The student's face is a clean, more expressive face. Students engage in more joking, but the working class has what we call a *budaya bisu,* a silent culture.

Recapitulating the experience of the students, the workers' socialist study classes soon turned to activism. "We began with small strikes in the factories. Then we organized PPBI, the Center for Indonesian Labor Struggle, a sort of labor federation. The workers chose Dita Sari as their chairwoman," Amir explains. "That was a time when students held demonstrations at the factory gates. Many times when the students demonstrated, workers joined them, and then the military repressed them both. We opened democratic spaces, and then the parasitic politicians used them."

The Founding of the PRD

By 1994, Hendrik Kuok explains, the student radicals had created three organizations: SMID, STN, and PPBI.

> We then brought all three of these—the student, peasant, and labor organizations, together in the People's Democratic Union, which we founded in 1994. We organized and carried out a debate within the People's Democratic Union around two points: first, the idea that students needed to unite with the people, with workers and peasants; and, second, that we needed a political party. Out of that discussion we transformed the People's Democratic Union into the People's Democratic Party.

Ma'ruf adds,

> There was a split at that time. One group felt it was not time to
> build a party, and they left us, formed the Movement for De-
> mocracy in Indonesia, and sought affiliation with the Socialist
> International. We disagreed. We believed, because of the radi-
> calization among peasants and workers, that they needed a
> party as a political vehicle to challenge the dictatorship, and we
> believed that none of the existing parties could serve as that
> vehicle. So we founded the PRD in 1996.

Sugeng Bahagijo, the chairperson, announced the founding
of the PRD at the Jakarta Legal Aid (LBH) office on May 2, 1994,
and welcomed "everybody as members, farmers, workers, students, intellectuals, and others, as long as they are concerned
about the development of democracy in Indonesia." With Marxism, Communism, and socialism illegal in Indonesia, the PRD
founding statement emphasized democracy, supported small-
and medium-sized national capitalism against multinational capital, but made no mention of socialism or revolution. Soesilo
Soedarman, the politics and security minister, immediately announced that the "PRD is not legal," because Indonesian law
permitted the existence of only three legally recognized parties.
He declared that "the government will take firm action."

At about the same time that it emerged as a party, the PRD
fell under the influence of another leftist organization, the Australian Democratic Socialist Party (DSP). The DSP had its ante-
cedents in the involvement of Trotskyist activists in the student
and antiwar movements of the 1960s. In the 1970s, the group
formed the Socialist Workers Party (SWP) of Australia, closely
aligned with the small political party of the same name in the
United States and with the Trotskyist Fourth International. Later
in the 1980s, both the Australian and the U.S. SWP broke with
Trotskyist theory and oriented toward support of the Nicaraguan
and Cuban revolutions. Together with the U.S. SWP, the Australian socialists came to reject Trotksy's theory of permanent revolution, the idea that the working class would have to carry out a

democratic and socialist revolution in a permanent and uninterrupted process. The DSP argued that in rejecting Trotsky, it was moving back toward Lenin's original theory of a workers' and peasants' government as the key to democratic revolution in countries dominated by imperialism. The group also changed its name to the Democratic Socialist Party and eventually broke off its relations with both the SWP in the United States and with the Fourth International.[4]

Having given up both its ideological and organizational ties to orthodox Trotskyism, the DSP adopted a theory and practice that had more in common with Maoism. Both the DSP and the Maoists emphasized the need for workers and peasants to join with other social groups, including small capitalists and national capitalists, to carry out a national democratic revolution. In Australia, the DSP built a small but strong socialist group active in many labor and political struggles, and in international solidarity work. The DSP's new organizational independence and its adherence to a two-stage theory of revolution facilitated a rapprochement with the originally Maoist PRD.

A few Australian DSP members spoke Indonesian, and one of them, Max Lane, had a long history of involvement with opposition currents in Indonesian cultural and political circles. For a small student group like the PRD, with relatively small numbers, virtually no financial resources, and few international contacts, the DSP represented an important overseas ally. Ever since its founding in 1994, the PRD has relied on the DSP for assistance of all sorts—moral, material, and political. At the same time, the DSP has had a significant ideological influence on the PRD, strengthening its Maoist tendency to see its job as allying with and pushing other classes to carry out a democratic revolution against "feudalism" and militarism, while putting off a struggle for socialism until a later date.

About the time of the founding of the PRD, the struggle against Suharto had begun to heat up. "We decided we had to organize bigger factories," Amir recalls.

In 1996, we organized a strike at GRI, or Great River Industry, a factory owned by former Labor Minister Abdul Latief, which produces shirts for Arrow and Triumph. The factory employed 15,000 workers. We organized the strike and then led the workers to parliament. Can you imagine what it was like when we mobilized workers to parliament? We said to them, just follow us. We divided them into groups to evade the military. We said, just follow us. So when a student stood, they stood. And when the student sat, they sat.

For most of those workers who were living and working in the industrial suburbs, that was the first time they had seen Central Jakarta. It was the first time they had seen the National Monument, the parliament, or even an elevator. Some of the workers were afraid to get on the elevator, because they had never seen one before.

The PRD began to lead other strikes throughout Java. "We organized in the Tandes, of Surbaya, an area of about 20 factories, and led out 12,000 workers. We were brutally repressed and students and workers were arrested. We organized at Sritex, a plant owned by Harmoko, the chairman of parliament, which makes uniforms for NATO and employs about 7,000 workers."

The PRD During the Crisis

The years of political crisis, 1996 and 1997, presented the PRD with a whole new series of challenges. In 1996, a dispute erupted within the Indonesian Democratic Party (PDI) between the old guard, loyal to the Suharto regime, and the supporters of Megawati Sukarnoputri, the daughter of former president Sukarno, who was fighting to take leadership of the organization. On the morning of July 1996, gangsters organized by the military regime attacked the PDI headquarters on Diponegoro Boulevard in the Menteng neighborhood of Central Jakarta. That afternoon there were riots throughout Jakarta, and many people were killed and injured in the melée. The government blamed the PRD for organizing the riot, and even went so far as to accuse it of attempting a coup d'état.

The riot was used as an excuse to ban various political organizations and arrest prominent political figures, such as Muchtar Pakpahan of the SBSI labor federation. The PRD, which had defended Megawati and her supporters in the PDI against attack by the government, was banned, as were its affiliated organizations (SMID, STN, and PPBI), and nine of its top leaders were arrested. The military also arrested or kidnapped and tortured many other PRD members, and generally terrorized the organization, its members, and its supporters. The PRD suffered more repression than any other opposition group in Indonesia. Two of its members, Gilang and Yusup Prizzal, were murdered. Four other members are still missing and presumed murdered: Herman Hendrawan, Bimo Petrui, Suyar, and Wijui Thukul. Another 14 PRD members were imprisoned by the Suharto government, and most were only released two years later. Many PRD members who were imprisoned suffered torture. Ironically, the repression also brought political influence. Magazines put the photo of PRD leader Budiman Sujatmiko on their covers, bringing national notoriety to the party for the first time.

Amir recounts, "After that, we had to organize underground again. Many of our members ran away at that time, though later they came back. We had only between 20 and 30 leaders of our organization, and about 50 members—only 100 altogether." So when the economic crisis hit Indonesia in 1997, the PRD had been reduced to a tiny organization of perhaps 100 activists operating underground and subject to the terror and torture of the police. "When the crisis began, we concentrated on work among students at the universities," says Ma'ruf. SMID had been banned along with the PRD, so the PRD members had to either organize new student groups, or join those that other students had organized. "We were involved in student groups such as City Forum (Kota Forum) and later the Big Family of the University of Indonesia (KBUI). Finally, we organized the Committee of Students and People for Democracy in Indonesia (KOMRAD). The students also organized student committees on other campuses,"

Ma'ruf remembers. These organizations would be among the most active and most radical of the Indonesian student groups that helped bring down Suharto.

"We also entered into the committees which had been organized by other groups to fight for our program. We wanted to focus on one set of national demands," explains Dita—not Dita Sari, but another PRD leader. This Dita, less than five feet tall, was shot with rubber bullets and then beaten by several policemen in an attack on a PRD demonstration. She is missing one front tooth, and the other turned black after she was struck in the face. From time to time as we talked, she winced with pain from the rubber bullet wound.

> Up to that point, because of the crisis, the students had only raised economic demands. In addition to the crisis, El Niño [the weather system] had caused a drought and a bad harvest, and many people were actually starving. We tried to convince the student movement that this struggle was not only economic, but also political. Our demands were: overthrow Suharto; end *dwifungsi,* the military's dual-function role; end the five political laws—that is, the laws governing political parties, elections, the parliament, mass organizations, and the referendum to change the constitution; higher wages; and meet the people's needs for nine basic commodities, such as rice, cooking oil, and so on.

The PRD members—by then more had begun to return to the party, and new recruits had started to join—attempted to galvanize the broader student and popular movement into action. The PRD called for demonstrations of students, workers, and the urban poor. Students were urged to reach out to the unemployed, housewives, and mothers. The PRD called on students and workers to engage in sit-ins in public places and to organize strikes against the regime.

The student movement grew in size from day to day, from hundreds to thousands to tens of thousands, and on a national scale to hundreds of thousands of student activists engaged in demonstrations. By May 1998, there were demonstrations of as many as 50,000 students in Jakarta, with many workers among them. By November 1998, after the fall of Suharto, the demonstrations against the proposed People's Consultative Assembly had grown to as large as 100,000. The PRD, while only one of many organizations involved across a wide political spectrum, played a dynamic and at times central role in the student demonstrations. No other group manifested the same consistent opposition not only to Suharto, but also to Golkar, the military, and the whole system of military state capitalism.

Mass Movements and Politics

The biggest challenge for the PRD was charting its course as it became clear that Suharto would fall and that Megawati would be the leading political candidate for president. No doubt because it was so deeply involved in the massive student movement—and what soon became a broader social movement of students, workers, the middle class, and even elite opponents of the regime—the PRD was subject to all sorts of political pressures from more conservative political forces. That it was subject to such forces is a testament to its non-sectarian and activist orientation; purist sects never face opportunist pressures because they fear moving with the real movement. The pressures of the real movement pushed the PRD toward Megawati and her wing of the PDI, the future PDI-Struggle (PDI-P). This was almost a natural evolution. In July 1997, the PRD began politically defending Megawati and the PDI against the attack by the military. This defense of democratic rights was quite remarkable, since Megawati had never said a word nor lifted a finger to support the young PRD activists who had been tortured to defend her rights. Some of the PRD leadership hoped to work with the left wing of the PDI, with which they had formed a practical alliance, and hoped to win over some of their ranks. But other PRD members simply began to drift toward the PDI. For members of a young and growing student movement, it was easy to move from support for the rights of another political party and its candidate to politi-

cal support for that party and its very popular candidate, and
that's what started to happen.

Another problem faced the PRD. The forces were flowing,
and then surging, toward Megawati, and the PRD's leaders felt
that the growing numbers behind Megawati could bring down
Suharto. The PRD wanted to be part of that mass movement, but
the leadership had not worked out clearly the question of the political independence of a working-class party. Perhaps the history
of the PKI and its role within the nationalist movement, and later
in Sukarno's government, had some influence here, but the key
problem was a lack of theoretical clarity.

The PRD had adopted the position that the task of the moment was the overthrow of Suharto's New Order, or—in Marxist
terminology—that bourgeois democratic revolution was the
agenda of the day. Nico Warouw, the PRD's international representative based in the Netherlands, wrote,

> What the dictatorship fears most is the formation of a broad
> coalition that can serve as an alternative government to bring
> the nation out of crisis. A coalition of competent and charis-
> matic leaders combined with mass-based organizations repre-
> senting the interests of the majority. Such a coalition would
> attract huge popular support.... The anti-Suharto coalition
> will be the embryo of a coalition government whose task is to
> create more democratic conditions under which all people are
> encouraged to participate in forming a democratic Indonesia.
> Central to creating this is abolition of all repressive laws [and]
> the social-political role of the armed forces, and the organizing
> of free and fair elections.[5]

But, eager to see that democratic revolution, the PRD found
itself attempting to push, cohere, and even advise the old parties.
In January 1998, the National Committee for Democratic Struggle (KNPD), a coalition of opposition forces, held a press conference at the LBH in Jakarta at which it "called on leaders of social
organizations and pro-democracy figures to form a council for
the salvation of the people's sovereignty." On January 16, the

PRD issued a statement giving "critical support to the call, but emphasized that [Amien] Rais [leader of one of the largest Muslim organizations] and Megawati should announce their political program and take a clear stand against the dictatorship."[6] Budiman Sujatmiko, the chair of the PRD, interviewed in prison in January 1998, said, "We have been involved in local coalitions uniting urban poor, students, workers, and Megawati supporters in a number of cities. Now we are focusing on a mass campaign to support Megawati in rejecting the reelection of Suharto."[7] This statement came dangerously close to simply endorsing Megawati and the PDI-P.

By suggesting that the radical movement support Megawati, the PRD risked disorienting its followers and members and moving them into the position of backing a conservative capitalist politician. In doing so it risked turning itself into an appendage of what would become Megawati's PDI-P party.

When the government announced elections, the PRD first called for abstention on the grounds that the old regime was running the elections. Later, however, the leadership changed its position and registered the PRD as a legal electoral party. Perhaps the leadership reflected on the disastrous experience of the CPP in the Philippines, which had boycotted the election at a critical moment in the country's history and had virtually fallen into oblivion. While calling for a coalition and tacitly supporting the PDI-P of Megawati, the PRD also created its only legal political party and sought election of its own candidates. But who did it really support—its own PRD candidates or Megawati? In the end, the PRD adopted the confusing political slogan, "Boycott the election or vote for the PRD." Yet many of its own members voted for the PDI-P because they wanted to ensure that Golkar would not return to power. In the end, the PRD candidates received less than 1 percent of the votes.

While the PRD, like the PBN, received less than 1 percent of the vote, the leadership argues that it approached the elections correctly and helped to build the party. Hendrik Kuok defensively explained, "At that time, in 1998, we sometimes supported Megawati because most people were backing her, and we thought it would advance the movement. We did get some democratic space, but since then she has become very conservative." Today, while still defending the democratic rights of the PDI-P and Megawati, the PRD strongly criticizes both.

People's Councils

But support for Megawati was not the PRD's only position in the crisis, and did not make up its entire program. The essence of PRD politics in the crisis was the call for "People's Councils." At student, worker, and peasant meetings, in leaflets and pamphlets distributed at demonstrations and strikes, the PRD argued: "An independent and sovereign People's Council [*Dewan Rakyat*] must be established to replace the function of the puppet DPR/MPR [the parliament and electoral congress]. It must be established at all levels: the hamlet, village, sub-district, city, regency, province, and nationally. People's Councils must also be established on campuses, schools, factories, and offices."[8]

Ma'ruf explains the significance of the People's Councils demand at that time:

> We called for the organization of People's Councils, which was really a call for a transitional government. We didn't want the old regime to run the elections for a new government. We wanted a transitional government to run the elections, and we rejected the idea of an elite transitional government made up of the old political parties and the military. We called for a real democratic transitional government made up of people from many sectors of society. We called for the organization of councils on the campuses, in the *kampungs,* or the villages, and in the factories. This sounds like a call for soviets, but the soviets led an insurrection. We were calling for elections.

Soviet is the Russian word for council, and in the socialist lexicon refers to the councils of workers first formed in the Russian Revolution of 1905 and again in 1917. Originally organized in the city of Petrograd (Petersburg, or Leningrad) to lead strikes during that first attempt to overthrow the tsar in 1905, the councils evolved into a kind of proto-government. During the Russian Revolution of 1917, councils of workers, peasants, and soldiers formed again and gradually became an alternative to the parliament. By October 1917, a situation of dual power had developed in Russia. There were two alternative governments, one a parliament dominated by parties committed to capitalism, and the other a soviet, or workers' council, dominated by socialist parties and led by the Bolshevik Party, committed to overthrowing capitalism and creating a workers' and peasants' government. Which would rule? The Bolshevik Party settled the matter by organizing an insurrection, dispersing the parliament, and thrusting power on to the soviets. The soviets thus became the government of Soviet Russia and later of the Soviet Union, a workers' government, at least for a little while. At the time, the Bolsheviks, or Communists, as they soon called themselves, argued that workers' councils represented a broader democracy, a democratic government of workers and peasants, and therefore a higher form of democracy than capitalist parliaments.

The PRD's call for People's Councils seemed to fall somewhere between the idea of parliament and the idea of soviets. Not well defined, not clearly linked to putting power into the hands of workers and peasants, and with too few cadres to really create them, the PRD's call for the councils never really took off. In 1998, with the entire nation oriented toward elections, the call for organizing councils found little response. Perhaps it would have resonated more broadly had there been a political impasse or had the economic and social crisis deepened. But at the time, the PRD's opportunistic support for Megawati had more impact than its idealistic call for People's Councils.

Ma'ruf told me in July 1999 that the next step for the PRD was party building:

> Today we have about 800 cadre members, full members. We have to concentrate our work among students, though in the long term we want to organize workers. But we need more

students, more educated people in order to reach those workers. Though about a third of our leaders are women, right now about 20 percent of our members are female.

We publish only about 1,000 copies of our 20-page paper. But during the elections, we put out ... 100,000 pamphlets and some 600,000 leaflets.

In 1999, one observer estimated that the PRD had 800 members, 8,000 sympathizers, and the capacity to mobilize perhaps 80,000 students across Indonesia. In addition, it had activists and supporters in the peasant and labor unions.

When I visited the PRD almost a year later, in June 2000, the party had grown tremendously and claimed to be more than 10 times larger than it had been a year before. Wilson, one of the PRD's top leaders, explained,

> Participating in the election really had an amazing impact on our party. Imagine, we had been an illegal party, and then suddenly we became a legal party. We were in the newspapers, on radio, and on television. Our best known leaders like Dita Sari and Budiman were on television talk shows. Even the Indonesian state radio, Radio Republik Indonesia, interviewed our party leaders.
>
> Before the election, we had about 15 or 20 branches and maybe 1,000 members. Today we have 54 branches and 10,000 members. We have found it amazing that there is a great sympathy for socialist ideas in many areas where we would never have expected it, including in the most fundamentalist Islamic areas. We receive messages all the time from students or activists who say, "We want to start a PRD branch." For example, we have a PRD branch in Aceh, one of the most fundamentalist areas. It's only 15 people, but we have a branch there. We have a branch in West Kalimantan, Borneo, where three years ago you could not imagine a socialist organization existing.

Where do the PRD recruits come from? I asked.

We have recruited from many different sorts of groups. Some of our members have come from the Islamic Student Association, or HMI, a conservative group whose leaders move into Golkar. Many of our members come from Plagar Islam Indonesia, the Indonesian Muslim students, a radical organization. Others have come from the Catholic Student Union. I find it amazing that they have come to join us, because it is so dangerous. They are risking their lives, because if there is an Islamic or military crackdown, their names would be on our membership lists.

The PRD recruits largely on the basis of its organizing campaigns, Wilson told me. "We organize student demonstrations to go after Suharto. We see Suharto as the symbol of the New Order regime that still retains a lot of power. We go after Suharto because that symbolizes democratizing society." The PRD's campaign proved successful in August 2000 when the government finally indicted Suharto for embezzlement, though later the courts decided he was too sick and psychologically disoriented to be tried. Wilson continues,

> Also today there are a lot of strikes, and the PRD must be involved in the workers' movement. We have called for a 100 percent increase in wages. Organizationally, we are trying to get all of our branches involved in labor organizing. Many of our members are active in the FNPBI, the union federation led by PRD member Dita Sari, and in other labor unions.
>
> We are also organizing to fight against neoliberalism and its effects on workers and the poor. We are taking on issues such as the liberalization of the tariff and cuts in education subsidies. The state is selling many state enterprises, such as Pertamina, the state oil company, and the state electric company. We oppose these privatizations. We call for the nationalization of all natural resources and public utilities. While it is true that many of the managers were corrupt under state-ownership, that does not mean that the answer is to sell off these properties to private industry.

Through such organizing the PRD continues to recruit new members. The new members present not only organizational but political challenges, says Wilson:

During the election, many students came to us to join the organization. These new members have an anti-military and anti-neoliberal consciousness, but they are not ideologically developed. We felt that we could not turn them away, but at the same time, not all of them should be PRD members, because we are a cadre organization. When we accept them as a member, we give them a political job to organize on their campus, in the community, or in the workplace.

We are trying to strengthen our propaganda. We publish a party magazine called *Pombebasan [Liberation]* that comes out every two weeks, and we have published 18 numbers so far. But we only print about 3,500 copies because we do not have the funds to print more. All of our members have to buy and sell the magazine. But our distribution system is still weak.

We have also developed a political education program. The new members study the national situation, our political program, the question of organization, the history of Indonesian society, and internationalism. The cadre program includes readings in what we call the classics—Marx, Lenin, Trotsky, Mao. And we read about contemporary socialist movements in countries such as Brazil, Mexico, and Germany.

The PRD would like to be involved in broader coalitions with other organizations, but has found that difficult.

We have had a big problem working in coalitions. The problem is not with us, but with the NGOs that don't want to work with the PRD. For example, in the big anti-debt coalition here, the NGOs excluded us. We are not sectarian, but the NGOs are very childish. They fear that because we are a party, we will monopolize the movement and dominate them. But we do work in coalition with some groups. We have a lot of contact with Islamic groups and student groups.

Many students are opposed to neoliberalism, and we can work with them. But there is still an anti-partisan consciousness among the students. They sometimes reject us, saying that we will try to control them. We do have a coalition with the Liga Mahasiswas Nasional Untuk Demokrasi [LMND], the National Student League for Democracy. LMND is made up of 29 student unions around the country and has an anti-militarist platform, and we work well with them.

In fact, the PRD helped to create the LMND, and a PRD member leads it, so this is not exactly a coalition activity.

The PRD remains quite involved in union organizing activities, Wilson told me. "We send organizers into the industrial areas and factories to set up unions. We organize workers, but they choose their own unions. We work closely with Kobar and with the FNPBI, but in the end the workers have to choose the union they want." The STN, the PRD's peasant union, is still organizing, but, said Wilson, "It is not growing as fast as the student movement or the workers' movement."

The PRD has no women's group, a surprising fact in any leftist organization after the international women's movement in the 1970s and 1980s. Wilson explained, "We still have no women's organization. Right now, our priority is on workers, peasants, students, and the urban poor. We concentrate on workers and students. Maybe when we have more cadres we would also set up a women's organization." The PRD's reluctance to organize women as women on feminist issues seems anachronistic and is in contradiction to its labor organizing among women.

The PRD has adopted an apparently contradictory attitude toward the government of Abdurrahman Wahid (Gus Dur). On the one hand, the PRD was the first party to come out against the Wahid government. According to Wilson,

> In February 2000, at the national capital in Jakarta, we organized an anti-neoliberal demonstration in which 2,000 PRD members participated, and where we declared our opposition to the program and policy of Wahid. We were the first group who openly declared our opposition. Also, on April 1, we organized a national action against neoliberalism in more than 50 cities, opposing the government's cuts in subsidies to electricity and oil. We had demonstrations on many different islands and in all the major cities.

On the other hand, the PRD also has a closer relationship to

Wahid's PKB than to any other party in the parliament. "After all, that was the only party to call for lifting the anti-Communist ban," Wilson explained. "Also some PKB members—though not the whole party—agree with us on ending *dwifungsi*. Of course this doesn't mean that we support the Wahid government. We oppose them strongly on neoliberalism. We only agree with them on this issue of lifting the anti-Communist ban." Wahid and other leaders of the PKB have held meetings with PRD leaders to discuss areas of possible cooperation, though little has come out of those meetings so far.

In just a few short years, the student radicals who created the PRD have seen some remarkable successes. Yet the PRD still represents a very small political party, one that merits our attention only because of the key role its small numbers have played in recent Indonesian history, particularly during the period leading up to the fall of Suharto. To become a national party such as the PKI was in the period between 1945 and 1965, the PRD would have to grow at least 100 times bigger than it is now. To lead a revolution, it would have to be perhaps 1,000 times bigger. While such growth is not impossible, it represents an enormous challenge. Certainly the PRD will have to professionalize its operations, improve its communications skills, develop its ability to enter into alliances and coalitions, and stimulate the creation of mass movements in which it can grow and develop.

The PRD Vision of Socialism

At the end of the twentieth century and the beginning of the twenty-first, the words socialism and communism sometimes seem bereft of all significance. The bureaucratic Communist states of the Soviet Union, China, Vietnam, Yugoslavia, and Cuba all called themselves socialist, and yet none had much in common with either the historic sense of the word, the idea of socializing the nation's and the world's wealth, or with the specifically Marxist idea of achieving that goal through a workers' revolution that would establish a democratically controlled economy. In the Communist countries, dictators like Stalin, Mao, and Ho

Chi Minh, or somewhat more charismatic and charming caudillos like Tito and Castro, headed up bureaucratic Communist parties that controlled the state, the economy, and the citizenry. The bureaucracies of those countries oppressed and exploited workers and peasants in ways not so different than the ways in which they were treated under capitalism, though it was all justified by a quite different ideology, a virtual state religion. At the same time, the Labor, Socialist, and Social Democratic parties of England, France, Germany, Spain, and Italy long ago gave up any idea of socializing the nation's or the world's wealth, and contented themselves with managing capitalism as junior partners in the firm.

What is the PRD's vision of socialism? Ma'ruf, editor of its newspaper, clarified for me a number of questions I had about the PRD's vision of socialism. In listening to Ma'ruf, it's clear that not only Lenin but also Marx has had an impact on the PRD.

"We want a classless society, a society that is not divided into social classes, but that's a long struggle," said Ma'ruf. He sees the organization of People's Councils, one of the PRD's long-term goals, as an important step in moving toward socialist revolution.

> The People's Councils represent an alternative system to parliament. The broad masses will organize through the councils for revolution. The party will work within the councils to raise the people's consciousness. The People's Councils will not be under party control, but the party will have to struggle within the councils to win them to its view. Today, the people still trust the parliament, but we have to organize now so that when the parliament's credibility is gone, the councils will be organized.
>
> In the beginning, while the bourgeoisie is still strong, the People's Councils will function like action committees and educational organizations, to educate the masses more broadly than the party can. Inside the People's Councils will be parties, trade unions, other organizations, and non-party individuals, but all will be in the same position within the councils.

Ma'ruf does not envision a one-party state. "In establishing socialism, we foresee relations with other parties. We are critical of the Cuban revolution because there is only one party. Where there is only one party, there is the danger that it will become a party of bureaucrats, like the USSR and China."

Ma'ruf also worries about the creation of a party army. "We feel it is dangerous if the party controls the military. The People's Councils should control the military. We also reject the Blanquist idea of a 'special force' to carry out the revolution," says Ma'ruf. Blanqui, a French revolutionary who was roughly a contemporary of Marx, had seen socialism as largely a problem of military organization and insurrection by an enlightened minority, rather than social and political organization of the working class. Ma'ruf continues, "Party control of the military led to problems in the Soviet Union and China. That is why the Chinese military is so corrupt today." The Chinese People's Liberation Army, in many ways much like the Indonesian Army, runs factories where it treats workers like virtual slaves.

Ma'ruf expanded on his concerns:

> In the insurrection, the "special force" [that is, the military organization] is secondary. The most important thing is the mass movement. The "special force" is a petty bourgeois concept, the idea of a hero who will save the people. In fact, such a special force has no mass base. This was a problem with Communist Party of the Philippines, where they had the New People's Army and the ABB. The ABB was a terrorist organization that assassinated people in the villages. We reject terrorism as an elitist concept. We support something like Trotsky's concept of armed struggle. Mass action is itself a kind of practice for an insurrection. Mass action leads to discipline under a single command.

Talking to Ma'ruf, it is clear that the study groups in the classics read not only Mao and Lenin, but also Trotsky and Marx. Ma'ruf conjures up a vision of a democratic socialist society based on humanistic values.

Indonesia and Socialism

One of the striking things about Indonesia is that while the country has many opposition parties, it has hardly any genuine reform parties. Only the PUDI and the PBN qualify, and neither of those has any significant following. Few major parties or political leaders call for ending the military's political role, and virtually no one calls for an end to the economic system dominated by the military generals, a handful of bankers and industrialists, and the multinational corporations, a system that excludes the vast majority of Indonesians and condemns between a quarter and a half of them to desperate poverty. Most other reform parties simply want to move from so-called crony capitalism to a somewhat more broadly based capitalist system, still dominated by the national and multinational corporations. Only the PRD stands opposed to this program and calls also for radical social change.

Whether the PRD will be able to transform itself from a student party into a real working-class party remains to be seen. When I spoke to PRD leaders in the summer of 2000, they seemed overwhelmed by the task of assimilating new members and building a real national organization in the new, somewhat more open atmosphere. The party still focused much of its attention on the student movement, seeing it as the source both of troops for the movement and of recruits. At the same time some party cadres were working among workers and in unions, mostly the FNPBI, but also a few in the SBSI. The party leadership had decided that their best course of action was building a movement against Golkar, *dwifungsi,* and the military, and against the government's neoliberal economic policies. But at the same time, the combination of the Maoist background and the DSP's advice seemed to be leading the PRD into an alliance with President Wahid. The contradictions between supporting Wahid, on the one hand, and objecting to his economic policies, on the other hand, can only in the long run weaken the party's influence in the mass movement. Still, Indonesia's only socialist party, the PRD continues to raise a radical political and economic alternative, a vision of democracy and socialism as the real alternative for the labor movement and for Indonesia.

1 For an example of dependency theory, see Andre Gunder Frank, *Capitalism and Underdevelopment in Latin America: Historical Studies of Chile and Brazil* (New York: Monthly Review Press, 1969).

2 Martin Jay, *The Dialectical Imagination: A History of the Frankfurt School and the Institute for Social Research, 1923–1950* (Boston: Little, Brown and Company, 1973); and Herbert Marcuse, *One Dimensional Man: Studies in the Ideology of Advanced Industrial Society* (Boston: Beacon Press, 1968).

3 A review of the literature that debates the history of the Communist Party of the Philippines can be found in Mark R. Thompson, "The Decline of Philippine Communism: A Review Essay," *South East Asia Research* 6 (July 1998): 105–29. For a personal account, see Dorothy Friesen, *Critical Choices: A Journey with the Filipino People* (Grand Rapids, MI: William B. Eerdmans Publishing Company, 1988), especially 183–213.

4 John Percy, "History of the DSP." Available on-line at http://www.dsp.org.au/dsp/hist1.htm.

5 Nico Warouw, "Building a United Front Against the Dictatorship," *Free Indonesia* 1 (1998): 3.

6 "Mounting Opposition" and "The Road to Overthrowing Suharto is Open," *Free Indonesia: Publication of the International Office of the People's Democratic Party* 1 (1998): 7.

7 "PRD Leader Speaks from Prison," *Free Indonesia* 1 (1998): 11.

8 "Continue to Raise the Banner of the People's Struggle," *Free Indonesia* 1 (1998): 14.

Chapter 10

Globalization, Indonesia, and International Labor Solidarity

The neoliberal globalization process—predicated upon the almost instantaneous movement of money capital (currency, derivatives, etc.) and the possibility of rapidly moving plants and production from one country to another—has tended to undermine labor unions in every country. U.S. corporations have moved plants and production to Latin America and Asia to escape trade unions and contracts, to avoid environmental and health and safety regulations, and, above all, to find cheaper labor. Multinational corporations frequently blackmail labor unions, threatening to move their plants if not granted concessions in wages, benefits, or conditions. Capital mobility and competition for cheap labor have weakened unions and contributed to stagnant or falling wages in the United States and other developed countries.

Even in Asia and Latin America, where workers' wages are already low, the multinational corporations may move to other countries that pay even more miserable wages. A corporation in Indonesia may move to China or Vietnam, for example, both for lower wages and because those even more authoritarian regimes mean workers are less likely to organize successfully to improve their wages or conditions. Workers around the world have been forced to compete with each other by working for ever lower wages, a cycle that has been called the race to the bottom.

What can and has been done by workers and their unions to resist these tendencies? The international mobility of capital and the movement of production facilities make clear the need for international organizations of labor. Since the nineteenth century, workers, unions, and labor political parties have taken numerous steps to build international solidarity, protect their wages and conditions, and advance their own political agenda. The challenge has been to create workers' organizations that can maintain their independence from governments and employers. The task has proven extremely difficult, and at times has seemed impossible. But the pressures of capitalism have constantly forced workers to seek new forms of international collaboration.

The Internationals: Working Men, Socialist, Communist

The attempt to build international workers' organizations has a long and rather complicated history. Between the 1860s and the 1930s, the workers' movement launched a series of radical and revolutionary attempts to build an international labor movement, and produced three workers' Internationals, as they were called. In the mid-nineteenth century, European workers created the International Working Men's Association (IWMA), also known as the First International, an alliance of labor unions and political organizations whose secretary was Karl Marx. In his inaugural address, he argued that the European ruling classes had

> taught the working classes the duty to master themselves the mysteries of international politics; to watch the diplomatic acts of their respective governments; to counteract them, if necessary, by all means in their power; when unable to prevent [them], to combine in simultaneous denunciations, and to vindicate the simple laws of morals and justice, which ought to govern the relations of private individuals, as the rules paramount of the intercourse of nations.[1]

The idea that workers and labor unions from different nations should cooperate to develop a common foreign policy based on the common interests of the world's workers represented an altogether new idea with radical and even revolutionary implications. The IWMA suggested that workers should support each other rather than their respective capitalist classes.

The IWMA broke up over the differences between anarchists and socialists, and died after the defeat of the Paris Commune, a socialist revolution in France in 1871 that sections of the international had supported.

Almost 20 years passed before radicals undertook the next effort to form an international labor organization. In the late 1880s, several labor and socialist parties came together to form the Socialist International, also known as the Second International. An alliance of socialist parties rather than labor unions, it was in effect a labor international because the most important unions were generally affiliated with the socialist parties. The movement spread across four continents (Europe, North and South America, and Australia), but with the exception of Japan had little influence in Asia or Africa, and had little to say to colonial peoples.

In the age of imperialism, the socialist workers pledged not to go to war as their governments and corporations fought for colonies. But World War I led to the breakup of the Second International as the conservative leaders of the socialist parties in each of the belligerent countries violated their pledges and supported their own governments in the war. Ironically, the labor union leaders were the most nationalistic and the most opposed to internationalism, precisely because they had the closest links to the corporations and capitalism.

Out of the horror of the war and the chaos of the collapse of the German, Austrian, Russian, and Ottoman empires came new hope for labor solidarity. From the ruins of the Second International rose the Third, or Communist, International led by Lenin, Trotsky, and the victorious Bolshevik Party in Russia. Those early Communists saw the Third International not as a federation of labor and socialist parties, but rather as a centralized, international revolutionary workers' party coordinating efforts to overthrow capitalism and install workers' power on a global scale.

As Trotsky wrote in 1919 in the first Manifesto of the Communist International to the Workers of the World, "If the First International presaged the future course of development and indicated its paths; if the Second International gathered and organized millions of workers; then the Third International is the International of open mass action, the International of revolutionary realization, the International of the deed." Unlike the First and Second Internationals, the Communist International worked not only to unite European workers and emigrants, but also workers in Africa, Asia, and Latin America. The colonial slaves and pariahs would join with the workers of Europe to overthrow capitalism and create a new socialist society.[2]

But the rise of Stalinism in the late 1920s and 1930s soon turned the Communist International (or Comintern, as it was called) into an arm of Soviet foreign policy, rather than a movement for workers' revolution. The Stalinist counter-revolution in the Soviet Union and subversion of the Comintern led Trotsky and his small bands of followers in a handful of countries to proclaim a Fourth International in 1939 to reclaim the hope and promise of the Third. But in the era of Hitler, Stalin, and World War II, there was no mass response and that effort also collapsed. The Chinese Communists under Mao and the Cuban Communists under Fidel Castro later set up international organizations aimed at exporting their versions of revolution. But their efforts tended to support political parties or armed organizations, and did not really take an active role in the area of international labor solidarity. In any case, Castro's alliance with Soviet Russia, and Mao's later tacit alliance with the United States beginning in the 1970s, undercut whatever value such movements might have held for international labor solidarity.

What has been Indonesia's role in the various Internationals? The First and Second Internationals, based in Europe and the

Americas, had little impact in Asia, though the Socialists did establish a party in Japan and the Comintern created a powerful party in China. The Comintern played a role in Indonesia, too, both in its idealistic phase from 1918 to about 1925, and in its Stalinist period from 1925 until the overthrow of Sukarno and the massacre of 1965. Unfortunately during the heroic period of the Comintern (1918–1925), the organization was too weak to offer much help to Indonesia, while it offered mostly poor models and bad advice during the Stalinist period.

Stalin's Soviet Communism and later Mao's Chinese Communism offered the model of a totalitarian state and bureaucratic collectivism rather than the ideal of labor solidarity fighting for democratic socialism. During Sukarno's presidency, the Communists led a peasant movement fighting for land reform and a labor movement fighting for the nationalization of the Dutch industries. But the Communists, politically subordinating themselves to Sukarno, found themselves caught in a contradiction. On the one hand, they led millions of peasants to challenge the landowners and the capitalists, a situation that could only lead to conflict with Sukarno and the government; on the other hand, they failed to create an independent political and military force to defend the peasants against repression. A party that calls for revolution, but then does not lay the basis to really carry it out, leads people to their slaughter. Consequently, when Suharto led the army in the coup that crushed the Communists, more than 500,000 perished in the holocaust.

The ILO and the Trade Secretariats

All of the internationals fought, and all failed, which meant that other forces would fill the vacuum. The U.S. government convened the first meeting of the International Labor Organization (ILO) at the end of World War I to promote a capitalist and corporate version of workers' rights. Founded in 1919, the ILO was based upon a tripartite organization of governments, employers, and unions intended to set internationally agreed upon labor standards. At first, the ILO set standards for particular trades or around particular issues, such as international child labor standards or guidelines for mine workers. It later took positions on workers' rights in the broad sense. ILO Convention 87, for example, states that workers have the right to join unions of their own choice. But the ILO does not have the authority either to obligate states to adopt its conventions or to enforce them once they do. With government and employers involved, the ILO represents not international labor solidarity, but rather international class collaboration, partnership writ large. Still, the ILO conventions often established a standard that workers could use to fight for improvements in their rights and conditions.

During the period roughly from 1890 to 1920, labor unions from different European countries and sometimes from the Americas established international labor ties based on trade or industry. Later, after World War II, these became the international trade secretariats (ITSs) organized by industry: chemicals, food, metal, transportation, and so on. Each of the ITSs has its own character, and some are more progressive than others. Most engage in some sort of international solidarity work, though for many it is largely of a literary or symbolic sort, such as letters of protest or at most an investigative delegation. But some of the secretariats are more aggressive and actually use their economic power. The Food Workers' International Trade Secretariat, the International Metal Workers' Federation, and the International Chemical Workers (ICEM) have been among the most successful in promoting international solidarity. The groups have called international labor mobilizations, including work stoppages in support of workers in other countries, though such displays of solidarity on an international scale remain relatively rare.

At the beginning of the Cold War in 1949, the international labor movement split into two factions, the International Confederation of Free Trade Unions (ICFTU), loyal to the Western capitalist countries, and the World Federation of Trade Unions (WFTU), dominated by the Soviet Communists. Both federations were compromised by their subordination to the foreign policy of their respective superpowers, the United States and the Soviet Union, and while each criticized the lack of labor rights in the other's sphere of influence, neither fought very hard for workers' rights in its own bloc. Before 1965, Indonesia's most powerful labor federation, SOBSI, led by the Communists, worked with the WFTU. But after the 1965 coup and massacre, Indonesia suddenly became part of the "free world," and its government and government-controlled unions cooperated with the ICFTU. Since the collapse of Communism, the ICFTU has become the home to most of the world's labor federations.

Today, the ICFTU links the most important labor unions throughout the world, acting as a clearinghouse for information and a center for international labor solidarity. However, since it is a loose federation of national labor unions that are themselves dominated by fairly cautious and moderate labor bureaucracies, the ICFTU tends to be bureaucratic and cautious itself. While the ICFTU publicizes violations of labor rights, files protests on behalf of national labor unions and workers, and intervenes in international organizations on behalf of labor, it has not proven capable of mobilizing unions and workers in mutual support across international frontiers, and it hesitates to call on workers to use their economic and political power to bring about social change.

The ICFTU is divided into various regional associations. In Asia, the ICFTU regional organization is the Asian and Pacific Regional Organization (APRO), established in 1951. While APRO proclaims that its goal is the protection of Asian workers from multinational corporations, it has not proven particularly effective. APRO seldom flexes the muscles of the world's largest labor force. Nihon Rodokumiai Sorengokai (Rengo), the Japanese labor federation, has played a particularly conservative role in Indonesia, supporting the state-controlled SPSI unions virtually until the fall of Suharto. In this way, it seems, Rengo has supported Japanese capital, the biggest foreign investor in Indonesia and the most likely to be hurt by the rise of independent labor unions.

Rengo exerts its influence directly and also through APRO, which it dominates. In July 2000, for example, APRO convened a conference made up almost entirely of conservative labor unions formerly affiliated with Suharto's New Order government and the Golkar party. Most of the unions in attendance came from the former state-controlled labor federation, SPSI, either from its status quo or Reformasi branches.[3] The conference proposed to create a new labor confederation in Indonesia. The new confederation, should it actually come into being, would intentionally exclude SBSI, a genuinely independent and more aggressive union, presumably because of its affiliation with the World Confederation of Labor (formerly a Christian trade union federation, now non-sectarian). The APRO conveners did not even invite the FNPBI, presumably because of its origins in the People's Democratic Party (PRD) and its radical, militant, and democratic approach to unionism. In its July 2000 *Monthly Report,* the U.S. American Center for International Labor Solidarity (ACILS) in Jakarta criticized APRO and the Indonesian unions involved in organizing the conference for "excluding all unions with a history of opposition to the Suharto regime."[4]

National Labor Federations: USAID and the AFL-CIO

National labor federations also play an important role in international labor relations, if not always in international labor solidarity. The problem is that most of the national labor federations, and especially those of the great powers, generally work closely with their countries' multinational corporations and with their national governments to promote the "national interest"—as opposed to the workers' international interests. The German labor federation, for example, is known for working to support the interests of German capital, even at times when those interests conflict with unions of other countries.

What is the role of the AFL-CIO Solidarity Center in Indonesia? Throughout the entire post–World War II period and up until the 1990s, the AFL-CIO had close ties with the U.S. State

Department and the Central Intelligence Agency (CIA). The federation supported the goals of the U.S. government in the Cold War and its struggle against Communist and nationalist movements that threatened U.S. political and economic interests. During those years, as today, the AFL-CIO was also an important part of the Democratic Party, which held power in the Congress and the White House throughout much of the Cold War period. The AFL-CIO virtually never disagreed with its party or with the government on major foreign policy issues between 1949 and the early 1990s. On the contrary, under the leadership of George Meaney and Lane Kirkland, the AFL-CIO worked closely with both the State Department and the CIA in the struggle against Communism and nationalism, and in support of U.S. corporations and their interests abroad.[5]

The negotiation of the North American Free Trade Agreement (NAFTA), which had majority support from both Republicans and Democrats, led to the first real break between the labor federation and the U.S. government in almost half a century. The passage of NAFTA also led to deeper divisions within the AFL-CIO, and was a factor in bringing about the election of John Sweeney as president of the federation in 1995. With the election of Sweeney's New Voices slate, a significant shift in the federation's approach to international affairs took place. Sweeney moved to put some distance between the federation and the government and to adopt a somewhat more independent foreign policy. In particular, Sweeney and the AFL-CIO continued to clash with President Clinton and the leadership of the Democratic and Republican parties over trade policy. The AFL-CIO opposed the expansion of NAFTA to other parts of Latin America, and differed with the U.S. government on the issue of granting "permanent normal trade relations" (PNTR) with China, as well as on other specific foreign policy issues. Under Sweeney, the federation has become much more critical of U.S. foreign policy, and far more independent. But while the AFL-CIO called for global justice, at times its leading officials, such as George

Becker, the president of the United Steel Workers of America (USWA), or James R. Hoffa, Jr., of the Teamsters, adopted a nationalist and protectionist rhetoric. Some local officials and rank-and-file members sometimes went beyond nationalism and used racist terms to characterize foreign workers.

The Sweeney leadership moved away from the old Cold War anti-Communist ideology and developed a new position, calling for "global justice."[6] But under Sweeney, the AFL-CIO also said that it wanted to raise productivity, increase quality and competitiveness, and work in partnership with the corporations for the good of U.S. workers and the U.S. public. The AFL-CIO leadership seems to want to recreate the social compact between capital and labor that existed in the period between the late 1940s and the 1980s, a social peace based on an expanding economy, Keynesianism, social welfare programs, and the regulation of corporations. At the same time, the federation has sought out unions in its work abroad that share its vision of a corporate-labor partnership for productivity. The AFL-CIO would like to work with those unions within the context of an internationally regulated regime of fair trade. So the AFL-CIO supports independent labor unions, but would prefer business unions with a vision of collaboration, not class conflict.

The problem is that U.S. business union partnerships are not compatible with international labor solidarity. If U.S. firms become more competitive, they drive foreign companies out of business, and foreign workers lose their jobs. A national economic partnership cannot coexist with international labor solidarity, at least not in the long run. Workers will be forced to choose between loyalty to their bosses or to their sisters and brothers in other countries.

Informed by this vision, the AFL-CIO reorganized its international program in 1997. Barbara Shailor, a progressive staff person from the International Association of Machinists, was appointed to head the International Affairs Department, while other progressives were appointed to head specific international desks and foreign offices. Sweeney and the AFL-CIO International Affairs Committee did away with the federation's four international institutes—the Free Trade Union Institute, the American Institute for Free Labor Development, the African-American Labor Center, and the Asian-American Free Labor Institute—all of which had been involved with the State Department and the CIA. The institutes were replaced with a new entity, ACILS. Sweeney and Shailor removed a number of CIA "spooks" who still haunted the house of labor, and in several cases brought in progressives to replace them.

Yet, despite these changes, there has never been a complete separation between the AFL-CIO and the State Department. The labor federation still maintains close ties to the department and financial ties to its subsidiary, the Agency for International Development (USAID). The August 1996 AFL-CIO Executive Council meeting had recommended that the new center and all future international activities "be funded without government supervision, foreign or domestic."[7] But this recommendation was never adopted. The AFL-CIO still remains economically dependent upon USAID to carry out many of its international labor solidarity programs. In Indonesia, the AFL-CIO and USAID continue to work closely together to influence the a new independent labor union movement.

The Role of USAID

It's important to understand the role of USAID if we are to understand the activities of the AFL-CIO and its Solidarity Centers. President John F. Kennedy created USAID by executive order at the same time that he signed the Foreign Assistance Act of 1961. Like the Peace Corps, it was intended as part of the struggle against Communism and radical nationalisms in other countries. USAID was established to implement the U.S. government's foreign economic and humanitarian assistance programs along lines that would resist Communism and promote U.S. interests.

During the glory years of the 1960s, USAID had 5,000 staff members in Vietnam, and thousands of others in countries around the world. Today, there are only about 1,000 foreign service staff and 1,000 civil service staff altogether both in Washington, D.C., and stationed at USAID offices around the world. Congress allocated $7 billion of the total foreign assistance budget for USAID for fiscal year 2001. Originally created as an independent agency, today USAID reports to the State Department, which oversees its work. USAID works in close cooperation with 3,500 U.S. businesses and 300 U.S.-based NGOs. In four regions of the world—Sub-Saharan Africa; Asia and the Near East; Latin America and the Caribbean; and Europe and Eurasia—USAID works in economic growth and agricultural development; population, health, and nutrition; the environment; democracy and governance; education and training; and humanitarian assistance. USAID's work with the AFL-CIO comes under the heading of democracy and governance.[8]

While described as an economic development and humanitarian aid agency, USAID exists to further the long-term policy goals of the U.S. government and, much like the Peace Corps, represents an organizational complement to the State Department, the CIA, and the military. USAID plays a secondary but very significant role in U.S. foreign policy. The U.S. State, Defense, and Treasury Departments, together with international institutions such as the IMF and the World Bank, stand at the center of U.S. foreign policy, including in Indonesia. But USAID does play an important role in terms of social policy, especially labor policy. As a USAID spokesperson in Jakarta told me, "Since the fall of Communism, the emphasis has changed to supporting U.S. trade and investment abroad."[9] Today, then, USAID represents another U.S. government vehicle for promoting free trade policies and what has come to be known as neoliberal globalization. Yet while supporting free market trade policies, USAID also ostensibly promotes political democracy, including workers' right to organize independent labor unions. The two policies—support for neoliberal globalization and for independent labor unions—may come into conflict, but there is no doubt which has priority. Capital before labor and dollars before democracy remain the fundamental principals.

The USAID budget for Indonesia has been increased dramatically from about $50 million in 1996–1997 to about $112 million for 1999–2000, with another $20 million in food aid. The average annual USAID budget for Indonesia is projected to be about $130 million for 2000–2003. Almost all USAID assistance is given in the form of grants rather than loans, and most of the money is usually given to NGOs or businesses, many of which have been contracted by the Indonesian government.

USAID in Indonesia funds three types of programs: economic recovery, maintenance of social standards (or prevention of social deterioration), and the transition to democracy. The latter is the basis for USAID's work with the AFL-CIO Solidarity Center in Indonesia. But USAID money is directed toward the labor movement with clear general goals. As a spokesperson for the USAID office in Jakarta told me, "We support labor unions that pursue objectives like labor unions in the United States, that is, as opposed to the objectives of European unions." He made it clear that that meant USAID supports unions that do not organize labor or socialist parties or take a prominent role in politics. "USAID is supposed to be non-partisan, so we cannot support a union that organizes a labor or socialist party. We would get in all kinds of problems with the Congress if we did something like that. Imagine what the Republicans would say—or even the Democrats."[10]

USAID and the AFL-CIO's ACILS in Indonesia

USAID has provided approximately $1 million a year to ACILS in Indonesia since 1997. During 1999 and 2000, the ACILS maintained an office in Jakarta with about 25 staff who worked on labor programs throughout the country.

According to a summary of the ACILS-USAID program written before the fall of Suharto, the goals of the ACILS-USAID program were: 1) to increase the number of freely negotiated collective bargaining agreements (CBAs), 2) to improve shop steward and grievance-handling performance, 3) to improve the research and financial/administrative capabilities of the unions to take advantage of the new bottom-up dues collection, 4) to integrate the SPSI (the state-controlled union) into the overall framework of this project, and 5) to promote alternative dispute resolution.[11]

Since the fall of Suharto, the ACILS office in Jakarta, headed by Tim Ryan, has turned its back on the former state-controlled unions and placed its emphasis on supporting the development of independent labor unions that engage in the negotiation of collective bargaining agreements. ACILS has provided labor education, offered technical support, and provided funding to the three major independent federations: SPSI-Reformasi, SBSI, and the FNPBI, as well as to specific labor unions and NGOs that work with labor. USAID provides most of the money that goes to support these programs. Thus the State Department is still the principal support of the AFL-CIO's work in Indonesia. The State Department and the U.S. Embassy have the power to veto USAID program proposals and to cut off funding for ventures that do not square with U.S. political and economic objectives.

ACILS sometimes works closely with Gregory Fergin, the U.S. Embassy's labor attaché. In the most important case, Fergin, Ryan, and a number of SPSI union officials came up with the idea of moving the state-controlled Indonesian labor federation in a new direction, toward reform. In March 1998, Fergin, with the help of Ryan, organized a dinner at his house to which SPSI, SBSI, and other union officials were invited to discuss the existing situation and alternatives. Given that push by the embassy and ACILS, the SPSI unions split, giving rise to SPSI-Reformasi.

Certainly at the time of its creation, SPSI-R wasn't a fully independent labor federation, wasn't free from corruption, and wasn't engaged in genuine collective bargaining, though for more than two years ACILS has propped it up and attempted to turn it into something like a genuine labor union federation.[12] While the U.S. Embassy was probably looking for a way to keep labor under a more moderate leadership, ACILS seems to have wanted to move labor in a more independent direction, and the two motives apparently coincided at that moment. But ACILS has also been a strong supporter of the independent SBSI, led by Muchtar Pakpahan, as well as the more radical FNPBI, led by Dita Sari of the PRD. In addition to its support for several independent unions and the three major independent federations, ACILS has been the principal force in the organization of several temporary and more long-term union alliances, such as the Labor Union Forum (FSU), which speaks out on broader issues such as labor law reform.

Some Indonesians are critical of ACILS for its role in the union movement in Indonesia. Indera Nababan, the idiosyncratic and irascible founder of the Urban Community Mission (UCM), a 17-year-old NGO that works with factory workers and unions in the Jakarta area, accuses ACILS of creating and controlling labor unions and federations. He urges the workers he works with to avoid SPSI-R, SBSI, and the FNPBI, in part because he sees them as fronts for ACILS. "We don't believe there is a national trade union yet. We encourage workers to organize a strong trade union in the plant, and later to link up and create sectoral unions. We don't trust the trade unions. We believe unions should come from the workers themselves. We want to extend solidarity among the workers. First we had government-controlled unions, now we have ACILS-controlled unions." Indera claims that ACILS finances the most malleable union and NGO leaders. "The American money will go to whoever does not ask questions. Whoever asks questions will get no money." He also accuses ACILS of corrupting and co-opting some Indonesian union and NGO leaders and activists. "There is no transparency about the money," he said. "They have been co-opted by ACILS."

Surya Tjandra, an attorney with LBH, the Legal Aid Institute in Jakarta, offers different and less acerbic criticisms of ACILS. For Tjandra, the big problem is that neither ACILS nor the Indonesian unions have a real plan for strengthening the workers' movement:

> ACILS gives a lot of money to the unions, but the unions just follow the ACILS programs. I don't think that ACILS has a perspective. They don't know what they want, and the unions don't know how to use the money. The Indonesian unions take the money, and they have to spend the money, but they don't know how to spend it in ways that help the workers. I don't think Tim Ryan [the head of ACILS] wants to control the workers. Some of the problem is here. I don't see any independent unions, except perhaps the FNPBI.

Dita Sari, the leader of the FNPBI, has more experience than almost any other Indonesian labor leader, excepting Muchtar Pakpahan, with attempting to raise money from other union federations. While her federation accepts funds from ACILS, she also has serious political criticisms of the AFL-CIO and USAID for the way in which they assist independent labor unions in Indonesia. When I asked her about this funding, she told me,

> In fact, the AFL-CIO recently arranged a trip for me to the United States, and the State Department paid my travel costs. I also had three meetings with the U.S. State Department while I was there. I think the U.S. State Department and USAID give this money to the ACILS in order to control and moderate third world unions. The AFL-CIO also wants to keep third world unions moderate and to keep the foreign unions from attacking U.S. corporations. The State Department and the AFL-CIO have a common interest. The State Department has an interest in controlling and moderating the third world unions because they can't use the CIA any more. So, to achieve their goals, they use an institution like the AFL-CIO because it has legitimacy as a labor organization.

Why then does the FNPBI take USAID and ACILS money? "We need money to be able to build our organization and our program," Dita explained. "But we want an independent union and we want to keep our own ideological views. We want to be able to explain those views to the workers. So we do not accept any financial aid that would affect our independence or our ability to run our own education program." In practice, the FNPBI negotiates with ACILS over possible programs:

> We propose some programs to ACILS that they accept, and some they don't. They propose some programs to us that we accept and some we don't. ACILS once said to us, "How about if we finance your magazine and educational materials?" But they said, "We can't finance you if you say you are against U.S. imperialism, because the U.S. Embassy would block that." So, we don't want to accept money for the magazine or education. We do accept money for computers or fax machines or other equipment that is helpful to our work. But we do not accept money with conditions that would limit our ability to explain our ideology.

Dita also gives another example:

> Once I asked ACILS for money for a strike fund, because every time we have a strike we need to provide food for the striking workers. When I said this, ACILS said, "But what if you had a strike against a U.S. corporation? How would it look that U.S. money was going to a union striking against a U.S. company?" In the end, they said they could not give money for a strike fund. ACILS would like to give money only to moderate unions. But when they see our work in organizing workers into real unions, they can't justify not funding us.

Asked about these conversations, an ACILS senior staff person denied that any such conversation with Dita Sari had taken place. ACILS staff and consultants deny that they promote one sort of union over another. They assert that they give money to all genuine independent labor unions that are free from corruption and engage in real collective bargaining, period. To its credit, on the basis that it supports genuine labor unions, the ACILS office in Jakarta has supported the entire spectrum of the new unions in Indonesia, from the conservative SPSI-R and the moderate SBSI to the radical FNPBI.

"Even though we are in a situation with many problems, ACILS is not a pragmatic solution for us," Dita explains. "We are trying to build our own basis of economic support from our members. But that is difficult. We can't get dues check-off, because the companies will generally only give it to SPSI." So Dita continues to accept money from ACILS for equipment, material, and specific programs, though she remains leery of both the AFL-CIO and the State Department.

I asked Dita if she had received help from other unions.

> The Canadian Labor Congress supported our May Day activities. And the Australian Construction, Forest, Mining, and Energy Union has also supported us. But, really, we get little support from other labor unions. Even though I have traveled around the world and met the unions, it is really not easy to get money from them. They see the character of our union: radical, opposing the government, and using direct action and mass mobilization to fight for our demands. That makes them uncomfortable. We have been to the Netherlands, Belgium, and England. In England, I met with the Trade Unions Congress, and they have money, but, no, not for radical unions.

Other Solidarity Movements

Unions represent the most important source of solidarity for workers in other countries because they broaden and strengthen the struggle against the corporations and capital. When workers find other workers who have built unions to confront their employer or employers in their industry, then they have a potentially powerful new ally in the international struggle against corporations. Unions can work together across international boundaries to confront employers, and can support each other in the struggles against their own states when the states support capital.

While international labor support may be the most important form of solidarity, it is not the only one. In the last few years, student movements, consumers organizations, and human rights groups have also played an important role in solidarity with workers in countries such as Indonesia. These groups have the capacity to conduct research, organize educational campaigns, develop corporate codes of conduct, conduct labor rights monitoring, lead boycotts, lobby politicians in their own countries, and bring human rights cases before international organizations. Support organizations and their campaigns are usually strongest when they work in conjunction with the workers and unions with whom they are in solidarity, though this is not always possible.

Jeff Ballinger, former head of the AFL-CIO office in Jakarta, created Press for Change to take on the Nike corporation, particularly in Indonesia and other countries in Southeast Asia, and was later joined by Global Exchange and other organizations that took up the crusade against Nike. Other NGOs working on Nike included the Resource Center of the Americas, the National Labor Committee, and the People of Faith Network. Working with UNITE! (the Union of Needletrades, Industrial, and Textile Employees), they were able to bring considerable pressure to bear on Nike, though the company often responded with evasion and deception.

United Students Against Sweatshops (USAS), a U.S. student group founded in 1997, demanded that whenever a university logo was used on clothing, those garments be made in decent working conditions. USAS conducted sit-ins, occupying university buildings at the University of Arizona, Duke University, the University of Michigan, the University of Wisconsin at Madison, Georgetown University, and the University of North Carolina at Chapel Hill to demand an end to university logos on the products of sweatshop labor—and all six sit-ins proved successful. USAS demanded that university manufacturers adopt a code of conduct regarding labor conditions and full public disclosure of plants used to make the product. They also insisted that the code should be overseen by an independent Workers' Rights Consortium (WRC).

By late 1998, USAS had grown to more than 100 chapters. In some places, students had begun to expand their efforts to work with campus workers and local labor unions. As part of their own education about workers' rights issues, USAS students traveled to various countries around the world, among them Indonesia.[13] In Indonesia, ACILS helped them to contact employers, unions, and workers so that they could see workers' conditions and judge for themselves. The USAS activists met with SBSI and FNPBI union leaders and activists and with Indonesian student groups such as those in PIJAR.

Whether or not the USAS and the Indonesian unions and workers will be able to develop a long-term relationship, and how effective such a relationship will be, remains to be seen. But the USAS approach of organizing students to meet with workers in countries such as Indonesia to form an international worker-student alliance represents an exciting development. Workers have to play the central role in their own emancipation, but students can offer them assistance, and can themselves become an important part of the struggle.

Pseudo-Solidarity Movements

During the 1980s and 1990s, not-for-profit groups and NGOs flourished, and in various countries came together, calling themselves the organized expression of civil society. Turning away from charity and social work, many of these NGOs began to take an interest in labor rights, civil rights, and politics. The NGOs became organizations of activists often closely linked to progressive social movements. In many cases they supported grassroots groups and rank-and-file labor organizations, and backed environmentalists and indigenous people. In authoritarian societies in Eastern Europe and Latin America, they generally took up the cause of democracy.[14] Governments and corporations soon recognized the potential of the NGOs to shape public opinion and direct social movements, and began to create their own government-sponsored or corporate-directed NGOs.

After the appearance of groups like USAS at more than 100 campuses in 1998, employers responded by sponsoring their own youth group. The International Youth Foundation, a corporate-sponsored NGO, created the Global Alliance for Workers and

Communities, which describes itself as "an alliance of private, public, and not-for-profit organizations to help improve the lives, workplace experience, and communities of young working people in global manufacturing and service companies."[15]

The alliance, with an initial budget of $10 million, said it would work to identify workers' aspirations and issues, assess worker and community needs, and then conduct education and training to help resolve the workers' issues. The alliance defined its primary concern as clothing, toy, and athletic footwear manufacturers in various regions of the globe, including Southeast Asia, with an initial focus on Thailand, China, Vietnam, and Indonesia.

At first blush, this sounds like a not-for-profit prepared to tackle notorious sweatshop manufacturers such as Nike and the Gap. But it turns out the founding members of the Global Alliance for Workers and Communities included the World Bank, the Gap, Nike, and St. John's University. Mattel and the John D. and Catherine T. MacArthur Foundation also supported the alliance. James Wolfensohn of the World Bank praised the organization, noting, "This approach of negotiation of standards between business, government, civil society, and international institutions seems to be the best way to deal with this issue."[16]

What did the alliance recommend for the low-income workers of Southeast Asia in its July 2000 *Progress Report*? The alliance did not call on the corporations to raise wages, improve working conditions, or create supplemental benefits. It did not call upon the corporations to recognize labor unions or sign union contracts protecting workers' rights. Nor did it call for an end to the dictatorial or authoritarian governments, or for political or civil rights in those countries. The Global Alliance's only recommendation in its report was to establish mechanisms to help young workers set up savings accounts. The report implies that workers' poverty is due to their reckless spending, rather than looking at the authoritarian governments, the lack of civil and labor union rights, the anti-union employer policies, and the starvation wages workers are paid.[17] The Global Alliance was perhaps intended to act as a shield for the corporations, and thus another weapon against the workers. However, even this corporate creation found it hard to ignore the atrocious conditions in Indonesia's factories, such as low wages, long hours, and abuse.[18] Despite their efforts, such pseudo-reform organizations have failed to hoodwink many students into joining. Student activists have generally rejected such employer fronts and worked to create genuine pro-worker groups such as USAS.

International Labor Solidarity: The Future

International labor solidarity necessarily represents a part of the broader fight for human rights. From February 23 to 25, 2001, approximately 150 people from across the United States, joined by many Indonesians, East Timorese, Europeans, Australians, and New Zealanders, met to form the Indonesia Human Rights Network, which is dedicated to changing the U.S. policy of support for the Indonesian military, as well as working on other humanitarian issues. Among its other activities, such an organization can play an important role in denouncing workers' rights violations and promoting international labor solidarity.

Beyond this promising development, what is the future of international solidarity, particularly solidarity between U.S. unions and those in Indonesia? Clearly, the AFL-CIO has moved a long way from the positions of George Meaney and Lane Kirkland in the heyday of the Cold War, when the federation worked closely with the State Department and the CIA. However, the federation has yet to cut its ties to USAID and the State Department, and remains dependent on them to carry out much of its labor solidarity work. The AFL-CIO should break completely with the State Department and USAID, and go to its member unions to ask for an increase in dues to pay for its programs. As long as the federation is linked to the government, its behavior must inevitably be influenced and its motives will be suspect.

Around the world from Mexico to China, the State Department pushes for free trade policies that support U.S.-based banks and multinational corporations and hurt U.S. workers. With the help and cooperation of the State Department, U.S. corporations frequently have moved operations abroad to take advantage of authoritarian and anti-union regimes. In general, the State Department acts to support policies conceived by the corporations, passed into law by corporate lawyers elected to Congress, and enforced by an executive branch staffed by former and future corporate executives and attorneys. The idea that the State Department and USAID might work to further labor unions or workers' interests flies in the face of past history and contemporary reality. At home, the U.S. government maintains anti-labor measures such as Taft-Hartley and striker replacement so successfully that only 13.5 percent of all workers and only 9 percent of private-sector workers in the United States are organized in unions, one of the lowest rates of union density in the industrialized world. How can anyone seriously believe that the United States, which pursues an anti-labor agenda at home, would pursue pro-labor policies abroad?

The AFL-CIO should break off its relationship to the State Department, USAID, and the embassies and their labor attachés. U.S. embassies abroad are staffed with career diplomats and among them some CIA agents whose lives have been dedicated to undermining the efforts of working people around the world. The AFL-CIO should also demand that the U.S. government stop supporting the corporations and stop meddling in the affairs of labor unions and workers in other countries.

Why is it that Sweeney's AFL-CIO, the most progressive labor leadership in 50 years, has been unable to emancipate itself from the State Department? The reason is that its foreign policy is a continuation of its domestic policy. In the United States, the AFL-CIO has adopted a policy it calls "partnership." That is, it seeks partnership with corporations in the battle for productivity, quality, and competitiveness on the world market. Such a policy means that the AFL-CIO supports U.S. corporations in their struggle to defeat foreign corporations in international markets.

But, of course, every victory for a U.S. firm is a defeat for a foreign firm and leads to wage cuts, layoffs, plant closings, and bankruptcies. When a U.S. firm wins, foreign workers lose. So partnership with U.S. corporations necessarily means rivalry with foreign workers. The AFL-CIO's relationship to the State Department flows logically from partnership with U.S. corporations.

Another reason that the AFL-CIO works with the State Department is that the U.S. unions have no independent political existence, but depend on their relationship with the Democratic Party. The Democrats and Republicans remain at their highest levels almost completely controlled by the banks and multinational corporations. The banks and corporations provide their funding, leadership, staff, and ideas. As long as labor remains a captive of the Democratic Party, it cannot develop an independent foreign policy and, consequently, cannot establish any real independence from the government, whether under Democratic or Republican administration.

If U.S. workers had a working-class political party, a labor party, they would at least be able to begin to work out for themselves the framework for an alternative democratic and pro-labor foreign policy. There are, of course, many more immediate reasons why U.S. workers need their own political party, from stagnant wages to lack of health care. U.S. unions, however, are not likely to push for the creation of a labor party under their current leadership.

The AFL-CIO cannot both stand by U.S. corporations and stand by labor unions in other countries. The AFL-CIO should stand on the side of Indonesian workers and workers in other countries against the U.S. corporations, but if it does not stand against these companies at home, how can it do so abroad? Moreover, a stand against the corporations would logically imply a stand against a government dominated by those corporations. Neither U.S. workers nor their union leaders have yet decided that their real allies are not necessarily their compatriots, but

rather members of their class in other countries. Clearly it is difficult to come to the conclusion as a U.S. worker that I may have
more in common with an Indonesian Muslim worker than I do
with the corporate executive who belongs to my church, speaks
English, and looks like me. But, in fact, that is the meaning of international labor solidarity—the idea that class has more meaning
than country, that I would support workers in another country
before I would support corporations in my own.

But then, we might ask, can the AFL-CIO give up its partnership policy with the corporations, break with the Democratic
Party, and refuse to continue to work with the State Department
and USAID? Would that be realistic? Would it be responsible?
The truth of the matter is that the current method is neither realistic nor responsible. For almost the last 50 years, the AFL-CIO
has pursued a policy of politics within the Democratic Party and
cooperation abroad with the U.S. State Department. What has
been the result? Union membership has fallen from 35 percent in
the 1950s to 13.5 percent in 2000. U.S. manufacturing plants
have relocated abroad, eliminating jobs, unions, and contracts. At
home, the corporations have polluted and contaminated our
country, and destroyed much of our environment and our natural
wilderness. Abroad, those corporations have worked both with
the State Department and with authoritarian foreign governments such as that in Indonesia to exploit workers and rape the
environment. The AFL-CIO's approach, believing that corporations would cooperate with unions in such a way as to benefit
workers, has proven to be completely unrealistic.

If this is so, can we expect the AFL-CIO leadership to see the
light and move toward a more independent position at home and
a more solidarity-based policy abroad? After all, during the last
few years, Sweeney has already moved the AFL-CIO to the left,
breaking with some of the worst aspects of the old union foreign
policy, and also moving toward organizing and militancy at
home. The AFL-CIO's reform under Sweeney was not the result
of any great rank-and-file upheaval in the labor movement,

though increasing working-class discontent did play a role in the election of the New Voices slate. Sweeney and the new leadership moved toward a more progressive position because of the deteriorating position of labor unions in the United States, particularly the declining number of industrial workers and labor union members, but also because of the difficulties in organizing new members, winning union contracts, and achieving meaningful wage gains. The leadership made that move for several reasons: to protect its own position, to protect its members' interests, and to head off the possibility of rising discontent in the unions. Couldn't the AFL-CIO continue to move to the left?

Sweeney and other leaders of the federation adopted reform and moved to the left primarily because they felt their own interests and those of their institutions to be threatened. As it has made this move, the Sweeney leadership has been buoyed by the support of a whole layer of rising union leaders, most of them between 40 and 55 years old, who became involved in union politics after having been influenced by the civil rights movement, the anti-war movement, and the women's movement. Those relatively younger leaders have both provided personnel to staff the new AFL-CIO and, more important, brought new policies and a new vision of the union movement. These local union activists, officials, staffers, and consultants—some of them former leftists who were once involved in the Maoist and Trostkyist party-building efforts of the 1970s or members or ex-members of the Communist Party and the Democratic Socialists of America—have now mostly adopted a social democratic political outlook that places them on the far left of the U.S. political spectrum. While these left-of-center secondary leaders have helped support the Sweeney reforms, they do not have an alternative program to put forward for the AFL-CIO; nor do they have an organizational vehicle for putting forward their ideas within the labor movement.

The AFL-CIO, having incorporated that younger layer of leaders produced by the last great series of social movements in the United States, seems unlikely to move any further left without pressure from below. As corporations and government employers continue to put pressure on the labor unions, and as workers' wages and conditions continue to stagnate or decline, we can expect at some time a workers' rebellion from below. If history is any guide, a rank-and-file workers' movement will raise demands for union democracy and militancy, forcing the leadership to move to the left or be swept aside by new leaders. At this point, it seems likely that that is the only way that the federation will be moved any further to the left.

What about the work of particular U.S. labor unions in the area of international solidarity? Several AFL-CIO labor unions and other independent unions have been involved in labor solidarity efforts, mostly with Mexico and Central America. UNITE!, the textile and garment workers union, the International Brotherhood of Teamsters (IBT), the United Steel Workers of America, the United Auto Workers (UAW), and the United Electrical Workers (UE) have all become involved to one degree or another in work with Mexican labor unions. U.S. labor unions have offered economic resources and educational programs, sent delegations to investigate conditions, and protested abuses of workers' rights to national and international bodies. While Mexican labor unions and workers have generally appreciated the gestures of solidarity, they have also been leery of being taken over by the U.S. unions, which have greater size, power, and, above all, treasuries. In addition, U.S. labor union officials have sometimes acted with insensitivity, presuming that they knew what was best for their Mexican brothers and sisters. Even with the best of intentions, such attitudes will provoke fear of U.S. trade union imperialism among Mexican unionists.

The most interesting and important of the recent international solidarity efforts by U.S. unions is a strategic alliance between UE and the Authentic Labor Front (FAT), an independent union in Mexico. Based on the principle of mutuality and reciprocity, the UE and the FAT have worked out an arrangement in which both unions offer each other organizing support. While each union remains in charge of these organizing efforts in its own country, they also help each other out by exchanging organizers and sharing resources. The collaboration, while not without its tensions, has led to growing mutual respect over the years, and to a deepening appreciation of both cultural differences and political similarities. The UE's ability to develop this relationship with the FAT has no doubt been made possible by the fact that the UE has historically rejected the partnership model of the AFL-CIO. (UE is not a member of the federation.) The UE-FAT experience represents a wonderful model of labor union and worker-to-worker solidarity on the North American continent, but whether such solidarity could be worked out across oceans and continents, as in the case of Indonesian unions and workers, remains to be seen. Certainly, cultural, religious, and linguistic challenges are greater, as are financial and logistical difficulties.

The AFL-CIO and most of its affiliated international or national unions remain committed to the partnership model, and therefore to international competition rather than solidarity. Only a broad reform movement driven by rank-and-file workers is likely to change the leadership, and that remains a difficult prospect. Even then, there is no guarantee that a more democratic and militant leadership arising out of a rank-and-file movement would necessarily be more internationalist in outlook, and it could possibly be even more narrowly nationalistic. But countervailing tendencies also exist, such as the growing immigrant composition of the workforce, including people who have organized in other countries with a more internationalist labor tradition, and the growing awareness among workers that their bosses operate globally. At present, there are few rank-and-file groups within labor unions, and those that exist—such as Teamsters for a Democratic Union (TDU) in the Teamsters and the New Directions Movement (NDM) in the UAW—do not tend to have developed political views on questions of international labor solidarity. While some TDU or NDM leaders may have internationalist views, the organizations have not generally educated their fellow members about those views very broadly or deeply. This means that labor union activists and union supporters must continue to raise the idea of international labor solidarity within their unions and among workers.

At present, most local unions and most workers have little or no idea of what it would mean to act to back workers in their own country, much less to support workers in another. Labor activists have to raise the idea of international labor solidarity as a moral, strategic, and long-term political issue. Workers may be won to the idea of international solidarity out of their existing ethical views based on religion or a humanist morality, an appeal to our common humanity. But they must also be won on the basis of self-interest to appreciate the strategic importance of an alliance between workers in different countries who will gain the economic power to confront and defeat the corporations. An international labor alliance would make possible coordinated strikes, boycotts, and political campaigns in two or more countries, thus undercutting the corporations' ability to pit workers against each other. Finally, workers must be won to an understanding of the importance of the labor movement developing an independent politics that will allow it to engage in genuine international labor solidarity.

The Question of Socialism

The debate and discussion over NAFTA; the protests in 1999 and 2000 against the World Trade Organization (WTO), the IMF, and the World Bank; and the fight over PNTR with China have led to a broader discussion about alternatives to the existing corporate-dominated free market trade relations. The critics of the WTO, IMF, World Bank, and PNTR for China argued that multinational banks and corporations undemocratically dominate all world trade arrangements, which benefit those corporations at the expense of working-class people and poor farmers or peasants. While the banks, corporations, and international financial institutions such as the IMF carry out a globalization from above, many anti-corporate activists argue that the world's people need to carry out a globalization from below.[19]

Various groups and individuals have raised ideas about what have come to be called "alternative architectures" for world trade, that is, other possible schemes for the organization of the world economy. Most of these alternative architectures call for a reduction in world trade, protectionism, a return to regulation of corporations, or the breaking up of corporate monopolies. The more radical proposals, which might be called conservative social- democratic conceptions, call for some form of international capitalist planning. The problem with all of these models is that they would leave the corporation as the dominant economic and social institution because they hesitate to raise the idea of a society without corporations, that is, a society without capitalism.[20]

While some currents in the international labor movement have promoted a social democratic vision of an alternative architecture—in an attempt to revive the idea of the welfare state managed by a labor or socialist party—the AFL-CIO has virtually nothing to say on the creation of an alternative vision for the world economy. As long as the AFL-CIO holds the view that it wants to be in partnership with U.S. corporations in the competition for world markets, it will be unable to develop any useful alternatives for U.S. workers or those in other countries.

If we were really to reject corporate domination and free trade, what could we say to U.S. and Indonesian workers? Wouldn't we have to say that the corporate-owned and managed world is inherently undemocratic and unjust? If we rejected that world, wouldn't we have to propose a world of democracy and social justice, a world of greater economic and social equality? Wouldn't this discussion lead us to the idea of the democratically controlled economy that has for the last 150 years been called socialism? Couldn't we build democratic national and international institutions to manage the world's economy, rather than let that economy periodically swirl out of control as it did in the Asian crisis of 1997 with such devastating effects?

While the AFL-CIO does not and is not likely in the near future to embrace the idea of a socialist reorganization of the world economy, that is, in fact, the logical choice for the world's workers. Those of us engaged in human rights work and in promoting international labor solidarity must not be afraid to explain that the logical expression of the more democratic and humane world that we strive for would be a socialist one.

Unfortunately, socialism was identified for almost a century either with capitalist welfare states in Western Europe or with the Stalinist Communist states of the Soviet Union or China. After the fall of Soviet Communism in 1989, the capitalist world claimed victory in the great struggle for world domination, and conservative commentators proclaimed socialism dead forever. But in the last decade a series of economic crises and the chronic problems of capitalism around the world—the millions of people living in poverty, hunger, and desperation—have called the entire system into question. At the same time, new social movements such as those described in this book have risen up to challenge the powers-that-be and raised the possibility of a new worldwide movement for democracy and equality.

The historic name for the democratic reorganization of the world's economic and social life is socialism. The PRD has raised the idea in Indonesia, and we should be prepared to raise it in ours. The future of the Indonesian movement, of our own society, and of the world depends on it.

1   Karl Marx, *On the First International,* ed. Saul K. Padover (New York: McGraw-Hill Book Company, 1973), 12.

2   Leon Trotsky, *The First Five Years of the Communist International* (New York: Pathfinder Press, 1972), vol. 1, 29–30.

3   The meeting organized by ICFTU-APRO, took place in Jakarta on July 27-28 and was attended by 23 different trade unions—TSK (Textile Workers' Union—Reformasi), Kahutindo (Woodworkers—Reformasi), Kahut (Woodworkers—Status Quo), SPMI (Indonesian Metal Workers' Union), Farkes (Pharmaceutical Workers' Union—both Reformasi and Status Quo), ASPEK, PGRI (Indonesian Teachers' Association), KEP (Chemical Workers' Union—Reformasi), PPMI (Printing Workers' Union—Reformasi), RTMM (Food and Beverage Workers' Union—both Status Quo and Reformasi), Construction Workers' Union (Status Quo), Air Transport Workers' Union, KPI (Indonesian Seamen's Union), SP BUMN (State Enterprise Workers' Union), Pariwisata (Tourist Workers' Union—Status Quo), Korpri (Civil Servants' Association), Sarbumusi, Gasbiindo, Plantation Workers' Union (Status Quo), Inland Road Workers' Union (Status Quo), and the Journalists' Union (Status Quo). The meeting was also attended by a number of international trade secretariats (ITS's), including ICEM, IFBWW, FIET, Education International, TWARO, and briefly, by the IUF. From ACILS, *Monthly Report* (July 2000), 20-21.

4   ACILS, *Monthly Report* (July 2000), 21.

5   Beth Sims, *Workers of the World Undermined: American Labor's Role in U.S. Foreign Policy* (Boston: South End Press, 1992); Hobart A. Spalding, Jr., "U.S. Labour Intervention in Latin America: The Case of the American Institute of Free Labor Development," in Roger Southall, *Trade Unions and the New Industrialization of the Third World* (Pittsburgh: University of Pittsburgh Press, 1988), 259-286.

6   Cite AFL-CIO web site 2000.

7   Rachel Hays, "AFL-CIO Restructuring Favors Cross-Border Solidarity," *Borderlines* 28 (October 1996). This article is available on-line at http://www.zianet.com/irc1/bordline/1996/bl28/bl28cio.html.

8   From USAID home page: http://www.usaid.gov, July 2000.

9   Interview with USAID spokesperson on condition of anonymity, USAID office, U.S. Embassy, Jakarta, Indonesia, June 13, 2000.

10   Interview with USAID spokesperson, USAID office, on condition of anonymity.

11   "Program Summary: ACILS-USAID Program (June 1998 – September 2000), a two-page document provided by the USAID office at the U.S. Embassy in Jakarta, Indonesia.

12   American Center for International Labor Solidarity (ACILS), *Monthly Report* (April 1998), 11.

13   In 1999, while working at Global Exchange, I was approached by USAS to take a group to learn about conditions in the maquiladoras at the U.S.-Mexico border, which we did. I was impressed when Jeremy Blasi called me and said, "We think if we are going to be speaking out on behalf of these workers, we should know what they think about the situation." This has been the admirable internationalist spirit of USAS in its solidarity work.

14   At the same time the very structure of the NGOs sometimes inhibited them or compromised their independence. Corporate foundations usually financed these NGOs; wealthy, professional and middle-class boards generally oversaw them; while liberal or social democratic directors ran them, hiring the radical organizers who often worked for them. The NGO organizers sometimes intervened in social problem areas and even directed social movements. Some NGOs became social vacuum cleaners sucking up discontent and redirecting it in reformist channels, rather than acting as vehicles for genuine social change. In the worst cases, the independent NGOs became sinecures for retiring revolutionaries, or money-pots that corrupted former activists. But, all of that said, many NGOs certainly contributed to the development of radical social movements.

15   See the Global Alliance web site: http://www.theglobalalliance.org/.

16   "Global Alliance Formed to Enhance Workers' Lives," press release, April 7, 1999, page 1. This press release is available on-line at http://www.theglobalalliance.org/content/news2.cfm.

17   Judith Bruce, "Viewpoint: Controlling Earned Income and Savings Opportunities: A Right for All—A Revolution for Young Working Women," in Global Alliance for Workers and Communities, *Progress Report* 1: 3 (July 2000): 3. Other articles in the report emphasize that workers are paid more than the minimum wage, and the entire issues focuses on savings accounts as the answer to workers' problems.

18   *Workers' Voice: An Interim Report on Workers' Needs and Aspirations in Nine Nike Contract Factories in Indonesia.* See the Introduction for my summary and assessment of this report.

19   For the "from below" point of view, see, for example, Daniel Singer, *Whose Millennium? Theirs or Ours* (New York: Monthly Review Press, 1999); and Kevin Danaher, *Globalize This! The Battle Against the World Trade Organization and Copororate Rule* (Monroe, Maine: Common Courage Press, 2000).

20   For critics who raise alternative global architectures but who then propose reforms short of socialism, see Jeremy Brecher, Tim Costello, and Brendan Smith, "Our Financial Architecture and Theirs" and Jeremy Brecher amd Brendan Smith, "The Global Sustainable Development Resolution," both available on-line at Z Net: http://www.zmag.org.

Epilogue

Socialism from Below

What are the essential steps to solving Indonesia's enormous economic problems? The first is the cancellation of Indonesia's foreign debt. Today, Indonesians labor under a foreign debt of about $100 billion, one of the largest in the world. Every year for many years, the Indonesian government will have to devote an enormous proportion of its gross national product to paying down the debt, depriving its citizens of money needed for infrastructure, basic housing and food subsidies, social programs such as health and education, and culture and the arts. The whole world recognizes that Suharto and his illegitimate dictatorship were responsible for those debts, many of them arranged to benefit him and his cronies. The Indonesian people should not be asked to pay the debts contracted by the despot who oppressed them. The multinational banks and corporations, foreign governments, and international financial institutions should cancel those debts in the interest of justice and fairness.

A second essential step in bringing justice to Indonesia is the expropriation and nationalization of all of the wealth of the Suharto family, of their cronies, and of the political and military leaders who continue to benefit from the crooked deals made by the old regime. By all rights, those fields and farms, mines and oil fields, factories and mills should belong to the people of Indonesia, and should be taken over by the government on their behalf. Article 27 of the Indonesian Constitution asserts that the Republic of Indonesia holds the national wealth on behalf of the people. This article provides a legal basis for the seizure, nationalization, and democratic administration of this property.

Finally, the people of Indonesia have a right to control their nation's banking system, its industry, and its foreign trade, the commanding heights of the archipelago's economy. For 400 years, Indonesians' labor as slaves, forced laborers, and later as wage laborers (but virtual wage slaves) produced the wealth of Indonesia's capitalists, whether they were indigenous Indonesians (*pribumi*), Chinese Indonesians, or foreign-owned or multinational corporations. The Indonesian working people, and the Indonesian people as a whole, have 400 years of sweat equity invested in that property, and it rightfully belongs to them. Of course, the three measures sketched out here (and it would be incredibly difficult to actually carry out such a tremendous economic, social, and political reorganization) represent only the beginning of the creation of a new Indonesia, for the real challenge would be to insert that Indonesia into a new context, that of a just and equitable world economic system: international socialism.

But what does socialism really mean? Since the beginning, the idea of socialism has been a contested terrain. Karl Marx and Friedrich Engels, the founders of modern socialism, already felt obligated in writing the *Communist Manifesto* in 1848 to differentiate their version of socialism from earlier ones.[1] Today, 150 years later, after dozens of countries have tried one or another sort of system called socialist or communist, the issue has become even more complicated and confusing. In a world cluttered with the remains of scores of socialisms, and several existing socialist or Communist parties and governments, how do we distinguish among them? Several years ago, a U.S. socialist named Hal Draper made the suggestion that we distinguish between what he called "the two souls of socialism," the advocates of socialism from above and socialism from below.[2]

Socialism from above refers to socialism created by an elite that argues it knows what is best for the people, and seeks to lead them to it or impose it on them. Even when these socialists seem well-intentioned and benevolent to begin with, Draper argued, they inevitably end up engendering authoritarianism, oppression, and exploitation. The great logical and moral contradiction of these socialisms from above is that the elite minority can never really know what is best for the majority; the few can never know what the many want and need. The missing element in this sort of socialism is democracy.

Draper saw the tradition of socialism from above as beginning with Ferdinand Lassalle, the founder of German socialism, and continuing through Friedrich Ebert in Germany and Joseph Stalin in the Soviet Union. Today, the principal advocates of some sort of socialism from above are the social democrats who in various countries in Western Europe administer (or hope to administer) capitalism and the Stalinists, or bureaucratic Communists (most accurately bureaucratic collectivists), who rule (or ruled) the Communist countries mostly in Eastern Europe and Asia. Without democracy, socialism tends to become a bureaucratic dictatorship, a command economy. Instead of a regime where people begin to realize their freedom, it becomes a prison.

Socialism from below, on the other hand, is predicated upon the notion that socialism must be democratic, and that the majority of the people must make the decisions that affect their lives under socialism. Socialism from below suggests that the making of a socialist society must be the work of working people themselves democratically transforming society through their own efforts. Self-emancipation, self-administration, and workers' control (*auto-gestion* as it is sometimes called) represent the touchstone ideas of socialism from below. This tradition calls for working people, the majority of society, to run everything, from their workplaces and communities to their national economy. Democratic socialism holds out the hope of a world organized by and for the people, a change brought about by a revolutionary upheaval from below. Thus, socialism from below stands in revolutionary opposition not only to capitalism, but also to the so-called socialisms imposed from above, such as social democracy and Stalinism.

Advocates of socialism from below can at present boast of no existing society where its principles are put into practice, but it cherishes the brief workers' revolutions and democratic socialist

experiences in Paris in 1871, in Russia in 1917, in parts of Spain in
the 1930s, and in Hungary in 1956, as well as scores of other attempts at workers' power in the Americas, Asia, and Africa.

Party and Class

In the practical struggle for socialism, one key factor determining
whether or not a social revolution terminates in a socialism run
from above or a socialism created and controlled from below
may be found in the relationship between a socialist party and the
working class. The question is: does the socialist party (or parties)
have a dynamic and democratic relationship to the working class
such that the party represents a genuine leadership (the historic
term is "the vanguard") of the working class, and not a substitute
for it? There can be many measures of that relationship: the
party's real rootedness in the working class; the role of party leaders in working-class organizations such as labor unions; the ability of working-class organizations to influence the party; and the
ability of the party to mobilize the working class in economic
struggle, in electoral contests, and in a direct challenge to the existing regime. A socialist political party also establishes its relationship to the working class through the strategy of the united front,
that is, entering into alliances with other political parties, labor organizations, and social movements in the fight for common goals
in the larger national framework. Only if the party represents a
genuine leadership of the working class with organic and democratic ties to the labor movements and the poor can one hope
that a revolution will lead to a democratic socialist society.[3]

The party relationship, however, is only one check on the
creation of an authoritarian socialism. Perhaps even more important is the role of democratic institutions of power through which
the working class (and, in countries like Indonesia, the peasantry)
can run a society. Historically, in situations of deep social crisis,
workers created their own institutions of struggle and power,
such as the neighborhood committees of the Paris Commune
and the workers', peasants', and soldiers' councils of the Russian
Revolution. Workers created representative leadership bodies

through which working people could elect a leadership and, if necessary, recall and change their leaders at will. The breakdown of both party democracy and the broader class democracy of the soviets under the tremendous crisis of war, revolution, and social collapse led to the failure of the experiment in socialism from below in Russia and to a counter-revolution, its replacement by Stalin's socialism from above.

Socialism is an abstraction and an ideal that has always been fought for in a world of concrete realities. The fight for working-class democracy necessarily takes place in hierarchical and authoritarian societies and in the midst of struggles that inevitably engender new power relationships. The history of the fight for socialism in Indonesia has been a tragic one, largely because the Dutch colonists who prided themselves on their parliamentary democracy at home ran a police state in their East Indies colonies. The Dutch used spies, police repression, exile, and imprisonment to control their subjects. On the broader political playing field, they encouraged racial and religious competition and conflict, leaving a legacy of hatred and violence. The imperial and colonial experience inhibited, undermined, and distorted the struggle for democracy, socialism, and humanitarian ideals, creating a less than ideal environment for the socialist experiment.

European immigrants and labor unionists introduced socialism to Indonesia in the late nineteenth and early twentieth centuries. The revolutionary socialist version of socialism, socialism from below, arrived with Henk Sneevliet and other Dutch socialists at the outbreak of World War I. Sneevliet and the Indonesian Semaun led the founding of the Indonesian Communist Party (PKI), the first in Asia in 1920. Under Indonesian leaders such as Semaun and Tan Malaka, the PKI had remarkable success in making inroads among Muslim workers, particularly railroad workers, and seemed well on its way to building a powerful national party, despite the repression of the Dutch.

But other PKI leaders, like Musso, apparently fearing that the Dutch were cornering them, were impatient for revolution and laid the plans for an insurrection in 1926. The Communist International, then led by Joseph Stalin, as well as the PKI chairman in exile, Tan Malaka, sometimes mistakenly described as a Trotskyist, both warned the PKI that the conditions for revolution were not ripe. They argued that the PKI had too few members, too weak an organization, and, moreover, faced a strong and united opposition. Nevertheless, the PKI went ahead with its uprising. In the event, it was a disaster, leading to imprisonment and death for many, and to the destruction of the party.

Throughout the 1930s and 1940s the PKI followed the many twists and turns of Stalin's Comintern, first rejecting all alliances with other left and labor groups in the "revolutionary" third period from 1929 to 1935, then turning toward a popular front with nationalists and Muslim organizations from 1935 to 1941. During the popular front period of the 1930s, a period of alliance between Communist and capitalist parties, the Dutch and Indonesian Communists even downplayed the demand for Indonesian independence. After the Nazis' attack on the Soviet Union in 1941, the PKI aligned itself with the Allies and with the government of the Netherlands, a position it retained throughout the war. This, of course, tended to isolate the PKI from the nationalist movement that saw its opportunities either in an alliance with Japan or in a guerrilla resistance movement against the Japanese now and the Dutch later.

With the end of the war in 1945, the PKI moved back toward the mainstream, returning to a popular front approach that submerged its differences with the nationalists led by Sukarno and Hatta. However, with the outbreak of the Cold War, the PKI shifted back into opposition to the nationalist leadership now seeking support from the United States. Friction increased between the Indonesian revolutionary government and the Communists, and Sukarno moved to drive the PKI out of leadership positions in the military. At the same time, the Communists may have thought that they could do in Indonesia in 1948 what they were doing in Czechoslovakia. In 1948 in Madiun a group of PKI military leaders initiated a local insurrection, and then succeeded in getting the national party to support it. The result was a military and political disaster that eliminated the party from national politics for several years.

Remarkably, the PKI had revived by the early 1950s, but now, under the influence of Stalin and the Soviet Union, it rejected its previous insurrectionary history and adopted a reformist strategy. More than reformist, the PKI adopted a position of supporting President Sukarno, even when he proclaimed his "Guided Democracy" dictatorship. This popular front—that is, this cross-class alliance with Sukarno and the ruling elite—created some organizing opportunities for the party, and it grew rapidly among the peasants and workers. But the price was high: it lost its political independence. Supporting Sukarno, the PKI also became dependent on him. When in the early 1960s Sukarno moved away from the Soviet Union and toward its rival, Mao's China, the PKI moved with him. The PKI's primary loyalty ceased to be to the Indonesian working class or even Stalin's Soviet Union, but became loyalty to Sukarno. Dependent on Sukarno's nationalist dictatorship and looking for inspiration either from Stalinist Russia or Maoist China, two totalitarian dictatorships, the PKI could develop no democratic strategy for revolution in Indonesia. The PKI's 1920 ideal of socialism from below had been supplanted by the idea of Sukarno and the PKI handing down socialism from above. Other strains of socialism existed in Indonesia at that time, the most interesting being Tan Malaka's attempt to fight for national independence and democracy while also pushing forward a fight for socialism.[4]

What is the most important lesson of the PKI experience from the 1920s to the 1960s? As long as the PKI drew workers and peasants into alliances where they were subordinated to nationalists, there was no hope of a democratic movement for socialism from below. The interests of the working class and the peasantry were subordinated to the interests of national and international capital or to the interests of the Communist states. At the same time, such alliances directed the labor movement into the struggle for power within a bourgeois framework, rather than attempting to rupture that framework and create new, more democratic, institutions as the expression of the power of the laboring majority. Only when the working class exercises complete political independence can it possibly build the mass movement from below necessary to overthrow capitalism.

Suharto's 1965 coup and the massacres of between 500,000 and 1 million Communists and their sympathizers destroyed the PKI and its labor unions and peasant leagues. Suharto's New Order regime cut off virtually all political and intellectual contact with Communist China and the Soviet Union, and only a tiny percentage of the Indonesian elite had any opportunity to learn anything about European social democracy. Only student exiles in Australia, the United States, or Europe were likely to learn about the traditions of revolutionary socialism from below, which had been reduced to tiny currents among intellectuals and activists in those countries. As already described, the People's Democratic Party (PRD) student activists started from scratch, taking some inspiration from the Maoist Communists of the Philippines to recreate a revolutionary socialist current.

The PRD

The PRD has just begun the process of creating a revolutionary party in Indonesia, and has still to develop that dynamic relationship between party and class that marks a healthy development in the creation of socialism from below. Whether or not it will actually accomplish the task of creating such a relationship remains to be seen. In my interviews with PRD leaders, I was struck by the fact that they remained in many ways a student group that has yet to come to grips with its relationship to workers, unions, and the working class. The young intellectuals and students who created the PRD have to be admired for their success in organizing several mass organizations, such as Students in Solidarity for Democracy in Indonesia (SMID), the National Peasant Union (STN), and the National Front for Indonesian Labor Struggle

(FNPBI). Through these organizations, they have begun to develop a broader social base within the Indonesian society and in the working class. The old style of labor organizing, based on responding to worker strikes or appearing at factories to call workers out, has given way to taking responsibility for leading workers' organizations that determine when to strike. The PRD as a party can now give a lead to the working class, but finds it must do so through discussions with small contingents of worker leaders and activists. The PRD's early role as a group outside the working class has been changed, and it is now a small force within the working class. While this represents an advance, it is little more than the first step.

In the past, the Suharto dictatorship's severe repression made it difficult to organize democratic party conferences or other public discussions of politics in Indonesia. While Indonesia remains far from a democratic society, the repression has eased up, and the PRD can now organize public events and debates. To take advantage of this opening, which is possibly a temporary one, the PRD understands that it will have to create a strong organizational structure, a real national newspaper, and regional newspapers. Only with a party press and party radio stations will the PRD be able to have the dynamic democratic relationship with the working class on which genuine socialism is predicated. At present, with its weak infrastructure and lack of economic resources, it does not yet have even the organizational basis that would make such a relationship possible.

Socialism from below and the democratic relationship between party and class also depend on the strategy of the united front. To influence other organizations, social movements, and political parties, the PRD has to be able to enter into alliances with such groups around specific economic and political issues. Activists tend to learn through experience, and it is only by going through experiences with other organizations that the PRD can test its positions and see if they prove correct in practice. When it does, it will win others to its views.

The PRD immersed itself in the student movement in the period from 1996 to 1998 in a real united front of social organizations, and proved to be among the most politically consistent of the student groups. Since that time, PRD leaders complain that they have found it more difficult to work with other organizations in the student movement or with other political parties. However, the PRD-inspired labor federation, the FNPBI, does seem to work in a united-front fashion with other unions, at least at certain times. The PRD has just begun the process of building a socialist party, establishing the organization, building a social base, organizing its own press, and developing a relationship to other movements, organizations, and parties. Whether or not it will be able to create a mass party of millions such as the PKI once was remains to be seen.

Democracy and Socialism in Indonesia

The PRD, or for that matter, any other leftist party in Indonesia, faces enormous challenges. The last time I talked with PRD leaders, in the summer of 2000, the party claimed to have 10,000 members throughout the islands and to be growing among young people.[5] Despite its still small size, the PRD aspires to lead workers and farmers in the struggle for democracy and socialism. But the task is a daunting one in a country that has only been partially democratized and where the military remains deeply involved in government. Indonesia, now embroiled in many national, religious, and ethnic conflicts across the archipelago, seems to face the threat of either a return to power of the military or the rise of Islamic fundamentalism. What are the prospects for democracy and socialism in such a society?

History never repeats itself, but capitalism, which has been a world system for the last 500 years, tends—even in very diverse cultural circumstances and in different conjunctures—to generate similar economic and political structures. In the competitive struggle for profit and accumulation, capitalism develops through long waves of expansion and contraction and through short-term business cycles. At the same time, it develops through experiences of political reaction and political liberalism, and produces both periods of stability and periods of crisis and potentially revolutionary situations. If history does not repeat itself, it does produce trends and patterns and reproduce structures and relationships. Consequently, similar problems and opportunities arise in different eras and different places. Revolutions in Europe in 1789, 1848, 1871, and 1917–1918, and in various parts of the world in 1946, 1956, 1959, and 1968–1975, presented similar historical problems though the economic, political, and cultural situations were different. The central question posed in each of those situations was: what class attempts to take power and reorganize society? Today, capitalism has reproduced in Indonesia a set of conditions parallel to those faced in other societies in the past and similar to other contemporaneous societies (such as China).

The conditions today in Indonesia bear a striking resemblance to the situation in Tsarist Russia at the beginning of the twentieth century. Under Suharto, Indonesia was a virtual monarchy. Like Russia, whose economy was dominated by French and English capital, Indonesia has been dominated by foreign capital, in this case, Japanese, off-shore Chinese, European, and U.S. Because of foreign investments and political-military alliances, Indonesia has grown dependent and, consequently, has a weak bourgeoisie, just as in Russia. And, like Russia at the opening of the twentieth century, Indonesia's people desire both democracy and improvements in their economic conditions. Finally, much as in Russia, organized religion by and large supports reaction. If the debates of Lenin, Trotsky, Stalin, and Mao have held an attraction for the Indonesian left and for the students and workers there, it is hardly surprising. The Indonesian student or worker activists seeing the Suharto dictatorship and the virtual enslavement of workers and poor peasants, must feel that they are re-living an earlier period of human history, one that should have been superceded long ago.

The problem in these societies, whether Russia in 1900 or Indonesia in 2000, is that the national elite cannot be relied upon to fight for democracy. The Indonesian capitalist class has since the 1940s preferred the security of military institutions.[6] Moreover, Indonesian bankers and industrialists have become so involved with and dependent on Japanese, off-shore Chinese, and U.S. capitalists that they have limited socioeconomic or political independence. The Indonesian capitalists hardly constitute a real capitalist class, in part because they have never created broad bourgeois institutions. It is the military or the Muslim organizations, for example, that have created Indonesia's think tanks and foundations, not the capitalists. Contrary to the claims of Western ideologues that capitalism and free markets spread democracy, they have done no such thing in Indonesia.

Indonesia's capitalists have never shown a vocation for democracy. Unlike the situations in Europe in the late eighteenth and early nineteenth centuries, the Indonesian bourgeoisie cannot be relied on today to lead a fight for democracy. The situation in Indonesia today is much more like that in Russia in 1900, when a dependent and cowardly capitalist class preferred the tsar to a struggle for democracy that might set the workers and peasants in motion. One only need look at the experience of the fall of Suharto to see the reactionary character of the Indonesian capitalists. Even with the fall of the dictator—brought about not by the capitalists but by students and the popular classes—not one of the major bourgeois political parties of Indonesia led a fight for democracy. Not one of those parties led a fight to purge the military from the government and create a genuinely democratic parliament. Not one of those parties called for full political and civil rights, including an end to Indonesia's religious laws.[7] In large measure, they did not do so because the military government served their interests. Only the PRD, a small socialist party, called for thoroughgoing democracy.

Because the Indonesian capitalists won't lead a fight for democracy against the military, that responsibility falls on the people of Indonesia. The people—that is, the majority of the people, the workers and farmers of Indonesia—find that they must push the bourgeoisie and other social classes toward the goal of democracy, and in doing so find that they must lead the fight for democracy themselves. But to lead such a fight, workers and farmers need strong organizations, labor unions, and farmers' associations. Most important, they need a political party that can coordinate that struggle for democracy. The PRD, almost unique in the Indonesian political spectrum, aims to be the party that will lead the Indonesian people in their struggle for democracy.[8]

After the fall of Suharto, the PRD proposed that the Indonesian people should fight for a genuine democratic government. At the same time, the party also urged the people to create their own democratic institutions, what it called peoples' councils, or councils of students, workers, and peasants. The PRD argued that only the people mobilized could create the political pressure that would lead to democracy. The call for people's councils of workers and peasants echoed the Bolsheviks' call for the workers' and peasants' councils (the soviets) to take power in Russia in 1917. While the PRD denied that it wanted these councils to take power, saying that it merely wanted them to ensure genuinely democratic elections, PRD leaders must have recognized that if such councils had been created (in fact, there was not much of a response and virtually none were established), the party would have found itself leading a parliament of workers and farmers in a struggle for power. What would it have done then?

If a party such as the PRD leads workers and peasants in the struggle for democracy, and those workers and peasants succeed in taking power either through control of a constituent assembly or parliament, or through their control of peoples' councils, why would that party wish to return power to Indonesia's capitalists who have for so long denied them their democratic rights and their workplace rights? Wouldn't the logic of events lead workers and farmers to assume responsibility for running the society? Would the workers' and peasants' fight for democracy become their fight for political power? And wouldn't the struggle for democracy tend to become a struggle for socialism?[9]

If what I have described above is true, then the logic of the situation facing the PRD demands that it ask: how do we become the leading and hegemonic party in society? How does a revolutionary workers' party take leadership of the labor unions, and the working class in general, and how does it give leadership to the farmers? I think that there are two answers to this question. First, such a socialist party must be the most consistent fighter for the democratic rights of all people, including the rights of workers and farmers, oppressed nationalities, minority religions, women, and gays and lesbians. A left party must be the spokesperson for all of the oppressed of society, what Lenin called "a tribune of the people." Second, a socialist party must speak to the needs and the economic and social interests of workers, farmers, and the poor. By taking up the fight for the interests of the majority, and by setting that majority in motion, a leftist party becomes a force for democracy in society. If such a party consistently leads the fight for democracy and becomes the leading party of the workers and peasants, it will enter the struggle for political power. If it succeeds in taking power, such a party will not surrender it to the Indonesian bourgeoisie, but will have to create a workers' government and begin the transition to socialism. The party's ability to engage in united front activities with other parties, labor unions, and social movements will largely determine its ability to gradually become the hegemonic group within the working class and then within society.

Of course, there may be more than one, and in fact there may be several working-class political parties and other parties, that would have to be recognized within the context of some new representative institutions. Socialism from below suggests a multiparty democracy where workers and their representatives could choose from alternative political programs.

Trotsky's description of "permanent revolution," the idea that the struggle for democracy becomes the struggle for socialism under the leadership of the working class, seems as applicable today as it was in Russia in 1905 and again in 1917, at least in Indonesia.[10] Indonesia has no capitalist class willing to fight for its national sovereignty and for democracy, and there seems to be little or no space for a democratic movement fighting for reform. The PRD, left organizations, the labor movement, and, most important, the people of Indonesia will have to arrive at their own conclusions through their own experiences. In the course of those experiences, they will no doubt raise new problems and questions, and possibly new solutions to old problems.

In the event of a socialist revolution in Indonesia, which is certainly not on the agenda at the moment or even in the near future, the country will face greater problems than even Russia faced. In 1917, Lenin and Trotsky argued that the Russian workers' seizure of power could succeed if they found allies in the European labor movement and particularly in the German workers' movement. However, a working-class victory in Indonesia would find itself surrounded by totalitarian Communist governments, such as those in China and Vietnam, and by reactionary capitalist governments, such as those in Japan and Korea. Above all, the Indonesians would confront the United States, the dominant world capitalist power. That makes it even more clear that the future of the Indonesian revolution will depend on international solidarity from the working people of the world. In a very real sense, the future of Indonesia also depends on us.

1   Karl Marx and Friedrich Engels, *The Communist Manifesto,* ed. D. Ryazanoff (New York: Russell & Russell, Inc., 1963), Part III, 54–68. Marx and Engels distinguished their version of socialism or communism from what they called "feudalistic socialism," "petty-bourgeois socialism," "German or 'True' socialism," "conservative or bourgeois socialism," and "critical-utopian socialism and communism." What distinguished their socialism from the others was its identification with the working class as the agent of social revolution.

2   Hal Draper, "The Two Souls of Socialism," in *Socialism from Below* (Atlantic Highlands, N.J.: Humanities Press, 1992), 2–33.

3   While written for another time, I still think that the collection of essays *Party and Class* (London and Chicago: Bookmarks, 1996) by Tony Cliff, Duncan Hallas, Chris Harman, and Leon Trotsky remains the best short discussion of this issue.

4   Arnold C. Brackman, *Indonesian Communism: A History* (New York: Frederick A. Praeger, Publisher, 1963. While this is a Cold War, anti-Communist history, it is nonetheless quite useful. For a time in this period the Praeger publishing house was used by the CIA, but I do not know whether or not this was a CIA-sponsored book. For a recent biographical essay on Tan Malaka, see Geoffrey C. Gunn, "Tan Malaka and the Indonesian Revolution," in New World Hegemony in the Malay World (Lawrenceville, N.J.: Red Sea Press, 2000), 27-60. See also Tan Malaka, *From Jail to Jail,* trans. and ed. Helen Jarvis (Athens: Ohio University Press [Ohio University Center for International Studies Southeast Asia Series Number 83], 1991).

5   Since then the PRD has suffered a split, so that there are now two rival socialist organizations: the PRD and the new and very small Democratic Socialist Association. Because I have not been able to talk with leaders of both factions since the split, I have decided not to attempt to deal with these recent developments.

6   The fact that the Chinese Indonesians so completely dominate the upper echelons of the Indonesian economic elite, but not necessarily its political elite, complicates the situation in Indonesia, and constantly raises the danger that democratic and working class struggles against the capitalists will be posed in racial terms and degenerate into racial pogroms. The vulnerability of the Chinese-Indonesian bourgeoisie has locked them into a pathological relationship to the Indonesian generals. Sections of the Chinese intelligentsia, it should be pointed out, have historically supported the struggle for democracy and the interests of the popular classes.The targets of ethnic programs are almost invariably ordinary Chinese people such as shopkeepers.

7   All Indonesians must by law adhere to the state doctrine, Pancasila, and belong to one of the five approved religions (Islam, Buddhism,

Hinduism, Protestantism, or Catholicism).

8   This is, in fact, one of the great debates of the history of the socialist movement, a debate that first took place in revolutionary Russia in the period between 1890 and 1920. In that debate, the Mensheviks argued that the workers and peasants had to press the bourgeoisie to take power. Lenin and the Bolsheviks argued that workers and peasants would have to take power and establish a democratic dictatorship of workers and peasants to bring democracy to Russia. Trotsky argued that having taken power, the workers would have to create a workers' government as a transition to socialism. The workers' allies in that fight, he argued, would be the peasants and the labor movement of Europe and the world. The situation in Russia at that time has been virtually reproduced in Indonesia today, and so it gives rise on the left to the same sort of debates. The PRD has entered into this debate both within the party and with other groups on the left, but its own position has been inconsistent, vacillating between the positions once taken by Mensheviks, Bolsheviks, and Trotsky. The left debate in Russia in the period between the 1890s and the 1920s over the relationship of the struggle for democracy and the struggle for socialism was exemplified by three positions. The Mensheviks or moderate socialists argued that workers would pressure the capitalist class to take power, or that, if the workers should inadvertently take power themselves, they would have to surrender power to the bourgeoisie. The Bolsheviks, led by Lenin, argued that workers would have to lead the fight for democracy and would have to create a workers' and peasants' government, a democratic dictatorship. Finally, Trotsky argued that the workers, in fighting for democracy, would find themselves fighting for socialism, and, having taken power, would have to keep it, creating a workers' government, if not yet a socialist government. For a discussion of the debates, see Tony Cliff, *Lenin,* Vol. 1, *Building the Party* (London: Pluto Press, 1975), Chapter 6, "Fighting the Liberals," and Leon Trotsky, *History of the Russian Revolution* (Ann Arbor: University of Michigan Press, 1964), Appendix III, "Historic References on the Theory of 'Permanent Revolution,' " 419–428.

9   The PRD has generally taken a position that seems to suggest a two-stage vision of revolution: first democratic revolution, and later socialist revolution. The PRD's position may reflect both the influence of Maoism (via the Philippines) and of the Democratic Socialist Party (DSP) of Australia, the foreign party that has been in a position to offer the most material assistance. See the DSP website for Doug Lorimer's article "In Defense of Lenin's Marxist Policy of a Two Stage, Uninterrupted Revolution" and other related documents. For an advocate of Trotsky's permanent revolution position (or something very close), see Tony Cliff, "Revolution and Counter-Revolution: Lessons for Indonesia,"

International Socialism 80 (Autumn 1998): 53–70. Cliff's main point in the article is the need for a revolutionary party and press.

10 Trotsky first made these arguments at the time of the 1905 Russian Revolution in the essays later published as *The Permanent Revolution and Results and Prospects* (New York: Pathfinder, 1970).

Key Acronyms

ACILS	American Center for International Labor Solidarity
APRO	Asian and Pacific Regional Organization
ASBI	Indonesian Workers Solidarity Action
BBI	Indonesian Workers Front
BTI	Indonesian Peasant Front
ELTRANS	Institute for Social Transformation
FNPBI	National Front for Indonesian Labor Struggle
FOKUBA	Indonesian Financial Sector Union
FPSI	Peasants Federation of Sumatra Indonesia
FSBI	All-Indonesia Labor Federation
FSU	Union Solidarity Forum
GABSI	Amalgamated Trade Unions of Indonesia
GASBINDO	Amalgamated Indonesian Islamic Labor Federation
GKMI	Indonesian Christian Student Association
HMI	Indonesian Muslim Student Organization
ICFTU	International Confederation of Free Trade Unions
ICMI	Indonesian Association of Muslim Intellectuals
ILO	International Labor Organization
IMF	International Monetary Fund
INFID	International NGO Forum on Indonesian Development
Infight	Indonesian Front for the Defense of Human Rights
Kobar	Workers' Committee for Reform Action
KOMRAD	Committee of Students and People for Democracy in Indonesia
KORPRI	Public Employees' Corps of the Republic of Indonesia
LBH	Legal Aid Institute
LBH APIK	Legal Aid Institute – Indonesian Women's Association for Justice
LMND	National Student League for Democracy
MPR	People's Consultative Assembly
NU	Nahdlatul Ulama
PBHI	Indonesian Legal Aid Foundation

PBN	National Labor Party
PDI	Indonesian Democratic Party
PDI-P	Indonesian Democratic Party of Struggle
PIJAR	Information and Action Network for Reform
PKB	National Awakening Party
PKI	Indonesian Communist Party
PNI	Indonesian Nationalist Party
PPBI	Center for Indonesian Labor Struggle
PPP	United Development Party
PRD	People's Democratic Party
PSI	Indonesian Socialist Party
PUDI	United Indonesian Democratic Party
SBJ	Serikat Buruh Jabotabek union
SBSI	Indonesian Prosperity Labor Union
SEATO	South East Asian Treaty Organization
SI	Serekat Islam
SMID	Students in Solidarity for Democracy in Indonesia
SOBSI	All-Indonesia Central Workers' Organization
SPSI	All-Indonesia Workers' Union
SPSI-R	Post-1998 Reformed All-Indonesia Workers' Union (Reformasi)
SPSI-Status Quo	Post-1998 Unreformed All-Indonesia Workers' Union
STN	National Peasant Union
TSK	Indonesia Textile, Garment, and Leather Workers' Union

Appendix:
Key Statistics

Area

Total: 1,919,440 square
    kilometers (sq km)
Land: 1,826,440 sq km
Water: 93,000 sq km

Land boundaries

Total: 2,602 kilometers (km)

Border countries

Malaysia: 1,782 km
Papua New Guinea: 820 km

Coastline

54,716 km

Maritime claims

*Measured from claimed archipelagic
baselines:*
Exclusive economic zone: 200
    nautical miles (nm)
Territorial sea: 12 nm

Climate

Tropical; hot, humid; more
moderate in highlands

Terrain

Mostly coastal lowlands; larger
islands have interior mountains

Elevation extremes

Highest point: Puncak Jaya:
    5,030 meters (m)
Lowest point: Indian Ocean: 0 m

Natural resources

Petroleum, tin, natural gas, nickel,
timber, bauxite, copper, fertile
soils, coal, gold, silver

Land use

Arable land: 10%
Permanent crops: 7%
Permanent pastures: 7%
Forests and woodland: 62%
Other: 14% (1993 est.)
Irrigated land: 45,970 sq km
    (1993 est.)

Population

224,784,210 (July 2000 est.)

Age structure

0–14 years: 30.57% (male
    34,932,102; female
    33,783,603)
15–64 years: 64.96% (male
    72,889,994; female
    73,124,821)

65 years and over: 4.47% (male
    4,413,268; female 5,640,422)
    (2000 est.)

Population growth rate

1.63% (2000 est.)

Birth rate

22.6 births/1,000 population
    (2000 est.)

Death rate

6.31 deaths/1,000 population
    (2000 est.)

Sex ratio

At birth: 1.05 male(s)/female
under 15 years: 1.03
    male(s)/female
15–64 years: 1 male(s)/female
65 years and over: 0.78
    male(s)/female
total population: 1
    male(s)/female (2000 est.)

Infant mortality rate

42.21 deaths/1,000 live births
    (2000 est.)

Life expectancy at birth

Total population: 67.96 years
Male: 65.61 years
Female: 70.42 years (2000 est.)

Total fertility rate

2.61 children born/woman
    (2000 est.)

Ethnic groups

Javanese: 45%
Sundanese: 14%
Madurese: 7.5%
Coastal Malays: 7.5%
Other: 26%

Religions

Muslim: 88%
Protestant: 5%
Roman Catholic: 3%
Hindu: 2%
Buddhist: 1%
Other: 1% (1998)

Languages

Bahasa Indonesian (official,
modified form of Malay),
English, Dutch, local dialects, the
most widely spoken of which is
Javanese

Literacy

*Definition: age 15 and over, able to
read and write:*
Total population: 83.8%
Male: 89.6%
Female: 78% (1995 est.)

Source: U.S. Central Intelligence
Agency (CIA), *World Fact Book
2001* (Washington, DC: CIA,
2000). On-line at:
http://www.odci.gov/cia/publica
tions/factbook/geos/id.html.

Table 1: Indonesian GDP Composition by Sector: 1999 Estimated

Sector	Percentage
Agriculture	21
Industry	35
Services	44

Source: U.S. Central Intelligence Agency (CIA), *World Fact Book 2001* (Washington, DC: CIA, 2000). On-line at: http://www.odci.gov/cia/publications/factbook/geos/id.html.

Table 2: Indonesian Labor Force by Sector: 1998

Sector	Percentage
Agriculture	45
Trade, Restaurant, and Hotel	19
Manufacturing	11
Transport and Communications	5
Construction	4
Other	16

Note: 88 million workers were in the Indonesian workforce in 1998. The unemployment rate in 1998 was between 15 and 20 percent.

Source: U.S. Central Intelligence Agency (CIA), *World Fact Book 2001* (Washington, DC: CIA, 2000). On-line at: http://www.odci.gov/cia/publications/factbook/geos/id.html.

Table 3a: Indonesia's Main Export Partners: 1999 Estimated

Country/Region	Percentage
Japan	18
European Union	15
United States	14
Singapore	13
South Korea	5
Hong Kong	4
China	4
Taiwan	3

Note: Indonesia's main exports are oil and gas, plywood, textiles, and rubber.

Source: U.S. Central Intelligence Agency (CIA), *World Fact Book 2001* (Washington, DC: CIA, 2000). On-line at: http://www.odci.gov/cia/publications/factbook/geos/id.html.

Table 3b: Indonesia's Main Import Partners: 1999 Estimated

Country/Region	Percentage
Japan	17
United States	13
Singapore	10
Germany	9
Australia	6
South Korea	5
Taiwan	3
China	3

Note: Indonesia's main imports are machinery and equipment, chemicals, fuels, and foodstuffs.

Source: U.S. Central Intelligence Agency (CIA), *World Fact Book 2001* (Washington, DC: CIA, 2000). On-line at: http://www.odci.gov/cia/publications/factbook/geos/id.html.

Select Bibliography

On Indonesia

This bibliography only includes books in English and is meant as a guide to the general reader interested in learning more about Indonesia, rather than a resource for the labor specialist.—D.L.

Benedict R. O'G. Anderson. *Java in a Time of Revolution: Occupation and Resistance, 1944–1946.* Ithaca: Cornell University Press, 1972.

Carmel Budiardjo. *Surviving Indonesia's Gulag: A Western Woman Tells Her Own Story.* London: Cassell, 1996.

Robert Cribb and Colin Brown. *Modern Indonesia: A History Since 1945.* New York: Longman, 1995.

Harold Crouch. *The Army and Politics in Indonesia.* Ithaca: Cornell University Press, 1978.

Herbert Feith. *The Decline of Constitutional Democracy in Indonesia.* Ithaca: Cornell University Press, 1962.

Vedi Hadiz. *Workers and the State in New Order Indonesia.* London: Asia Research Centre and Routledge, 1997.

D.G.E. Hall. *A History of South-East Asia.* Third Edition. New York: St. Martin's Press, 1970.

Robert W. Hefner. *Civil Islam: Muslims and Democratization in Indonesia.* Princeton: Princeton University Press, 2000.

———. *The Political Economy of Mountain Java: An Interpretation.* Berkeley: University of California Press, 1990.

Chalmers Johnson. *Blowback: The Costs and Consequences of American Empire.* New York: Henry Holt and Company, 2000.

Audrey R. and George McT. Kahin. *Subversion as Foreign Policy: The Secret Eisenhower and Dulles Debacle in Indonesia.* New York: New Press, 1995.

George McT. Kahin. *Nationalism and Revolution in Indonesia.* Ithaca: Cornell University Press, 1952.

Raden Adjeng Kartini. *Letters of a Javanese Princess.* Preface by Eleanor Roosevelt. Ed. and intro. by Hildred Geertz. New York: University Press of America and the Asia Society, 1985.

Sartono Kartodirdjo. *Modern Indonesia: Tradition and Transformation.* Yogyakarta, Indonesia: Gadjah Mada University Press, 1991.

Damien Kingsbury. *The Politics of Indonesia.* Oxford: Oxford University Press, 1998.

Ira M. Lapidus. *A History of Islamic Societies.* New York: Cambridge University Press, 1989.

Tan Malaka. *From Jail to Jail.* Trans., ed., and intro. by Helen Jarvis. Athens: Ohio University Center for International Studies, 1991. 3 Vols.

J.D. Legge. *Sukarno: A Political Biography.* New York: Praeger Publishers, 1972.

J.C. van Leur. *Indonesian Trade and Society: Essays in Asian Social and Economic History.* The Hague and Bandung: W. van Hoeve Ltd., 1955.

Andrew MacIntyre. *Business and Politics in Indonesia.* North Sydney: Asian Studies Association of Australia, with Allen and Unwin, 1991.

Carolyn Marr. *Digging Deep: The Hidden Costs of Mining in Indonesia.* London: Down to Earth and Minewatch, 1993.

Ruth T. McVey. *The Rise of Indonesian Communism.* Ithaca: Cornell University Press, 1965.

Goenawan Mohamad. *Sidelines: Thought Pieces from Tempo Magazine.* Trans. Jennifer Lindsay. N.p.: Lontar, 1994.

Multatuli (Eduard Douwes Dekker). *Max Havelaar: Or the Coffee Auctions of the Dutch Trading Company.* Amherst: University of Massachusetts Press, 1982.

Rob Nieuwenhuys. *Mirror of the Indies: A History of Dutch Colonial Literature.* Singapore: Eric Oey, 1999.

People's Democratic Party, with Action in Solidarity with Indonesia and East Timor (ASIET). *The Struggle for Democracy in Indonesia: Introducing the People's Democratic Party.* Broadway, Australia: ASIET, 1996.

Anthony Reid. *Southeast Asia in the Age of Commerce, 1450–1680.* New Haven: Yale University Press, 1988.

Richard Robinson. *Indonesia: The Rise of Capital.* North Sydney: Asian Studies Association, 1986.

Maxime Rodinson. *Muhammad.* Trans. Anne Carter. New York: Pantheon, 1971.

Adam Schwarz. *A Nation in Waiting: Indonsia in the 1990s.* Boulder: Westview Press, 1994.

James Scott. *The Moral Economy of the Peasant: Rebellion and Subsistence in Southeast Asia.* New Haven: Yale University Press, 1977.

Takashi Shiraishi. *An Age in Motion: Popular Radicalism in Java, 1912-1926.* Ithaca: Cornell University Press, 1990.

Pramoedya Ananta Toer. *This Earth of Mankind.* Trans. and afterword Max Lane. New York: Penguin, 1990. (See also the other three volumes of *The Buru Quartet.*)

———. *The Mute's Soliloquy: A Memoir.* New York: Hyperion, 1999.

Anders Uhlin. *Indonesia and the "Third Wave of Democratization": The Indonesian Pro-Democracy Movement in a Changing World.* New York: St. Martin's Press, 1997.

Jeffrey A. Winters. *Power in Motion: Capital Mobility and the Indonesian State.* Ithaca: Cornell University Press, 1996.

On Globalization

This bibliography lists a number of popular and academic books dealing with the issue of globalization, with a particular emphasis on Asia.—D.L.

Walden Bello. *People and Power in the Pacific: The Struggle for the Post–Cold War Order.* San Francisco: Pluto Press, with Food First and the Transnational Institute (TNI), 1992.

Jeremy Brecher, Tim Costello, and Brendan Smith. *Globalization from Below: The Power of Solidarity.* Cambridge: South End Press, 2000.

Noam Chomsky. *The New Military Humanism: Lessons from Kosovo.* Monroe, Maine: Common Courage Press, 1999.

———. *Profit Over People: Neoliberalism and Global Order.* New York: Seven Stories Press, 1999.

Noam Chomsky and Edward S. Herman. *The Washington Connection and Third World Fascism.* Boston: South End Press, 1979.

Kevin Danaher, ed. *Corporations Are Gonna Get Your Mama: Globalizaiton and the Downsizing of the American Dream.* Monroe, Maine: Common Courage Press, 1996.

———, ed. *50 Years Is Enough: The Case Against the World Bank and the International Monetary Fund.* Preface by Muhammad Yunus. Boston: South End Press, 1994.

Kevin Danaher and Roger Burbach, eds. *Globalize This! The Battle Against the World Trade Organization and Corporate Rule.* Monroe, Maine: Common Courage Press, 2000.

Mike Davis. *Late Victorian Holocausts: El Niño, Famines, and the Making of the Third World.* New York: Verso, 2001.

Peter Gowan. *The Global Gamble: Washington's Faustian Bid for World Dominance.* London: Verso, 1999.

William Greider. *One World, Ready or Not: The Manic Logic of Global Capitalism.* New York: Simon & Schuster, 1997.

Paul Hirst and Grahame Thompson. *Globalization in Question.* Second edition. Cambridge: Polity Press, 1999.

Gabriel Kolko. *Confronting the Third World: United States Foreign Policy, 1945–1980.* New York: Pantheon, 1988.

David C. Korten. *The Post-Corporate World: Life After Capitalism.* West Hartford, Connecticut: Kumarian Press and Berrett-Koehler Publishers, 1999.

———. *When Corporations Rule the World.* West Hartford, Connecticut: Kumarian Press and Berrett-Koehler Publishers, 1995.

Walter LaFeber. *The Clash: A History of U.S.–Japanese Relations.* New York: W.W. Norton & Company, 1997.

Daniel Singer. *Whose Millennium? Theirs or Ours?* New York: Monthly Review Press, 1999.

George Soros. *The Crisis of Global Capitalism: Open Society Endangered.* New York: Public Affairs, 1998.

Interviews

Many Indonesians use only one name, in which case I have listed that name alphabetically as if it were a family name. In addition to the individuals listed here, I also conducted informational interviews among various groups of workers, such as the CALTEX petroleum workers of Riau, Sumatra; the Maspion and Sony workers of Jakarta, Indonesia; and women workers from the Citra Abadi plant in the Jabotabek industrial belt.—D.L.

See Key Acronyms for organization names.

Amir (pseudonym), PRD leader, interviewed on August 7, 1999, in Jakarta, Indonesia.

Asnitriyanti Damanils, coordinator of legal service for LBH APIK, interviewed on August 8, 1999, in Jakarta, Indonesia.

Augustinus Santoso, staff member, FNPBI, interviewed on July 30, 1999, in Jakarta, Indonesia.

Anonymous, USAID representative, interviewed on June 13, 2000, in Jakarta, Indonesia.

Djufnie Ashary, staff member, ACILS, interviewed on July 21, 1999, in Jakarta, Indonesia.

Rustam Askam, president, TSK-SPSI-R, interviewed on July 27, 1999, in Jakarta, Indonesia.

Suko Bandiyono, APU, demographer and specialist in migrant labor, Indonesian Institute of Sciences, interviewed on August 10, 2000, in Jakarta, Indonesia.

Ikrar Nus Bhakti, professor, Center for Political and Regional Studies at the Indonesian Institute of Sciences, interviewed on August 10, 1999, in Jakarta, Indonesia.

Roderick Brazier, director of the Small and Medium Enterprises project, Asia Foundation, interviewed on July 29, 1999, in Jakarta, Indonesia.

Bob Buckingham, Australian national, construction contractor, interviewed on July 22, 1999, in Jakarta, Indonesia.

Victor Butar-butar, professor, Career and Entrepreneurship Development Center, University of Riau, interviewed on July 22, 1999, in Jakarta, Indonesia.

Chandra, manager of a palm oil plantation, interviewed on June 16, 2000, in Medan, North Sumatra.

Desy, member of PIJAR, interviewed on June 10, 2000, in Jakarta, Indonesia.

Rudolfus Pejkalis Dhika, former textile worker, staff member, SBJ union, interviewed on July 31, 1999, in Bekasi, suburb of Jakarta, Indonesia.

Dita, leading member, PRD, interviewed on July 29, 1999, in Jakarta, Indonesia.

Christian "Cass" Evert, member of PIJAR, interviewed on June 10, 2000, in Jakarta, Indonesia.

Mansour Fakih, director, Institute for Social Transformation, interviewed on August 4, 1999, in Yogyakarta, Indonesia.

Muhammad Farid, director, Samin, a center for child labor studies, interviewed on August 4, 2000, in Yogyakarta, Indonesia.

Gregory Fergin, labor attaché, U.S. Embassy, interviewed on June 12, 2000, in Jakarta, Indonesia.

Mary Anne Forbes, staff member, ACILS, interviewed on July 21, 1999, in Jakarta, Indonesia.

Haikal, member of PIJAR, interviewed on June 10, 2000, in Jakarta, Indonesia.

Father Padmo Harsono, S.J., head of the Bureau of Labor Services of Lembaga Daya Dharma, Roman Catholic Archdiocese of Jakarta, interviewed on July 29, 1999, in Jakarta, Indonesia.

Ance Hotlina, worker, PT KDS electronic company, interviewed on July 31, 1999, in Bekasi, suburb of Jakarta, Indonesia.

Hudaya, Deputy General Secretary, the Teachers' Association of the Republic of Indonesian, interviewed on June 19, 2000, in Jakarta, Indonesia.

Jannes Hutahaean, member of the Labor Solidarity Committee, interviewed on June 14, 2000, in Medan, North Sumatra.

Inyo, member of PIJAR, interviewed on June 10, 2000, in Jakarta, Indonesia.

Lisa M. Isa, employee of Bank Sumitomo and general secretary, Fokuba, the Indonesian Financial Sector Union, interviewed on July 26,1999, in Jakarta, Indonesia.

Iwan, a leading member of the PRD, interviewed on June 17, 2000, in Jakarta, Indonesia.

Paul Keys, staff member, International Department, SBSI, interviewed on July 20, 1999, in Jakarta, Indonesia.

Hendrik Kuok, former representative of the People's Democratic Party to the National Election Commission, now a leader of the Democratic Socialist Faction, interviewed on July 29, 1999, and June 9, 2000, in Jakarta, Indonesia.

Max Lane, authority on Indonesian literature, translator, and leading member of the Democratic Socialist Party of Australia, interviewed on August 8, 1999, in Jakarta, Indonesia.

Togar Marbun, SBSI regional coordinator for North Sumatra, interviewed on June 15, 2000, in Medan, North Sumatra.

Ma'ruf, newspaper editor and leading member of PRD, interviewed on July 29 and August 12, 1999, in Jakarta, Indonesia.

H. Sutanto Martoprasono, leader of SARBUMUSI, the Muslim labor federation, interviewed on July 28, 1999, in Jakarta, Indonesia.

Haris Rusly Moti, PRD leader in Yogyakarta, interviewed on August 2, 1999, in Yogyakarta, Indonesia.

Mulyono, Vice-General Secretary, SBSI, interviewed on August 9, 2000, in Jakarta, Indonesia.

Indera Nababan, chairman of the Urban Community Mission, interviewed on June 9, 2000, in Jakarta, Indonesia.

B. Nainggolan, employee of Indonesia Management Resources, subcontracted to CALTEX in Riau, Sumatra, plant leader for SBSI union, interviewed on July 22, 1999, in Jakarta, Indonesia.

Carla June Natan, staff, Center for Indonesian Migrant Workers, a sister organization of the Urban Community Mission, interviewed on June 9 and 10, 2000, in Jakarta, Indonesia.

Ocip, independent researcher on labor issues, interviewed on August 10, 1999, in Jakarta, Indonesia.

Muchtar Pakpahan, founder and General Secretary of the SBSI, interviewed on August 9, 2000, in Jakarta, Indonesia.

Patuan, director of the Research Department of SBSI, interviewed on July 22, 1999, and June 12, 2000, in Jakarta, Indonesia.

Pelikson S., steering committee coordinator, Consortium for Indonesian Migrant Workers Defense, interviewed on August 13, 1999, in Jakarta, Indonesia.

Hendra Permana Sitinjak, SBSI organizer in area of immigrant and domestic workers, interviewed on August 9, 2000, in Jakarta, Indonesia.

Varena Retno, staff member, the Bureau of Labor Services of Lembaga Daya Dharma, Roman Catholic Archdiocese of Jakarta, interviewed on July 29, 1999, in Jakarta, Indonesia.

Reza, a leading member of the PRD, interviewed on June 17, 2000, in Jakarta, Indonesia.

Rindorindo, one of the national chairs and also head of the PGRI Foundation, associated with the Teachers' Association of the Republic of Indonesian, interviewed on June 19, 2000, in Jakarta, Indonesia.

Rohman, Holland Bakery salesman, interviewed on August 2, 1999, in Yogyakarta, Indonesia.

Endang Rokhani, a labor attorney for Urban Community Mission, interviewed on June 9, 2000, in Jakarta, Indonesia.

Tim Ryan, director of ACILS, interviewed on August 10, 2000, in Jakarta, Indonesia.

Bambang Purnomo Saeri, Vice-President of the SBSI banking union, interviewed on July 28, 1999, in Jakarta, Indonesia.

Soleh Sahab, the chairman of the SPSI-Status Quo union and leader of the strike at Maspion in Cibitung, Bekasi, interviewed on June 13, 2000, in Jakarta, Indonesia.

Sangsu, volunteer with FNPBI, interviewed on July 19, 1999, in Jakarta, Indonesia.

Bismo Sanyto, head of the International Department of SBSI, interviewed on June 12, 2000, in Jakarta, Indonesia.

Dita Sari, leader of the FNPBI, interviewed on July 30, 1999, and on June 17, 2000, in Jakarta, Indonesia.

Setiyono, chairman, SBJ, interviewed on July 31, 1999, in Bekasi, suburb of Jakarta, Indonesia.

Daulat Sihombing, works with the organization formerly called the Communication Forum for Community Development, which is now known as ELTRANS, interviewed on June 14, 2000, in Medan, North Sumatra.

Rekson Silaban, Director of International Department, SBSI, interviewed on July 28, 1999, in Jakarta, Indonesia, and on February 11, 2000, in San Francisco, California.

Timbul Simanungkalit, an attorney who works as an organizer and negotiator for ELTRANS, interviewed on June 14, 2000, in Medan, North Sumatra.

Sinal, a leading member of the PRD, interviewed on June 17, 2000, in Jakarta, Indonesia.

Afra Siowarjay, staff member, Bureau of Labor Services of Lembaga Daya Dharma, Roman Catholic Archdiocese of Jakarta, interviewed on July 29 and July 31, 1999, and June 13, 2000, in Jakarta, Indonesia.

Sjamsudin, PRD leader in Yogyakarta, interviewed on August 2, 1999, in Yogyakarta, Indonesia.

Roger A. Smith, consultant and staff member, ACILS, interviewed on several occasions in July 1999 and June 2000, in Jakarta, Indonesia.

Amin Soleh, child laborer on a Jermal (fishing platform), interviewed on June 14, 2000, in Medan, North Sumatra.

Ir. Suhardi S., General Secretary, Marhaenist Labor Union, and staff member of Universita Bung Karno, interviewed on August 14, 1999, in Jakarta, Indonesia.

Yatini Sulistyowati, chairwoman of the Food, Drink, Restaurant, and Hotel Sector of SBSI, interviewed on July 28, 1999, in Jakarta, Indonesia.

Ari Sunarijati, Director of the Women's and Children's Bureau of SPSI-Reformasi, interviewed on June 20, 2000, in Jakarta, Indonesia.

Susetiawan, professor of sociology, Gadjah Mada University, Yogyakarta, interviewed on August 2, 1999, in Yogyakarta, Indonesia.

Tartia, childcare worker and former migrant worker in Malaysia, interviewed on June 10, 2000, in Jarkarta, Indonesia.

Surya Tjandra, public defender and specialist in labor law for LBH, interviewed on July 26, 1999, and June 13, 2000, in Jakarta, Indonesia.

Pramoedya Ananta Toer, novelist, interviewed on August 12, 1999, in Jakarta, Indonesia.

Tono, staff member, Bureau of Labor Services of Lembaga Daya Dharma, Roman Catholic Archdiocese of Jakarta, interviewed on July 29 and July 31, 1999, in Jakarta, Indonesia.

Roem Topatimasang, staff member, Research Education and Dialogue, Yogyakarta, Indonesia, interviewed on August 4, 1999, in Yogyakarta, Indonesia.

Lut Vasant, Belgian labor unionist from the Confederation of Christian Trade Unions, working for the SBSI International Department, interviewed on June 9, 2000, in Jakarta, Indonesia.

Tri Wartri, worker in shoe plant producing for Adidas, interviewed on July 31, 1999, in Bekasi, suburb of Jakarta, Indonesia.

Lukas Gathay Widyanata, staff member, Bureau of Labor Services of Lembaga Daya Dharma, Roman Catholic Archdiocese of Jakarta, interviewed on July 29 and July 31, 1999, in Jakarta, Indonesia.

Wilson, a leading member of the PRD, interviewed on June 17, 2000, in Jakarta, Indonesia.

Judy Winarno, chairman of the union and of the strike committee at PT Sony Electronics of Indonesia, interviewed on June 13, 2000, in Jakarta, Indonesia.

Sri Wiyanti E., coordinator of public outreach for LBH APIK, interviewed on August 8, 1999, in Jakarta, Indonesia.

Vina, member of PIJAR, interviewed on June 10, 2000, in Jakarta, Indonesia.

Yono, LDD Bureau of Labor staff member, interviewed on July 13, 1999, in Jakarta, Indonesia.

Yoseph, member of PIJAR, interviewed on June 10, 2000, in Jakarta, Indonesia.

M. Rusli Yunus, Deputy General Secretary, Teachers' Association of the Republic of Indonesian, interviewed on June 19, 2000, in Jakarta, Indonesia.

Fatiwanolo Zega, head of the SBSI metal workers' sector, interviewed on June 15, 2000, in Medan, North Sumatra.

Index

offices of, 229, 231–32, 245;
politics and, 179, 218, 236–37,
243–45; PRD in, 287, 289, 293,
336–37; radicalism of, 173,
250, 312; repression of,
247–48; staff, 233–35
FOKUBA (Indonesian Financial
Sector Union), 180–86
footwear industry, xi–xiii, 35, 121,
145, 159
forced labor: under Dutch, 42,
59–60, 63–68, 94, 107; under
Japanese, 88–89, 94, 99, 107
Foreign Affairs, xvi
foreign investment. *See*
investment, foreign
Forum for Justice and Prosperity
(FAS), 194, 196
Foundation of Indonesian
Consumer Institutes (YLKI),
130
Foundation of Indonesian Legal
Aid Institutes (YLBHI), 131
Fourth International, 276–77, 298
FPSI (Peasants Federation of
Sumatra Indonesia), 6
France: capitalism in, 42–43, 57;
colonialism of, 30, 92; Paris
Commune, 297, 332;
Revolution, 62, 75
Frank, Andre Gunder, 259
Frankfurt School, 260–61, 264
Freeport McMoRan Copper and
Gold Inc., 35
French Confederation of
Christian Workers (CFTC),
199
Friedrich Ebert Foundation, 175

FSBI (All-Indonesia Labor
Federation), 122–23, 169
FSU (Union Solidarity Forum),
171–72, 243, 309
Fujiyama, Colonel, 87
Fukuda, Takeo, 47

G

GABSI (Amalgamated Trade
Unions of Indonesia), 108
Gabungan Serikat Buruh Vertikal
Indonesia (GSBVI), 108
Gandhi, Mohandas, 75, 76
Gap Inc., xi, xiii, 24, 35, 121, 315
garment industry: FNPBI union,
234, 235–36, 242;
manufacturing for U.S.
companies, 35, 121, 205; PRD
in, 278; SBSI union, 205, 207;
TSK union, 176–79, 238, 250;
women in, 145
GASBINDO (Amalgamated
Indonesian Islamic Labor
Federation), 91, 108, 176
General Motors Corporation, 47,
121
Gerakan Kesadaran Perempuan
(Movement of Conscious
Women), 271
Germany: capitalism in, 42–43,
45, 46, 302; Indonesia and, 37;
World War II and, 43, 86, 89,
112, 117, 334
Geyl, Pieter, 58, 59
Gilang, 279
GKMI (Indonesian Christian
Student Association), 196, 205,
207

L

labor costs, 178, 192

Labor Day, 239. *See also* May Day

labor movement. *See* international labor movement; unions

labor parties: activists and, 26, 172, 185, 243–44, 247; in U.S., 318. *See also specific organizations*

Labor Solidarity Committee of Medan, 24

land: during colonial period, 63, 65, 67, 74; ownership, 4–5, 10–12, 67, 263, 272–73; reform, xviii, 31, 92, 108–9, 113, 299

Lane, Max, 277

Lassalle, Ferdinand, 331

Latief, Abdul, 278

Latin America, 155–56, 249, 321

LBH (Legal Aid Institute): APIK (Indonesian Women's Association for Justice), 140–42, 148–49, 150, 152; description of, 131–33; labor movement support, 10, 135–39, 183, 239

LDD (Lembaga Daya Dharma), 153–58

Legal Aid Institute. *See* LBH

Legge, J.D., 85

legislation: Anti-Subversion Law, 17; on foreign investment, 117, 118–19; on labor, 123–24, 145, 221; on land, 5, 31

Lembaga Daya Dharma. *See* LDD

Lenin, Vladimir: study clubs on, 261, 264–66, 270, 274, 288, 292, 339; theories of, 43, 232–33, 277, 291, 342–43, 345n8; Third International leadership, 297–98

Lenin on the Trade Unions (Lenin), 232–33

Leopold, King, 69

Letters of a Javanese Princess (Kartini), 70–71, 76

liberation theology, 9–10, 155–56, 159, 164n13

Liem Sioe Liong, 6, 118

Linggu, Jefri Aries, 255

LMND (National Student League for Democracy), 288–89

Luxemburg, Rosa, 43

M

Madiun Affair, 56n1, 92, 93, 334–35

Maeda, Rear Admiral, 88

Mahendra, Oka, 197

Malaka, Tan, 81, 101–2, 258, 333–34, 335

Malari incident, 117, 118–19, 131

Malaysia, 56n16, 90, 92, 179

Manchuria, 44–45, 86

Mandela, Nelson, 20–21

manufacturing: conditions of, 8, 161–63; foreign investment in, 24–25, 35, 46–47, 260, 319; industrial capitalism and, 43, 45, 119–21; unions in, 219–21, 242, 277–78; women in, 121, 137–38, 144–47, 151, 160–61. *See also* industries

Mao Tse-tung: influence of, 258, 267, 277, 320, 339; leadership of, 93, 109, 117, 290–91,

About the Author

Dan La Botz is a Visting Professor at Miami University in Oxford, Ohio. He is the author of two previous books with South End Press, *Mask of Democracy* and *Democracy in Mexico,* and is the editor *of Mexican Labor News and Analysis.* His writing appears regularly in *Against the Current* and *Labor Notes.* He lives with his family in Cincinnati, Ohio.

Books by the Author

The Crisis of Mexican Labor. New York: Preager,1988.

Rank-and-File Rebellion: Teamsters for a Democratic Union. New York: Verso, 1990.

The Troublemaker's Handbook: How to Fight Back Where You Work and Win! Detroit: Labor Notes, 1990.

Edward L. Doheny: Petroleum, Power, and Politics in the United States and Mexico. New York: Praeger, 1991.

Mask of Democracy: Labor Suppression in Mexico Today. Boston: South End Press, 1992.

Democracy in Mexico: Peasant Rebellion and Political Reform. Boston: South End Press, 1995.

About South End Press

South End Press is a nonprofit, collectively run book publisher with more than 200 titles in print. Since our founding in 1977, we have tried to meet the needs of readers who are exploring, or are already committed to, the politics of radical social change. Our goal is to publish books that encourage critical thinking and constructive action on the key political, cultural, social, economic, and ecological issues shaping life in the United States and in the world. In this way, we hope to give expression to a wide diversity of democratic social movements and to provide an alternative to the products of corporate publishing.

Through the Institute for Social and Cultural Change, South End Press works with other political media projects—Alternative Radio; Speakout, a speakers' bureau; and *Z Magazine*—to expand access to information and critical analysis.

To order books, please send a check or money order to: South End Press, 7 Brookline Street, #1, Cambridge, MA 02139-4146. To order by credit card, call 1-800-533-8478. Please include $3.50 for postage and handling for the first book and 50 cents for each additional book.

Write or e-mail southend@southendpress.org for a free catalog, or visit our web site at http://www.southendpress.org.

Related Titles

East Timor's Unfinished Struggle: Inside the Timorese Resistance
By Constâncio Pinto and Matthew Jardine

Mask of Democracy: Labor Suppression in Mexico Today
By Dan La Botz

Democracy in Mexico: Peasant Rebellion and Political Reform
By Dan La Botz

Globalization from Below: The Power of Solidarity
By Jeremy Brecher, Tim Costello, and Brendan Smith

Disposable Domestics: Immigrant Women Workers in the Global Economy
By Grace Chang

Sweatshop Warriors: Immigrant Women Workers Take on the Global Factory
By Miriam Ching Yoon Louie

Resource Rebels: Native Challenges to Mining and Oil Corporations
By Al Gedicks

Propaganda and the Public Mind: Conversations with Noam Chomsky
By Noam Chomsky and David Barsamian

Year 501: The Conquest Continues
By Noam Chomsky

The Washington Connection and Third World Facsism
By Noam Chomsky and Edward S. Herman

See previous page for ordering information.